THE PRACTICAL WOODWORKER

THE PRACTICAL
WOODWORKER

A COMPLETE GUIDE TO THE ART
AND PRACTICE OF WOODWORKING

Written and Illustrated by Experts

and Edited by

BERNARD E. JONES

Editor of " Work," " The Amateur Mechanic," etc.

VOLUME 3
MAKING FINE FURNITURE

POPULAR WOODWORKING BOOKS

Printed in the United States of America

978-1-4403-3869-4

T3826

popularwoodworking.com

A division of F+W, A Content + eCommerce Company

CONTENTS

CONTENTS

LIST OF THE CHIEF CONTRIBUTORS

H. ALEXANDER	Machine Woodworking
I. ATKINSON	Toys, etc.
A.M.	Upholstery
W. A. C. BALL	Examples
J. D. BATES	Metal Fittings
R. V. BOUGHTON	Drawing
G. S. BOULGER	Woods and Timber
JOHN BOVINGDON	Veneering and Examples
R. S. BOWERS	Examples
C. W. D. BOXALL	Equipment, Examples, etc.
SYDNEY CAMM	Aeroplane Woodworking
A. CLAYDON	Examples, etc.
T. W. CORKHILL	Joint Making, Construction, etc.
J. L. DEVONSHIRE	Examples
G. ELDRIDGE	Examples
H. E. V. GILLHAM	Examples
P. R. GREEN	Examples
R. GREENHALGH	Tools, Processes, etc.
T. HOLT	Joint Making
W. J. HORNER	Turning, Pattern Making, etc.
H. JARVIS	Joint Making, etc.
F. W. LOASBY	Billiard-table Making
R. H. LOMAS	Barrow Making
W. J. MOSELEY	Wood Finishing
G. F. RHEAD	Inlaying, etc.
W. S. ROGERS	Picture Framing, etc.
C. F. SHACKLETON	Examples
G. STRETHILL-SMITH	Examples
C. S. TAYLOR	Upholstery, etc.
H. TURNER	Wood Carving
C. E. A. WYATT	Examples

Occasional Tables

SIMPLE OCCASIONAL TABLE

THE neat little occasional table shown by the half-tone reproduction (Fig. 1) is stronger in construction and better finished than the majority of such tables, yet it will be found very simple to make. The dimensions are given in the drawings of an elevation and plan shown by Figs. 2 and 3.

The first part to prepare is the top, which must be 1 ft. $8\frac{1}{4}$ in. long by 1 ft. $2\frac{1}{2}$ in. wide ; that is, the size without the moulding on the edges. This will require to be in two pieces of board $\frac{3}{4}$ in. thick, jointed together by planing one edge of each perfectly straight and square, so that they fit together quite close like one piece of wood. These edges are warmed and fixed

Fig. 1.—Simple Occasional Table

together with hot, rather thin glue, rubbing together a little to work out the surplus glue, then left in accurate position in a dry place to set thoroughly. In the meantime the legs may be planed straight and square, each the exact length, 2 ft. $2\frac{1}{2}$ in. by $1\frac{1}{4}$ in. square. Two pieces of stuff about $\frac{3}{4}$ in. thick are next required, 1 ft. $3\frac{1}{2}$ in. long by $3\frac{1}{2}$ in. wide, planed and squared on the top edge and the ends, the lower edge to be shaped to a slight curve. These are joined to the legs by $\frac{3}{8}$-in. wood dowels, the outer surface of the rails being $\frac{1}{16}$ in. in from the outside surface of the legs. Two more rails similar to these are required, but only $9\frac{1}{2}$ in. long, to be joined to the legs to complete the upper frame of the stand. In joining these the dowels should be a

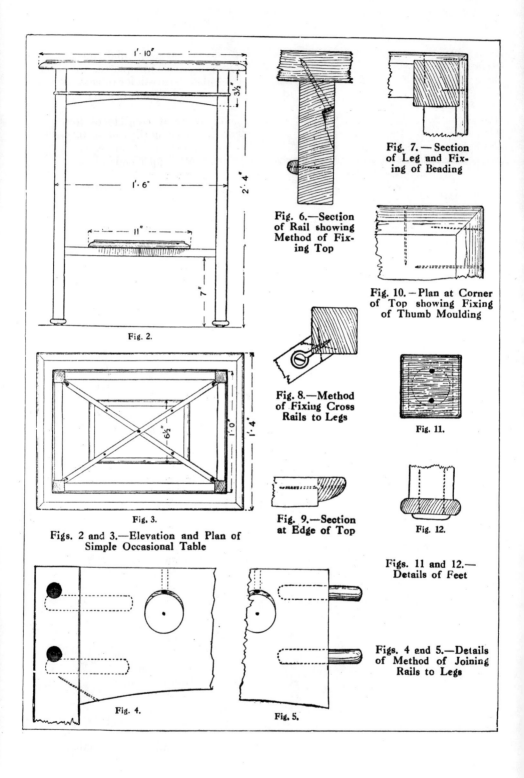

Fig. 2.

Fig. 6.—Section of Rail showing Method of Fixing Top

Fig. 7. — Section of Leg and Fixing of Beading

Fig. 10. — Plan at Corner of Top showing Fixing of Thumb Moulding

Fig. 8.—Method of Fixing Cross Rails to Legs

Fig. 11.

Fig. 3.

Figs. 2 and 3.—Elevation and Plan of Simple Occasional Table

Fig. 9.—Section at Edge of Top

Fig. 12.

Figs. 11 and 12.— Details of Feet

Figs. 4 and 5.—Details of Method of Joining Rails to Legs

Fig. 4.

Fig. 5.

little higher, to miss cutting through the others, but may just cut a little into them (*see* Figs. 4 and 5). These show the inner side of the rails, and it will be noticed that there is a circular impression made by boring on the slant with a 1-in. diameter centre-bit, and a screw-hole slanting through the upper edge of the rail. These are for fixing the table top (when it is ready), as in Fig. 6, which also shows the small beading fixed along the rails and round the legs, as further shown by Fig. 7. Glue and very fine panel pins are used for fixing. The beading can easily be made by a small smoothing plane.

Two cross-rails to support the shelf may next be fitted. They are of $\frac{7}{8}$-in. by $\frac{5}{8}$-in. section, halved into each other where they cross at the centre. The ends are fitted and fixed to the legs, as in Fig. 8, but should also be glued in addition to the screw-eye fixing and pins. The shelf can then be made 10 in. by $5\frac{1}{2}$ in. ; that is the size without the moulding. Both the shelf and the top should be planed on the top surface and edges perfectly level. The thumb-shaped moulding round the top is $\frac{3}{4}$ in. by $\frac{5}{8}$ in. in section, and can easily be made with the smoothing plane. It is shown in Figs. 9 and 10, fixed with glue and the fine pins. The shelf is done in the same way, but the moulding may be a little smaller. It is fixed in place by means of screws through the cross-rails, as seen in Fig. 3.

Four pieces of firm wood are now required, $1\frac{5}{8}$ in. square by about $\frac{1}{2}$ in. thick, to be rounded bead-like on the edges, and fixed on the ends of the legs with glue and two fine nails, as in Figs. 11 and 12, which also indicate a set of gliders that are put on finally. The table is now ready for finishing. It must be well smoothed with glasspaper, rubbing down slightly all very sharp corners. Pin-heads should be punched down a little and the holes filled with putty, also any other small defects that there might be.

CHESS AND DRAUGHTS TABLE

Devotees of the ancient game of chess will appreciate the small table shown by Fig. 13, with its top subdivided into the requisite number of squares, and a small cupboard underneath for tobacco sundries. An elevation and plan are given by Figs. 14 and 15.

Structurally it consists of four $1\frac{5}{8}$-in square legs having their outer faces tapering downwards to $\frac{7}{8}$ in. square at the bottom. The upper ends of the legs can be stub-tenoned or dowelled to the table top, which will be described later. At a height of 1 ft. 4 in. above the floor they are notched to receive a square framework of $1\frac{3}{4}$-in. by $\frac{3}{4}$-in. stuff, mitred and halved or tenoned as at A in Fig. 16, which shows an

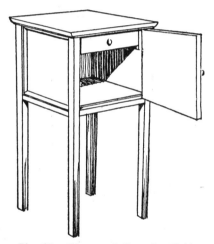

Fig. 13.—Chess and Draughts Table

angle cut out to suit the notch in one of the legs (indicated by dotted lines). This framework should finish flush with the legs, and is partially shown on plan at B in Fig. 17. This figure shows how, by means of small quadrant mouldings C, mitred round each of three sides, the sides of the cupboard can be fixed in position as at D without the necessity for grooves or rebates. These sides can be $\frac{1}{2}$ in. or even less in thickness, and when they are in position, a thin bottom, as at E in Fig. 18, can be fitted, its front edge serving as a stop to the door.

The door should be made to match the sides, with a moulding mitred round its outer edges, and if the small internal drawer is required, it must be hinged so as to open right back (*see* Fig. 19), and leave this free to be pulled out without encountering any obstruction. The table top can be a $\frac{7}{8}$-in. board with moulded edge projecting about 1 in. beyond the legs and having the quadrant mould fixed to its

woods, such as sycamore and mahogany, and glued to a deal baseboard F, the edges being finished with a larger moulding than in the simpler case, mitred round.

A possible addition to the table would be a couple of thin hardwood slides to pull out from under the cupboard to take the

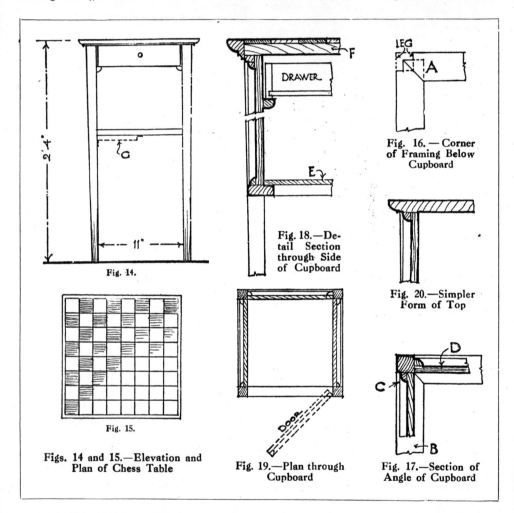

Fig. 14.

Fig. 15.

Figs. 14 and 15.—Elevation and Plan of Chess Table

Fig. 18.—Detail Section through Side of Cupboard

Fig. 19.—Plan through Cupboard

Fig. 16. — Corner of Framing Below Cupboard

Fig. 20.—Simpler Form of Top

Fig. 17.—Section of Angle of Cupboard

underside, as in Fig. 20, in which case the light and dark squares would probably be stained or painted on it. For a more elaborate piece of work, however, the arrangement shown in Fig. 18 would be preferable. Here the squares are each cut and fitted separately in two contrasting

captured pieces of each opponent. These could slide in strips of brass bent and screwed in position, as at G in Fig. 14, on opposite sides of the table, and should have small stops on their undersides to obviate any chance of being pulled out too far.

SMALL TEA-TABLE WITH PANELLED FALLS

The construction of the useful little tea-table shown by Figs. 21 to 23 should offer no difficulties to the amateur woodworker. The table is arranged with two panelled falls, which when opened form an extension of the lower shelf.

The table is 2 ft. 5 in. high, and the top should finish $\frac{1}{2}$ in. in thickness, the legs being square wrought and 2 ft. $4\frac{1}{2}$ in. high by $1\frac{1}{4}$ in. square. The top rails should have a bead on the lower edge. The open ends should be framed together first, the joints, of course, being mortised and tenoned together and the legs mortised for the diagonal stretcher stub-tenons. The stretcher is halved together in the centre, and is fixed in position when the com-

Fig. 21.—Small Table with Panelled Falls

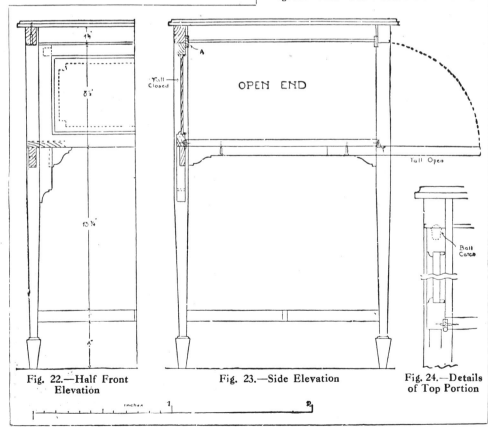

Fig. 22.—Half Front Elevation

Fig. 23.—Side Elevation

Fig. 24.—Details of Top Portion

plete frame is glued up, together with the lower shelf. This shelf should be fastened by screwing up through the spandrels on the ends. The top, which is 1 ft. 8 in. by 1 ft. 8 in., should project $\frac{1}{2}$ in. beyond the frame all round, and should now be fixed in position. This is secured either with screws through the top rails, or with wooden buttons. If the latter are used, provision will have to be made for them, and the four top rails must be grooved inside before the table is put together.

Next proceed with the falls, and

they are closed, and a small brass knob should be screwed in to allow of easy opening. A check or box line in the top and panels are additions that tend to improve the design.

SMALL TABLE WITH RISING TRAY

A small table of somewhat novel construction is shown by Fig. 25. When the top (which is divided down the centre) is raised a tray or cellaret is lifted out of the

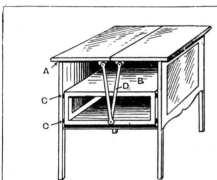

Fig. 25.—Table with Rising Tray with One Panel Removed

mortise and tenon these together, allowing for a stub-tenon on the two small brackets underneath the bottom rail. The fall should be $\frac{7}{8}$ in. thick. The reason why the " horns " are left on the fall " uprights " or " stiles " is that when the falls are opened and in position, the horns swing under the lower shelf and effectively prevent the falls from dropping lower than shown in Fig. 21. When hinging the falls in position care must be taken to sink one half of the hinge in the fall, and the other half in the edge of the shelf, as shown in Fig. 24. The centre of the hinge knuckle must be exactly in line with the bottom edge of the fall and shelf. A wood stop (Fig. 23) should then be screwed into the top rail to prevent the fall from being pushed in too far. A small spring ball-catch should be fixed in the top edge of the falls to fasten them when

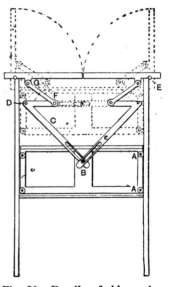

Fig. 26.—Details of Alternative Form of Tray-lifting Mechanism

hollow part of the table to the normal level of the table top. In the figure one panel of the table is removed in order that the interior arrangement may be seen. The illustration shows a table 2 ft. by 2 ft. The shelf rises 9 in., and the guide frame is 9 in. deep. The height of the table is 2 ft. 6 in. The top of the table opens in two flaps hinged on the outside at A. A sliding shelf B has a framework underneath, to each corner of which is fixed two roller wheels C to prevent friction when the shelf is raised and lowered. Four arms D, two on each side, work loosely on pivots attached to the frame. The upper ends of the arms are attached to the underside of the flaps as shown. The lifting of one flap would raise the two, thus preventing any tipping of the shelf. A spring catch (fixed in the front of the outer case and near the top) to shoot into or under the shelf when raised would prevent the flaps closing until required.

Fig. 26 shows another arrangement, in

pin D fixed to the inside surface of the table. The flaps are hinged at E, and connected to cranks by rods working loosely on centre pins F and G. A strong fixed iron pin B having a short piece of tube revolving thereon to form a roller projects from the sliding frame, and works through both the slots of the cranks. The top of the frame is solid to form a shelf. Two wheels A (eight in all) should be fixed close to the top and bottom corners of the frame to prevent friction. The centre of

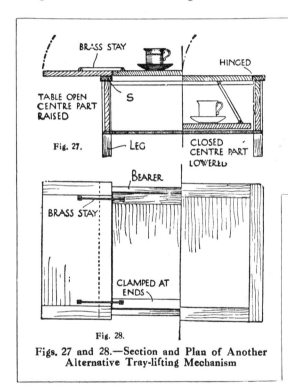

Fig. 27.

TABLE OPEN CENTRE PART RAISED

BRASS STAY

HINGED

S

LEG

CLOSED CENTRE PART LOWERED

BEARER

BRASS STAY

CLAMPED AT ENDS

Fig. 28.

Figs. 27 and 28.—Section and Plan of Another Alternative Tray-lifting Mechanism

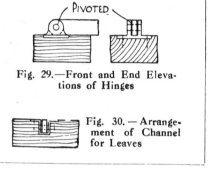

PIVOTED

Fig. 29.—Front and End Elevations of Hinges

Fig. 30. — Arrangement of Channel for Leaves

pin D to centre of F is twice that of centre of hinge E to centre of pin G ; centres D to B are twice centres D to F. A spring catch should be fixed in front to shoot into the frame when raised to prevent the flaps falling.

Still another arrangement of the lifting-mechanism is shown by the part section and the plan Figs. 27 and 28.

Two strips S (Fig. 27) are secured by dowels or screws to the end bearers, and to these the leaves are hinged. Four pivoted brass stays connect these with the centre portion, so that when the table is open the section will be that shown in the left of Fig. 27. When the leaves are folded over, the centre part will descend until it assumes the position shown in the right of Fig. 27. In the plan of the device shown by Fig. 28, it will be seen that to avoid warping it is advisable to clamp the various portions at the ends.

which levers and cranks are used for raising the flaps of the table both at the same time, and consequently keeping the sliding shelf level as it rises and falls, leaving only a small part of the connecting levers exposed above the top when the flaps are open. Of course, the arrangement of levers here shown must be in duplicate, at the two ends of the table. In this figure C is a slotted crank made at an angle of 45°, and working on a centre

It must be noted that care must be taken to close the leaves simultaneously if the centre part is to be kept level while in motion, a condition essential if it is to carry tea-cups. Details of the brass stay are shown by Fig. 29. If the surface of the table is desired flush, the stays could be fitted into channels, as in Fig. 30, without interfering in any way with the movement.

obtained. Sufficient allowance should be made in length, width, and thickness for working. The sizes of the table shown by Fig. 31 are : top, 1 ft. 6 in. square by $\frac{5}{8}$ in. thick ; legs, 2 ft. 4 in., tapering from $1\frac{1}{4}$ in. square at the top to $\frac{13}{16}$ in. square at the bottom ; width outside the legs, 1 ft.

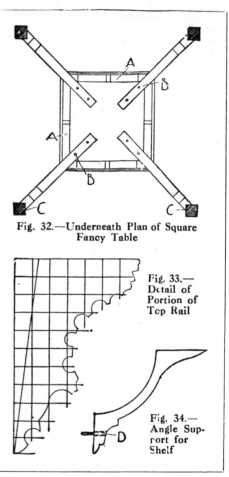

Fig. 32.—Underneath Plan of Square Fancy Table

Fig. 33.—Detail of Portion of Top Rail

Fig. 34.—Angle Support for Shelf

Fig 31.—Square Fancy Table

SQUARE FANCY TABLE

Suggested woods for the fancy table shown by Fig. 31 are birch for the legs and the other parts of pine and all finished in white enamel. If, however, the tables are required to match other articles of furniture, such as mahogany, American walnut, or satinwood, these woods, finished with french polish, would be quite suitable. First set out a full-size elevation of one side, and a plan of the design chosen from the dimensions given ; then the sizes of the various parts can be

1 in. at the top and 1 ft. 5 in. at the floor line ; deepest part of shaped top rails, 1 1 in. by $\frac{5}{8}$ in. thick. The central shelf is 8 in. square by $\frac{5}{8}$ in. thick, the top of the shelf being 1 ft. 1 in. from the floor. The top sides of the angle supports, where connected to the legs, are 9 in. from the floor. An underneath plan of the table is shown by Fig. 32.

To facilitate the copying of the curves or the shaped parts, the diagram Fig. 33 should be spaced out in lines at right angles to each other, forming 1-in. squares. The short spandrels A (Fig. 32) under the central shelf are $6\frac{3}{8}$ in. by $1\frac{1}{2}$ in. A moulding is worked round the upper edges of the table top. The shaped top rails under the top are tenoned into the legs, and stand back $\frac{1}{8}$ in. from the face of the legs. The top is secured with screws driven in a

Fig. 35.—Octagonal Fancy Table

slanting direction through the inside of the top rails and then into the table top. The shaped angle supports to the central shelf are screwed from the underside into the shelf, as shown at B (Fig. 32), and the opposite ends are fitted to the leg with a V-shaped end, as at C, and fixed with short dowels or screwed from the inside as at D (Fig. 34). The small spandrels of the central shelf are fitted between the angle supports and secured with glue, and are screwed from their under edges into the central shelf.

OCTAGONAL FANCY TABLE

Another fancy table, but of octagonal shape, is shown by Fig. 35. The design of this is based upon very similar lines to

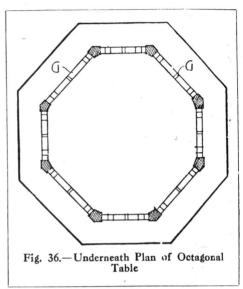

Fig. 36.—Underneath Plan of Octagonal Table

the last one described, and will lend itself equally well to the same treatment as regards material and finish, etc.

The general dimensions of this are:

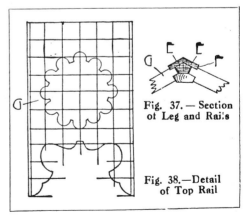

Fig. 37. — Section of Leg and Rails

Fig. 38.—Detail of Top Rail

Extreme width of top, 1 ft. 10 in. ; sides, about 9 in. ; thickness, $\frac{5}{8}$ in. The legs, shown in cross section in the plan (Fig. 36) and in detail section in Fig. 37, are 2 ft. 4 in. long; extreme width, $1\frac{3}{8}$ in.; thickness, $1\frac{1}{8}$ in. The two outer faces E (Fig. 37) are $\frac{3}{4}$ in. wide, and the sides F are bevelled to fit the right-angled shoulders of the shaped top. rails G, which are shown enlarged by Fig. 38. Each angular face

$\frac{3}{16}$ in. deep into the sides of the legs, and the spindles housed their full thickness into the spindle rails and the shelf beneath.

HEXAGONAL OCCASIONAL TABLE

This useful table (Fig. 39) should be made in mahogany, oak or walnut.

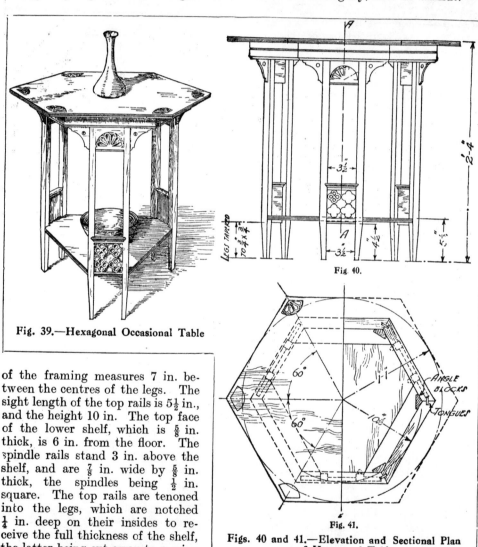

Fig. 39.—Hexagonal Occasional Table

Fig. 40.

Fig. 41.

Figs. 40 and 41.—Elevation and Sectional Plan of Hexagonal Table

of the framing measures 7 in. between the centres of the legs. The sight length of the top rails is $5\frac{1}{2}$ in., and the height 10 in. The top face of the lower shelf, which is $\frac{5}{8}$ in. thick, is 6 in. from the floor. The spindle rails stand 3 in. above the shelf, and are $\frac{7}{8}$ in. wide by $\frac{5}{8}$ in. thick, the spindles being $\frac{1}{2}$ in. square. The top rails are tenoned into the legs, which are notched $\frac{1}{4}$ in. deep on their insides to receive the full thickness of the shelf, the latter being cut away to receive the legs. The shelf is then secured with glue and slanting screws from the underside of the shelf. The ends of the spindle rails should be housed

All necessary dimensions and details of construction are given in the elevation and plan (Figs. 40 and 41) and the detail drawings. It will be seen that the hexagonal frame is tongued and glueblocked at its angles (Fig. 41). It is also grooved on its inner face to receive the " buttons," and embellished with a small moulding and $\frac{1}{4}$-in. bead (Fig. 42). The three pairs of legs are tenoned to the frame, the full size of the leg ($1\frac{1}{8}$ in. by $1\frac{1}{8}$ in.) being let in to a depth of $\frac{1}{8}$ in., as are also the upper ends of the brackets and top carved panels. The leg tenons are 1 in. by 1 in. and 1 in. long (see enlarged section, Fig. 43), and the lower part of the legs are tapered on three sides to $\frac{3}{4}$ in. by $\frac{3}{4}$ in. The housing of the panels and brackets to the legs is indicated in the detail drawings (Figs. 44 and 45) by means of dotted lines, and should be no more than $\frac{1}{8}$ in. deep in each case. The panels have a shoulder formed $\frac{3}{16}$ in. back from the uncarved face, and the brackets also have a shoulder $\frac{3}{16}$ in. back from the face. The legs, panels and brackets are dowelled and glued together; and here it should be noted that the brackets must be fixed to the legs before these latter are assembled to the frame. A $\frac{1}{4}$-in. bead is run round the edges of the top and all visible edges of the undershelf. Six " buttons " hold the top to the frame, and the undershelf is fitted in between the legs and secured to each by means of a screw-eye and screw (see Fig. 42).

The carving to the panels and top is incised and recessed to a depth of about $\frac{1}{16}$ in., and the recessed portions either treated with a carver's punch to give a rough texture, or they may be worked to a smooth face according to taste ; but in no case should these surfaces be polished

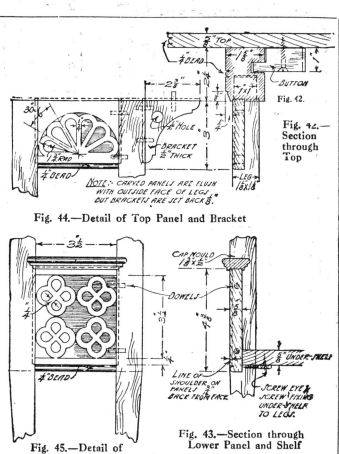

Fig. 42.

Fig. 42.—Section through Top

NOTE :- CARVED PANELS ARE FLUSH WITH OUTSIDE FACE OF LEGS, BUT BRACKETS ARE SET BACK $\frac{3}{8}$.

Fig. 44.—Detail of Top Panel and Bracket

Fig. 43.—Section through Lower Panel and Shelf

Fig. 45.—Detail of Lower Panel

to a shine. They should either be left clean or treated with a dull polish in contrast to the rest of the work.

In the case of the panels the carved effect may be obtained by cutting out the design in $\frac{1}{16}$-in. fretwood, and applying this as an overlay to the panels, a method which is often employed where the edges of the overlay can be concealed. This cannot be done with the six ornamentations on the top, and it is advisable to carve these.

The moulded capping to the lower

the top is folded the whole answers as a side table. The wood for the top should be well seasoned, as, being connected to the table frame by a centre only, it is liable

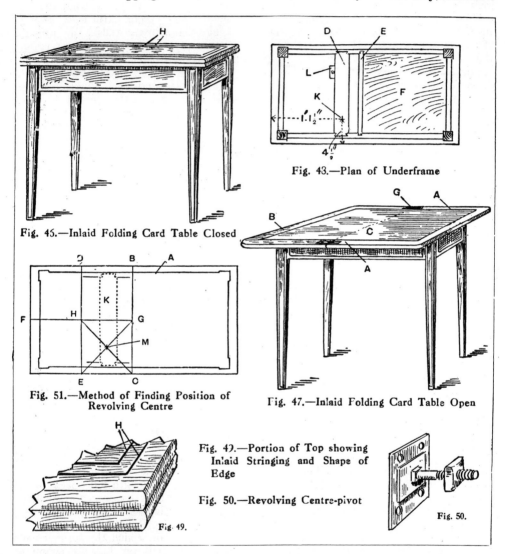

Fig. 46.—Inlaid Folding Card Table Closed

Fig. 43.—Plan of Underframe

Fig. 51.—Method of Finding Position of Revolving Centre

Fig. 47.—Inlaid Folding Card Table Open

Fig. 48.—Portion of Top showing Inlaid Stringing and Shape of Edge

Fig. 50.—Revolving Centre-pivot

Fig. 49.

Fig. 50.

panels is returned on the outer faces of the legs, as shown in the illustrations.

INLAID FOLDING CARD-TABLE

The card-table shown closed by Fig 46 and open by Fig 47 is made so that when

to warp if not thoroughly dry ; mahogany is suitable. The ornamental lines are inlaid (inlay and veneer work are dealt with in a later section) with satinwood or boxwood stringing, which can be obtained from most cabinet-makers or veneer merchants. Instead of the inlaying, the lines can be incised with a tool shaped like a **V**, or a small gouge. If not to be inlaid, the table could be made of pine, with birch legs, and afterwards stained, painted, or enamelled.

The following are the dimensions of the stuff required, allowing a little for working : Two pieces for the top, 3 ft. by 1 ft. 6 in. by 1 in. ; four legs, 2 ft. 5 in. by 1¾ in. by 1¾ in. ; two side rails, 2 ft. 9 in. by 4¼ in. by 1 in. ; two end rails, 1 ft. 4 in. by 4¼ in. by 1 in. ; two strips of veneer A (Fig. 47) for the top, 3 ft. by 2 in. ; strips B (Fig. 47) for gluing round the inside of the tops to form a recess for the cloth, 1 ft. 3 in. by 2 in. (endway of grain) ; one cross-rail D (Fig. 48), on which the top revolves, 1 ft. 4 in. by 3 in. by 1 in. ; one inside rail E (Fig. 48), which forms the inside end of the box for holding cards, etc., 1 ft. 4 in. by 3½ in. by 1 in. ; and one piece for the bottom of the box F (Fig. 48), 1 ft. 4 in. by 1 ft. 5 in. by ½ in. The bottom F can be kept in position with ½-in. strips nailed or screwed to the side and end rails.

To proceed with the making, plane the tops to thickness and take to length and width. Next mark, with a toothing plane, the inside face of the top, which makes the cloth and the veneer borders stick better. The veneer, A and B (Fig. 47), can then be laid, the end pieces being endwise, and the grain running the same way as that of the top. Then insert the stringing H (Figs. 46 and 49) in the uppermost side of the top when the table is closed ; the outer line should be 1¼ in. from the edge and the inner line 2 in. from the edge. If desired, the corners of the top may be rounded as shown in Fig. 47. When the veneer and stringing are dry, the two outside edges and ends of the top can be rounded, as shown in Fig. 49, the two inside edges, which are hinged, being left square. The top should then be cleaned up and glass-papered ready for hinging, as shown at G (Fig. 47). The legs should be squared up to 1¾ in., and the side and end rails planed and taken to width. Before tapering the legs they should be mortised to receive the tenons on the ends of the rails. Allowing for the legs to stand in underneath the top 1¼ in. at the ends and ½ in. at the sides,

the length from shoulder to shoulder of the side rails will be 2 ft. 6 in., and of the end rails 1 ft. 1½ in. The legs should be tapered to 1¼ in. square at the bottom, beginning the taper 4½ in. from the top. The stringing is inlaid in the legs ¼ in. from the edge, and in the rails ½ in. from the edge. Before gluing the frame together, the inside rail E (Fig. 48) should be fitted either with stub tenons or dovetails 1 ft. 5 in. from the end rail. The later rail is ¾ in. narrower than the other rails, which allows the bottom of the card-box to be screwed underneath it. The cross-rail D (Fig. 48) can be dovetailed into the side rails when the frame is together.

When the frame is together, the top should be hinged and the centre may be fixed. The hinges (*see* Fig. 47) and the revolving centre (Fig. 50) can be obtained of most ironmongers. The position for the revolving centre is shown at K (Fig. 48), 1 ft. 1½ in. from the end of the top and 4½ in. from the side. For instructions on fixing card-table hinges, see an earlier chapter. Folding and revolving card-table tops are, as a rule, made exactly square when open ; therefore, when closed, the width would be half the length. When this is the case, a ready way of finding the centre is as follows : Place the leaf (which is to be fixed to the frame) underside on the bench, the other leaf being hinged to it at the side E and C (Fig. 51). Next turn the table frame upside down, and adjust it to its exact position as regards projection at the sides and ends ; then mark round the frame with a pencil, as at A (Fig. 51). Now take off the frame, and divide the top at the centre of its length B C. Next bisect the half length at D E, and the width at F G. Draw diagonal lines G E and H C, and the intersecting point is the position of the centre on which the top revolves. The dotted lines on Fig. 51 show the position of cross-rail K through which the centre works. If the width of the top is not exactly half the length, mark the centre lines B C and F G as before. Now mark on line F G the point H at the same distance from G as from G to C. The line H E, drawn parallel to G C, and the diagonals as before, give the centre. The point M is transferred by measurement from the top to the frame.

The large plate of the revolving centre is screwed to the underside of the top, the

should be pasted down after the table has been polished. Suitable baize or cloth can be obtained from dealers in upholsterers' materials. When applying the paste, see that it does not ooze through the baize.

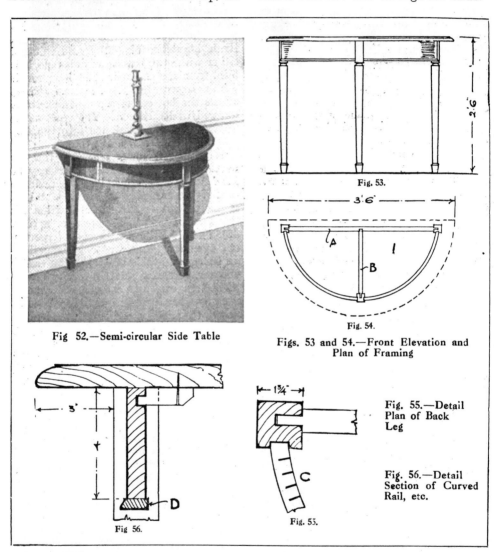

Fig 52.—Semi-circular Side Table

Fig. 53.

Figs. 53 and 54.—Front Elevation and Plan of Framing

Fig. 54.

Fig. 55.—Detail Plan of Back Leg

Fig. 56.—Detail Section of Curved Rail, etc.

Fig 56.

bolt goes through the rail D (Fig. 48), and the nut screws up underneath. To prevent the top turning too far when opened, as in Fig. 47, a piece of wood L (Fig. 48) about 1 in. wide is screwed to the underside of the top. The cloth C (Fig. 47)

SMALL SEMI-CIRCULAR SIDE TABLE

It is strange that tables of the type shown by Fig. 52, while often found in old houses, are not more extensively used at the present day. In form they are un- doubtedly simplified versions of the massive marble and gilt " console " of the palace and mansion, and are particularly graceful in appearance and convenient in shape for a variety of purposes. They are much associated with the work of the brothers Adams, whose characteristic type of ornament can very suitably be applied to their edges and framing, or they might be enriched in the style of Sheraton with inlay and banding.

In the example shown, and of which Figs. 53 and 54 are a front elevation and plan respectively, the top is an exact semicircle of 3 ft. 6 in. diameter, moulded on its periphery and overhanging the legs, to the extent of 3 in. The framing consists of three $1\frac{3}{4}$-in. square legs, tapered and worked to any desired extent, the back ones having a 4-in. by 1-in. rail tenoned into them, as at A in Fig. 54. In the centre of this rail, and at right angles thereto, is dovetailed a shorter one B,

table edge. This is bent by means of a series of saw-kerfs on the inside, as at c in Fig. 55, and is finished with a thin

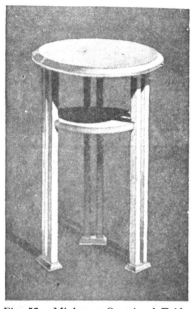

Fig. 57.—Miniature Occasional Table

moulded slip along the bottom, as at D in Fig. 56, which also indicates the fixing by means of rebates and oak buttons of the top to the various rails.

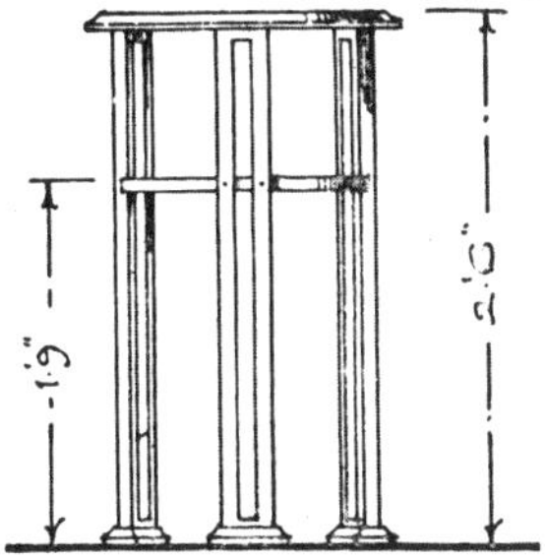

MINIATURE OCCASIONAL TABLE

The little occasional table shown in the photographic reproduction (Fig. 57) would look well in oak. It consists of a 1-in. circular top with chamfered edge, supported on three pairs of 1-in. square uprights. Elevation and plan are shown by Figs. 58 and 59.

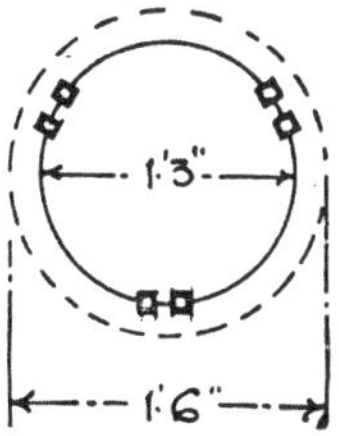

Each pair of uprights has a 1-in. distance piece at top and bottom, as at A in Fig. 60, the upper ends being housed $\frac{1}{2}$ in. into the under-side of the table top, and the bottoms similarly let into a 4-in. by 2-in. by 1-in. chamfered base next the floor, and screwed from below. About

Figs. 58 and 59.—Elevation and Plan of Miniature Occasional Table

Fig. 58.

Fig 59.

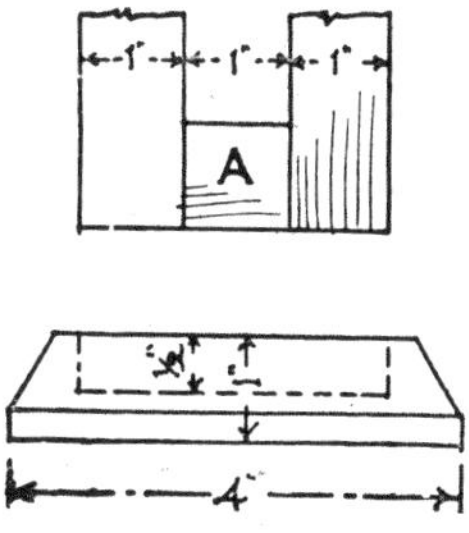

Fig. 60.—Detail of Bottom of Leg

tenoned into the front leg. Connecting the legs and slightly housed into them is a curved 4-in. by $\frac{3}{4}$-in. rail parallel to the

8 in. below the top a shelf 1 ft. 3 in. in diameter is fitted in order to stiffen the uprights, to suit which it should be very accurately notched out at the six points required. The uprights can be nailed to this shelf and the holes stopped, or they may be secured with brass round-headed screws.

SMALL CIRCULAR TABLE

An occasional table, equally suitable for a circular or octagonal top, of exceedingly

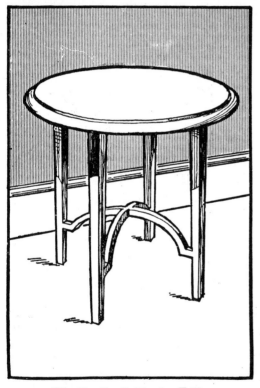

Fig. 61.—Small Circular Table

simple construction is shown by Fig. 61. With a view to giving the worker as nearly as possible the exact style he happens to prefer, two alternative elevations are shown, the actual construction being identical in both cases. As will be seen, the alternative in Fig. 62 has turned legs, while that in Fig. 63 has simply square

tapered legs. In this latter case the ties or stretchers between the legs near the floor are shown of a different outline, which is, of course, interchangeable with the first.

Briefly reviewing the construction of the first alternative, this should consist of a circular top, $\frac{3}{4}$ in. or $\frac{7}{8}$ in. thick, 2 ft. 7 in. in diameter, with a moulded or simply a chamfered edge, and made up of, say, three widths cross-tongued together. This is supported on four legs turned out of, say, $1\frac{1}{2}$-in. stuff, which would in the majority of cases have to be bought ready or made to order, and are intended to be fixed in the positions denoted by small crosses in Fig. 64. Their upper ends are tenoned into horizontal bearers on top rails each about $1\frac{1}{2}$ in. square, as shown by the isometric sketch (Fig. 65). The positions of these bearers are indicated by the dotted lines in Fig. 64. They have shaped ends, and are halved together where they cross in the centre, as in Fig. 65. Their upper edges will need to be planed and tested until perfectly true, in order properly to take the top as first described. The ties might be about $4\frac{1}{2}$ in. above the floor level, and are placed immediately under the bearers. They should be kept light in section, say about 1 in. high and $\frac{3}{4}$ in. thick, each being cut out of one flat piece and notched in the centre to form a halved joint with the other, in the same way as shown for the bearers. Their ends are tenoned into the upright legs. The worker will probably have the turned legs prepared for him, and should have them kept simple and restrained in outline, as a lot of detail will only detract from the appearance of the table.

As previously stated, the construction for the alternative design need not differ from that already described; but the legs should be kept square, and tapered from about $1\frac{1}{2}$ in. at the top to 1 in. next the floor. Figs. 66 and 67 will be found to give full details concerning the setting-out of the work, the centres from which the curves of the ties are drawn, etc. The

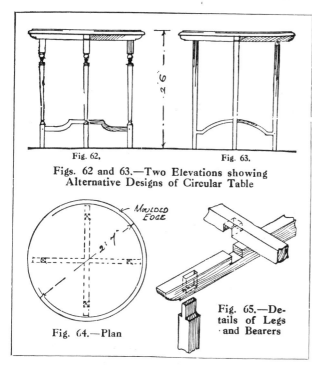

Fig. 62.

Fig. 63.

Figs. 62 and 63.—Two Elevations showing Alternative Designs of Circular Table

MOULDED EDGE

Fig. 64.—Plan

Fig. 65.—Details of Legs and Bearers

are of the better kind. A good quality of mahogany should be chosen, especially as the quantity being small, the cost will not amount to much. The delicate construction requires a good sound material. If old mahogany is used, with good workmanship, they can be made to strongly copy genuine antiques. Fig. 70 shows how they may be made to take apart by screw threads being turned on the pins, though this is not really necessary. The stem of the table (Fig. 69) is turned in one piece, with a plain pin to fit into the top collar.

The first table (Fig. 68) is 1 ft. 8½ in. high, with a 1-ft. diameter tray top, and has an inlaid "fan centre." The second (Fig. 69) is 1 ft. 7¼ in. high, the top being 11 in. in diameter, ornamented by

various details can be readily transposed from one design to the other, or replaced with other simple treatments of the same general construction.

COFFEE TABLES

The reproduced photographs (Figs. 68 and 69) show two different patterns of wine or coffee tables, as they are called. They will be of special interest to the woodworker who can do turning, as they are all lathe-work except the legs. Woodturning is dealt with in a later section. There are a variety of patterns in these tables, but the two here to be described

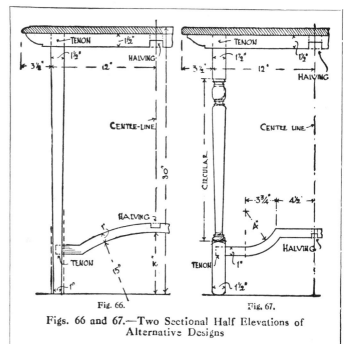

Fig. 66.

Fig. 67.

Figs. 66 and 67.—Two Sectional Half Elevations of Alternative Designs

carving the marginal bead into sections. The line drawings given on page 843 are all to the same scale. Figs. 71 to 76 refer to

sional wood-turner, it will be necessary to make a cardboard pattern for the turned stems and collars, as shown by Figs. 71

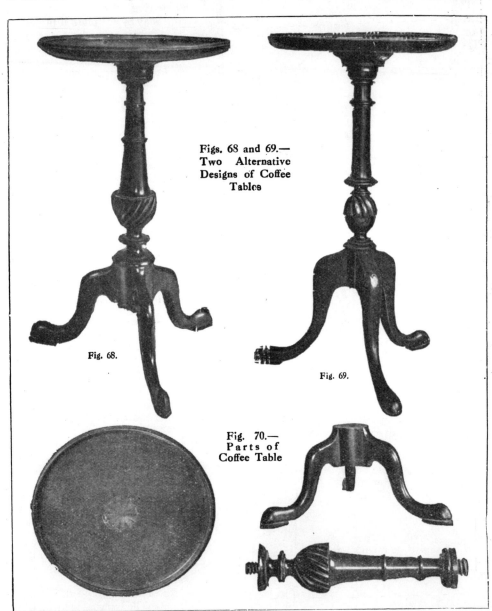

Figs. 68 and 69.—Two Alternative Designs of Coffee Tables

Fig. 68.

Fig. 69.

Fig. 70.—Parts of Coffee Table

the table (Fig. 68), and Figs. 77 to 81 refer to Fig. 69. Whether the worker does his own turning, or gets it done by a profes-

and 77 ; also for tops, as in Fig. 72. The stem (Fig. 71) will require 3-in. diameter material to finish $2\frac{3}{4}$ in. ; and Fig. 77

requires 2-in. stuff to finish 1¾ in. The collars are 5 in. in diameter by 1 in. thick, and the tops are of the same thickness.

The patterns for the legs are easily drawn by ruling a piece of cardboard with 1-in. squares, and forming the curves as in Figs. 73 and 79. They must be cut out (Fig. 71), and Fig. 81 is somewhat similar, but reversed, for the stem (Fig. 77). Fig. 78 shows the carved work on the top of the table (Fig. 69); but it is not essential, and may be left plain if preferred.

When the turning is done the next thing is to mark out the part of the stem

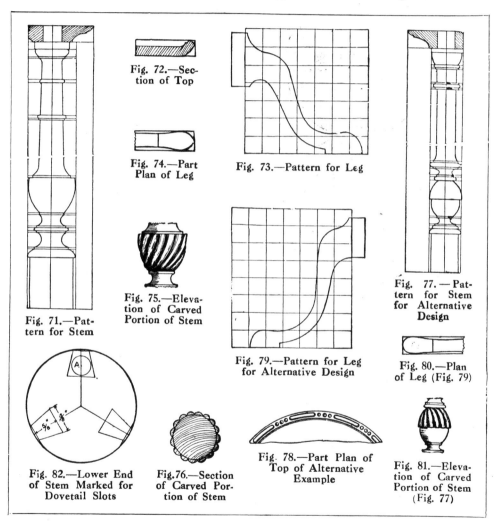

Fig. 72.—Section of Top

Fig. 74.—Part Plan of Leg

Fig. 73.—Pattern for Leg

Fig. 75.—Elevation of Carved Portion of Stem

Fig. 71.—Pattern for Stem

Fig. 77. — Pattern for Stem for Alternative Design

Fig. 79.—Pattern for Leg for Alternative Design

Fig. 80.—Plan of Leg (Fig. 79)

Fig. 82.—Lower End of Stem Marked for Dovetail Slots

Fig. 76.—Section of Carved Portion of Stem

Fig. 78.—Part Plan of Top of Alternative Example

Fig. 81.—Elevation of Carved Portion of Stem (Fig. 77)

with a sharp-pointed knife, to be used for marking out on the 1-in. thick board. When the legs are cut, other patterns, as Figs. 74 and 80, are required for marking the shape of the feet. Figs. 75 and 76 show the carved work on the stem to be carved. The carving is done simply with a ⅜-in. bevelled paring chisel. The lower part of the stem must be set out for making the three dovetail slots for joining on the legs, as in Fig. 82. First find the three angle points on the circumference, and mark lines from these to the centre point. These lines must also be marked perpendicularly up the stem, and other lines $\frac{3}{8}$ in. at each side of them. The $\frac{3}{4}$-in. space

then be chiselled off to the shape, and the upper side of the leg rounded. With these legs the underside also is rounded, but oftener they are left flat. In any case

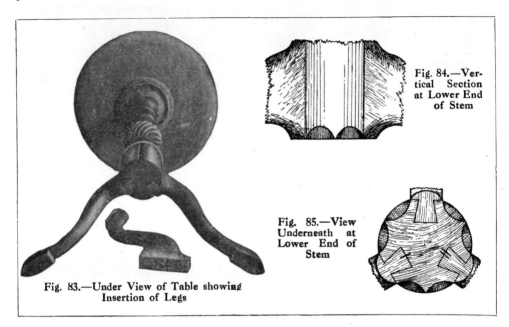

Fig. 83.—Under View of Table showing Insertion of Legs

Fig. 84.—Vertical Section at Lower End of Stem

Fig. 85.—View Underneath at Lower End of Stem

between these lines must be chiselled flat, and the centre lines marked again ; also other lines $\frac{3}{16}$ in. at each side of them. These latter indicate the narrow opening of the dovetail slot, which must spread to $\frac{5}{8}$ in. and $\frac{5}{8}$ in. deep. The waste is removed first by boring from the end, as shown at A (Fig. 82). They are then sawn at the lines and cleaned out with the chisel and mallet.

The trimming up and fitting of the legs is an interesting piece of work to a woodworker. First the dovetails should be marked on the part allowed for joining, and the cuts on the sides of the leg may be made. By fixing a wood hand-screw in the bench-vice the awkward handling is overcome. The point of the feet may

they require continual judging with the eye to obtain a pleasing shape. To form the shoe, they are cut with the fine saw $\frac{1}{16}$ in. deep, and pared with the chisel to make the line more distinct. The dovetail pins may then be sawn and trimmed carefully to fit. They should taper slightly, and be tried in place, but should not be driven in too tightly, to be taken out again for gluing. They must be marked before taking out to know their correct positions (Fig. 83), and both the slots and pins must be glued. The top is fixed with three screws through the collar. The square corner on the lower end of the stem between the legs is "thumb" notched with a $\frac{5}{8}$-in. gouge (Figs. 84 and 85).

Gate-leg Tables

OVAL GATE-LEG TABLE

THE construction of a gate-leg table as shown by Fig. 1 appears to be somewhat it measures 3 ft. 6 in. by about 1 ft. 8 in., and when placed against a wall makes a convenient side or auxiliary table. The working diagrams are to the scale given on

Fig. 1.—Oval Gate-leg Table

complicated, but when carefully considered it is easily within the scope of the amateur woodworker.

The illustration shows a table 4 ft. 6 in. by 3 ft. 6 in. When both leaves are down page 846. Figs. 2 and 3 show two elevations. The gate-leg principle is handy and decorative in smaller sizes, and the illustrations may be adapted by making a new scale. For dining-tables, 2 ft. 4½ in.

is the usual height, and for smaller occasional tables the height ranges from

draw the outlined oval of the top, make a horizontal line 4 ft. 6 in. long, and a

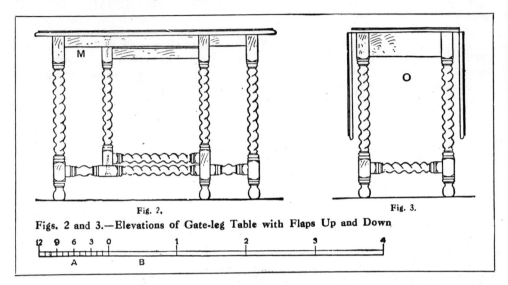

Fig. 2.   Fig. 3.

Figs. 2 and 3.—Elevations of Gate-leg Table with Flaps Up and Down

2 ft. upwards, according to requirements or special considerations.

central vertical line 3 ft. 6 in. long (*see* dotted lines in Fig. 4). With a radius of

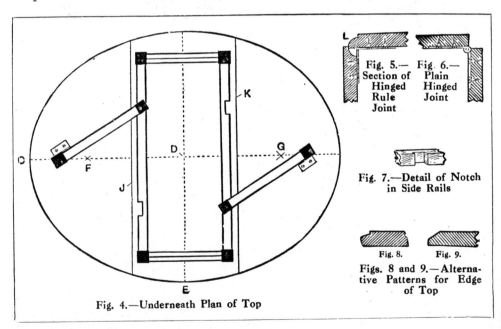

Fig. 4.—Underneath Plan of Top

Fig. 5.— Section of Hinged Rule Joint

Fig. 6.— Plain Hinged Joint

Fig. 7.—Detail of Notch in Side Rails

Fig. 8.   Fig. 9.

Figs. 8 and 9.—Alternative Patterns for Edge of Top

First make full-size working drawings on sheets of paper gummed together. To

half the length, c to d, draw an arc, taking e as the centre, and where it cuts the horizontal line at F and G drive two nails through the paper and into the floor, and another nail at E. Stretch and tie a length of string extending round E, F, and G, forming a triangle. Remove the nail at E only, and draw the outline of the oval by keeping a pencil upright, pressing against the inside of the string. The above rule applies to an oval when the length and width are first decided on. The two vertical lines J and K, 1 ft. 6½ in. apart, represent the hinged joints of the leaves and the bed.

dowelled. When making up the widths of the leaves, a saving in length of wood may be made by noting where the joints come, and allowing for the gradual lessening of the oval end. If the hinged joints of the table are to be of the rule-joint kind, as in Fig. 5, then the projecting part L must be added to the bed. This joint is usually made with special planes ; it has a very neat appearance, forming an ovolo moulding when the leaves are down. If the table is used only with the leaves raised, then the ordinary joint, as at

Fig. 10.—Another Example of Gate-leg Table

The legs may be about 2¼ in. square ; for a 3-ft. 6-in. table about 2 in. ; for a 2-ft. 6-in. table about 1⅝ in. The gate-legs may be about ¼ in. less than the corner ones, also the turned cross-rails. Before proceeding with the plan (Fig. 4) draw the side elevation (Fig. 2) and the end elevation (Fig. 3). It is advisable, before proceeding further with the table, to obtain the timber for the legs.

The table top should be of 1-in. stuff (¾-in. for smaller tables), the centre part and the leaves being made up of available widths of board jointed together and

Fig. 6, is sufficient. The side top rails M (Fig. 2) are dovetailed into the tops of the legs ; the end rails O (Fig. 3) and the lower side and end rails have tenons fitting in mortises in the legs. Very thick screws may form the centres on which the gates move, the one at the top being inserted before the table top is fixed with screws to the under-framing. To allow for the gate-legs closing against the upper and lower side rails, the latter must be notched for nearly half their thickness, and the gate-legs to correspond (see Fig. 7). The table top may have a moulding, as in Fig. 8, or a simple bevelled edge, as in Fig. 9.

necessary elevations and plan are given by Figs. 11, 12 and 13. The main dimen-

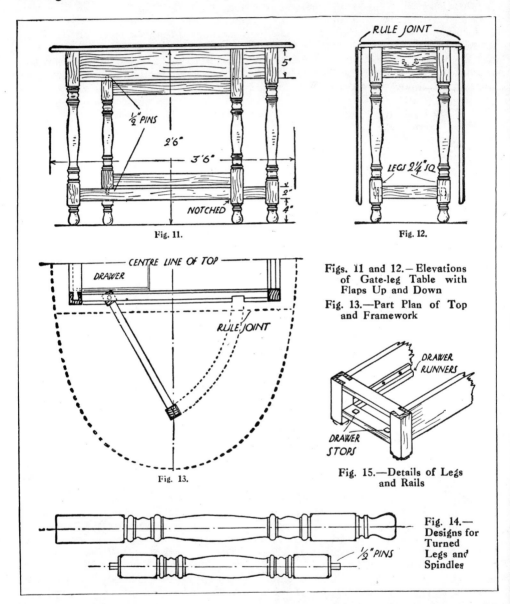

Fig. 11.

Fig. 12.

Figs. 11 and 12.—Elevations of Gate-leg Table with Flaps Up and Down

Fig. 13.—Part Plan of Top and Framework

Fig. 13.

Fig. 15.—Details of Legs and Rails

Fig. 14.—Designs for Turned Legs and Spindles

ANOTHER EXAMPLE OF GATE-LEG TABLE

Another gate-leg table of different design is shown by Fig. 10, while the

sions of the table are 5 ft. 9 in. long over all, 3 ft. 6 in. wide, and 2 ft. 6 in. high. The most suitable material for the table will be, of course, good-quality oak.

The legs, of which there are eight,

should be prepared first, the four main ones being 2¼ in. square and the legs of the two " gates " a little lighter—2 in. square. Fig. 14 suggests the patterns for the legs. The rails of both the table and the gates can be prepared, after which the actual construction can be commenced. Details of this are shown in Fig. 15, the central table being framed up in the usual way, the lower rails of 2-in. square stuff and the upper 5-in. by 1-in. The two gates, which are framed up with the ordinary mortise-and-tenon joints, swing between the rails of the centre portion, for which purpose ½-in. pins are turned at each end of the hinging legs. The outer or meeting legs are notched or halved into the upper and lower rails of the table, so that the whole lies flush when the gate is closed. As the upper rail of the table is of only 1-in. material, a ⅜-in. iron pin might be substituted for the one turned on the end of the hinging leg. In each case care must be taken that the centre of the upper pivot is vertically over the centre of the lower to ensure the gate swinging true. Provision is made for a drawer at one end of the table, the runners for which are screwed to the inner side of the rails (*see* Fig. 15). The drawer could, if desired, be partitioned off for cutlery.

The top, of ⅞-in. material, is in three portions, the centre and two leaves or flaps, the shape of the whole being that indicated in the plan (Fig. 13). It is slightly fuller at the ends than a true ellipse, which, although possibly having a better appearance, would be less economical in material and accommodation than the shape suggested. The three portions will probably have to be jointed up from two or more widths of timber each, preferably being dowelled together. The rule joint shown in Fig. 12 is the best to employ when hinging the flap, as it presents a good appearance when it is folded down. This may, with care, be worked with a suitable pair of hollow and round moulding planes, and three strap hinges fitted to the underside as shown. The centre of the top is fastened to the framework by sinking channels on the inner side of the top rails with a gouge, and screwing from beneath. When the three parts have been fitted and hinged the whole top may be finished to shape and a simple thumb moulding worked on the edge. A couple of small wedge-shaped stops might be fixed to the underside of the leaves to keep the gates in their correct position, and the construction is completed.

Draw and Extending Dining Tables

MEDIÆVAL DRAW TABLES

THE dining table, so much in evidence now, is usually constructed on the telescope or dovetail-slide principle and, like others characteristic of European countries, the method of extension is based upon a telescope or dining-table screw.

justified, for by no other system can such a length be obtained so compactly, or be operated in such a simple fashion with a single or double screw. For tables, however, that are not required to extend to quite twice the length of the bed frame, it is extremely doubtful whether the dovetail slider or telescope

Fig. 1.—Elizabethan Draw Table with Carved Legs and Inlaid Rail

The advantages of this system lie in the great length to which these tables can be extended, and, conversely, to the comparatively small space they occupy when closed, it being no uncommon thing to manufacture tables which, when closed, occupy a space not more than 4 ft. long, and which may be extended to a length of 16 ft. or even 18 ft. It is in this way that the telescope system of extension is

system is the better. There are draw tables—so named from their peculiar construction—which dispose of the least satisfactory features of ordinary dining tables, and combine in a marked degree the essential feature of utility and the excellent feature of artistic merit. The latter is a difficult problem with modern table-designers. The draw table is of considerable antiquity, although there are modern developments, patented, embracing a slight improvement in the slider action.

most furniture of the time, it is made in an extremely strong fashion, and stands

Fig. 2.—Elizabethan Table and Joint Stool

Figs. 1, 2 and 3 show three examples of the mediæval type, the constructional features of each being practically the same. Fig. 1 is a fine example of to-day in almost the same condition as when it left the craftsman's hands four hundred years ago. The tops are framed together, the stuff is about $1\frac{3}{4}$ in. thick,

Fig. 3.—Draw Table with Bottle-shaped Legs

Elizabethan woodwork. It is essentially mediæval in character, and, similarly to

and in the large top there are six panels firmly mortised and tenoned together. A top of this character that has to stand alone, without any fixing to the framing rails, as is usual with ordinary dining tables, has, it will be obvious, to be

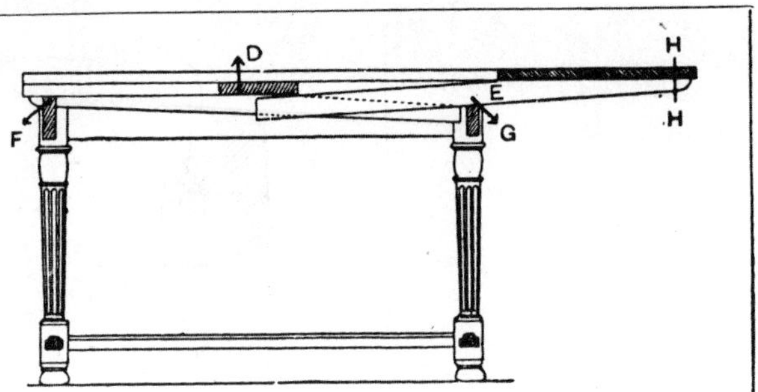

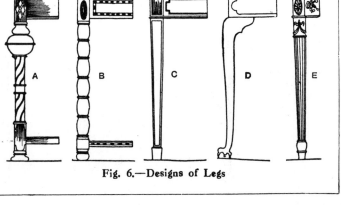

Fig. 4.—Sectional Elevation under Top of Draw Table

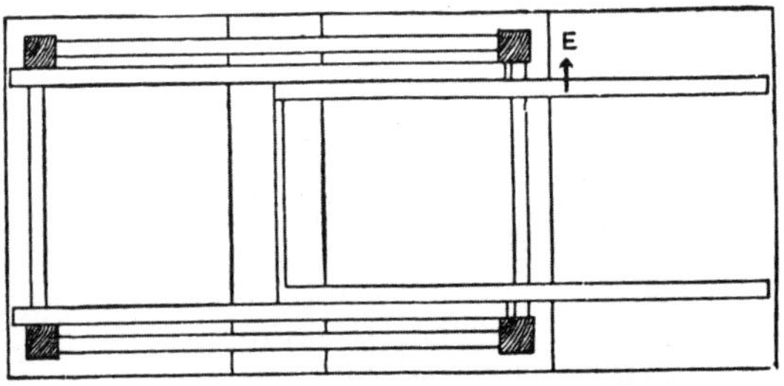

Fig. 5.—Plan Under Top of Draw Table

INCHES· SCALE·

specially well constructed in order to stand flat and be kept free from warping. Underneath the main top there are two smaller ones in leaves, to give them their correct designation (*see* Figs. 4 and 5). These also are specially constructed, being mitre-clamped together with mortise-and-tenon joints.

From the design point of view (Elizabethan) there is much to be learned from this piece and that illustrated by Fig. 2. The legs are those technically known as

Fig. 6.—Designs of Legs

acorn shape. The leaf carvings on the legs are particularly good Elizabethan detail, as is also the inlay work on the side and end rails. Although the proportion between the carved cappings of the legs and the swelled part or shaft are at first sight disproportionate, a sympathetic study of this style will reveal in these unique proportions a massiveness and richness of effect which is eminently suited to dining-room furniture. Some modern furniture experts query the suitability of under-framing on dining tables, which, incidentally, can only be introduced in the fixed types, or with draw tables. It is generally agreed that mahogany tables to which a high degree of finish has been imparted, are spoiled by the continual action of boots upon the under frames. But where oak is the material employed, with a dull or fumed finish, no

detrimental effect is produced by using them fairly as foot-rests. Many of these old types, and indeed nearly all of the mediæval draw tables, were provided with foot-rests, and the evidences of wear they exhibit testify to their appreciation by the users. Fig. 3 is another fine example brackets are added underneath the rails, a detail peculiar to the Dutch types, a somewhat unnecessary detail, however,

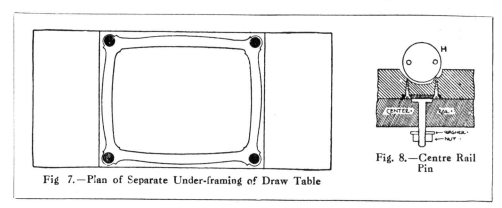

Fig 7.—Plan of Separate Under-framing of Draw Table

Fig. 8.—Centre Rail Pin

of a draw table in the Elizabethan style. The similarity between this and Fig. 1 will be noted, and it is interesting as showing the variation of details, with almost the same outlines and general treatment. The rails exhibit carved nulling, a popular detail in Elizabethan and Jacobean woodwork, especially the former. The acorn or bottle-shaped legs shown in the previous examples are Dutch in character, and were developed from the bulbous-shaped legs introduced into England from the Continent. Such an example is that shown in Fig. 3; it is

for dining tables, which are nearly always covered when in actual use. Gadrooning is another detail very much used in Elizabethan turning and carving. It resembles somewhat the nulled decoration of the rails, or it may be defined as inverted fluting. That shown in the legs in Fig. 1 is very good, the strapwork surrounding each inverted flute being a detail that should be particularly noted.

Although draw tables are chiefly made in the Elizabethan style, there is no specific reason why their production should be confined to these periods of

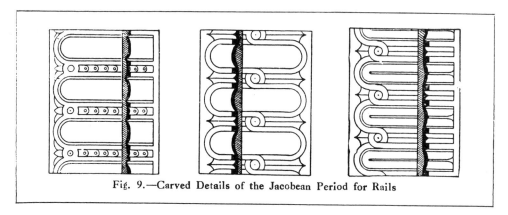

Fig. 9.—Carved Details of the Jacobean Period for Rails

a particularly good specimen. In addition to the leg and rail decoration it will be seen that small pierced or fretted design. They can be produced to advantage in woods such as mahogany and Italian walnut, and give a good scope for the ingenuity of the designer in decorating them. The legs, for instance, can be turned, or even thurmed in square moulded legs, of which an example is shown by D (Fig. 6). A carved or recessed knee part adds to the general effect. A and B show two alternate treatments for turning suitable for furniture based on the eighteenth-century styles. They are also produced with twisted turning based on the Cromwellian and Early Queen Anne periods. When inlaid, with legs tapered and inlaid as at C (Fig. 6), they are quite in accordance with the delicacy peculiar to Sheraton work, whilst D shows a "Queen

structive feature of this example, which can be extended to a variety of other furniture, lies in the construction of a framed-up shape, made completely independent of the legs or rails, and secured to the legs by the toes. This is effected by stopping the legs immediately above the position of the under-framing, and boring a hole 1 in. in diameter about 2 in. into the bottom part of the leg. The toes or feet are turned up into corresponding pins or dowels in the solid, which pass through holes in the under-framing. When all are glued in position, a particularly strong job is effected.

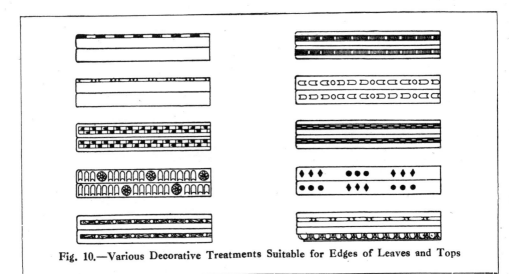

Fig. 10.—Various Decorative Treatments Suitable for Edges of Leaves and Tops

Anne" design, and E an "Adams" treatment. The essential factor to consider in designing these tables to harmonise with definite period work is proportion and ornament, and the former is not a difficult matter to a designer conversant with the historical periods. Under-framings would hardly be in line with the eighteenth-century periods ; but when they are designed in William and Mary, Queen Anne and Early Georgian lines, they can be introduced with considerable effect. Fig. 7 shows the application of under-framing to an Early Georgian example executed in Italian walnut. The construction

Reverting to the photograph reproduced by Fig. 3, this fine specimen is of Dutch origin, and shows excellent bottle-shape legs. From this source, it should be noted, much furniture of the seventeenth century in England was developed. Considering the date of this piece, one is struck by the refined lines and detail of the design. A pleasing feature is the "thimble" carving on the knee part—and above the feet—of the legs ; the brackets underneath the rails are also excellent detail.

Regarding the construction of these tables, reference should be made to

Fig. 4, in which is shown a longitudinal section through the table, illustrating the system of extension. It will be observed from this diagram that a centre rail D is fixed to the framework, and sliders E (Figs. 4 and 5) operate under the centre rail and above the end rails, these being notched out to receive them. The complete success of the action depends on these sliders, and, assuming that the top and leaves in this case are each $1\frac{3}{4}$ in. thick, the rail should be so notched at the part marked F (Fig. 4) to allow a clear space equal to the thickness of the top

withdraw a leaf, it is simply pulled out, this causing the top to rise slightly, and where the leaf is pulled out to its fullest extent, the top will drop and rest on the bearer as shown in the sectional view. It should here be noted that the top is secured to the fixed centre rail with two card-table movements, consisting of a plate sunk into the underside of the top. A pin passes from this plate through the centre rail, and a nut screwed into same and carefully adjusted allows the top to be raised (Fig. 8). When it is required to close the table up, the centre top is raised

Fig. 11.—Extending Top Dining Table

that has been withdrawn. Or, again, the part G showing above the leg must equal the thickness of the top, and the slider or bearer at H must equal the space from underneath the top to the bottom of the notch in the rail.

The plan view (Fig. 5) shows how the two pairs of sliders are arranged. Two run inside the pair on the opposite side, and, to prevent them working apart, they are connected with a rail dovetailed into their ends. All sliders are screwed to the underside of the leaves or small tops, and blocks between the outside sliders and the rails facilitate their working action. To

slightly and one leaf can then be pushed in, the operation being repeated at the other end. The modern development of this action, previously mentioned, is a patent lever arrangement fixed under the leaves, by which means the centre top can be raised sufficiently to permit of the entry of a leaf. Two are, of course, fixed, one in each table ; the centre also has an action to facilitate the action of the sliders. With this it is necessary to also fix runners to the framework, these, together with the sliders, being channelled out to admit the insertion of small wheels. This latter development, while it certainly renders the opening and closing process somewhat easier, involves a good deal of extra labour, and, excepting the very large illustrated and described. Fig. 10 shows various decorative treatments suitable for the edges of the top and leaves.

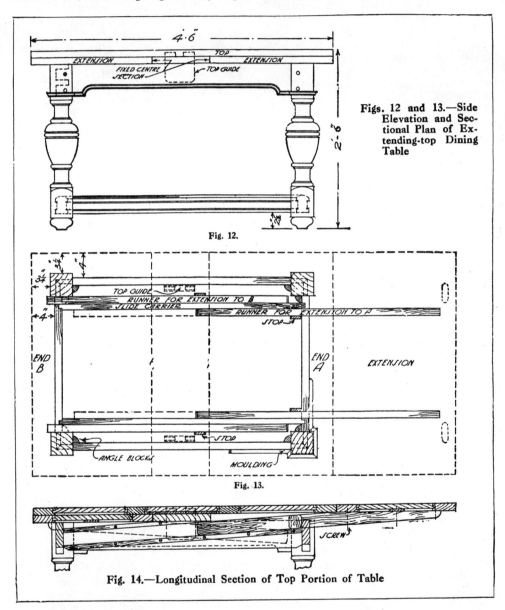

Figs. 12 and 13.—Side Elevation and Sectional Plan of Extending-top Dining Table

Fig. 12.

Fig. 13.

Fig. 14.—Longitudinal Section of Top Portion of Table

or heavy types, it is unnecessary. In Fig. 9 are shown various decorative details which could be employed to advantage on the rails of tables similar to those

EXTENDING-TOP DINING TABLE

The method of extension embodied in the table shown by Fig. 11 is a modern adaptation of the old-fashioned principle previously described. Modern constructional features are also introduced.

extending operation, the fixed centre section, and the two extensions. A plan and longitudinal section are shown by

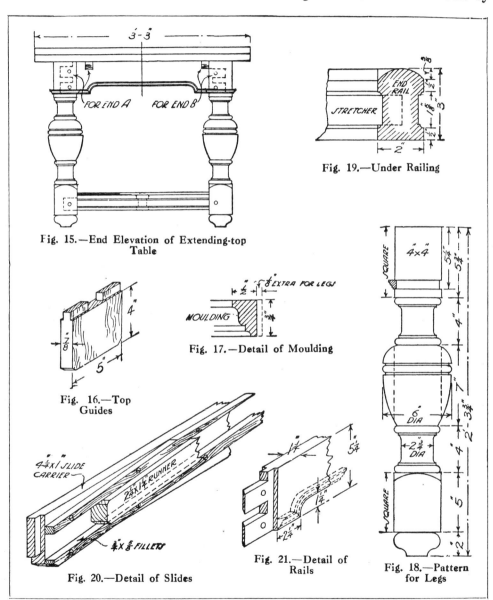

Fig. 15.—End Elevation of Extending-top Table

Fig. 19.—Under Railing

Fig. 16.—Top Guides

Fig. 17.—Detail of Moulding

Fig. 20.—Detail of Slides

Fig. 21.—Detail of Rails

Fig. 18.—Pattern for Legs

Fig. 12 is a side elevation of the table closed, and in this same figure appear the names on parts concerned, these being the top, which rises and falls during the

Figs. 13 and 14, and an end elevation by Fig. 15. To extend the table an extension is pulled out from the end, and it will be seen on reference to Fig. 14 that these are each carried on runners working in slides which are oblique, so that on the extension reaching its outward limit it will have

member is fully out and the two parts become flush. The section shows the table with one end extended. The top

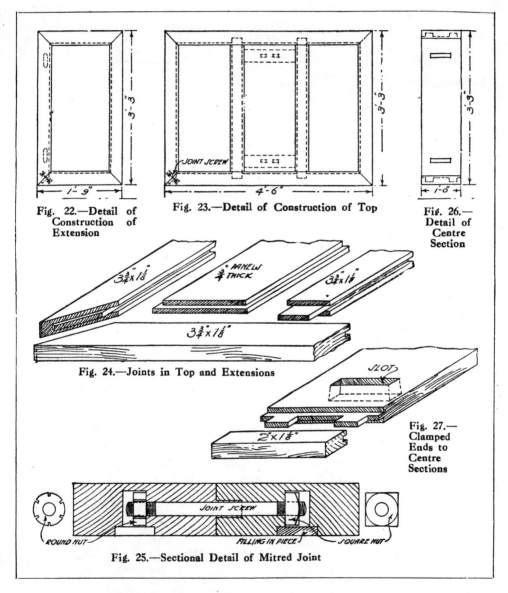

Fig. 22.—Detail of Construction of Extension

Fig. 23.—Detail of Construction of Top

Fig. 26.—Detail of Centre Section

Fig. 24.—Joints in Top and Extensions

Fig. 27.—Clamped Ends to Centre Sections

Fig. 25.—Sectional Detail of Mitred Joint

risen above its former level to the extent of the thickness of the top (in this case $1\frac{1}{8}$ in.). During this operation the top is lifted by the moving extension, but falls back to its normal position when that

guides, shown dotted in the illustrations and detailed in Fig. 16, are stub-tenoned into the underside of the top and work in slots cut in the fixed centre section to keep the top in position and ensure its falling correctly. Both ends of the table act similarly, and to close it the top must be lifted by hand sufficient for the introduction of the edge of the extension, which is then pushed in.

As regards the construction of the table, the legs and rails are framed together with haunched tenons, draw-bored and dowelled, and blocks are glued in angles to add strength. A slight difference occurs with the rail tenons for the end B, owing to the notches for the runners coming close up to the legs, and this is indicated in Fig. 15. The moulding, of which a detail is given (Fig. 17), is planted on the face of the rails and carried round the legs, these being recessed $\frac{1}{8}$ in. to receive it. Lines dotted on the detail of the turned legs (Fig. 18) show where the 4 in. by 4 in. must be packed out for turning to the larger diameter. The two end under-rails are tenoned and dowelled in place, and the long stretcher rail is tenoned to these, the rounding on the former members being stopped in the middle where the stretcher abuts (see Fig. 19). Fig. 20 is a detail of the slides, consisting of $4\frac{1}{4}$ in. by 1 in. slide carriers with a pair of oak fillets screwed to each side, one pair running up as shown, and the other pair running up from the opposite end. These must, of course, be very carefully set out full-size, as accuracy at this point is essential to the proper working of the table. The slope required is one that gives a rise of $1\frac{1}{8}$ in. in a distance of 1 ft. 9 in. The fact that the top fillet comes to a feather-edge is not of consequence, as the thrust from the runner when the extension is out is taken by the fixed centre section, the fillet at this point merely acting as a packing piece. Six screws are used to fix each extension to the hardwood runners placed where indicated in Fig. 14, and it will be observed that a packing piece is necessary under the middle screws as the extensions are not flush on the underside. Stops are fixed to each runner, those at the end A (Fig. 13) striking on the inner face of the rail and those at the end B striking on the legs. Both end rails have, of course, to be notched for the passage of their respective pairs of runners. A detail of the rails is shown by Fig. 21. The top, etc., above the rails will now be dealt with.

Dealing first with the top and extensions, the method of construction is shown in Figs. 22, 23, 24 and 25, and it will be seen that they consist of a frame of $3\frac{3}{4}$-in. by $1\frac{1}{8}$-in. stuff (finished) tongued and grooved at the mitres, and further strengthened at these joints with joint screws. The frames, including muntins in the case of the top, are grooved $\frac{3}{8}$ in. by $\frac{3}{8}$ in. to receive $\frac{3}{4}$-in. panels, all being flush on the top side. Two finger grips are sunk in the underside of the extensions where indicated, and packing pieces, 3 in. by $\frac{3}{8}$ in., are fixed across the middle panel of the top to obtain a deeper mortise for the fixing of the top guides.

Figs. 26 and 27 show the centre section which is of $1\frac{1}{8}$-in. stuff (finished thickness) throughout. It has both ends clamped and is, as previously mentioned, slotted in suitable position for the two top guides, the slots being a snug fit to these on the top side, but slightly tapered outwards at their ends towards the bottom, to allow for free movement of the guides when the top is lifted and in a tilted position. The centre section is fixed to the side rails with screws.

If casters are added to the table, the height of the legs should be reduced correspondingly.

SCREW-OPERATED DRAW TABLE

The telescopic dining table shown by Fig. 28 is the usual type in which the legs are moved with the top. The table shown is a fairly good size when drawn out, being 14 ft. long and 4 ft. 6 in. wide. It will bear a much greater weight than any other expanding table, but more material is required, consequently it is more expensive than other kinds. It is essential that the larger tables should be made completely of hardwood. The under-construction of the sliders, etc., bears a tremendous strain when the table is drawn out full size, and the sliders being composed of short lengths, must be sufficiently strong at those parts of lapping when the sliders are at the top. Fig. 29 shows a plan of the table without the top.

The legs having been chosen of the desired pattern should be 4½ in. square at the top. These are joined together in pairs by the under-framing at the desired height of the table, minus the thickness of the table top and height of the caster-wheel. These rails A (Fig. 29) are 4½ in. deep and 1⅜ in. thick. The distance between the legs is 3 ft. 5 in., which is the same distance as the shoulders apart on

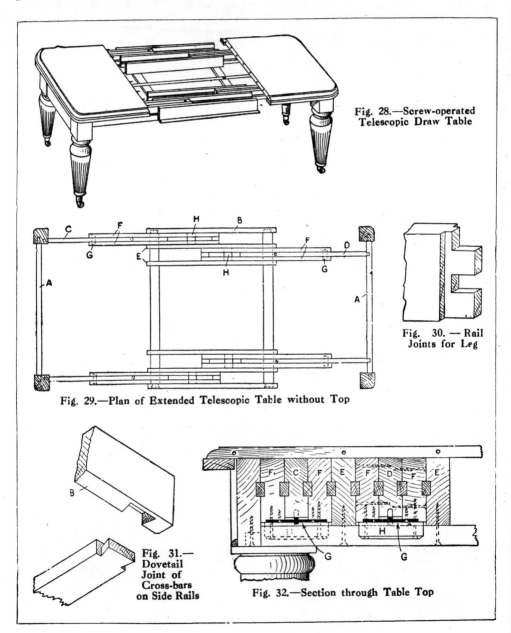

Fig. 28.—Screw-operated Telescopic Draw Table

Fig. 30. — Rail Joints for Leg

Fig. 29.—Plan of Extended Telescopic Table without Top

Fig. 31.—Dovetail Joint of Cross-bars on Side Rails

Fig. 32.—Section through Table Top

the rails. The tenon at each end will be 2½ in. long, so it is necessary to cut the rails to 3 ft. 10 in. long. Fig. 30 shows the method of making these strong joints. The tenon is ⅝ in. thick, and when driven rail at the other end of the table. There are sixteen sliders, eight on each side, all of them being 1¼ in. thick. The four fixed sliders F are made the full depth of 3½ in., as shown in Fig. 32. These are

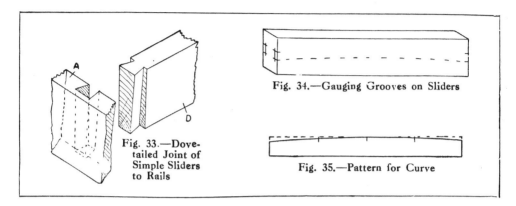

Fig. 33.—Dovetailed Joint of Simple Sliders to Rails

Fig. 34.—Gauging Grooves on Sliders

Fig. 35.—Pattern for Curve

together the face of the rail is ¾ in. beyond the face of the leg. The two side rails B (Fig. 29) are 3 ft. 6 in. long, 4½ in. deep, and 1⅛ in. thick, framed together by two cross-bars 3 in. by 1 in., which are dovetailed underneath about 2 in. from each end. The dovetails are 1 in. long and lapped into grooves ¾ in. deep, as shown in Fig. 31. The distance outside the rails B should be 4 ft. 1½ in.; this will allow the side rails to be just within the face of the legs when closed up. The dovetailed frame gives a space above the cross-bars of 3½ in., in which the sliders work.

The sliders, excepting the four single

secured with screws through the cross-bars underneath. The double sliders E are ¼ in. less in depth (3¼ in.), and the single sliders ½ in. less (3 in.). The section of half the table (Fig. 32) shows them clearly. When all the sliders are prepared to size, they should be laid together in position and exact measurements taken for the joints of the single sliders. Those marked C are mortised and tenoned into the legs, as shown in Fig. 30. These should be draw-bored and pinned from the inside when finally fixed together, as these joints are in tension and have to receive great strain. The sliders

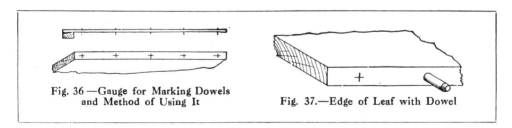

Fig. 36.—Gauge for Marking Dowels and Method of Using It

Fig. 37.—Edge of Leaf with Dowel

ones, are 3 ft. 6 in. long. The single sliders C are 2 in. longer to allow for a tenon into the leg at each side, and those marked D are 3¼ in. longer, because they are extended to make a fixing on to the

D are dovetailed to the rail, as in Fig. 33. The dovetails for these joints are ⅞ in. long and are slightly tapered as shown.

An important part in the making of the table is the grooving and tongueing of the sliders. This must be done so as to make the table top slightly arched shape when extended. By making the grooves in each piece a trifle convex at the top, the centre portion of the table will rise when drawn out to the extent of $\frac{1}{4}$ in. to $\frac{1}{2}$ in., according to the size of the table. This will counteract any tendency of the table to sag, which would be sure to take place if the grooves were made straight. The grooves should be $\frac{3}{4}$ in. wide by $\frac{1}{4}$ in. deep in the middle of the sliders. Fig. 34 shows one of the sliders gauged for the width and depth of the grooves on each side and end. The $\frac{3}{4}$-in. grooving plane is guided by a piece of wood temporarily nailed on. This piece of $\frac{3}{8}$-in. or $\frac{1}{2}$-in. boarding must be convex $\frac{1}{8}$ in. at the middle, and the curve must be regular. It is hardly possible to strike this portion of a circle in the usual way, so proceed to mark it as shown in Fig. 35. The length is divided into four parts, the ends are marked $\frac{1}{8}$ in. down, and the points between the middle and the ends $\frac{1}{16}$ in. below. This edge is rounded off with a smoothing plane. When all the grooves have been made in this way, prepare the hardwood tongues 3 ft. 6 in. long by $\frac{3}{4}$ in. by $\frac{1}{2}$ in. These are glued on both sides of the four single sliders C and D, and on the outsides of the double sliders. Short ends about $2\frac{1}{2}$ in. long are cut off the single sliders and fixed at the ends of the double sliders, as shown in Fig. 29. These are secured by screwing from the outside, with one or two pieces of paper packing each side to give freedom to the sliders.

The end rails and single sliders should now be smoothed up, glued, and cramped into the legs, after which the whole should be placed together and the pieces B secured by gluing and screwing on the cross-bars. The fixed sliders E are secured with screws through the cross-bars underneath. The stops should now be fixed to the sliders so as to allow them to lap about 14 in. when drawn full out. An iron plate G is screwed underneath the ends of the double sliders, and an iron pin driven in underneath the single slider to catch against the plate. This pin is adjusted to give the desired lap. The double sliders

have a block H screwed across underneath to catch against the cross-bar as required. At this stage the double winding screw should be obtained and fixed. The tongues of the sliders are blackleaded to make them work freely.

By allowing the table top to overhang the legs 2 in. at the sides and ends, the boards are cut off so as to finish 4 ft. 6 in. long and 2 ft. $3\frac{1}{2}$ in. wide. The number and widths of the extra leaves or flaps should be ascertained, all of which are cut off to a finish at 4 ft. 6 in. long. The undersides of all boards are then planed true, the edges being shot and planed to their correct widths. The ends are planed square, and all the boards laid together. Now mark for the dowels on each edge. These should be equally spaced, and the end ones about 2 in. from each end of the joint. Fig. 36 shows a gauge which should be made for marking the holes. A small block is fixed on to a strip of wood, and brads driven through at the required distances. Care should be taken to see that the dowels are marked from the same ends of all the boards. Then gauge from the undersides to half the thickness, and bore with a $\frac{3}{8}$-in. twist-bit, all the holes being 1 in. deep. Glue and drive in all the dowels, making sure they are driven in on the same edge, say the right edge of each board. Then cut them off so as to project $\frac{3}{4}$ in., and use a dowel rounder to trim off the corners (Fig. 37).

The table top is fixed with screws from underneath, holes being bored in the usual way through the rails A and the single sliders. There is $\frac{1}{16}$ in. of packing between the rails and the top to facilitate the free working of the curved tongues. This is done by gluing pieces of veneer on the top of the rails each side of the screw-holes. After the tops are screwed on the table should be screwed up tight, the top planed true, and the moulding worked and fixed on as required. The extra leaves are then placed in one at a time and finished off flush with the fixed top. When all are finished, place them in altogether, and scrape and glasspaper to a good surface. The casters are then screwed on, when the table is ready for polishing.

ANOTHER SCREW-OPERATED TELESCOPIC TABLE

The screw-operated extension table is still preferred by many people. The table shown by Fig. 38 is constructed with this system of operation. Fig. 39 is a side elevation of the table fully extended and with the extra leaves A in position, while Fig. 40 shows it in the act of being opened, and Fig. 41 is a plan with the top removed. A section is shown by Fig. 42.

The screw can be obtained from any large furnishing ironmonger.

In constructing the framework, first plane the stuff to the sizes given, and then set out the mortises of the legs and the tenons of the rails, as shown by dotted lines in Fig. 39. The mortises for the inner sliding rails are farther from the front edge of the legs than those for the outer rails, as shown in Figs. 41 and 45. The inner rails or slides c should be ploughed from their top edges, 1 in. wide and ½ in. deep. This groove can be made with a ½-in. plough-iron, or with a rebate plane by fixing a piece of wood at the right distance parallel to the top edge.

Fig. 38.—Screw-operated Telescopic Table

The table is of average simple construction and should be of mahogany, oak, or walnut. When closed this table is 6 ft. long, and it has been designed to extend to 9 ft. with the addition of two 1-ft. 6-in. leaves. The legs, if preferred, can be obtained ready turned, or can be worked as shown from stuff about 4½ in. square. The outer rails for the framework may be solid, or the outside portion may be of ½-in. stuff glued to a pine backing, as shown at B in Fig. 43. The inner rails or slides and the two cross-rails should be of cheap hardwood, such as beech or birch. The former are marked c in Figs. 39 to 43, and the latter D in Figs. 41 to 44 inclusive.

Pieces of hardwood should be planed so as just to fit in the grooves as at E in Figs. 43 and 45, and glued into the grooves of the inner rails. The moulding on the bottom of the outer rails F (Fig. 43) should next be fixed with glue and screws. The cross-rails D should be dovetailed to the inner sliding rails in one case and into the projecting moulding at F in Fig. 43, as sketched in Fig. 44, in the other. Care must be taken in making these dovetails, or the rails, not being parallel, will prevent proper working. When all the joints fit properly, those between the legs and the rails, and between the cross-rails and the latter, should be glued together, keeping

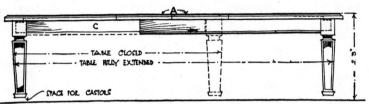

Fig. 39.—Side Elevation of Screw-operated Telescopic Table (Fully Extended)

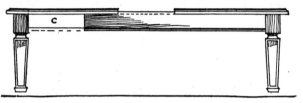

Fig. 40.—Side Elevation of Table (Partly Extended)

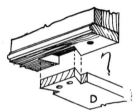

Fig. 44.—Dovetail Joint of Cross Rail and Outer Sliding Rail

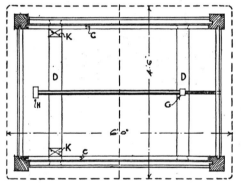

Fig. 41.—Sectional Plan of Table (Closed)

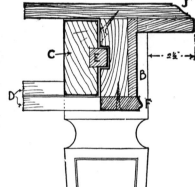

Fig. 43. — Enlarged Sectional Detail at Corner

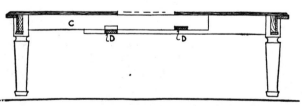

Fig. 42.—Cross Section of Table (Partly Extended)

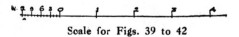

Scale for Figs. 39 to 42

SCALE OF INCHES

the legs and rail square. The cross-rails should also have a couple of screws inserted, as shown in Fig. 44.

The table top must be of well-seasoned material. If it can be obtained in about 1-ft. 6-in. widths, each half will require only one joint. The leaves are also 1 ft. 6 in. wide. The top should be dowelled and glued, and the undersides of the top and leaves trued up. Next join together the two portions of the permanent top and the two leaves, and dowel them with hardwood pins about

other end of the barrel being secured at H to the underside of the top, to which it may be necessary to fix a wood block for this purpose. Next tighten the screw a little so as to hold the top firmly together, plane the top and leaves, and work the moulding round the edges shown at J in Fig. 43. The thicknessing fillet shown fixed round the edge of the table top in Fig. 43 should next be prepared. It should be mitred at the angles (which might alternatively be formed as in Fig. 47), fitted round the tops of the legs, and

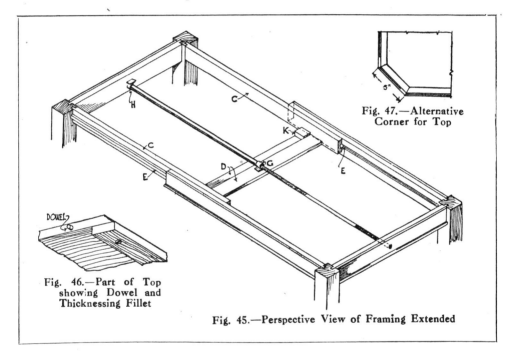

Fig. 47.—Alternative Corner for Top

Fig. 46.—Part of Top showing Dowel and Thicknessing Fillet

Fig. 45.—Perspective View of Framing Extended

$\frac{3}{8}$ in. in diameter, projecting about $\frac{5}{8}$ in. (*see* Fig. 46). The whole should then be stretched out to its full length, as shown in Fig. 39, turned bottom side up, and the framework fastened to the two permanent parts of the top with screws inserted obliquely, as shown in Fig. 43.

The screw and barrel should now be fixed, the handle end of the screw being secured to the end rail of the table. The box in which the screw works, and which holds one end of the barrel, can be fixed to the cross-rail at G (Figs. 41 and 45), the

fixed with glue and screws. It is best to have the two side pieces long enough to reach from end to end, thus taking in the two leaves, afterwards cutting with a fine saw where the joints of the leaves should occur. Two stops K (Figs. 41 and 45) prevent the framework moving too far. This table would be firmer if it extended to 8 ft. 6 in. only, the leaves being then only 1 ft. 3 in. wide ; but at the same time is quite suitable under ordinary conditions for the full-length extension of 9 ft. previously mentioned. The legs are shown square, tapered and simply shaped, the panel effect being produced either by means of an inlaid banding or a sinking on

the outer faces of each leg. In setting out the legs, allowance must be made for the casters in calculating the total length.

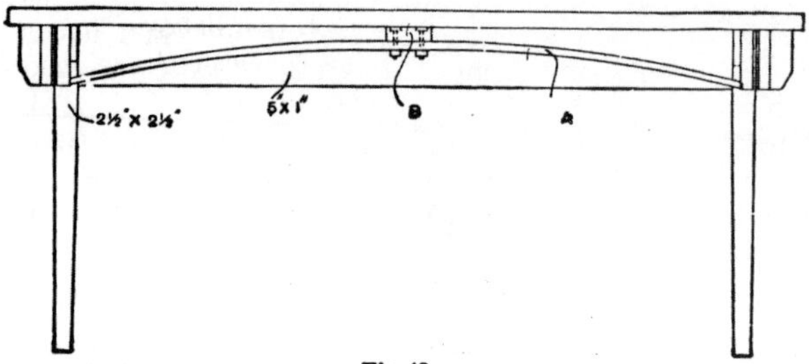

The invisible type, working in a slot cut in the end of each leg, are to be recommended.

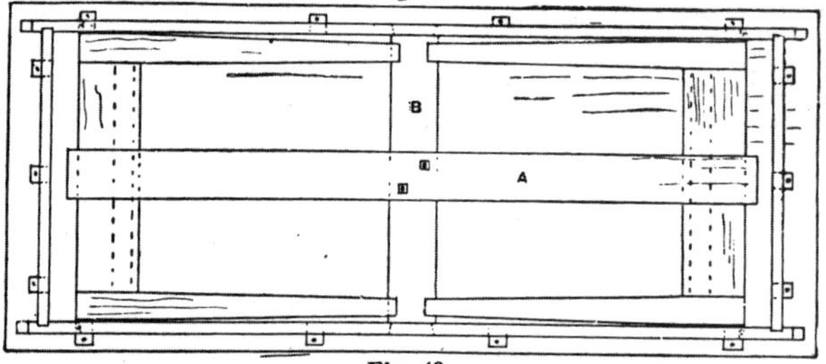

COLLAPSIBLE DINING TABLE

This dining-table is made so that the legs can be folded up within the depth of the side rails, thus making it portable and convenient for stacking away when not in use. The legs are secured, when the table is in use, or when folded up, by means of a wooden spring. The table is an ordinary one in appearance ; but the sectional elevation as shown by Fig. 48 illustrates the wooden spring A for strutting the legs to a rigid position. Fig. 49 is a plan of the underside of the table when folded up. The sizes given are of a table 6 ft. long and 2 ft. 6 in. wide, which is nearly the minimum in length to allow folding space for the legs. If a table of a larger or different size be required to act on this principle, the members of the table should vary accordingly.

Whatever timber is used for the table, it is essential to use oak for the spring A. It is a straight piece of wood 4 in. wide, $\frac{3}{4}$ in. thick in the middle, and is made

Fig 48.

Figs. 48 and 49.—Sectional Elevation and Plan (Legs Folded) of Underside of Collapsible Table

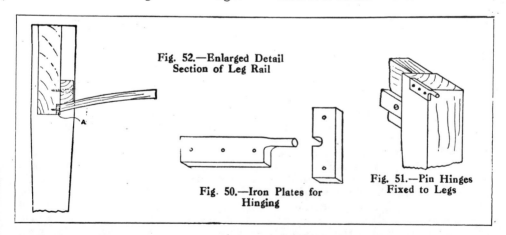

Fig. 52.—Enlarged Detail
Section of Leg Rail

Fig. 50.—Iron Plates for Hinging

Fig. 51.—Pin Hinges Fixed to Legs

thinner to $\frac{1}{2}$ in. at the ends. The length, for the present, should be cut so as to fit between the end rails. This spring is fixed with two $\frac{3}{8}$-in. bolts to the cross bearer B, which can also be of oak, 4 in. by 1 in., dovetailed to the top edges of the side rails before the table top is fixed. The legs, although shown square, can be turned to any shape required, and framed together in pairs by means of rails, as shown in Fig. 49. The rails should be as wide as the side rails, about 5 in. or more, and jointed strongly into the legs, so as to ensure the table being rigid. The plan (Fig. 49) shows the legs folded in with about 2-in. clearance at the ends, and about $\frac{1}{2}$-in. space between the legs and the side rails. The space between the leg rails and the end rails is about $2\frac{1}{2}$ in. to 3 in. The arrangements for hinging the legs are shown by Fig. 50. The hinge plates are made of 1-in. by $\frac{3}{8}$-in. iron. A round end or pin $\frac{3}{4}$ in. long and $\frac{3}{8}$ in. in diameter is filed on the longer piece, and a notch is made to receive this pin on the other piece as shown. The plate with the pin is fixed with screws to the inner top corners of the legs, as shown in Fig. 51,

and the notched plate is let in flush on the side rails. It will be seen that the open notch is uppermost, allowing the leg frames to be lifted out when the table top is off.

The leg rails have a fillet on the inside to make a rebate to receive the wooden spring, which should be fixed $\frac{5}{8}$ in. from the bottom edge of the rails. An iron plate 6 in. long by $\frac{1}{2}$ in. by $\frac{1}{8}$ in. is let flush into the rails, and screwed so as to take the thrust of the spring when the table is erected. Fig. 52 shows a section of leg rail with the fillet and the small iron plate A. Now fix on the table top by the usual method or by means of small iron plates, as indicated in Fig. 49. These plates can be let in flush on the top of the rails, and project over to take a screw for fixing the top. If the pin hinges are fitted properly, the legs should not open beyond the vertical position. The ends of the spring should then be cut off, so as to give a tight thrust to the legs when in position.

To fold the table it is only necessary to lift the spring from the recess of the leg rails.

Chairs

TWO DINING-ROOM CHAIRS

THE chair shown by the half-tone reproduction (Fig. 1) is slightly more difficult to make than the one illustrated by Fig. 2, which is of a somewhat simplified form. Two elevations of this latter are shown by Figs. 3 and 4. The differences may be pointed out, and the reader left to adopt whichever scheme he may prefer, or feel best qualified to undertake.

In the half-tone the two back rails are very slightly curved in plan, and the front of the seat is also curved a little, thus adding somewhat to the finish and appearance of the chair, although these details are not actually essential for its comfort. In this case, also, it will be observed that the lower rails which connect the legs in the simpler design (Fig. 2) do not appear, thus making the whole construction

Fig. 1.—Dining-room Chair

depend for strength on first-class workmanship in the joints between the legs and seat rails.

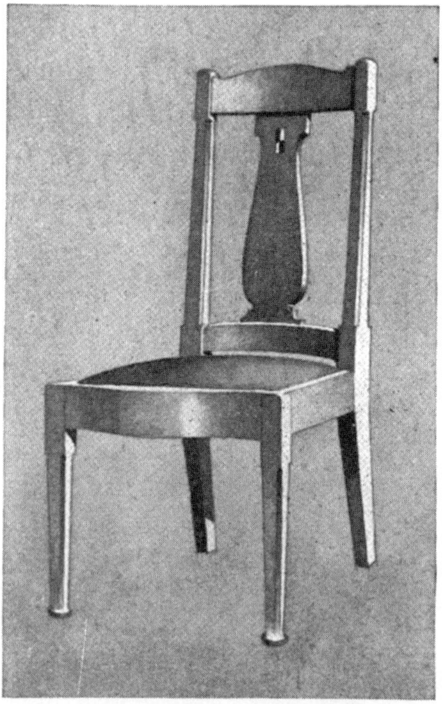

Reverting to the chair shown by Fig. 2, the front legs should be $1\frac{1}{2}$ in. square (finished sizes are given throughout), splayed at the angles as at A in Fig. 5, the splays or chamfers widening downwards, and the four square sides tapering, until just above the floor the legs form in section an octagon contained in a square of 1-in. sides as at B. Below this each leg curves out to a circular foot of about $1\frac{1}{2}$ in. diameter, as clearly indicated in the same figure.

Each back leg should be worked up from a piece $2\frac{1}{4}$ in. by $1\frac{1}{2}$ in. and 3 ft. 7 in. long, the sides of which are shown by the dotted lines at c in Fig. 5, which shows the lower half of one back leg in side elevation. At seat level, and measuring from the dotted line on the left, the

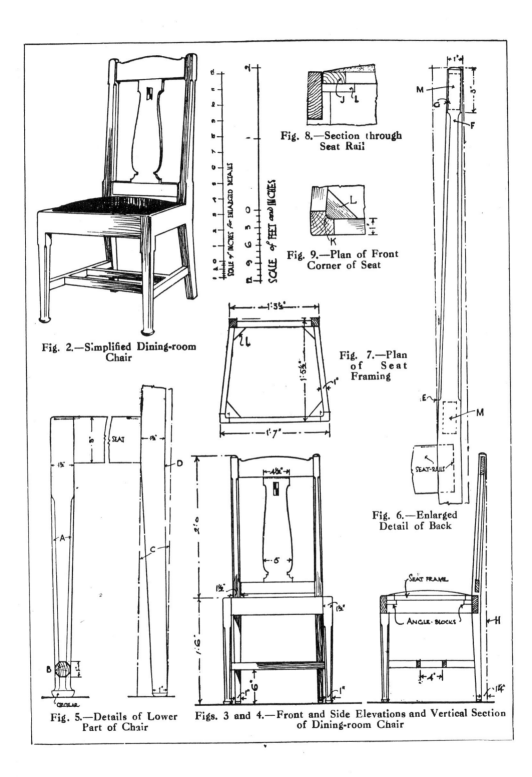

Fig. 2.—Simplified Dining-room
Chair

SCALE OF INCHES for ENLARGED DETAILS

SCALE of FEET and INCHES

Fig. 8.—Section through
Seat Rail

Fig. 9.—Plan of Front
Corner of Seat

Fig. 7.—Plan
of Seat
Framing

Fig. 6.—Enlarged
Detail of Back

Fig. 5.—Details of Lower
Part of Chair

Figs. 3 and 4.—Front and Side Elevations and Vertical Section
of Dining-room Chair

leg is 1⅛ in. wide, whence it tapers downwards to the extreme right of the 2¼ in. width as shown. Next to the floor it to a very slight curve, as at D. In front elevation, the back leg is 1½ in. wide at seat level, and it tapers down to 1 in.

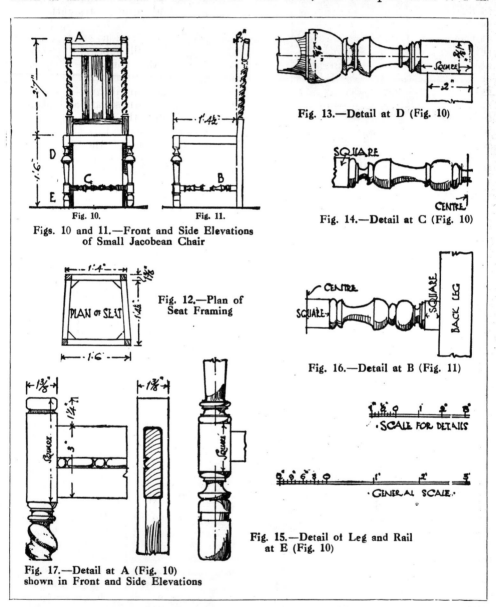

Fig. 13.—Detail at D (Fig. 10)

Fig. 14.—Detail at C (Fig. 10)

Figs. 10 and 11.—Front and Side Elevations of Small Jacobean Chair

Fig. 12.—Plan of Seat Framing

Fig. 16.—Detail at B (Fig. 11)

Fig. 15.—Detail of Leg and Rail at E (Fig. 10)

Fig. 17.—Detail at A (Fig. 10) shown in Front and Side Elevations

is 1 in. wide, and rounded underneath to obviate the need for casters. It should be noted that while the left-hand or front edge is straight, the back edge is finished next to the floor, as clearly shown on the left-hand side of Fig. 3.

The upper part of each back leg is rather more elaborate, being tapered from $1\frac{1}{2}$ in. square at seat level to 1 in. square at the extreme top, the end being slightly rounded, as in Fig. 6. In addition to this tapering, the edges are chamfered as shown, the chamfers being very slight at their start 3 in. above the seat rail E (Fig. 6), and increasing until the leg is nearly octagonal in section at the level of F. Above this the leg is square, but very slightly chamfered off as at G. The method of stopping the larger chamfers by means of a quadrant curve outwards will be noticed. When framed up the back legs slope back as in Fig. 4, the top overhanging the bottom to the extent of $1\frac{1}{4}$ in., as explained by the dotted line H, this being vertical.

The four seat rails are 3 in. by 1 in., and set out in accordance with Fig. 7, tenoned joints being used. Removable padded seats upholstered in leather, etc., on a $1\frac{1}{2}$-in. by $\frac{3}{4}$-in. frame J (Fig. 8) should be adopted for this class of chair. They should be very accurately fitted into the opening formed by the seat rails, the inner angles of the front legs being cut away to suit them, as at K in Fig. 9, and they should be supported on small angle-blocks housed into the latter, as at L in Figs. 7, 8, and 9. The four small rails connecting the legs should be about $1\frac{1}{4}$ in. by $\frac{7}{8}$ in. or $\frac{3}{4}$ in., stub-tenoned in position. Two horizontal rails are required for the back, the lower one 2 in. by $\frac{7}{8}$ in., and the top one $2\frac{1}{2}$ in. by $\frac{3}{4}$ in., this one being shaped, as in Fig. 3, to a very slight curve on the top. Both should be tenoned centrally into the back legs, as at M in Fig. 6, and between them is stub-tenoned a shaped centre slat, 5 in. across at the widest point, $\frac{1}{2}$ in. thick, and relieved with a spot of inlay, as in Fig. 3. Finally the top edges of the front legs and outer angles of the seat rails should be rounded slightly.

SMALL JACOBEAN CHAIR

The characteristic features of the Jacobean style have been retained in the elaborate turning and spiral turning, and the tall, almost upright, back of the chair shown by the two elevations (Figs. 10 and 11). A plan of the seat framing is shown by Fig. 12. There is no curved work, and the framing together will be found quite straightforward. Particular care should be devoted to the turning (*see* later section), as it is on this that the effect will depend. It will be noticed that the spirals of the back uprights both wind outwards, or in other words, wind in opposite directions. The back legs are shown square and plain in order to simplify the work ; but in old work they are usually turned.

Enlarged details of the turning are given by Figs. 13, 14, 15 and 16, the portions left square being noted in all cases. The rail B in the side elevation (Fig. 11) occurs at each side, while that at C in the front elevation (Fig. 10) crosses from side to side in the centre of the two rails at B. The back has a filling of one wide and two narrow uprights with inch spaces between, the narrow ones as well as the top rail having a sunk beaded ornament incised as in the detail, Fig. 17. Alternatively, a narrow cushion might be contrived on the back of the chair : it should be long so as to suit the outer uprights.

The seat might very appropriately be filled in with rush-work, or removable seats, consisting of light padded frames, upholstered with leather or leather-cloth, could be made or obtained, the angle-blocks to support them being indicated on the plan of seat.

Walnut and oak will be found suitable materials.

BEDROOM CHAIR

Lightness and simplicity of design are the usual characteristics of bedroom chairs, and, in their making, any difficulty of construction that may present itself is merely due to the necessity of securing sufficient strength consistent with lightness. The chair shown by Figs. 18 to 21 has been designed with these requirements in view, and their achievement has been chiefly secured by the inclusion of the lower rails, which materially add to the strength of the chair, but do not give it any appearance of clumsiness as would be the case if heavier material was used. As regards the actual construction, this follows almost

good depth (2½ in.) is allowed for the upper rails in order to secure strength, but the deep appearance of these is relieved by the curved lower edge of the

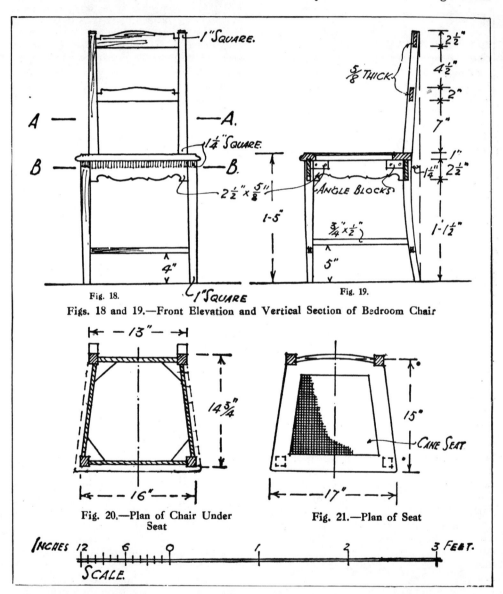

Fig. 18.

Fig. 19.

Figs. 18 and 19.—Front Elevation and Vertical Section of Bedroom Chair

Fig. 20.—Plan of Chair Under Seat

Fig. 21.—Plan of Seat

exactly upon the lines as the chair described earlier in this section (Fig. 2), and therefore repetition is unnecessary. All dimensions are given in the figures. A

rail. In order not to unduly weaken the legs the front and side lower rails are placed on two levels at heights of 4 in. and 5 in. respectively.

A cane seat is shown (Fig. 21), and the fitting of this will probably be beyond the sphere of the worker, but it will be an easy matter to get done, or as an alterna-

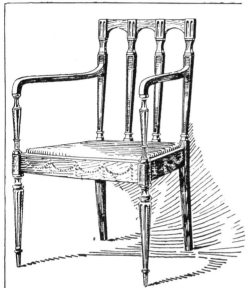

Fig. 22.—Sheraton-Heppelwhite Elbow Chair

tive one of the many prepared seats could be fitted.

TWO SHERATON-HEPPELWHITE ELBOW CHAIRS

Figs. 22 and 23 are modest examples of elbow chairs of the Sheraton style, late eighteenth century, which is no doubt the nearest to our present-day taste. The designs of the Sheraton school are, without question, worthy to rank with other earlier masters, such as Chippendale, Heppelwhite, and Adam. These Sheraton chairs are usually executed in mahogany with satinwood inlay. Light and graceful in construction they are sometimes found with round legs, fluted or reeded, and, as in the example shown, with square tapered legs and toe. Similar designs were also executed with loose upholstered seats covered in various silks.

The general proportions of the various members may be gleaned from the front and side elevations, Figs. 24 and 25, and Figs. 26 and 27. The part plans (Figs. 24 and 26) show the framing and shaping of the seats. Throughout the whole of the framing all the joints should be neatly executed with mortise and tenons of the greatest practicable length according to situation. Due regard, of course, must be observed in the shaping of the various members, viz., arms, back, and seat framing.

SHERATON DINING-PARLOUR CHAIR

Fig. 28 illustrates a fine example of what was known as a dining-parlour chair, also of the Sheraton style. As will be seen the two front legs are not square and tapered as in the two preceding designs, but round and fluted, tapering

Fig. 23.—Alternative Design for Sheraton-Heppelwhite Elbow Chair

to toe, while the two back legs are of square section. Here also will be noted a suggestion of Heppelwhite in the semi-circular detail of the back, with tapered

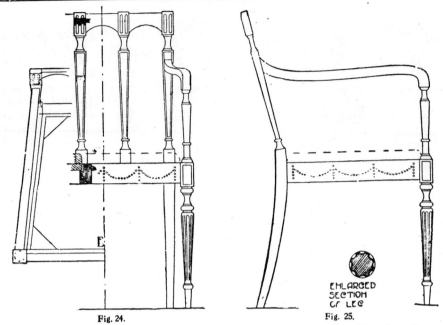

ENLARGED
SECTION
OF LEG

Fig. 24.

Fig. 25.

Figs. 24 and 25.—Part Plan and Part Front Elevation and Side Elevation of Elbow Chair (Fig. 22)

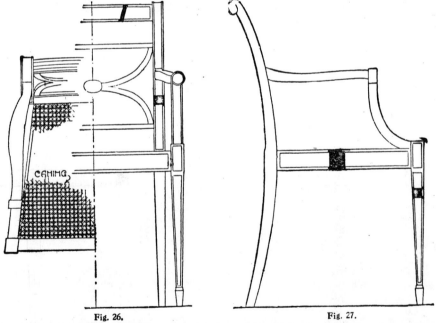

CANING

Fig. 26.

Fig. 27.

Figs. 26 and 27.—Part Plan and Part Front Elevation and Side Elevation of Elbow Chair (Fig. 23)

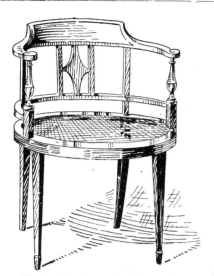

Fig. 28.—Sheraton Dining-parlour Chair

uprights, ornamented with flutes and sinkings. As shown in front elevation (Fig. 29) the framing of the seat is delicately enriched with inlays of satinwood, or coloured woods, festooned, or in many instances hand-painted decorations are applied. The seat in this example is a thinly upholstered loose seat covered in silk, which should sink almost flush with the top of framing. A side elevation is shown by Fig. 30.

CHAIR WITH ADJUSTABLE SEAT AND BACK

An adjustable chair of simple design that could easily be made by anyone with a little knowledge of woodworking is shown by Fig. 31. Front and side elevations and plan are given by Figs. 32, 33 and 34 respectively.

There are four short legs, connected

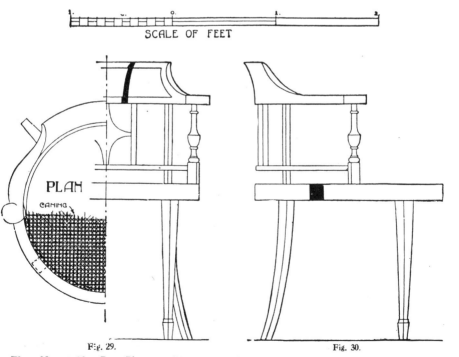

SCALE OF FEET

PLAN

CANING

Fig. 29.

Fig. 30.

Figs. 29 and 30.—Part Plan and Part Front Elevation and Side Elevation of Dining-parlour Chair at the tops by four rails and at the centre by stretchers. Four supports for the arms are fixed at the corners of the lower framing. The arms are given additional over the stuffing. Along each top rail of the seat framing four rollers are pivoted, on which the seat slides (Fig. 35). The back of the seat is pivoted to the bottom

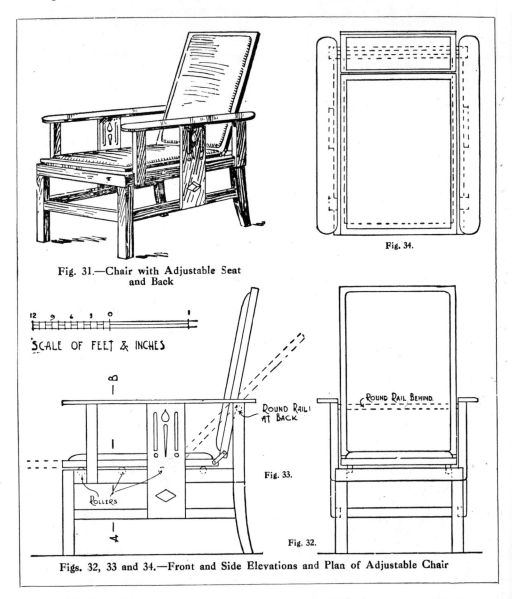

Fig. 31.—Chair with Adjustable Seat and Back

SCALE OF FEET & INCHES

ROUND RAIL AT BACK

ROUND RAIL BEHIND.

ROLLERS

Fig. 32.

Fig. 33.

Fig. 34.

Figs. 32, 33 and 34.—Front and Side Elevations and Plan of Adjustable Chair

support in the middle by the two decorated brackets shown. The seat and back consist of wooden frames with webbing underneath and a suitable covering tacked edge of the back. The seat may therefore be brought forward to any position, and the back adjusted to any inclination. In order to keep the seat in the desired position, a removable peg could be inserted through one of the arm supports to fit into a series of holes bored along the edge of the seat. A better method would be to make a number of saw-teeth-like indentations in the back, and make the back rail of a suitable section to fit into them. By simply lifting the back, sliding the seat forward and lowering the back, the chair could be adjusted and fixed in the desired position.

TWO QUEEN ANNE CHAIRS

During recent years there has been a marked tendency to go back to the old styles in furniture, and not without good reason. It would seem that popular taste had been degenerating. For good design, comfort, and conscientious workmanship it is necessary to go back from fifty to two or three hundred years. Although the old styles are being copied they are usually modified, with a view of keeping them as inexpensive as possible,

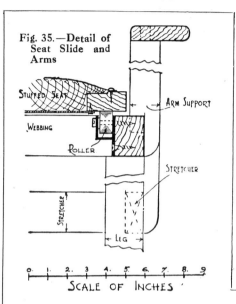

Fig. 35.—Detail of Seat Slide and Arms

STUFFED SEAT

ARM SUPPORT

WEBBING

ROLLER

STRETCHER

STRETCHER

LEG

SCALE OF INCHES

Fig. 36.

Fig. 37.

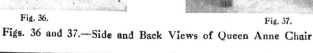

Figs. 36 and 37.—Side and Back Views of Queen Anne Chair

Fig. 38.—Front View of Queen Anne Chair

thickness. It is fitted with the ordinary stuffed loose seat to fit in the rebate, indicated by dotted lines in Figs. 43 and 44. The seat frame is of beech, mortised and tenoned together in the usual way, webbed, canvased, hair-stuffed, and covered with leather. That, of course, is a detail, as it might be covered in tapestry or in any other suitable material.

To make such a chair frame, it is recommended first to draw full half elevations of the front, back, and side parts, also plan, and cut out cardboard patterns to same. The back uprights, top rail, splat and back seat rail may be cut out in the solid and worked approximately to the shape for jointing together, the veneering to be done afterwards. Fig. 46 shows the shape it should be when veneered, at a point about the middle of the first curve above the back leg, from whence it tapers to the top. The joint to the shaped top rail is shown

to comply with modern requirements. At present, one of the most popular styles for furniture suites is that known as the Queen Anne style. The name applies principally to the chair frames, the couch and " easy " chairs being generally of the stuff-over make, showing nothing but the legs in woodwork.

In the first instance details of a genuine old chair will be given, followed by the necessary instructions for making a replica. Figs. 36, 37 and 38 show various views of the old chair, Fig. 39 gives a more detailed view of the carved leg, and Figs. 40, 41 and 42 are enlarged views of the carving. On many of the old chairs the carving is much simpler, and others again are quite plain. The principal measurements are given in Figs. 43, 44 and 45. Solid walnut is the wood used, the back being cross-veneered with " figured " walnut of about $\frac{1}{10}$ in.

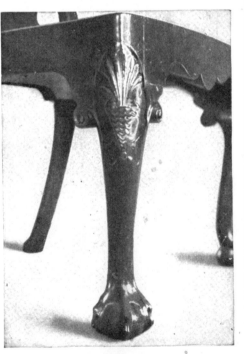

Fig. 39.—Detail View of Carved Leg

by Figs. 47 and 48; but the back seat rail must first be mortise-and-tenon lower edge (*see* Fig. 38); but the upper edge is quite straight to receive the

Fig. 40.—Detail View of Carving on Leg

Fig. 41.—Detail View of Foot

Fig. 42.—Detail View of Carving on Top of Back

jointed in position. The shape of the back rail is a simple curve cut out of the moulded base piece for the splat. This is seen in Fig. 43. The splat is jointed

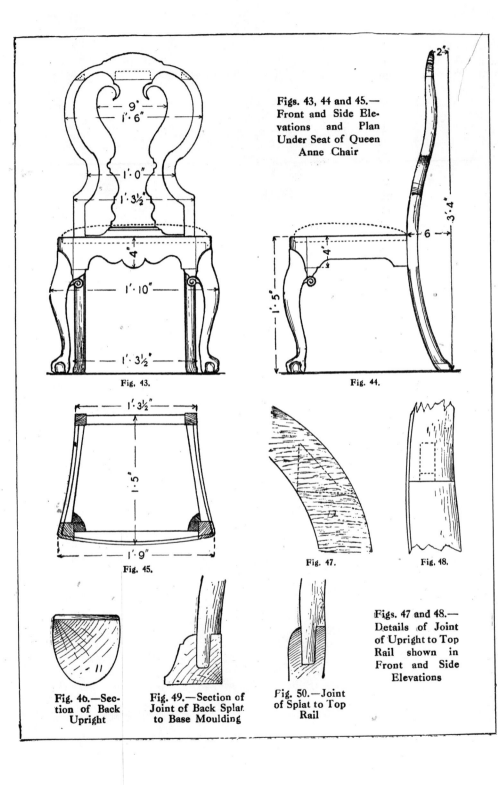

Figs. 43, 44 and 45.—
Front and Side Ele-
vations and Plan
Under Seat of Queen
Anne Chair

Fig. 43.

Fig. 44.

Fig. 45.

Fig. 47.

Fig. 48.

Figs. 47 and 48.—
Details of Joint
of Upright to Top
Rail shown in
Front and Side
Elevations

Fig. 46.—Sec-
tion of Back
Upright

Fig. 49.—Section of
Joint of Back Splat
to Base Moulding

Fig. 50.—Joint
of Splat to Top
Rail

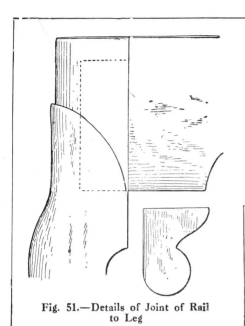

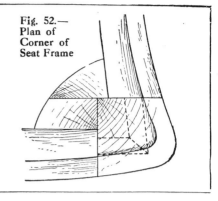

Fig. 52.—Plan of Corner of Seat Frame

Fig. 51.—Details of Joint of Rail to Leg

into it, as shown in Fig. 49. The upper end of the splat is jointed in a similar manner to the top rail (*see* Fig. 50). The uprights and rails may be jointed permanently to be trimmed when set to the correct shape before gluing the splat with base in place.

The front legs will require to be cut out of stuff $2\frac{3}{4}$ in. square, to be mortise-and-

Fig. 53.—Modern "Queen Anne" Chair

Fig. 54.—Detail View of Leg

tenon jointed to the front rail, the scroll blocks being cut separate (*see* Fig. 51). Before being glued, the joints of the side

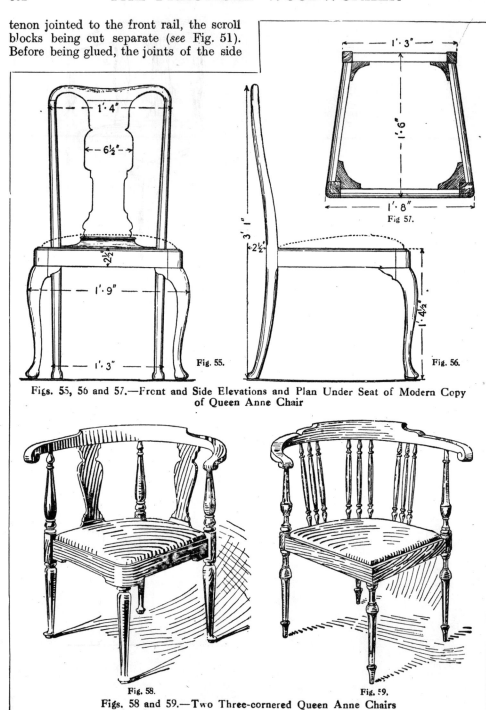

Figs. 55, 56 and 57.—Front and Side Elevations and Plan Under Seat of Modern Copy of Queen Anne Chair

Fig. 58.

Fig. 59.

Figs. 58 and 59.—Two Three-cornered Queen Anne Chairs

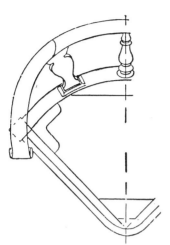

Fig. 61.—Part Plan of Three-cornered Chair (Fig. 58)

Fig. 60.—Another Design for Three-cornered Queen Anne Chair

CENTRE →

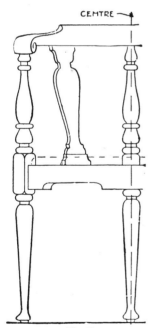

Fig. 62.

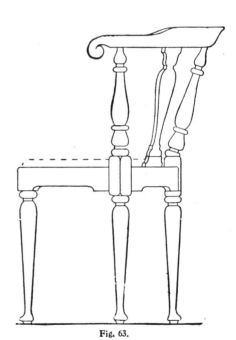

Fig. 63.

Figs. 62 and 63.—Part Front Elevation and Side Elevation of Three-cornered Chair (Fig. 58)

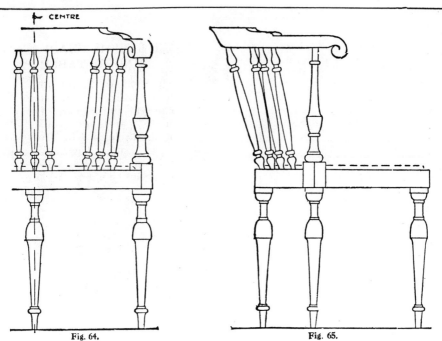

Fig. 64. Fig. 65.

Figs. 64 and 65.—Part Front Elevation and Side Elevation of Three-cornered Chair (Fig. 59)

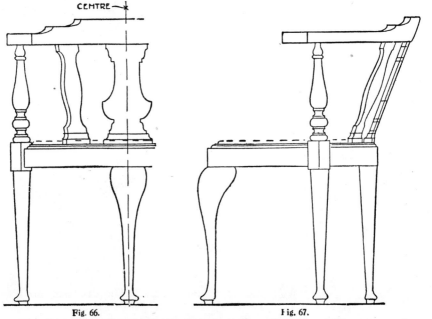

Fig. 66. Fig. 67.

Figs. 66 and 67.—Part Front Elevation and Side Elevation of Three-cornered Chair (Fig. 60)

FEET.

rails must be made, and the rebating done to all three rails and tops of the legs, also the carving. When they are glued up, the scroll blocks may be carved to something near the mark to be carefully fitted, toothed, and well glued in place, to be trimmed to the finished shape when thoroughly set. To give further support, the blocks which are glued in the corners must come well down behind them. These blocks also give strength and rigidity to the frame (see Fig. 52), which also shows how the tenons should fit inside the legs.

The finished work should be carefully trimmed up and french-polished.

Fig. 53 shows a modern copy of a much plainer design, made in mahogany. The loose seat was upholstered in green morocco leather. Fig. 54 gives a more complete view of the leg. The method of construction may be as described for the old chair, the measurements being given in Figs. 55, 56 and 57.

THREE THREE-CORNERED CHAIRS

The three-corner, or what are known as " roundabout " chairs, illustrated by Figs. 58, 59 and 60, are after the Queen Anne style. These chairs appeal to many for their charm of simple design and solid construction, remarks which apply generally to the furniture of that period. The prevailing wood for furniture construction of the Queen Anne period was walnut, as oak was for earlier times. The reproduced drawings (Figs. 61 to 67) are to scale and provide a sufficient guide to the intending constructor.

A characteristic of the design shown by Fig. 65 is the splay or rake given to the splats, which overhang the framing of the seat some six inches. This not only adds to the comfort but also to the general character of the design. In some instances these splats were shaped so as to fit the shoulders, and certainly gave additional comfort. In each case the chair is fitted with a loose frame seat which is upholstered and covered in various materials.

CHILD'S HIGH CHAIR WITH HINGED TABLE

The chair shown in the photographic reproduction (Fig. 68) is constructed of oak. The seat and legs are of 1-in. stuff, three small panels of $\frac{1}{4}$-in. stuff, the frame of the table of $\frac{1}{2}$-in. stuff, and the rest of $\frac{3}{4}$-in. stuff. The sizes given are suitable for a child of average size, and the footrest can be unscrewed and lowered

Fig. 68.—Child's High Chair with Hinged Table

as required. The drawings are to scale, and from these the work should be set out on a board full size, and the angles and lengths measured from it. The seat is fixed with four brass screws, whose heads are sunk into the rails underneath (inside). Fig. 69 is a front elevation with the table

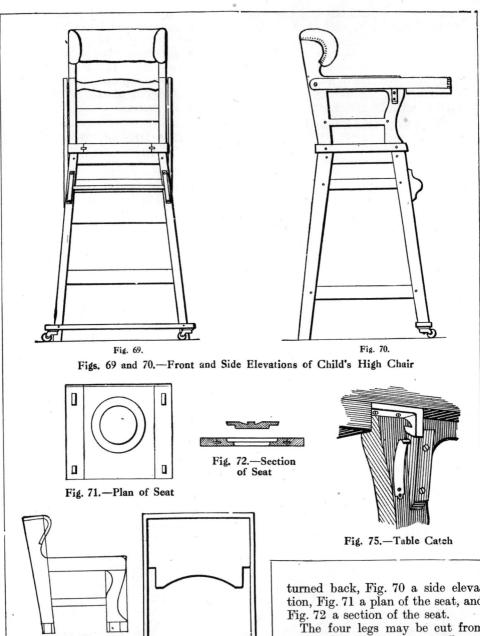

Fig. 69.

Fig. 70.

Figs. 69 and 70.—Front and Side Elevations of Child's High Chair

Fig. 72.—Section
of Seat

Fig. 71.—Plan of Seat

Fig. 75.—Table Catch

Fig. 73.—Arm
Framed Up

Fig. 74.—Plan of Table

turned back, Fig. 70 a side elevation, Fig. 71 a plan of the seat, and
Fig. 72 a section of the seat.

The four legs may be cut from
4 ft. of 1-in. by 7-in. stuff, and
in all eleven rails (in addition to
the footrest) and three small panels
will be required. In framing up,
the parts are all draw-bored and
pegged, the tenons not coming

quite through except in the case of the seat and the bottom front rail for the casters. The two arms are framed up as in Fig. 73,

Fig. 76.—Another Design for Child's High Chair

and the curves afterwards cut with the bow-saw. The piece which comes out at the elbow is glued on again higher up, and a rebate ½ in. wide is sunk ⅛ in. for the upholstery. The turned rail in the back forms a convenient handle for moving the chair, but it may be replaced by a plain straight rail if necessary. The table (Fig. 74) swings on two stout brass screws, and drops on to stops on the arms. To prevent the child from lifting the table, a catch is fitted outside one arm. Fig. 75 shows its arrangement, and to lift the table the spring is pressed in by the thumb; simply dropping the table fastens it down. This fitting may

be made up in brass; let the spring be well hammered, and make the holes as low down it as possible.

When all the parts are put together, the sharp edges should be carefully removed, more especially above the seat, and the finishing should be three coats of good oil varnish.

ANOTHER DESIGN FOR CHILD'S HIGH CHAIR

Probably the most essential portion of the high chair shown by the half-tone reproduction (Fig. 76) is the actual seat, as it is into this that both the upper and lower framings are tenoned.

Front and side elevations are shown by

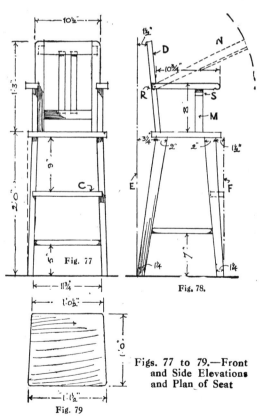

Figs. 77 to 79.—Front and Side Elevations and Plan of Seat

Figs. 77 and 78. The seat should be shaped, as in Fig. 79, out of wood at least 1 in. thick, and can be left quite flat or slightly " dished " in the centre as preferred. The under-framing consists of several rails and four legs, the latter 1 in. thick, tapered from 2 in. to 1½ in., and fixed sloping as in Fig. 78, and sloped slightly outwards towards the bottom as seen from the front (Fig. 77). They are intended to be fixed ⅞ in. from the back and front edges and ¾ in. from the sides,

Figs. 77 and 78, of each leg. Oak or ash rods of ¾-in. diameter are employed to connect the legs at the levels indicated. They can be tapered slightly at the ends and should be tightly fixed into sockets about ½ in. deep. At the level of c in Fig. 77 is a 3-in. by ¾-in. footrest, let into grooves in the front legs, and rounded on the front corners.

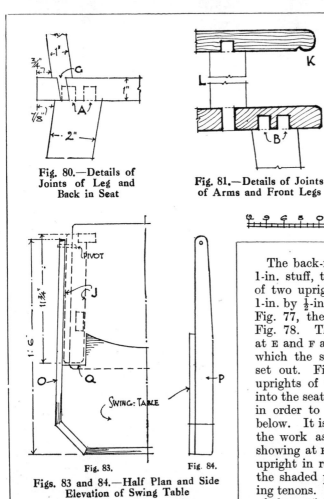

Fig. 80.—Details of Joints of Leg and Back in Seat

Fig. 81.—Details of Joints of Arms and Front Legs

Fig. 82.—Plan of Corner of Seat

Figs. 83 and 84.—Half Plan and Side Elevation of Swing Table

The back-rest is composed of 1½-in. by 1-in. stuff, tenoned together in the form of two uprights and two rails, with two 1-in. by ½-in. slats down the centre as in Fig. 77, the whole sloping as at D in Fig. 78. This figure incidentally shows at E and F a couple of vertical lines from which the several slopes can readily be set out. Fig. 80 shows at G how the uprights of the back should be tenoned into the seat, this operation requiring care in order to avoid the joints of the legs below. It is accomplished by setting out the work as in Fig. 82, which is a plan showing at H the outlines of a leg and an upright in relation to one another, while the shaded portions indicate the projecting tenons. It will be seen that the tenon of the upright is cut back on the left, in order to almost completely avoid the back tenon of the leg ; and as the latter does not go right through the seat, the actual overlapping of the two joints is negligible.

Arms 2 in. by 1 in. should be arranged

by means of double-stopped tenons ⅝ in. long, as at A in Fig. 80 and B in Fig. 81, the joints being carefully adjusted with the bevel to suit the two slopes, as in as dotted at J in Fig. 83, parallel to the sides of the seat, notched into the sloping uprights, and shaped on the front ends as at K in Fig. 81, which shows at L the method of fitting upright supports as at

necessary adjunct, and is explained by Figs. 83 and 84. It consists of $1\frac{1}{2}$-in. by $\frac{1}{2}$-in. arms, as at O and P, fixed to a $\frac{3}{8}$-in. flat table-top, curved on the inner edge and cut away to clear the arms of the

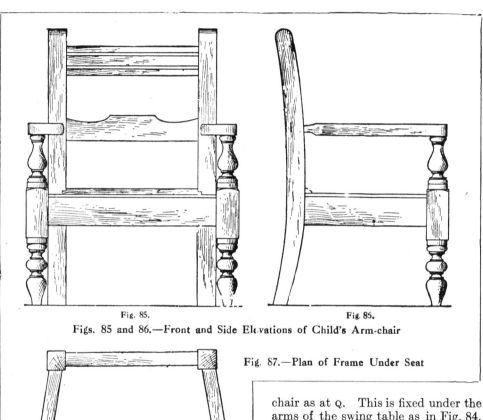

Fig. 85.

Fig. 86.

Figs. 85 and 86.—Front and Side Elevations of Child's Arm-chair

Fig. 87.—Plan of Frame Under Seat

chair as at Q. This is fixed under the arms of the swing table as in Fig. 84, these arms forming a ledge to it on the sides. The ledge is carried round the outer edges in the form of a beading to match the arms, strengthened, if necessary, at the mitres with small brass plates screwed on. The arms of the swing table are pivoted on oak dowels in the chair arms at R, and have stops to keep it level as at S, both in Fig. 78, and a catch might be provided to fasten it down when required.

M in Fig. 78. These are stop-tenoned into the undersides of the arms, and through-tenoned into the seat, where in this case they can be kept well away from the leg joints below.

A swing table, as at N in Fig. 78, is a

CHILD'S ARM-CHAIR

Figs. 85 and 86 show two elevations of a child's small arm-chair of very sturdy construction.

57—N.E.

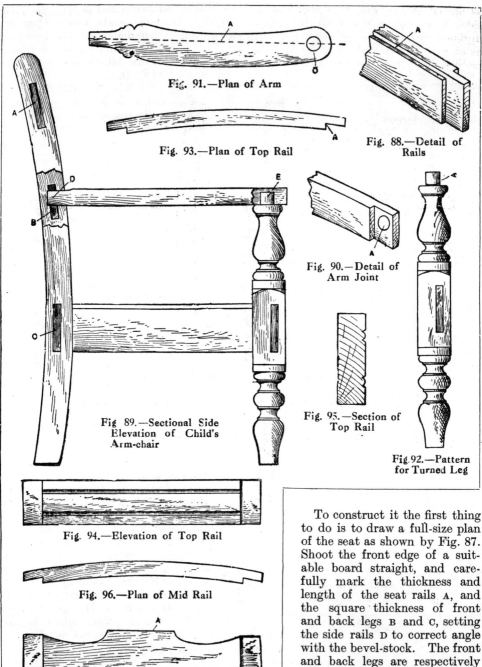

Fig. 91.—Plan of Arm

Fig. 93.—Plan of Top Rail

Fig. 88.—Detail of Rails

Fig 89.—Sectional Side Elevation of Child's Arm-chair

Fig. 90.—Detail of Arm Joint

Fig. 95.—Section of Top Rail

Fig. 92.—Pattern for Turned Leg

Fig. 94.—Elevation of Top Rail

Fig. 96.—Plan of Mid Rail

Fig 97.—Elevation of Mid Rail

To construct it the first thing to do is to draw a full-size plan of the seat as shown by Fig. 87. Shoot the front edge of a suitable board straight, and carefully mark the thickness and length of the seat rails A, and the square thickness of front and back legs B and C, setting the side rails D to correct angle with the bevel-stock. The front and back legs are respectively dressed 1½ in. and 1¼ in. square, the curve of the back legs being drawn to 3-ft. radius, which, failing a proper trammel, can be drawn with a thin lath of wood pivoted on a bradawl. The finished size of the seat rails is $1\frac{7}{8}$ in. by $\frac{7}{8}$ in. thick. The framing is prepared with $\frac{5}{16}$-in. mortise-and-tenon joints, glued and cramped together. The front rail and side rails are also rebated on the inside upper edges to take the bottom as shown at A (Fig. 88). Fig. 89 is a section of the chair showing the setting out of

the centre for prong-and-poppet chucking to turn the tenon ends, and the tenons are turned $\frac{5}{8}$ in. in diameter, also the beading, as shown at B, and the hole C bored with a $\frac{5}{8}$-in. centre-bit to suit the front-leg tenon A (Fig. 92).

The top back rail is $\frac{5}{8}$ in. thick and 2 in. deep, sawn out, as in Fig. 93, to a curve of 2-ft. radius, the tenons being shouldered to the front side as at A. It is finished

Fig. 98.—Chair-table in the Seventeenth-Century Style

the back-rail mortises A and B and seat-rail mortise C, and how the arm tenon D pins into the back leg through the back-rail tenon (as indicated by the hole A in Fig. 90); also the method of fixing to the front leg by the pin E. The arms, a plan view of which is shown by Fig. 91, are of $\frac{3}{4}$ in. thick stuff, the pieces being 2 in. wide before turning and sawing out to the curved shape. The dotted line A indicates

with flush scratched beadings as shown in Fig. 94, and also in the enlarged section of the top rail (Fig. 95). The mid back rail (Fig. 96) is similarly sawn out, but from $1\frac{3}{4}$-in. stuff, and afterwards finished to the shape shown in Fig. 97, the upper part A being smoothly rounded both for appearance and to prevent it hurting the child's back.

In putting the chair together, the back

leg mortises and back-rail tenons are brushed with hot glue of medium thickness, and quickly but carefully cramped together. Any exuded glue should at once be wiped off with a hot, damp rag. The front legs and front rail being simi-larly treated, the job may be placed aside to let the glue set; or the side rails can be at once glued in and the frame made ready for the bottom, which for strength should be about $\frac{7}{16}$ in. thick, and if possible in one solid width.

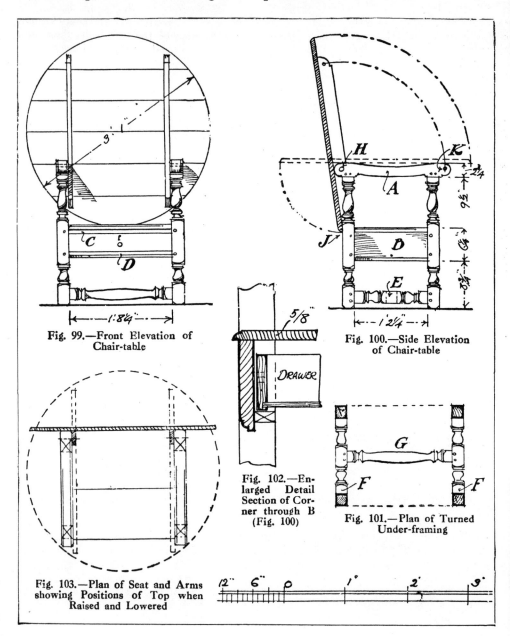

Fig. 99.—Front Elevation of Chair-table

Fig. 100.—Side Elevation of Chair-table

Fig. 102.—Enlarged Detail Section of Corner through B (Fig. 100)

Fig. 101.—Plan of Turned Under-framing

Fig. 103.—Plan of Seat and Arms showing Positions of Top when Raised and Lowered

CHAIR-TABLE IN THE SEVEN-
TEENTH-CENTURY STYLE

What is sometimes known at South Kensington Museum as the "miser's chair"—probably owing to the facilities it offers its occupant for guarding the contents of the drawer below the seat—is a substantial oaken piece of furniture, having a circular back pivoted in such a way that it can be lowered until it rests in a horizontal position on the arms at each side. The photographic reproduction (Fig. 98) shows the chair-table from the front with its top just slightly raised from the level position. It being thought that the idea involved might appeal to a number of readers in search of something a little unusual, therefore it is proposed to describe the chair-table as it exists.

The main supports consist of four upright legs each 2¼ in. square, shown in elevation by Figs. 99 and 100, and in plan at the corners of Fig. 101. It may here be mentioned that the square corners at the end of each part left square are rounded off a little. Each pair of legs is tenoned at the tops into the underside of a shaped arm-rest, as at A (Fig. 100), with its top slightly rounded in section, the joints here and throughout the job being secured with oak pegs, and the arms made so that the flat top will rest evenly on them, as shown by the dotted horizontal lines in Fig. 100. Under the arms, and at each side of the actual seat, pieces as at B (Fig. 100), are fixed by tenoning into the legs flush with them; it is beaded along the bottom outer edge and measures 5⅝ in. wide by 1 in. A similar piece, without bead, is fixed at the back. An enlarged detail section through B is given in

Fig. 102 showing a ⅝-in. seat (which is in two pieces, as indicated in Fig. 103) with rounded projecting edges on the top, a drawer-runner marked with a diagonal cross, and the side of an ordinary drawer in oak with a 1-in. front, small lock and round knob. In the front above the drawer is a bearer C 2 in. by 1 in. high for the edge of the seat, while below is a piece D tenoned and pegged in position, about 1½ in. by 1¼ in. high, at the same level as, and beaded to match, the lower edges of the side pieces B.

The third connection between the front and back legs on each side is made ¾ in. above the floor by a 2¼-in. square rail E (Fig. 100) and F (Fig. 101), tenoned at each end as before and partially circular-turned in the manner shown. The square central portion is left to receive a tie G (Fig. 101), almost the whole of which is turned, as will be seen from the photograph, and this completes the main framing, leaving the top to be described.

The top consists of an approximate circle of 3 ft. 1 in. diameter, having a rounded edge and being made up of six widths of ½-in. oak on a couple of ledges of a somewhat eccentric cut outline. These are shown in Fig. 100 in a simplified form, and are pivoted by means of oak centre-pins driven tightly through the arms, as at H (Fig. 100), with ends projecting about 1½ in. on the insides, on which projections the two ledges of the top work loosely. The whole is so arranged that the bottom edge of the top overlaps the back of the seat at J (Fig. 100) about ½ in. when the top is upright. At the front extremes of the arms are small holes, as at K (Fig. 100), with corresponding ones in the ledges, so that by the insertion of a pin the top may be fastened in its horizontal position when desired.

Stools

PLAIN STOOL

A STRONGLY-MADE stool of the type shown by Fig. 1 is likely to prove of service in an office, shop, or even about a house, where it would be of use for standing on occasionally. Two elevations and two plans are shown by Figs. 2, 3, 4 and 5. The principal part of its framing consists of the legs, each 2 ft. 5¼ in. long, 2 in. by 2 in. square at the top, and with two outer faces straight and vertical when in position. The inner faces, however, are only vertical for the top 3 in., below which they taper downwards to 1¼ in. at the bottom, as in Fig. 2. At the tops they are mortised ¾ in. deep, in accordance with the dimensions in Fig. 6, to receive the shouldered tenons on the ends of 3-in. by 1-in. top rails, part of one of which is there shown.

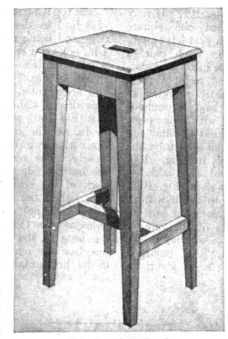

Fig. 1.—Plain Stool

Each pair of legs should be linked up with a 1½-in. by 1-in. rail, as at A in Fig. 5; tenoned into them 7 in. above the floor level, as at B in Fig. 6, the end of the rail (apart from the tenon) being accurately sloped very slightly to fit the tapered leg. This also shows at C the end of a 1½-in. by 1½-in. cross-rail, as at D in Fig. 5, tenoned into the two other rails centrally and completing the framing.

The seat is 14 in. by 12 in. square, and has rounded edges and a " dished " hole in the centre for lifting. It can be fixed by means of small angle-blocks on the underside, screwed to it and to the rails ; but a better method, allowing for any slight shrinkage, would be to secure it with "buttons," as in Figs. 4 and 7, fitting grooves in the longer top rails. At completion the stool should be stained to a serviceable colour and varnished. It would be quite possible to finish it with a padded seat covered with leather or "Pegamoid" if preferred.

LUGGAGE STOOL

A luggage stool is a useful piece of furniture for the bedroom, especially

the legs and 1 ft. 1 in. outside the legs at the ends, the extreme height from the floor being 1 ft. 6 in. The legs are 1½ in. square at the top, tapering to 1 in. square at the bottom. The shaped side and end rails are of 1-in. stuff and 5½ in. wide. The rails are tenoned into the legs, and stand back ¼ in. from the face of the

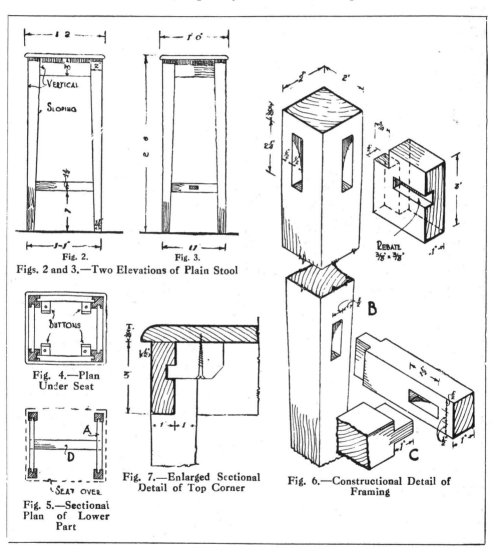

Figs. 2 and 3.—Two Elevations of Plain Stool

Fig. 4.—Plan Under Seat

Fig. 5.—Sectional Plan of Lower Part

Fig. 7.—Enlarged Sectional Detail of Top Corner

Fig. 6.—Constructional Detail of Framing

when made so as to serve also as a seat when not otherwise in use. The stand illustrated by Fig. 8 is 2 ft. long outside

legs. To facilitate the drawing of the shaped rails, diagrams are given by Figs. 9 and 10. These are set out in squares, each representing 1 in. The top frame is of 1-in. stuff, and projects $\frac{3}{4}$ in. beyond the outer faces of the legs. The side and end rails are $2\frac{1}{4}$ in. wide, and there are five cross-rails $1\frac{1}{4}$ in. wide fixed at an equal distance apart. Both end rails and cross-rails are tenoned into the side rails. The frame is secured with screws driven slant-wise from inside the shaped rails.

The cross-rails connected with the lower parts of the legs are $1\frac{3}{8}$ in. wide and $\frac{7}{8}$ in. thick, or as thick as 1-in. stuff will allow. They are halved where they intersect, and may be tenoned into the legs. Tenoning, however, has a tendency to weaken the legs. Another way is to secure them with a brass screw-eye and short dowel. Fig. 11 shows a portion of a leg cut away to receive the end of the

The wood should be chosen to match the other furniture of the room. The necessary dimensions and details of the various joints are given in Figs. 14, 15 and 16. It is best to cut out all the stuff first, and plane up to the finished sizes as follows :—

	Length.	Width.	Thickness.
	ft. in.	*in.*	*in.*
FOR THE STAND—			
Four legs	1 6	$1\frac{1}{4}$	$1\frac{1}{4}$
Two side rails ..	1 8	$2\frac{1}{2}$	$\frac{3}{4}$
Two end rails ..	1 1	$2\frac{1}{2}$	$\frac{3}{4}$
Two end lower rails	1 1		$\frac{3}{4}$
One stretcher rail..	1 $9\frac{1}{2}$		$\frac{3}{4}$
FOR THE TOP—			
Two pieces	2 2	$2\frac{1}{4}$	$\frac{3}{4}$
Six pieces	$10\frac{1}{2}$	$2\frac{1}{4}$	$\frac{3}{4}$

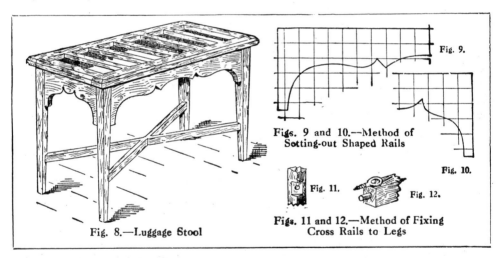

Fig. 8.—Luggage Stool

Figs. 9 and 10.—Method of Setting-out Shaped Rails

Fig. 9.

Fig. 10.

Fig. 11.

Fig. 12.

Figs. 11 and 12.—Method of Fixing Cross Rails to Legs

rail and the dowel, while Fig. 12 shows the rail upside down with the screw-eye fixed to it. The screw-eye is first screwed into the leg, after which a screw is driven through the eye to secure it to the cross-rail.

The stand should be made of the same wood as the surrounding furniture ; but if the latter is painted, birch should be used.

ANOTHER LUGGAGE STOOL

Fig. 13 shows another design for a luggage stool of a plainer style.

Allow 1 in. for turning the plain taper and ball feet, and 1 in. at the top end for making the joints.

The two end frames should be made first, the joints being mortised and tenoned, as shown in Fig. 15, and when glued and cramped up may be left to set awhile. In the meantime the top can be put together. The main thing to observe is that the six bars are exact in length and square at the ends ; also that the joint edges of the long pieces are straight and square. The setting out of the dowel points must also be accurate ; but this can be managed easily enough with care in using the marking gauge and a pair of compasses. One inch waste is allowed at each end of the long pieces, as shown in Fig. 16, to avoid splitting. The gluing up

feet to keep the legs from being strained in or out in fitting the stretcher. The joints for this are dovetailed and V-joints. Fig. 17 shows the end of the stretcher, the dovetail pin being cut to within about

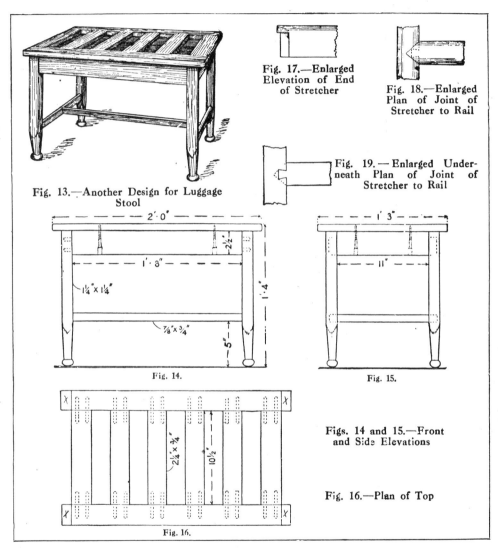

Fig. 13.—Another Design for Luggage Stool

Fig. 17.—Enlarged Elevation of End of Stretcher

Fig. 18.—Enlarged Plan of Joint of Stretcher to Rail

Fig. 19.—Enlarged Underneath Plan of Joint of Stretcher to Rail

Fig. 14.

Fig. 15.

Figs. 14 and 15.—Front and Side Elevations

Fig. 16.—Plan of Top

Fig. 16.

and cramping should be done quickly, and the work left in a dry place. The two end frames of the stand can now be connected by the long rails, the joints being dowelled as shown in Fig. 14. When this is done laths should be nailed temporarily on the

$\frac{1}{4}$ in. from the rounded top edge, which is cut to a V-shape. It is let into the rail as shown by Figs. 18 and 19.

The stand and top may then be trimmed up and glasspapered, all corners being rubbed down slightly round. Middle

No. 2 glasspaper is the best, with No. 1 to finish up with. The top is secured with eight 2½-in. screws through the rails, as

The stand is now ready for finishing; but as it is an article which has to stand a considerable amount of rough usage, a

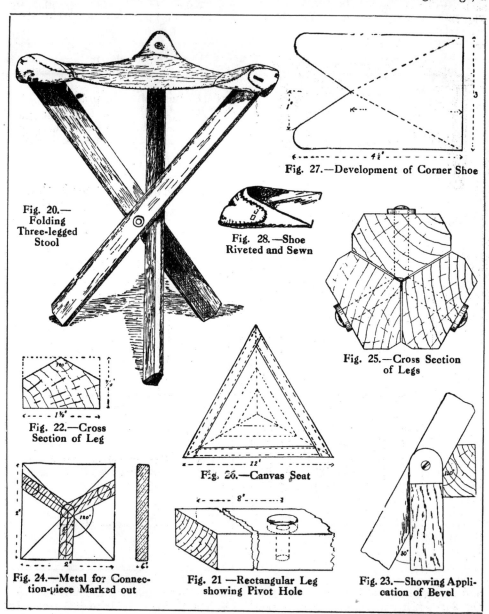

Fig. 20.—Folding Three-legged Stool

Fig. 27.—Development of Corner Shoe

Fig. 28.—Shoe Riveted and Sewn

Fig. 25.—Cross Section of Legs

Fig. 22.—Cross Section of Leg

Fig. 26.—Canvas Seat

Fig. 24.—Metal for Connection-piece Marked out

Fig. 21.—Rectangular Leg showing Pivot Hole

Fig. 23.—Showing Application of Bevel

shown in Figs. 14 and 15, the holes where the screws are sunk being filled with wood dowels to give a neater finish.

very fine polish is not necessary. If made in oak or walnut it could be wax-finished; mahogany should be french-polished.

FOLDING THREE-LEGGED STOOL

The stool shown by Fig. 20 is one largely adopted by anglers for its portability and strength. It is strong, durable, and easy to make, and, as will be seen, possesses three legs pivoting about a central three-way piece, to which they are attached by riveting, and when not in use folds up quite flat.

The seat is made, in a way to be explained, from canvas riveted and sewn to corner shoes or pockets of leather, which take the strain admirably. For the legs three straight-grained pieces of sound oak are preferable, although beech that has not dried and perished, or birch that is hard and tough, will do almost as well. Plane the three strips of wood to a rectangular section, $1\frac{3}{8}$ in. by $\frac{7}{8}$ in. exactly, and ascertain before gauging these to width and thickness that the face sides and edges are quite true, since oak has a tendency to spring from the straight when sawn down the grain. Cut off to a length of 18 in. On the face of each piece, 8 in. from one end and exactly in the middle of the width, bore a hole $\frac{1}{2}$ in. in diameter for a depth of $\frac{1}{8}$ in., continuing right through to the other side with a bit boring a $\frac{1}{4}$-in. hole (see Fig. 21). Each leg must then be planed exactly to the section shown by Fig. 22, the face side being worked so that a ridge is left down the middle, the two surfaces meeting in an angle of 120°. To accomplish this satisfactorily it will be found best to fix each leg securely, and one at the time, on the edge of a short board, which is then fixed in the bench vice. Two small blocks nailed on the edge of the board, one at each end of the leg with a space for a pair of wedges, will effectively hold the work while being planed.

Set a bevel to an angle of 150°, and with a plane carefully remove the waste wood from the middle outwards on one side until the bevel fits accurately (see Fig. 23); then remove the leg, and treat the two others similarly. Again set the bevel, this time to an angle of 120°, and remove the waste from the remaining portion of the face side until the bevel

once more fits, when it will be found that the three pieces if held together will fit accurately. For the present, the legs, although unfinished, must be put on one side and the three-way piece proceeded with. This is made from a piece of 2-in. by $\frac{1}{4}$-in. mild steel (see Fig. 24). To set out, chalk over one side of the steel, draw the diagonals with a blacklead pencil, and from the centre thus obtained strike a circle as large as can be drawn within the limits of the metal. Step the radius round the circle, and from every other point thus marked on the circumference draw lines meeting in the centre. Each of these three lines is the axis of one of the arms, and therefore the width of each arm must be accurately and equally divided on each side of the axis. The width should be $\frac{5}{16}$ in., and by describing circles having this diameter, one at the intersection of the three axes, and one near the end of each axis, lines tangential to the circles can be drawn, which will then be parallel to their respective axes. Although this explanation is necessarily somewhat involved, it is hoped that Fig. 24 will assist in making clear what is a fairly simple operation.

As all this marking out has been done with pencil, the arms must be gone over once more with a scriber, the end of a file, bradawl, or nail answering the purpose. The waste metal has next to be sawn out with a hack-saw, and it is well in using this tool to proceed slowly, keeping the blade moving in one plane as far as possible, a sudden wrench, a false stroke, or undue force being almost certain to snap the blade. The waste removed, each arm has to be filed round so that the legs may move freely when in position. This does not mean that they must be made exactly circular in section, an approximation to this shape being adequate for the purpose. The end of each arm, however, must be such that a $\frac{1}{4}$-in. washer just fits over without being loose. The legs can now be tried in position on the three-way piece, and any irregularity in the fit corrected. If the pins are too tight, the holes must be enlarged with a pin bit; if the legs do not meet easily at the centre, the larger hole in the ridge of each must be slightly deepened with gouge or chisel. The opening and closing of the legs when in use is made easier if slight draught or a gap is left between the

the washers too much force must not be used, or it may result in the bending or weakening of the arms. This finished, plane down the corners of the legs until they appear as in Fig. 25, and remove the

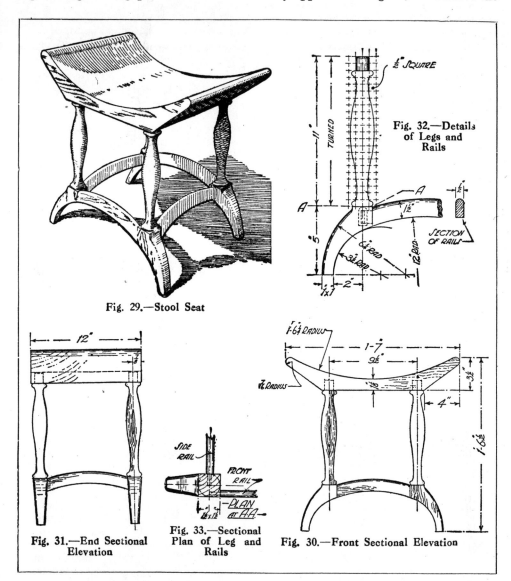

Fig. 29.—Stool Seat

Fig. 32.—Details of Legs and Rails

Fig. 31.—End Sectional Elevation

Fig. 33.—Sectional Plan of Leg and Rails

Fig. 30.—Front Sectional Elevation

meeting surfaces, as shown in Fig. 25. The legs and three-way connection are now ready for putting together, and in riveting the ends of the arms over on to

arrises. The object of keeping the connecting piece out of the centre of the leg's length is to give a greater spread to the top, and hence a large seat. Stand the stool on the table until the lower ends of the legs are spread about 9 in. apart, and with a straightedge mark off the top ends, so that when sawn they will lie in a plane parallel to the table. With a chisel pare off all corners at both ends when the construction of this part of the work is complete.

A good material from which the seat can be made is that commonly sold for jack towels, a better fabric being willesden canvas. On a length of this mark out an equilateral triangle of 12-in. side, and when cutting out leave a good wide margin, say $\frac{3}{4}$ in., for turning under. Two thicknesses machine-sewn together, as in Fig. 26, will be strong and durable, and with fair wear and tear will last a long time.

Fig. 34.—Chair Stool for Boot Cleaning

Fig. 35.—Alternative Design for Chair Stool for Boot Cleaning

Three pocket-pieces or shoes, of the developed shape shown by Fig. 27, must be cut from thin, pliant inner sole or upper leather. Turn the stool upside down on the table, and fold the leather round the end of one leg, when the best position in which to place the rivets can be seen at a glance (see Fig. 28). Three bifurcated rivets will be sufficient here, while for securing the canvas seat to the shoes thus made, four more for each will be required. If in addition to the rivets the shoes are hand-sewn with thread, and also sewn to the canvas, a good, strong job will be the result. The seat, instead of being made separate from the legs as in this case, can be permanently fixed to the leg ends with slight modification

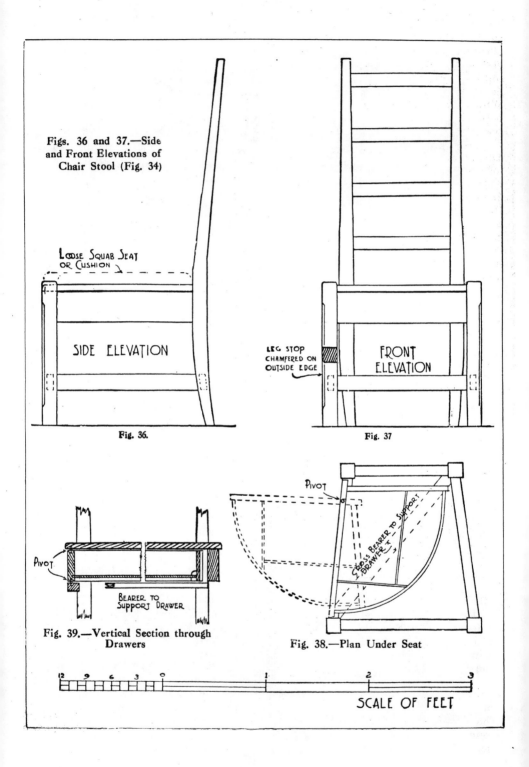

Figs. 36 and 37.—Side and Front Elevations of Chair Stool (Fig. 34)

LOOSE SQUAB SEAT OR CUSHION

SIDE ELEVATION

Fig. 36.

LEG STOP CHAMFERED ON OUTSIDE EDGE

FRONT ELEVATION

Fig. 37

PIVOT

BEARER TO SUPPORT DRAWER

Fig. 39.—Vertical Section through Drawers

PIVOT

CROSS BEARER TO SUPPORT DRAWER X

Fig. 38.—Plan Under Seat

SCALE OF FEET

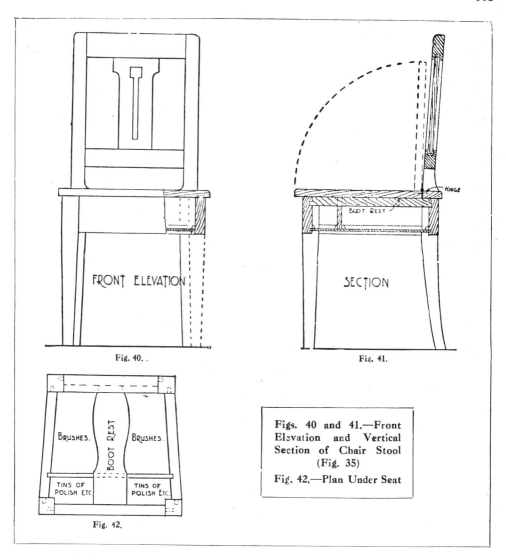

FRONT ELEVATION

Fig. 40.

SECTION

BOOT REST

HINGE

Fig. 41.

BRUSHES. BOOT REST BRUSHES.

TINS OF POLISH ETC.

TINS OF POLISH ETC.

Fig. 42.

Figs. 40 and 41.—Front Elevation and Vertical Section of Chair Stool (Fig. 35)

Fig. 42.—Plan Under Seat

of the shoes, only care must be taken that the folding of the stool is not impeded in any way.

A coat or two of varnish on the legs aids in the preservation and appearance of the finished work.

STOOL SEAT

The stool shown by Fig. 29 will prove a useful and attractive addition to any home, and would be found very handy when forming the family circle round the fire ; or, by increasing the height, it could be used as a music-seat. Front and side elevations are shown by Figs. 30 and 31.

The job would look well in oak, fumed or polished, or in ash stained green and polished, or there is no reason why it should not be painted and enamelled, in which case the top could be of a softer and cheaper wood, such as American white wood. In each case the legs should be of one of the harder woods, to avoid the risk of splitting where they curve away from the straight grain. In forming the concave seat surface much of the stuff may be removed by two oblique cuts with the hand saw, and if the craftsman is not fortunate enough to possess a compass plane with which to work this to a true and smooth face, a mallet and a sharp chisel must be used, and the operation finished with a steel scraper. A template of thin wood made to the seat curve should be used to ensure accurate shaping. As will be seen from the detailed drawings of the legs, (Figs. 32 and 33), these have pins 1 in. in diameter by 1 in. long formed on their upper ends, and these are glued and driven into holes bored in the seat.

The top edges of the rails are rounded to a semi-circle, and the two outside angles on the curved part of the legs are also rounded. The rails are tenoned into the legs as shown in the detail.

TWO CHAIR STOOLS FOR BOOT CLEANING

Two alternative designs of chair stools for boot cleaning are shown by Figs. 34 to 42. The first example (Fig. 34) is shown in front and side elevations by Figs. 36 and 37, and Fig. 38 shows a plan of the seat framing and drawer. Regarding the construction, the only part necessary to mention is the drawer, for the framework is on the plainest and simplest lines. A study of the plan will show that the drawer is pivoted at the back of the left-hand seat rail. The entire framework of the chair should be made first and temporarily fitted together, when it will be an easy matter to determine the shape and size of the drawer by the use of a large piece of cardboard. The pivoting of the drawer is clearly shown in the section (Fig. 38); one pivot works in the rail and the other in the underside of the wooden seat.

The other chair (Fig. 39) has a lift-up seat with a receptacle for containing the brushes, etc. Fig. 40 shows a front elevation and Fig. 41 a vertical section. Details of the seat compartment are shown by Fig. 42. Grooves are ploughed in the bottoms of the inner faces of the seat rails in order to support the bottom of the brush box. The boot rest should be of stout wood tenoned into the front and rear rails. Details of the hinging of the seat are shown in the section (Fig. 41). Care should be taken that the joint is sufficiently far forward to allow the seat to fall well back and remain in that position.

Footstools

FOOTSTOOL SLIPPER BOX

THE footstool shown by Figs. 1 and 2 is an article which can be made from material such as can mostly be found about the house.

the four box sides, the bottom and the lid. They are nailed together, as shown by Fig. 3, the lid being hinged with a strip of leather or strong canvas about 2 in. wide, which can be fixed with ordinary tacks. There will also be required enough flock

Fig. 1.—Footstool Slipper Box (Open)

Fig. 2.—Footstool Slipper Box (Closed)

Fig. 3.—Wood Box for Footstool

A useful size for the stool complete is 1 ft. 2 in. long by 10 in. wide by 7 in. high. The first thing is to make the wood box, for which is required two pieces 1 ft. 2 in. long and two pieces 9 in. long by 4 in. wide, also two pieces 1 ft. 2 in. long by 10 in. wide, all ½ in. thick. These are for

or other stuffing to cover the lid about 1½ in. thick when pressed down with the hands, also sufficient material to cover the top and sides of the box. This may be of tapestry, velvet or leather. In case these be not obtainable about the house, a local upholsterer would be able to supply them cheaply, as he often has odd pieces of stuff suitable for such purposes.

The top will need a piece 1 ft. 4 in. by

Fig. 4.—Foot tool of Old Design

1 ft., and the sides one long strip 5½ in. wide, or it may be made by sewing together four pieces each 1 in. longer than the box sides, ½ in. being taken up at each end by the seams. It should be made like a band, to fit fairly tight round the box, with a seam at each corner. Before putting it on it will be an improvement to line the box with glazed lining or paper. Oil baize or leather cloth are even better still, and it may be fixed with strong paste. It may turn over the edges to a little over the outside of the box; the same with the lid. The band of outside material may now be put on in a way that no tacks will be seen. To do this it should be inside out and be drawn over the lid and ½ in. on to the box sides, and be tacked round, keeping the tacks well up to the edge on the front and two short sides. Then the stuff can be drawn down into place, leaving ½ in. of stuff beyond the bottom to be tacked underneath. The upper edge of the stuff at the back may be tacked to the edge of the lid. The stuffing may next be packed evenly on the lid, and the cover placed over and tacked round the edges, which are to be finished with a leather banding or gimp fixed with brass-

headed nails; but a button-hole piece of leather must be fixed on the lid to fit a button or stud on the front side as a simple fastening. At each end of the box a strap handle may be fixed with four brass nails at each end, and a stay-strap should be put inside to keep the lid from falling back.

The rounded wooden feet can be fixed with screws the heads being countersunk in, and then stained, enamelled, or gold-painted.

FOOTSTOOL OF OLD DESIGN

The footstool shown by Fig. 4 is a reproduction of a typical specimen of old-fashioned furniture, thoroughly well made and in the best quality materials.

Fig. 5 is an under view, showing the shape of the framework and the webbed and canvas bottom, and Fig. 6 shows the finished shape of the upholstered top.

The construction of the framework is shown by Figs. 7 and 8, the legs being of walnut 2 in. square in section, sawn

Fig. 5.—Underside View of Footstool

Fig. 6.—Top View of Footstool

approximately to the shape and finished by carving. The rails are of birch, and should be sawn to the bow curves, shown in Fig. 8, 3 in. by 1 in. in section. They are mortise-and-tenon jointed to the legs, as shown at A in Figs. 7 and 8 ; but before gluing up, the lower edge of the rails must be sawn to the curves following the inner outline of the legs. Slips of walnut are required sawn to the same shape and also

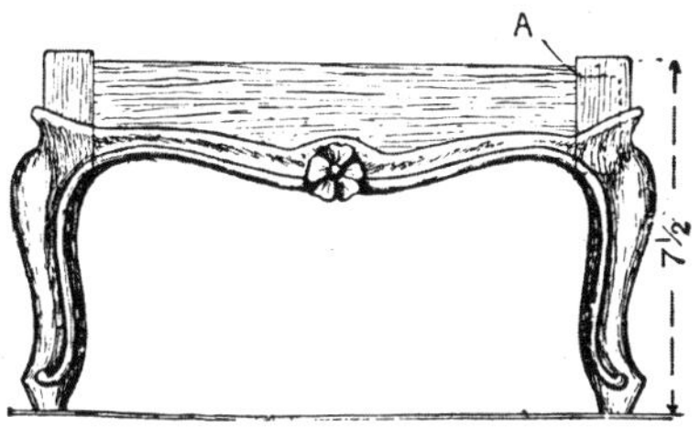

Fig. 7.

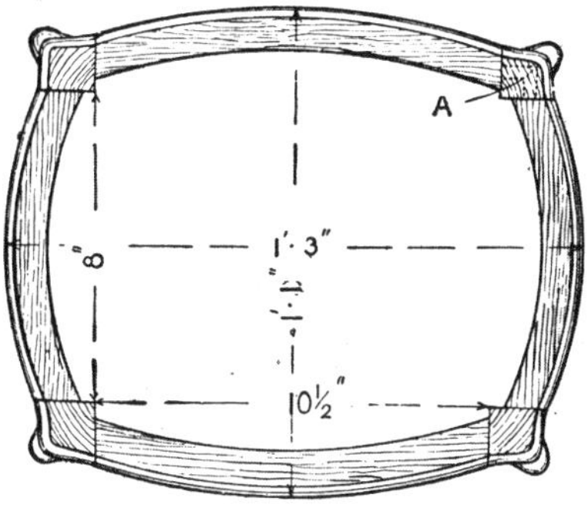

Fig. 8.

Figs. 7 and 8.—Elevation and Plan of Framework of Stool

Fig. 9.—Section of Rail

Fig. 10.—Section of Leg

to the bow curves. They must be $1\frac{1}{2}$ in. by $\frac{1}{2}$ in. in section, to be planted on the birch to follow out the carving of the legs. Fig. 9 is a section of the finished rail near the carved flower in the centre, and Fig. 10 a section of the leg just below the joint.

When the framework is made it may

be rubbed with linseed oil and french-polished, or well wax-polished and then upholstered.

"QUEEN ANNE" STOOL

A stool made in the so-called " Queen Anne " style is shown by Fig. 11. The cover of the stuffed loose seat (*see* Figs. 12 and 13) is made of narrow strips of leather woven together in the diagonal manner shown ; each diamond is stamped with a small pattern.

The woodwork of the stool will be found fairly simple to a moderately advanced worker, except the legs, which require to be carefully worked and well judged. But that is only in the rounding with the spokeshave and chisel. Fig. 14 gives the necessary measurements. The first thing to do is to make a cardboard pattern for the legs. This is easy to draw if lines are ruled over, forming 1-in. squares, as in Fig. 15. It is in two parts, the large part A to be marked round on the wood (mahogany) $2\frac{1}{2}$ in. square in section. When marked on one side and cut to the shape, the pattern is laid on the front cut surface, and marked to be cut the same again. Of the small piece B, eight are required, cut from material $\frac{3}{4}$ in. thick. Figs. 16 and 17 show half patterns for the long and short rails, the dotted lines indicating the tenons for jointing to the legs. The material for the rails should be about 1 in. thick, and the joints may be made before the legs are rounded ; but are not to be glued up until the legs and rails are worked to the correct shape. The rails are rebated on the top edge, as in Fig. 18 ; also the top end of the legs, as in Fig. 19, which also shows the manner of strengthening the joints by glue-blocking. The small curved pieces B (Fig. 15) are rounded in completing the shape of the legs, and neatly fitted and glued in place ; they are further strengthened with a small triangular block glued behind, as shown in Fig. 20.

The frame for the stuffed work is made of deal, of about $2\frac{1}{2}$-in. by 1-in. section, the joints being mortised and tenoned. It must fit in the rebate, allowing equal space all round for the upholstery, in this case $\frac{3}{16}$ in. ; but it is well to bevel it in a little on the edges, so that it will fit in with ease when finished and be tight when pressed down. It is webbed and canvased in the usual way, and simply stuffed with hair covered with calico. The leather cover is then put on, and a banding of the same material $\frac{3}{4}$ in. wide to cover the uneven edges, fixed with No. 12 copper studs along the upper edge, to show just above the rounded edge of the stool when in place. The lower edge of the banding requires fixing with fine tacks, which will be hidden in the rebate.

The woodwork should be well smoothed with glasspaper, and all sharp square corners rubbed down slightly round.

Fig. 11.—Queen Anne Stool

ADJUSTABLE LEG-STOOL

Fig. 21 shows a double-action adjustable leg-rest or stool which can be raised or lowered as required, and also set at an angle. It consists of three frames hinged together, the uppermost being stuffed

Fig. 12.—Top View of Queen Anne Stool

and covered, and the bottom one fitted with four legs to raise it from the ground. The rest is raised by means of struts which are framed together and fixed to the frames with rivets. The struts fit into notched rails fixed to the inside of the frames, as shown at Fig. 22, the rest being raised or lowered, and set at the required angle by regulating and setting the struts into the notched rails. Beech, walnut, or mahogany may be used for the construction, the following quantity being required : 18 ft. 6 in. of stuff 2 in. wide by 1 in. thick ; 8 ft. of stuff 1 in. square, one piece 1 ft. 4 in. long by 3 in. wide by $\frac{3}{4}$ in. thick ; and one piece 1 ft. 7 in. long by $1\frac{1}{2}$ in. square for the turned legs.

The three frames A (Fig. 22), a part plan of which is shown at Fig. 23, are 1 ft. 9 in. long by 1 ft. 4 in. wide ; the framework is 2 in. wide by 1 in. thick, framed together, as shown at Fig. 23. The back B of the top frame is 3 in. wide by $\frac{3}{4}$ in. thick ; the top corners are rounded over, and the back is fixed to the frame with

Fig. 13.—View of Stool with Top Removed

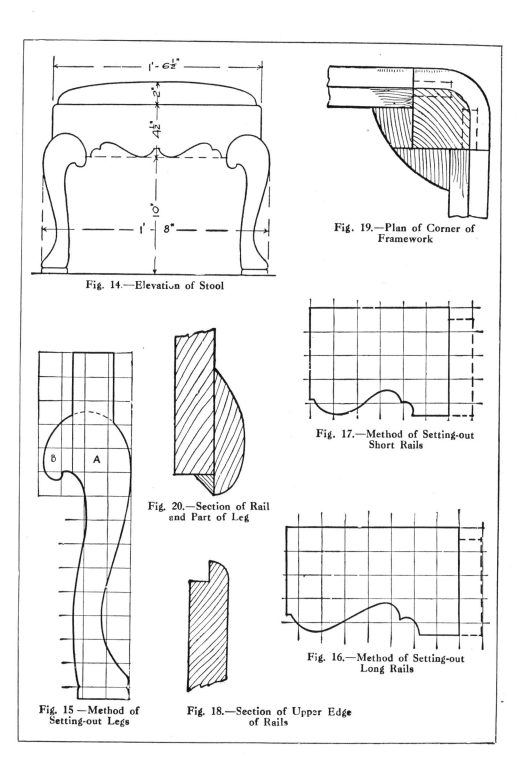

Fig. 14.—Elevation of Stool

Fig. 19.—Plan of Corner of Framework

Fig. 17.—Method of Setting-out Short Rails

Fig. 20.—Section of Rail and Part of Leg

Fig. 16.—Method of Setting-out Long Rails

Fig. 15.—Method of Setting-out Legs

Fig. 18.—Section of Upper Edge of Rails

screws from underneath. The turned legs which are fitted to the bottom frame are 4 in. high, having dowels on the top end which fits into corresponding holes in framed together with a centre bar, the framework being 1 in. square in section ; they are 11¾ in. wide by 9 in. deep, the ends being cut away to fit into the

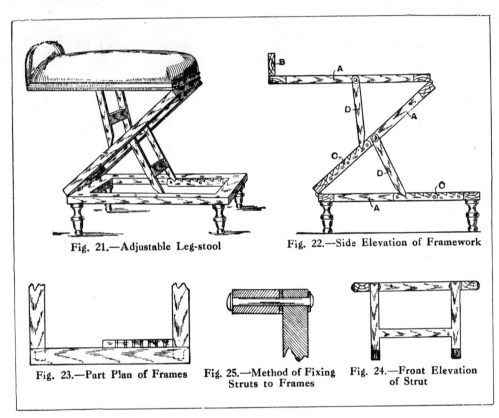

Fig. 21.—Adjustable Leg-stool

Fig. 22.—Side Elevation of Framework

Fig. 23.—Part Plan of Frames

Fig. 25.—Method of Fixing Struts to Frames

Fig. 24.—Front Elevation of Strut

the frame, to which they are fixed with glue. The frames are fixed together with 1½-in. butt hinges, as shown at Fig. 22. The notched rails c are 1 in. square in section, the notches being cut in them about 1 in. apart. These rails are fixed to the inside of the middle and bottom frames with screws. The struts D, a front view of which is shown at Fig. 24, are notches. The struts are hinged to the frames with ⅜-in. rivets which pass through the frames and struts, and are riveted over on the inside, as shown at Fig. 25.

When completed, the top frame and back should be stuffed with horsehair and covered with rep, the woodwork being either polished or enamelled.

Frames for Upholstered Furniture

EASY CHAIR

THE only exposed portions of the frame of the chair shown by Fig. 1 are the legs. Figs. 2 to 4 show the chief views.

stained and polished. The back (Fig. 4) should first be taken in hand. The legs are 2 in. thick, and cut to the outline shown in Fig. 3 from stuff 4 in. wide, tapered at the bottom as shown. The

Fig. 1.—Easy Chair

Birch or beech might be employed for the main framework, the legs being veneered or worked from the solid in mahogany or oak, or perhaps merely

head rail is out of 4-in. by 2-in. stuff, curved on the crown. The stuffing rail A is $1\frac{1}{2}$ in. by $1\frac{3}{4}$ in., and the seat rail B 4 in. by 2 in. These rails should be tenoned, draw-bored and pegged to the legs, thus completing the back frame.

The front legs c (Figs. 2 and 3) are 2½ in. square, tapering to 1½ in. at the bottom, the top portions being cut down to half-thickness, as in Fig. 2. Fig. 5 is a plan of the seat frame, the front rail of which should be tenoned into the legs. The back and front will then be ready for

WING EASY CHAIR

Approximate dimensions for all parts of the frame of the chair, shown by Fig. 6, will be found in the illustrations. Hardwood should be employed for the legs, which are the only parts not concealed by the covering material, and beech is recommended for the other portions. Front

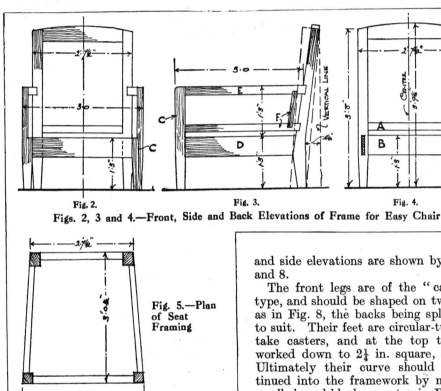

Fig. 2. Fig. 3. Fig. 4.

Figs. 2, 3 and 4.—Front, Side and Back Elevations of Frame for Easy Chair

Fig. 5.—Plan of Seat Framing

jointing together, as in Fig. 3. The seat rails D are tenoned in position, the exact rake of the back being set accurately before measurements for the arm rails E are taken. These rails are housed into the legs, glued and nailed, and stuffing rails, as at F, added last. Rasp or shave off all sharp angles, and fit the legs with casters having plates, not sockets.

The upholstering of chairs, seats, settees, etc., is dealt with in a later section.

and side elevations are shown by Figs. 7 and 8.

The front legs are of the "cabriole" type, and should be shaped on two faces, as in Fig. 8, the backs being splayed off to suit. Their feet are circular-turned to take casters, and at the top they are worked down to 2¼ in. square, as at A. Ultimately their curve should be continued into the framework by means of small shaped blocks, as at B in Figs. 7, 8 and 9, by this means avoiding the necessity of cutting inordinately large pieces of wood to waste.

The back legs can be set out from Figs. 8 and 10, the raking line at c indicating where the hardwood foot is spliced and screwed to the rough upper portion. The seat rails should be strongly tenoned into the legs (the front ones being carried up 1 in., as at D in Fig. 7, to strengthen the joints); but for the rest of the framework halved or dowelled joints should suffice. In view of the illustrations given, a

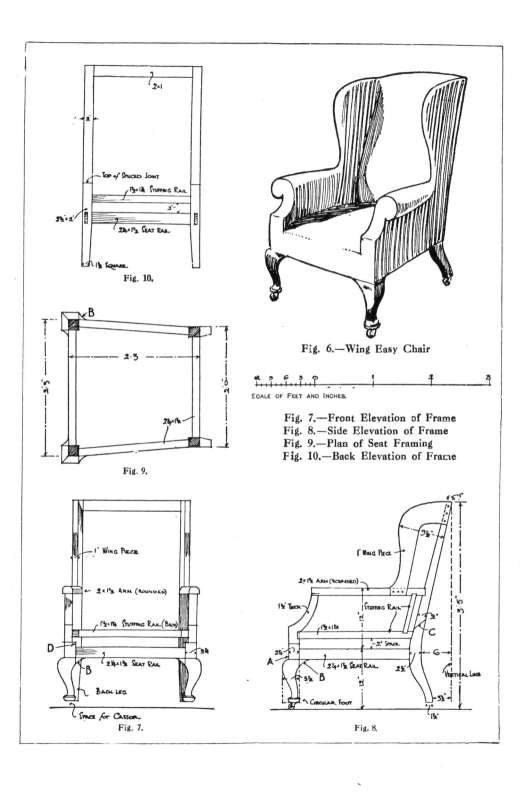

Fig. 10.

2×1

Top of Spliced Joint

1¾×1¼ Stuffing Rail

1″

2¾×2″

2¼×1½ Seat Rail

1½ Square

Fig. 6.—Wing Easy Chair

SCALE OF FEET AND INCHES.

Fig. 7.—Front Elevation of Frame
Fig. 8.—Side Elevation of Frame
Fig. 9.—Plan of Seat Framing
Fig. 10.—Back Elevation of Frame

B

2·3

2·5

2·0

2¼×1½

Fig. 9.

1″ Wing Piece

2×1½ Arm (Rounded)

1½×1¼ Stuffing Rail (Back)

D

2¼

2¼×1½ Seat Rail

B

Back Leg

Space for Castor

Fig. 7.

1″ Wing Piece

9½″

2×1½ Arm (Rounded)

1½ Thick

Stuffing Rail

2″

1½×1¼

2″ Space

C

2½

A

2¼

3½

B

2¼×1½ Seat Rail

2½

Circular Foot

Vertical Line

3½

1½

Fig. 8.

detailed description is hardly necessary ; but it may perhaps be pointed out that the " wings " could be built up of several pieces if desired, also that the head of the back might be curved instead of straight as shown. All framing should finish flush on the outsides and back, with the single exception of the rounded arm rails, which project outwards a little. It will be seen

holstery is required in the making of a settee of the type known to the dealer as a " box ottoman," and shown by Fig. 11. It forms a useful adjunct to the bedroom or nursery, as its seat forms the lid of a large box, the upper portion of which could be fitted with shallow lift-out trays if desired. Its length can be varied according to circumstances, and if long

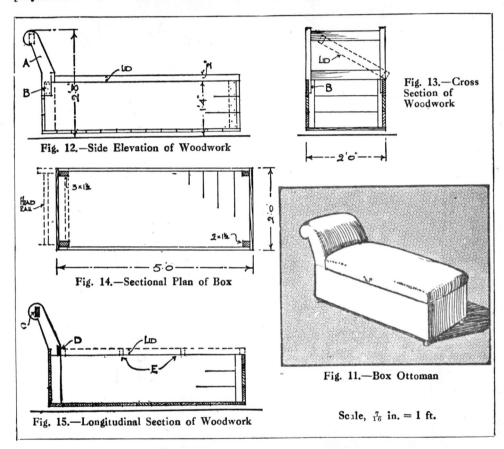

Fig. 13.—Cross Section of Woodwork

Fig. 12.—Side Elevation of Woodwork

Fig. 14.—Sectional Plan of Box

Fig. 15.—Longitudinal Section of Woodwork

Fig. 11.—Box Ottoman

Scale, $\frac{7}{16}$ in. = 1 ft.

from Fig. 9 that the chair narrows towards the back, so that a careful setting-out will be necessary in order to obtain the correct bevels for the joints. A full-size setting-out, based on Fig. 8, will also be very necessary.

BOX OTTOMAN

Nothing more than the most elementary knowledge of woodwork and simple up-

enough a head might be fitted at the ends. A padded back is sometimes included, but will obviously complicate the work and interfere with the free opening of the box.

The woodwork involved is practically of the packing-case order, the sides and bottom of the box consisting of stout boarding (Figs. 12, 13 and 14), preferably tongued, nailed to corner uprights

(Fig. 14).   These uprights are about 2 in. by 1¼ in. at the foot, and 3 in. by 1¼ in. at the head, where they are halved to the shaped side-rails A in Fig. 12.   The long sides are first put together, then connected by short lengths of boarding to form the ends, and the whole stiffened with boards running from the back to the front to form the bottom.   In working out the height of the box (1 ft. 4 in. from floor to

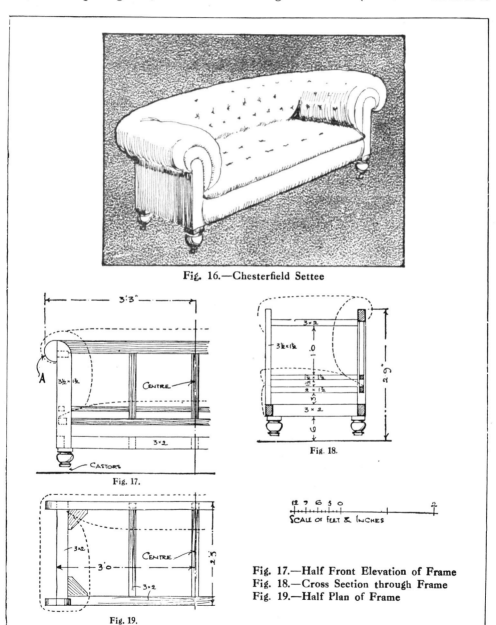

Fig. 16.—Chesterfield Settee

Fig. 17.

Fig. 18.

Fig. 19.

Fig. 17.—Half Front Elevation of Frame
Fig. 18.—Cross Section through Frame
Fig. 19.—Half Plan of Frame

top) an allowance should be made for casters or turned feet if these are required. They can easily be fixed at the corners, where the work is strengthened by the uprights previously mentioned. The shaped rails for the head can be solid or built up, and are halved and screwed to the uprights, as at B in Figs. 12 and 13, in such a way that their outer faces are flush with the boarding. They should be connected up with rails, as at C and D in Fig. 15, to take the upholstering, which must be quite thin at D in order to permit a close

be covered separately, its underside lined with some suitable material, and the whole hinged in position and fitted with a couple of stays of webbing to prevent it from opening too far back. A small handle will facilitate its opening, and the interior of the box can be painted or lined with paper, etc.

CHESTERFIELD SETTEE

A settee such as that shown by Fig. 16 can be from 5 ft. 6 in. to 7 ft. in length,

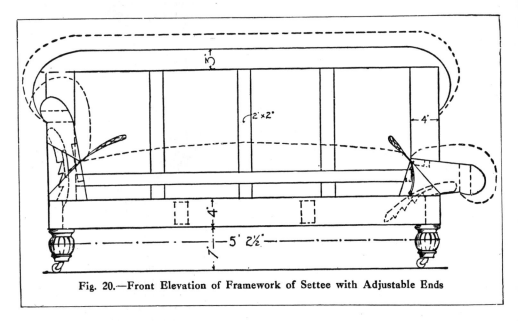

Fig. 20.—Front Elevation of Framework of Settee with Adjustable Ends

fit with the lid. The latter can next be put together from stuff about 2 in. by $1\frac{1}{2}$ in., halved neatly at the angles and stiffened with a couple of cross-rails, as at E in Fig. 15.

This framework can readily be webbed and padded, as can also the roll of the head, which can be finished smooth, or stabbed through and buttoned as desired. The sides of the box are merely covered with the selected material on a backing of canvas, stretched tightly and turned over at the edges, where it can be secured with coloured cord and gimp-pins, or, if desired, small brass-headed nails. The lid should

and the rough framing is of a very simple character, as will be gathered from Figs. 17 to 19. Simple halved or tenoned joints will suffice, provided the work is strongly screwed. Approximate sizes are shown, but need not be rigidly adhered to. Curved blocks, as at A, should be added to the tops of the uprights at the front and the back. The short legs should be in hardwood, circular-turned as shown, or square and tapered if preferred, and they can be dowelled in position. It should be noted that the shaded portions in Fig. 17 occur at the back only, as will be seen on reference to Fig. 18.

The approximate outlines of the finished upholstering are indicated by the curved dotted lines, and full instructions on this part of the subject will be found in a later section.

SETTEE WITH ADJUSTABLE ENDS

A settee with two adjustable ends is shown in front and end elevation by Figs. 20 and 21. Plain birch is recommended as the most suitable wood for making the framework; but oak or any

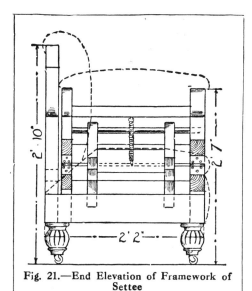

Fig. 21.—End Elevation of Framework of Settee

other wood could be used for the legs or "stumps," as they are called.

The four lower rails—one front, one back, and two ends—are of 4-in. by 2-in. section stuff, to be dowel-jointed together, the space being divided by two inner rails of nearly the same strength. The back framing is of 2-in. thick material, and could be made separate, to be strongly jointed on at the five uprights. The two front scroll uprights are the same thickness and 6 in. wide at the base, tapering to 4 in. Two similar ones are required in 1½-in. thick material for the back. These are

to be made into two frames for the adjustable ends, the back scroll uprights being ½ in. from the back frame. They are connected by a rail 4½ in. wide by 1½ in. thick at the scroll end, and another 6 in. by 1 in., even with the slant edge and 3 in. from the lower end. They can be jointed and glued up, and then a rail of ¾-in. diameter may be inserted at a point 1 in. below the scroll rail and ½ in. from the outer edge. It is fitted simply by boring holes, but must not be permanently fixed. The two scroll frames could then be dowelled in place. When they are set the V-shaped pieces may be cut out for making the ends to let down. The cuts are made at ¾ in. and 9 in. from the lower rail on the outer edge to the centre of the 6 in. wide piece at the slant edge, which has to be divided lengthwise. To make sure of not making a false cut, experiment with a cardboard pattern.

When the V-cut end frame is right it may be hinged and the wood ratchet pieces made. For these, tough wood 1½ in. thick should be used. They are about 1 ft. 2 in. long, slightly curved, and divided into ratchet teeth beginning 5 in. from the top end. These are connected by a flat piece about 1 ft. 3 in. long by 4 in. wide and 1 in. thick, jointed at about the centre. The rounded rail has to go through the top ends, just free enough to allow it to move easily. The teeth have to rest on the lower rail to keep the end up. To let it down, a loop of upholsterers' cord is attached about the centre of the connecting piece, to pull the ratchet forward so that the teeth miss the rail. The loop can be pushed in between the stuffed parts out of sight (see details in Fig. 20).

A coil spring has yet to be added to pull the teeth automatically on to the rail. This is attached to the connecting piece and the scroll rail by means of strong screw-eyes, as shown in Fig. 21. In the ½-in. space between the back frame and the fixed lower end of the scroll upright, wood may be glued in and screws inserted through to fix them firmly, giving strength to both. The lower frame should be strengthened with glued blocks at the corners, or by braces.

STUFF-OVER SOFA FRAME

The reproduced drawings, Figs. 22 and 24, are front and end elevations of a sofa frame to be stuffed all over, the four

in that the back of the sofa is made in one flat frame, which can be unscrewed from the ends and separately upholstered. A plan is shown by Fig. 23.

The four feet (Fig. 25) are turned out of wood $3\frac{1}{2}$ in. square, and mortised to receive the front, back, and end rails 3 in. deep by $1\frac{3}{4}$ in. thick, which should

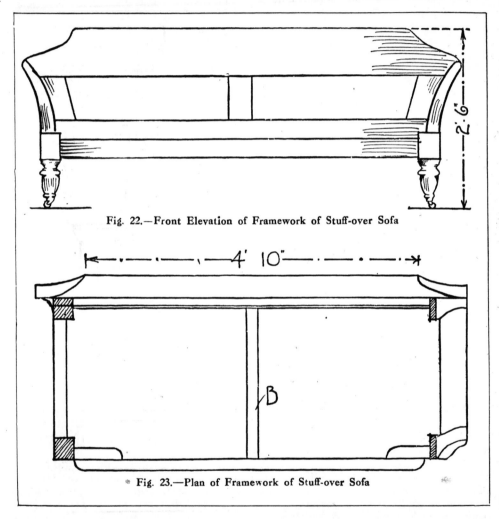

Fig. 22.—Front Elevation of Framework of Stuff-over Sofa

Fig. 23.—Plan of Framework of Stuff-over Sofa

turned feet only being seen, which could be made of mahogany, walnut, or oak. The frame is intended to be made of pine and birch. The construction of the frame differs somewhat from the usual method,

be flush on the outside edges. The bottom edges of the seat rails are kept $\frac{1}{2}$ in. above the turning, and the tops of the feet are left projecting 1 in. above the rails.

The measurements of the seat frame

are : Length across the end rails, 5 ft. 9 in.; width at middle, 2 ft. 5 in.; width at ends, 2 ft. 3 in. The break on the front rail shown in Fig. 24 is seen in detail in Fig. 26. Prepare two short rails A (Fig. 26) 1 ft. long by 3 in. deep by $1\frac{1}{2}$ in. thick. Tenon one end of each to fit the mortises in the front feet. Then cut the long rail 5 ft. 1 in. long by 3 in. deep by 2 in. thick, and round off each end. Glue and screw the short rails to it, showing the shoulders projecting $\frac{1}{2}$ in. over the rounded ends. A few dowels through the joint will further strengthen it. When the seat frame is cramped up, an iron strap B (Fig. 23) $1\frac{1}{2}$ in. by $\frac{1}{4}$ in. thick should be fitted to,

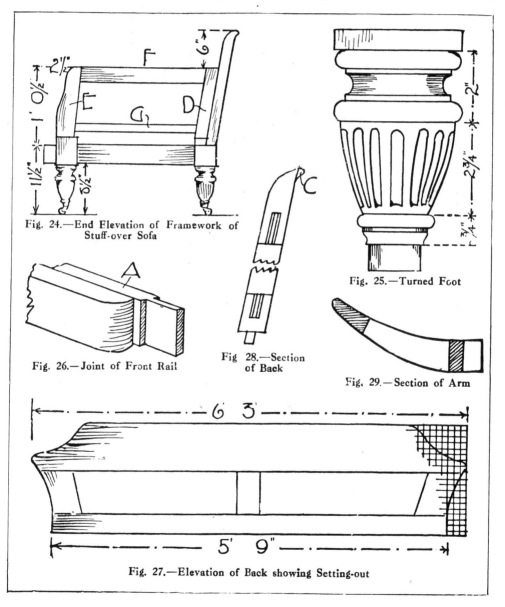

Fig. 24.—End Elevation of Framework of Stuff-over Sofa

Fig. 25.—Turned Foot

Fig. 26.—Joint of Front Rail

Fig 28.—Section of Back

Fig. 29.—Section of Arm

Fig. 27.—Elevation of Back showing Setting-out

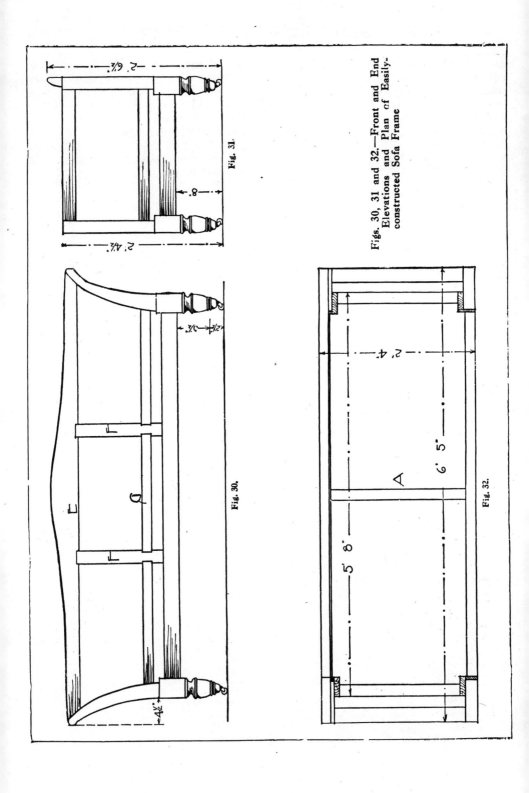

Figs. 30, 31 and 32.—Front and End Elevations and Plan of Easily-constructed Sofa Frame

Fig. 31.

Fig. 30.

Fig. 32.

and sunk flush with, the under edges of the front and back rails, and fixed with screws. This strap prevents the rails yielding to the strain of the girths when upholstering the seat. Sometimes a wood rail is substituted for the strap.

The back (Fig. 27) can next receive attention, and for this 1½-in. white pine is required. Cut out the top and bottom rails about 6 ft. 4 in. long, making the former 8 in. wide and the latter 3½ in. wide. The two end rails are about 1 ft. long by 6½ in. wide, and the middle rail 3½ in. wide. Mortise the top and bottom rails to receive the short end and middle rails at the positions shown in Fig. 27. To obtain the flat curve on the edge of

them to the stumps with ⅜-in. dowels, allowing a clear space of 2 in. above the seat rail. The back of the sofa has an incline of 1½ in., measuring from the top of the seat rail to the top of the elbow rail.

After cramping the arms together, they should next be dowelled to the feet, using four ⅜-in. dowels for each stump. Note the position of the back stumps, placed 1½ in. back from the back feet to allow the pine back to overlap.

The pine back can now be fitted to the back stumps, and fixed with strong screws. A few dowels fixed to the bottom rail of the back will steady it to the top edge of the seat rail. Fit cup casters to the feet, and polish. All the corners should be well

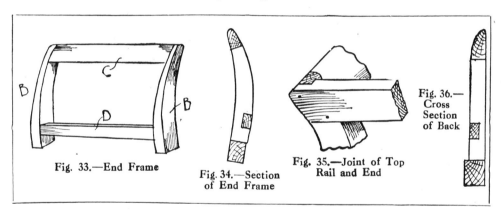

Fig. 33.—End Frame

Fig. 34.—Section of End Frame

Fig. 35.—Joint of Top Rail and End

Fig. 36.—Cross Section of Back

the top rail shown at c (Fig. 28), glue a piece of pine 2 in. wide by 1 in. thick to the back edge of the rail, and when hard, round the rail over at the front, using a round-soled plane or flat gouge to fit the curve at the back. The shape of the back at the ends is shown in Fig. 27, but before cutting out, the two arms should be proceeded with. Fig. 24 shows a side view, and Fig. 29 a section. The back stumps D (Fig. 24) are cut out of 2-in. birch, and shaped to the line shown on the back (Fig. 27). The front stumps E (Fig. 24) are cut out of birch 2½ in. thick, and are shaped on the face the same as the back stumps. They are also shaped at the side, as shown in Fig. 24. The elbow rails F are 2¼ in. by 1½ in. thick, and the stuffing rails G 2 in. by 1¼ in. Dowel

rounded over with a rasp before starting to upholster.

EASILY-CONSTRUCTED SOFA FRAME

Figs. 30 and 31 show another sofa frame that is to be stuffed all over except at the four turned feet. A plan is shown by Fig. 32.

Mahogany or walnut would be suitable for the feet and birch for the frame. Begin by marking the feet for the mortises to receive the front, back, and end rails, which are 3 in. wide by 1¼ in. thick, and leave the top ends of the feet projecting 1 in. above the edges of the rails for strength. The frame, when cramped together, should be 5 ft. 8 in. long by 2 ft.

4 in. wide, and an iron strap A (Fig. 32), 1½ in. wide by ¼ in. thick, is screwed to the bottom edges of the front and back rails, across the middle, to prevent the rails yielding to the strain of the girth webs when being upholstered. For the two sofa ends (Fig. 33) the stumps B are 2 in. thick, and cut to the curves shown in Figs. 30 and 34. The top rails C (Fig. 33) are 2¼ in. wide by 1½ in. thick, and are rounded to the outline of the stumps and dowelled to them. The stuffing rail D, 1½ in. wide by 1¼ in. thick, is mortised to the stumps, keeping the inside edges of the stumps and rail flush, and allowing a space of 2 in. between the bottom edge of the stuffing rail and the top edge of the seat rail. When the two ends are cramped together, as in Fig. 33, they should be dowelled to the top ends of the feet, using four dowels ⅜ in. thick for each stump.

For the back rail E (Fig. 30), pine 1½ in. thick may be used. At the middle it is 4½ in. wide, the ends being 2½ in. wide and half-checked to stumps, and glued and screwed, as shown in Fig. 35. The inside edge of the rail should be well rounded over. The two upright rails F (Fig. 30) are shown in section in Fig. 36. They are 2 in. wide by 1½ in. thick, and dowelled to the top edge of the seat rail, the top ends being housed into the bottom edge of the top rail and glued and cheek nailed. The stuffing rails G (Fig. 30) are similar to those in the ends, but are housed in the uprights and cheek nailed. The feet are turned to the pattern shown in Figs. 30 and 31, and fitted with cup casters.

Overmantels and Mirrors

PIER-GLASS FRAME

THE framework of the pier-glass or overmantel shown by Fig. 1 and in front and side elevations by Figs. 2 and 3, consists of one base rail, $4\frac{1}{2}$ in. by $1\frac{1}{2}$ in., one top rail out of 10 in. by $1\frac{1}{2}$ in., and two uprights 2 in. wide by $1\frac{3}{4}$ in. thick. When these are prepared, a double rebate for glass and backboard must be run along one edge of each, as in Figs. 4 and 5. The face of the sides and top are moulded, as shown in Fig. 5, etc., the top rail mitreing with the sides which die out against the base, as at A (Fig. 2). The top rail must be mitre-face tenoned to the sides, as in Fig. 6, the tenon B coinciding with the face between the two rebates, as at C in Fig. 5. The lower ends of the uprights are halved to the base, and screwed as at D in Fig. 3, this detail being better shown at D (Fig. 7).

Before the joints are fixed, the curved

Fig. 1.—Pier Glass

top rail must be got out. This, if in one piece, would require to be got out of a 10-in. board $1\frac{1}{4}$ in. thick, but for economy three pieces of $\frac{3}{4}$-in. oak may be jointed in a manner to give space for the curved rail, a suitable template for which should previously have been made in cardboard or stiff paper set out from Fig. 2. This will make the oak facing, and the back part of the rail may be made of deal or white wood 1 in. thick ; but the joints must not come directly behind those in the oak. What time may appear to be lost in doing this is saved by cutting the deal $\frac{3}{8}$ in. narrower than the facing, so that when glued together the curved rail is rebated for the glass, although a rebate for the backboard will still be required. This will, however, save the difficult task of rebating the solid oak. In fastening the facing, hot glue should be used on both pieces, which should be pressed well together with several hand-screws until thoroughly set. When the rail is fitted, the frame may be finally put together with glue. It will be necessary to cramp the joints up immediately, and they should all be secured with countersunk screws from the back. It is most

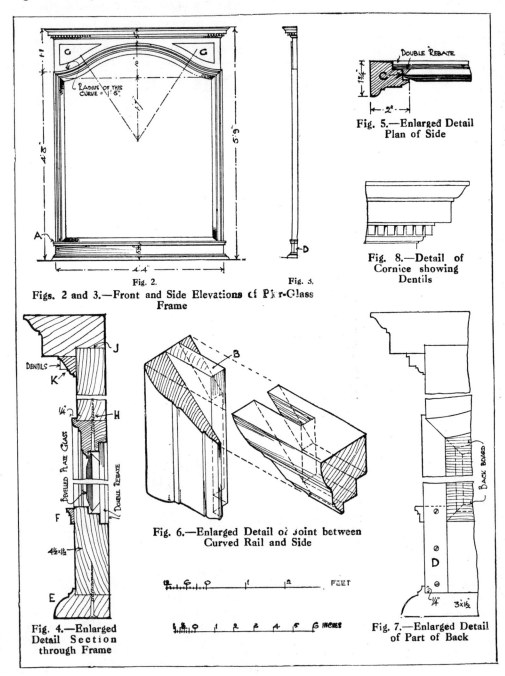

Fig. 2.

Fig. 3.

Figs. 2 and 3.—Front and Side Elevations of Pier-Glass Frame

Fig. 5.—Enlarged Detail Plan of Side

Fig. 8.—Detail of Cornice showing Dentils

Fig. 6.—Enlarged Detail of Joint between Curved Rail and Side

Fig. 4.—Enlarged Detail Section through Frame

Fig. 7.—Enlarged Detail of Part of Back

important to see that the frame is quite square, and out of winding, before it has had time to set.

The bottom rail is finished with a solid base 3 in. by $1\frac{1}{2}$ in., moulded and returned at the ends, and sunk $\frac{1}{4}$ in. on the top to receive the rail, to which it should be countersunk-screwed, as at E in the detail section (Fig. 4). A moulded fillet, as at F in the same figure, should be planted on and mitred and returned at the ends.

For the work at the top double spandrels, as at G (Fig. 2), will be required. They can be in one or two pieces, and might be clamped at the exposed ends. They are $1\frac{1}{2}$ in. thick, and after being carefully cut to the required bottom outline, should be let into slight sinkings previously prepared in the top of the curved rail, and well screwed from the glass rebate, as shown in Fig. 4 at H. The panel effect, shown in Fig. 1, is produced by sinking the entire surface of the spandrel about $\frac{1}{8}$ in., with the exception of a $\frac{3}{4}$-in. margin. A moulded cornice will be required to crown the whole, and should be carefully set out from Fig. 4. The main portion measures $4\frac{1}{4}$ in. by 2 in. and is moulded on the solid on the front and ends. It is rebated, as at J, to suit the spandrel, to which it can be screwed from above. The bed mould K (shown in the same figure) is mitred round under the main portion of the cornice. It measures $1\frac{1}{4}$ in. by 1 in., and has a dentil-course composed of square blocks, as shown in Fig. 8, separated by neatly-finished raking cuts as in Fig. 4.

When ordering the mirror send a template in any dry thin board nailed and glued, to ensure its not being put out of square. It should fit loosely, yet evenly, and, in fact, it will be well to allow $\frac{1}{8}$ in. play all round. The template with more timber fixed across will afterwards serve as the backboard. The frame is placed face downwards, and the mirror put gently in ; then small three-cornered blocks, as in Figs. 4 and 5, are glued round to regulate it to show the bevel evenly, and when these are sufficiently set the backboard may be put in.

OVERMANTEL FOR A LOW CHIMNEY-PIECE

The shortcomings of the low cast-iron mantelpiece, which it is the custom of the builders to fix in the least important bedrooms, are very apparent, and the overmantel shown by Fig. 9 is designed

Fig. 9.—Overmantel for Low Chimney-piece

with the idea of effecting some improvement in their appearance. The ordinary overmantel would be too low for the mirror to be of service unless elevated off the shelf, as the usual height of these mantels does not exceed 3 ft. 6 in.

The illustrations give all necessary dimensions and indicate the method of construction, the frame being a very simple piece of mortise-and-tenon work and quite straightforward. Front and side elevations are shown by Figs. 10 and 11, and a half sectional plan by Fig. 12. The introduction of the picture-frame moulding to take the mirror plate (see Fig. 13) is somewhat unusual. This

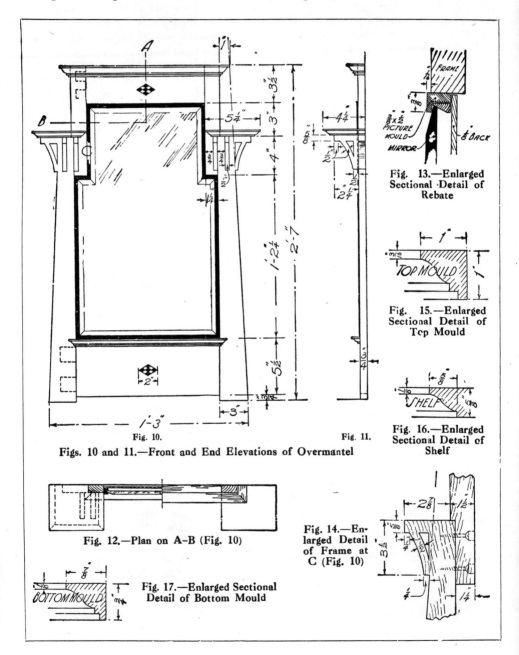

Fig. 13.—Enlarged Sectional Detail of Rebate

Fig. 15.—Enlarged Sectional Detail of Top Mould

Fig. 16.—Enlarged Sectional Detail of Shelf

Fig. 10.

Fig. 11.

Figs. 10 and 11.—Front and End Elevations of Overmantel

Fig. 12.—Plan on A–B (Fig. 10)

Fig. 14.—Enlarged Detail of Frame at C (Fig. 10)

Fig. 17.—Enlarged Sectional Detail of Bottom Mould

is one of those plain ebonised mouldings which have been used a great deal in recent years for framing etchings and photographs. It is bradded in place with its face projecting $\frac{1}{16}$ in. in front of the face of the oak frame. The top and bottom rails are relieved by diamond-shape inlays of ebony and red fibre—a non-conducting material used by electricians—and these simple features, together with the black inner frame, give the overmantel a very attractive touch. Glue and dowels secure the four front brackets in place, or they may be screwed from behind, and the two shelves are dowelled where they bed on these brackets and on the frame (Fig. 14). The rebate of the picture-frame moulding is stained black to avoid a conspicuous reflection of those surfaces when the mirror plate is in position, and the mirror is held by twelve wedge-shape blocks, each 2-in. long, and fixed with brads. Sections of the mouldings are shown by Figs. 15, 16 and 17. A pair of brass hanging plates, screwed to the back of the frame affords means of fixing the overmantel to the wall.

Fig. 18.—Hanging Mirror

HANGING MIRROR

A hanging mirror-frame (suitable for a hall or bedroom) into which an inlaid panel is introduced as decoration is shown by Fig. 18. The design lends itself to

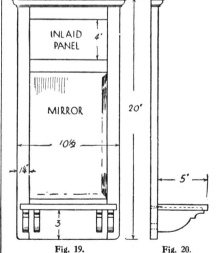

Fig. 19.   Fig. 20.
Figs. 19 and 20.—Front and Side
Elevations of Hanging Mirror

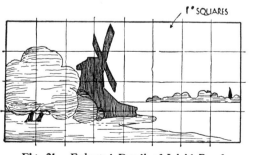

Fig. 21.—Enlarged Detail of Inlaid Panel

a fairly wide choice of material, oak or walnut probably being the most suitable for. the frame proper. This should be framed up in the usual way with mortise-and-tenon joints, the various dimensions being given in the elevations (Figs. 19 and 20). The cornice moulding is an easily-worked ovolo fixed to the frame with three ⅜-in. dowels. The lower shelf and brackets are of ⅝-in. material, the brackets, of which there are four, being

woods should be obtained of veneer thickness, when the method of procedure briefly will be as follows : The veneers are laid one on the other, with paper and a little thin glue between each one. When this is dry, the pattern should be transferred to the top piece, cut out with a fine fretsaw, and the various pieces separated. Each piece of the design should now fall into its place, and the whole be first glued to paper, and

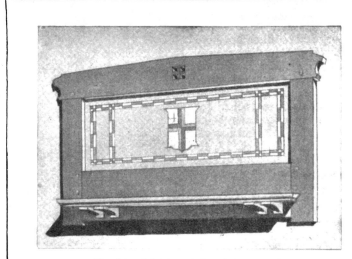

Fig. 22.—Inlaid or Painted Overmantel

tenoned into the frame and dovetail-housed into the shelf. The shelf is also secured to the back by means of screws (see Fig. 20). The shape of the brackets is, of course, capable of great variation.

The inlaid panel is an example of the form of inlay known as intarsia or pictorial inlay. Fig. 21 gives an enlarged detail of this, which should be drawn full-size. The choice of woods is left largely to the worker. The following, however, is a suggestion—the sky of greywood, water of holly, the windmill, walnut, the trees of burr walnut, which is excellent for obtaining foliage effects, and the foreground of cedar. These

finally, with the aid of a caul, to the panel. Both the veneer and the base should be well " toothed " or roughened before gluing. When dry the panel may be cleaned up with scraper and glass-paper, and fitted in the frame by means of a beading and panel pins. Inlay and veneer work are more fully dealt with in a later section.

The mirror should be held in position by a backboard of three-ply or other thin material pinned in, rather than by the usual method, as this will enable the frame to lie close against the wall. A dull waxed finish will be most suitable, and instructions on obtaining this finish are given on other pages.

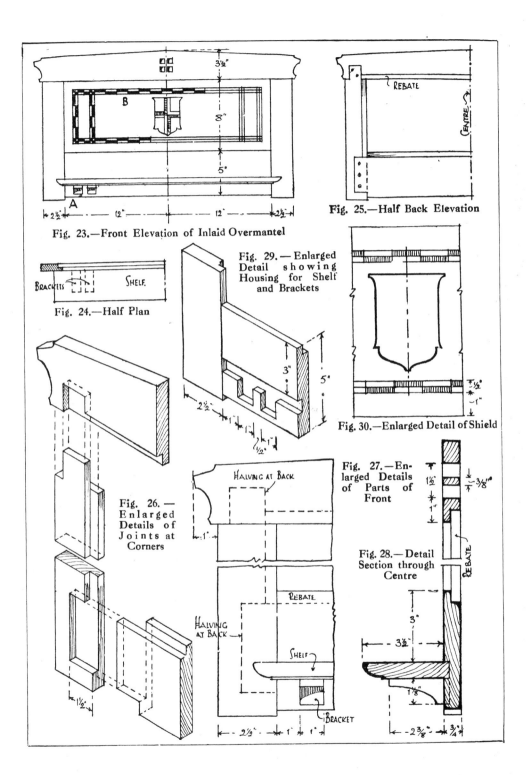

Fig. 23.—Front Elevation of Inlaid Overmantel

Fig. 25.—Half Back Elevation

Fig. 24.—Half Plan

Fig. 29. — Enlarged Detail showing Housing for Shelf and Brackets

Fig. 30.—Enlarged Detail of Shield

Fig. 26. — Enlarged Details of Joints at Corners

Fig. 27.—Enlarged Details of Parts of Front

Fig. 28.—Detail Section through Centre

INLAID OR PAINTED OVERMANTEL

This overmantel (Fig. 22) is designed to hang on the wall, at a convenient level above a mantelshelf. Its main interest centres in a painted shield or crest, providing a note of interest and colour very suitable to its position, which is the most important one in most rooms. Heraldic devices are usually eminently decorative, and if one having a local or personal application can be chosen, the result should be particularly appropriate. At the same time, if preferred, the panel can be adapted in size and shape to suit a picture or mirror. The shelf also is optional, and if employed can be fixed either with or without the small shaped brackets shown in the illustrations; it is thought that their use gives greater strength.

Oak will be very suitable for the framework, although other materials can be adopted; but in most cases a rather dark finish is likely to give the best results. The general dimensions are given in the elevations (Fig. 23). A half plan is shown by Fig. 24. Stuff $\frac{3}{4}$ in. thick should be used, $2\frac{1}{2}$ in. wide for the upright ends, $3\frac{1}{4}$ in. for the top and 5 in. for the bottom rails. The four pieces are rebated about $\frac{1}{2}$ in. by $\frac{3}{8}$ in., and halved and screwed together at the angles, as shown by Fig. 25, the simple joints necessary being elucidated by the isometric views of the various parts separated in Fig. 26. Forms of the dovetail could be used in such cases; but if halved and well screwed, the work should be thoroughly sound, and no joints will show on the exposed edges. Alternately the joints might be pegged together, as was often done in old work, the pegs sometimes being allowed to project slightly beyond the general surface. Note that the lower edge of the bottom rail finishes $\frac{1}{4}$ in. above that of the upright (A, Fig. 23). The top rail tapers from full width in the centre to about $3\frac{1}{4}$ in. at each end, where it is shaped as in Fig. 27, the projection not requiring to be more than 1 in. A central ornament consisting of four small squares (dimensioned in Fig. 28) can be pierced

or inlaid on it; or other small devices can be adopted at will.

The shelf shown is $3\frac{3}{4}$ in. by $\frac{3}{4}$ in. and 2 ft. 2 in. long, worked to a simple moulding along the front and end edges, and housed about $\frac{1}{4}$ in. into the bottom rail, as in Fig. 29. The ends can be cut back $\frac{1}{4}$ in. in order to butt against the uprights, as it would be unnecessary to house them at these points. The brackets shown under the shelf (Fig. 23) are optional; but if adopted can consist of shaped pieces $2\frac{5}{8}$ in. by $1\frac{1}{8}$ in. by 1 in., housed into the bottom rail in the positions shown in Fig. 29, and secured to the underside of the shelf by means of fine wire brads.

The panel might be drawn and painted in oils on wood or artists' canvas; or cheap cloth could be made to serve the purpose, provided that it is first stretched and prepared with several coats of paint to form a ground on which to work. Another course would be to use tempera or body-colour (that is, powder colours mixed with gum and white) on paper, in which case it would be advisable to place the panel under glass, although with oil-colours a coat of varnish would be sufficient protection. A strong outline of a fairly dark colour should be employed on a rather sombre ground, perhaps of a grey or brownish tone, the better to set off the bright heraldic colouring.

A suggested form of shield, suited for any ordinary case, is given to scale in Fig. 30, and part of the chequered border is also shown. This latter is worked on a series of three lines $\frac{1}{4}$ in. apart, and might be of vermilion, green, or dark brown, in conjunction with white or cream according to circumstances, any irregularities being toned down by the dark outline, which should be very carefully gone over last of all. The little rectangles should be kept rather long in proportion to their width, and care is necessary in spacing them to see that no two dark spaces come together at the angles, also that there is an odd number of divisions in the lines, as at B in Fig. 23. If this is not the case the ends will be the reverse of one another, instead of corresponding square for square.

MIRROR AND RACK

The mirror shown by Fig. 31 is of a generally useful type, but fitted with hat pegs or hooks as illustrated ; it is, on the former the suggested dimensions are given.

The framework generally should finish $\frac{7}{8}$ in. or $\frac{3}{4}$ in. thick, and can be either tenoned together in the orthodox manner,

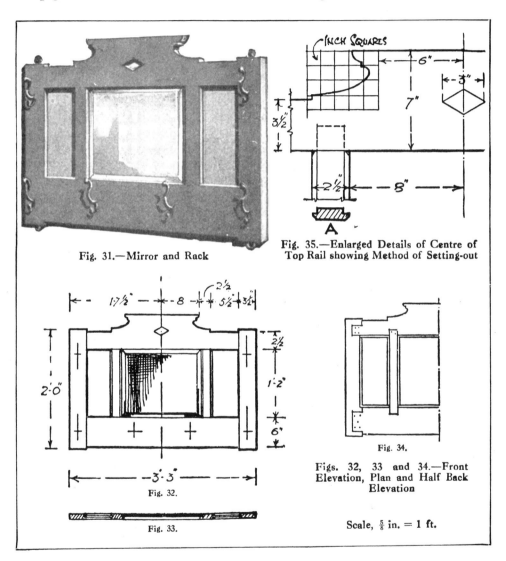

Fig. 31.—Mirror and Rack

Fig. 35.—Enlarged Details of Centre of Top Rail showing Method of Setting-out

Figs. 32, 33 and 34.—Front Elevation, Plan and Half Back Elevation

Scale, $\frac{5}{8}$ in. = 1 ft.

Fig. 32.

Fig. 33.

Fig. 34.

of course, especially suitable for use on the hall wall. Without these hooks it might, with slight modification, form an acceptable overmantel. An elevation and plan are shown by Figs. 32 and 33, and or for an easy job halved and screwed at the back, as shown by Fig. 34. The edges of the two middle uprights are slightly chamfered, as at A in Fig. 35. In the centre opening a piece of silvered plate glass, which should have bevelled edges, is placed, the rebate to receive this being ploughed out of the rails and uprights. The small side panels may be filled in with thin stuff in grooves or rebates, or they can be merely left open. The wide top rail is cut to shape, as in Fig. 35, with a band-saw, and pierced with a diamond-shape in the centre. The screwholes for the pegs and hooks having been set out, the woodwork should be polished before they are fixed.

Four strong brass plates are used to fix it to the wall. These could be bought or cut out of $\frac{1}{16}$-in. sheet brass.

If mahogany or walnut has been used, the work should be french-polished ; but if made of oak or teak.it would look well cleaned up, rubbed over with wax, and left dull. The glass for the mirror should be bought ready silvered and bevelled.

BEDROOM OVERMANTEL

The simple type of overmantel or mantel-mirror shown by Fig. 36 is designed for a bedroom, and alternative treatments are suggested by which it could be made to harmonise with the existing furniture. With reference to Fig. 36, in which the general effect can be seen, the left-hand portion is a suggestion for execution in oak with inlaid panels ; while the alternative on the right could be carried out in mahogany, the panels in this case being decorated by the use of finely-figured veneers (see later section).

In each case the construction of the framework is straightforward enough, the $1\frac{1}{2}$-in. framing being jointed up with the type of tenon shown by Fig. 37. It will be noted that the rebates on the outer edges of the two inner stiles must not be carried right through, but stopped where the short top rails are tenoned into them. When the framing is set out and jointed, it may be glued and cramped together and the mouldings proceeded with. Fig. 38 gives details of these, a plain ovolo shown at A for oak, and a slightly more elaborate form for mahogany at B. The dentils forming part of the latter must be accurately set out and cut,

otherwise they will easily appear irregular. The cornice moulding in each case can be fixed to the framing by dowelling, while the light base moulding can be either screwed or secured with fine pins.

The side panels may now be proceeded with. These are of $\frac{5}{8}$-in. material, bevelled on the back and fitted into the rebate of the frame with a small beading pinned round. Before the back of the panels are bevelled, however, the decoration of them should be carried out. The inlaid pattern for execution in oak, shown by Fig. 39, is an example of inlay pure and simple (as distinct from marquetry), that is, each piece of the design is cut out separately, laid on the groundwork, marked round, and a recess cut for it with chisel and gouge. The design should first be drawn full-size and traced, by means of carbon paper, on to the wood. The shape of each piece should then be transferred to the inlaying wood (which should be about $\frac{1}{8}$ in. thick), cut round with a fretsaw and finished to shape with fine files. It will help a good deal in fitting if the edges of these pieces are cut with a slight bevel, slightly smaller on the underside. The flowers are built up, as in Fig. 40, of five pieces of wood, glued first to paper, shaped and let into the ground, when the holes for the centres can be drilled with a Morse drill and small ebony pegs driven in. The marking out of the recesses should be done with a fine marking point, occasionally a sharp hard pencil will be preferred. In cutting these recesses—an operation which must be carried out with care—one or two carver's gouges and a bent background tool are useful. When ready the various pieces may be glued and lightly hammered in, and after the whole has thoroughly set, the panel may be cleaned up with a finely-set plane and finished with glasspaper.

The alternative pattern for mahogany is a fairly simple piece of veneering. A couple of well-figured " curls " should be chosen, and an unobtrusive banding laid round, as shown in Fig. 36, the edges of the panel being cross-banded. When completed, the panels may be fitted to the framework.

The mirror itself, which should be of good stout plate, has a ¾-in. bevel, and is fitted by means of small triangular blocks glued round the rebate. Before actually fitting the mirror, however, the inside of the rebate and the edges of the

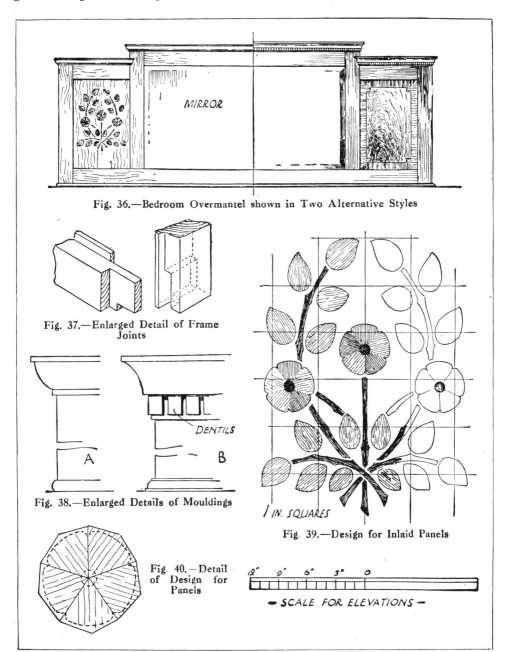

Fig. 36.—Bedroom Overmantel shown in Two Alternative Styles

Fig. 37.—Enlarged Detail of Frame Joints

DENTILS

A   B

Fig. 38.—Enlarged Details of Mouldings

1 IN. SQUARES

Fig 39.—Design for Inlaid Panels

Fig. 40.—Detail of Design for Panels

SCALE FOR ELEVATIONS

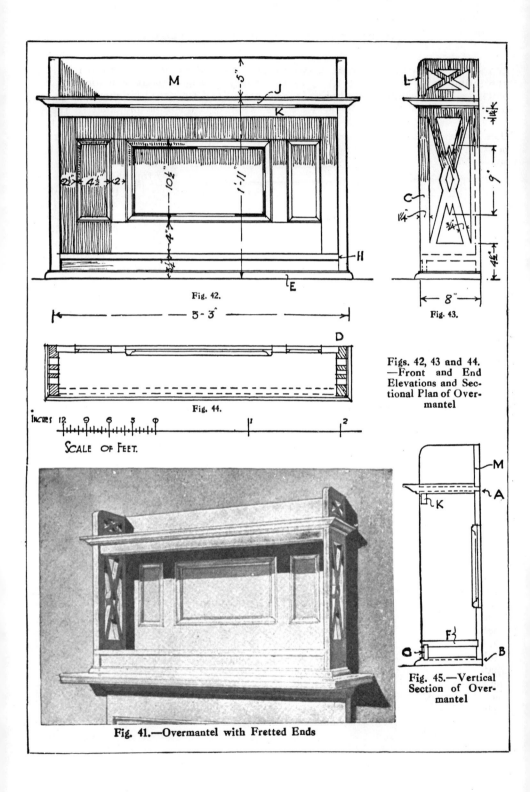

Fig. 42.

5 - 3"

Fig. 44.

Inches 12 9 6 3

Scale of Feet.

Fig. 43.

Figs. 42, 43 and 44.
—Front and End
Elevations and Sectional Plan of Overmantel

Fig. 45.—Vertical
Section of Overmantel

Fig. 41.—Overmantel with Fretted Ends

glass should be well blacked, to avoid unsightly reflections. A mixture of lampblack and french-polish is useful for this, being applied with a brush.

The finish depends on the material. Oak should be lightly fumed and waxpolished, while mahogany could be darkened and french-polished.

OVERMANTEL WITH FRETTED ENDS

The overmantel shown by Fig. 41 should be made to match in width the mantel or fireplace surround on which it is to be placed. Its fretted ends constitute a change from the class of work most usually employed, and its three panels can be filled with wood, silvered glass, or pictures. There are also several variations possible for the panels, such as the use of a mirror or suitable picture central between two wood panels ; or perhaps a mirror between two small decorative pictures, any variation which harmonises being suitable.

The suggested sizes are given in the two elevations (Figs. 42 and 43). Fig. 44 shows a sectional plan, but these may have to be altered to suit differing circumstances. The main back consists of a piece of framing finishing about $\frac{3}{4}$ in. thick, tenoned or halved together in the form of three panels, filled as desired, the end ones having a small moulding mitred round, while the centre has a much bolder moulding. The framing extends from A to B in Fig. 45, as do also the main ends C (Fig. 43). These are easily set out and fretted, and should be at least 1 in. thick in order to produce a substantial effect. They are slightly rebated for the main back, as at D in Fig. 44, and housed into a simply moulded baseboard E (Fig. 42), which should be rebated for the back, as at B in Fig. 45. The substantial appearance so very desirable in this type of work is increased by thickening out this base with a shelf, as at F in Fig. 45, and a small upright G recessed $\frac{1}{16}$ in. on the face. To avoid opening joints, all this work should be housed together, the shelf F being stopped

back $\frac{1}{4}$ in. from the face in order to show a straight joint, as at H in Fig. 42.

For the top, a $1\frac{1}{4}$-in. moulded shelf J (Fig. 42) should be prepared to the required size, and the sides and back jointed to it in eaxctly the same manner as to the base E. A thin rail about $1\frac{1}{2}$ in. deep should be fixed along the front edge of the top shelf K (Figs. 42 and 45), also housed in position and recessed $\frac{1}{16}$ in. Above the top shelf are two small fretted ends L (Fig. 43), and a plain back M (Figs. 42 and 45). These should exactly match the work below in width, thickness, and position, and can be screwed from the underside of the top shelf before the lower portions are finally secured to it. They are rebated together as at D in Fig. 44.

The backs of the panels should be well protected from possible dampness in the wall behind, and if glass, etc., is used, in the case of a new building, it might be desirable to cover them with thin zinc.

OVERMANTEL WITH CUPBOARDS

This overmantel is of more elaborate construction than those previously described, and it is designed on altogether different lines. Fig. 46 shows its general appearance, and two elevations and sectional plan are shown by Figs. 47, 48 and 49. Fig. 50 is a section through the centre.

Regarding construction a start can be made with a moulded base A (Figs. 47 and 48), grooved as necessary to receive the various portions above. At each end is a tall narrow cupboard, consisting of plain sides tongued or housed at the tops into small moulded shelves B (Fig. 47). The cupboard fronts have narrow frieze pieces let in at the top, with a small necking mould as at C (Fig. 47), the whole being set back sufficiently to enable the moulding to butt against the sides as shown. The lower parts have small framed doors, without mouldings, but rebated on the inside to receive leaded glazing, which should have rather wide cames. Door stops should be fixed inside. and shelves if required. The bottom rails of the doors are made 4 in. wide in order to line with the top of a central boxing. For the back of the cupboards thin boarding will suffice ; but for the central portion with the semicircular head, a piece of framing with a panel in the centre would be preferable.

The panel can be veneered, or it can take the form of a framed picture or mirror. The curved head should be cut out of one piece, joining the uprights at a point level with the centre from which

Fig. 52, the proved lasting qualities of the material recommending it for such a purpose. The time required to execute such decoration in gesso would not be comparable to carving it, whilst the result, if required for gilding, would be quite as satisfactory. Fig. 53 shows one repeat of a design of simpler character than the foregoing that would form a pleasing frame and be within the capabilities of an amateur worker to produce.

Oak would be the best material to

Fig. 46.—Overmantel with Cupboards

the curve is struck. The beaded ornament which surrounds the panel should be boldly carved. It can be worked separately, and glued and bradded in position with very fine wire brads. Alternatively it can be cut on the solid edge of the framing, as shown in section by Fig. 51.

CIRCULAR MIRROR-FRAME

A very fine circular mirror-frame in the South Kensington Museum, the ornamentation of which is executed in a gesso composition and gilt, is shown by

employ for the making, though any wood that can be cleanly moulded with a scratch-tool could be used. The frame could be made of any dimensions, a thickness of $\frac{5}{8}$ in. to 1 in. being requisite. If it is necessary to " butt " together two boards to make up the width, the joining edges must be accurately planed, and after applying the heated glue, rubbed well together to secure a good join all along, as any disposition to come apart later would be disastrous. Mark out the outer and inner circles and saw round with a pad-saw, truing up with a spokeshave so as to obtain outlines as correct as possible, as they will serve as a guide for the scratch-tools that form the mouldings. The frame will require to be very firmly fixed to the work bench whilst the mouldings are being made, either with cramps, the arms of which are carefully padded where they come in contact with the surface of the wood, or with carvers' "snibs" which consist of a piece of hardwood, one end projecting to hold the panel, the snib being fixed to the bench by means of a screw (*see* Fig. 54).

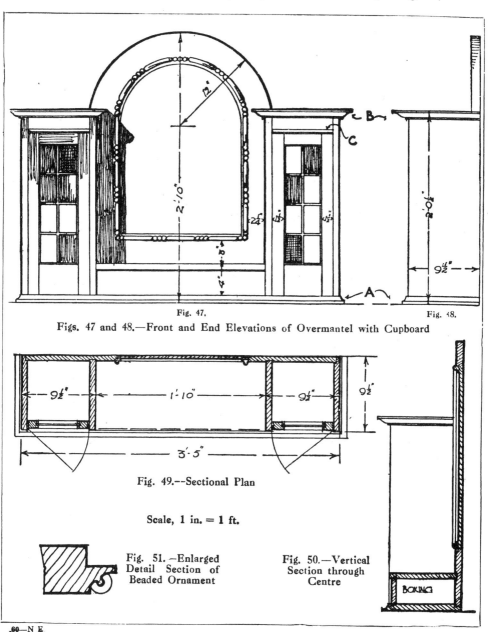

Fig. 47.

Fig. 48.

Figs. 47 and 48.—Front and End Elevations of Overmantel with Cupboard

Fig. 49.--Sectional Plan

Scale, 1 in. = 1 ft.

Fig. 51.—Enlarged Detail Section of Beaded Ornament

Fig. 50.—Vertical Section through Centre

The required section of moulding should be first drawn out full-size (*see* Fig. 55), the first process being to cut two grooves at A, as shown in Fig. 56. For this work it will be necessary to make a stock similar to that shown in Fig. 57, consisting of two pieces of ¾-in. beech shaped

away from the operator, taking care to keep it in alignment with the centre of the frame throughout the whole circumference. The groove is gone over repeatedly until the depth of it equals the projection of the cutter, the inner line being scored from the inside edge. The

Fig. 52.—Circular Mirror-frame

as shown, the cutter being held firmly between by tightening up with three gutter-bolts. The blade for this particular job is shaped as shown by Fig. 58, consisting of a sharpened piece of steel which is adjusted in the stock at the required distance from the guide. Fig. 54 shows the grooving in progress, with the scratch-stock in position, the tool being worked

iron is necessarily adjusted accordingly, whilst the snibs holding the frame in position are fixed on the outside edge. The grooves having been cut, the next operation will be to remove the waste between them (*see* Fig. 56). This can best be done with a chisel, a " router " being useful for levelling the sunken ground. This tool consists of a small block of hardwood with a perfectly flat sole. A slot is cut in the centre, one side of which is sloped to accommodate the wedge that holds the cutter in place. This is a piece of sharpened steel—a broken chisel serving admirably. Cut a little of the wood away as shown by A

After the mouldings of the frame have been completed, the whole of the front of the work is given a coat of thin glue in which some whiting has been dissolved, and allowed to dry, when it is lightly glasspapered over and the design traced on the surface.

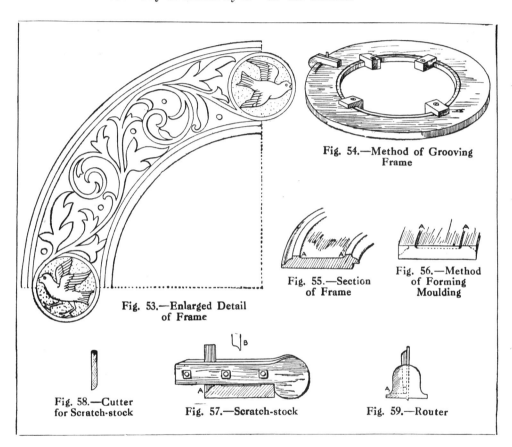

Fig. 54.—Method of Grooving Frame

Fig. 53.—Enlarged Detail of Frame

Fig. 55.—Section of Frame

Fig. 56.—Method of Forming Moulding

Fig. 58.—Cutter for Scratch-stock

Fig. 57.—Scratch-stock

Fig. 59.—Router

(Fig. 59) to allow for clearance. The cutter is adjusted so as to project the amount of the depth of the groove, the ends of the soles resting on the surface of the frame ; thus, by scraping, the hollow can be perfectly levelled. The mouldings of the frame are then completed by scratching the outer moulding with a cutter shaped as A (Fig. 57), and the inner one as B, the final operation being the cutting of the rebate at the back to take the glass.

There are two methods by which such a design as shown by Fig. 53 could be executed. First is to model one repeat of the pattern in plasticine and make a plaster cast of it, and then take what is known as a " squeeze " from the mould in composition, the process being repeated until the frame is covered. The other method is to paint the design in with a gesso composition which will render it in low relief. In the case of the first process, one-quarter of the pattern shown by Fig 53 could be modelled actually on the frame, then oiled, and a mould made. Composition, now known as "compo" in the trade, is a purchasable article. A little is pressed into the mould and levelled. Paint the pattern in with glue or gold-size roughly on the frame, and press the mould with the composition in it down to the surface, the material attaching itself sufficiently to be drawn out of the mould. It is then pressed well in contact, the same process being gone through in the case of the three other quarters, the bird panels being done separately. After the composition has set hard the frame can be prepared for gilding. In executing in "gesso" the material is applied in the form of a thin cream, that sets slowly and dries with a hard smooth surface. It is easy to use, being just painted on thickly. It will normally assume a smooth rounded surface of its own accord if of the right consistency, and as many coatings as necessary may be applied until the required degree of relief has been obtained.

A sable brush is the best to use, though a good camel-hair one will serve. The gesso mixture should be stood in a bowl of hot water whilst working. The design can then be painted in, keeping to the traced lines. For very low relief one application is sufficient, but for greater relief the work can be gone over repeatedly.

In the execution of the design (Fig. 53), the bird form would be most effectively executed in higher relief than the rest of the ornamental border, which is kept more or less flat, with just a little variation in the case of the larger leaves. A good effect will be produced if a little modelling is attempted in the case of the birds, by raising those parts that come in front, as in the case of the nearest wings, rounding off the head and body, whilst the legs are left in low relief. For work required in very high relief it is desirable to thicken the gesso with tow snipped into short lengths to bind it. It may be mentioned that gesso lends itself to colouring with either oil-colour or water-colour. Some examples of gesso work are so richly coloured as to appear almost like an illuminated manuscript; for such a purpose as the frame described, the use of bright hues for picking out the small details will yield a more pleasing result than dull tones employed in large masses. The use of oil-colour has the advantage that the scheme can be altered at will, by painting over what has already been applied, until a perfectly pleasing effect has been secured.

TWO REPRODUCTIONS OF OLD-STYLE MIRRORS

The use of mirrors is a revival of an old custom, it being the practice as early as the seventeenth century to introduce these in furnishing. During the Queen Anne period particularly some fine examples were produced, which for beauty of line, detail and figuring are hard to excel.

The Queen Anne style is regarded amongst designers as the purest of English styles of furniture design, and the ornament of this period owes less than any other style of furniture to foreign inspiration. Quite a feature of this period are the fine shapings of the glass heads, both in toilet and hanging mirrors. The most famous craftsman of the Queen Anne period was Grinling Gibbons, who was first discovered by Evelyn about 1670, and was introduced by him to the King, who gave him an appointment in the Board of Works. Grinling Gibbons as a carver has never been excelled from the point of view of technique, but the strictly natural effects he aimed at in his works are copied from nature, and are necessarily weak from the point of view of ornament. He nearly always carved in lime wood, which is soft and close-grained, and admirably adapted to the elaborate treatment and undercutting of his designs. In addition to executing floral devices, he made much use of cherubs' heads in his compositions, and fine examples of this style can be seen above the choir stalls of St. Paul's Cathedral. Grinling Gibbons made a special feature of pictures or mirrors above the fireplace, and embellished these with magnificent carvings in the shape of " swags " and " festoons."

tion, as his examples closely follow—in general treatment—French examples. He later made a number of small wall mirrors, termed " girandoles," which were most

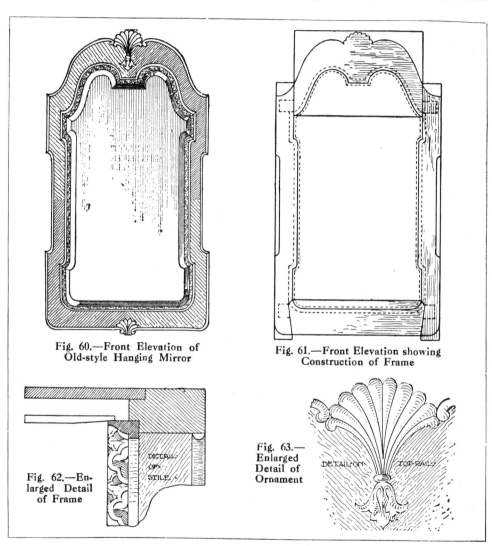

Fig. 60.—Front Elevation of Old-style Hanging Mirror

Fig. 61.—Front Elevation showing Construction of Frame

Fig. 62.—Enlarged Detail of Frame

DETAIL OF STILE

Fig. 63.—Enlarged Detail of Ornament

DETAIL ON TOP RAILS

Thomas Chippendale in his early work used the wall mirror very largely in conjunction with console tables, the former being supported by the table in halls and reception rooms. Both their shape and decorative treatment suggest that he went to the Louis XV. style for inspira-

elaborately carved, and are now much sought after by collectors. They were made with a large centre mirror and with delicate tracery round the sides, through which silvered glass gave a striking effect. Some of his girandoles are fitted with sconces for candles, which enhanced the general effect when hung in a room lighted only with candles.

The brothers Robert and James Adam also executed many mirrors of this type, generally more delicate in character than Chippendale's, and executed largely in stucco richly gilded. The round and oval examples of the brothers Adam are now much copied, and used as centre-pieces in recesses and panels in interiors.

In Fig. 60 is shown a modern rendering of a Queen Anne wall-mirror with characteristic curves and ornament. English walnut was the material most used for these mirrors, and although now English walnut is difficult to obtain, it gives a better appearance to the work than Italian or Circassian walnut, which is the best substitute. English walnut belongs to the same botanical order as the Italian and Circassian varieties, and it is characterised by a lighter groundwork—sometimes almost a golden colour—with very dark brown streaks or markings. The carved moulding round the opening should be gilded similarly to the small centre ornaments at the top and bottom of the frame. A high polish is not desirable in this work, and waxing is therefore more usual ; but an excellent effect can be obtained by completing the polishing in the usual way, and reducing it by means of powdered pumicestone in order to remove the brightness of the finish. A little wax and turpentine may then be rubbed in, which imparts a soft tone or finish to the work.

An elevation of the mirror is shown by Fig. 61, which illustrates the construction of the frame. A wide-top rail is introduced, and is tenoned between the two stiles with long and short shouldered joints, these being necessary in order to fill the rebates cut from the opening moulding and the back. It will be seen from the constructional diagram that the inside lines of the stiles must be cut square to the required shape before mortising is proceeded with. The rebating on the centre part can be done with a rebate plane. The top and bottom parts must be cut away with chisels, and then finished with a scratch-stock worked

off the edge of the material, thus cleaning the rebate to the desired distance in the back and also regulating the depth. At the bottom of the frame it will be seen that a bevelled shoulder is introduced, and this has the effect of strengthening an otherwise weak part. A small bevel connects the inside line of the rail with the shoulder, and short grain is thus obviated when the inside corners are rounded. The mortising and tenoning should be effected first, shaping and rebating comes next, and then the frame is glued up and stood aside to dry. The shaping of the head and bottom is the next step, and it is essential that the frame be quite symmetrical when shaped. To ensure this a piece of strong paper should be cut to coincide with half the top shape, and this is then laid on the work and worked round with a sharp pencil. The paper is then turned over on to the other side of the centre line and worked round again. An alternative method of constructing the frame is to mortise and tenon two rails and two stiles together, the pieces being arranged so that the finished shape can be cut out. The pieces are glued up true, and then the inside and outside shapes are cut out and filed true. Rebates must then be cut on both the back and the face side, which is an easy matter if a spindle machine is available ; if not, the superfluous wood must be chiselled out, and then finished as indicated previously with scratch-stocks.

To prepare the frame for veneering (see later section) it should be well toothed on the face side and glued, then the veneer can be cut and laid with a veneering hammer. If a veneering press or even a dozen hand-screws are available, it will be found a cleaner way to execute the work by building the veneers on paper, and then gluing the whole down together with a heated caul and pressure. Round the edges of the frame cross-banded beads should be fixed to the section shown in the enlarged detail (Fig 62), these being carefully connected to thin pieces of walnut cut to outline for the top (Fig. 63) and bottom ornaments.

These should, of course, be glued to the frame before carving is proceeded with.

The carved ornaments are essentially Queen Anne in treatment, and are frequently used in the knee parts of legs, centre of spandrels, and pediments of the period.

Fig. 64 shows a half elevation of a horizontal or "landscape" mirror based on the designs of the brothers Adam.

firms who make a speciality of this class of work. It the different parts are not obtainable ready built up and suitable in size it is not a difficult matter to get the design made up from stock units, which are cut and bent to the required pattern. Composition ornament of this character can be made plastic by putting it into a shallow tray of hot water, which acts on the glue and oil, and permits it

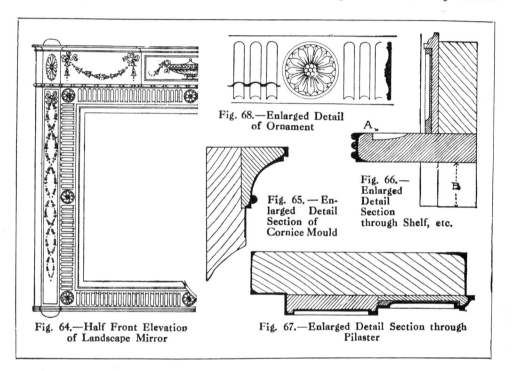

Fig. 68.—Enlarged Detail of Ornament

Fig. 65.—Enlarged Detail Section of Cornice Mould

Fig. 66.—Enlarged Detail Section through Shelf, etc.

Fig. 64.—Half Front Elevation of Landscape Mirror

Fig. 67.—Enlarged Detail Section through Pilaster

In making a mirror of this type the chief thing, of course, is the applied ornament. The brothers Adam introduced this kind of decoration, and largely employed it in decorating furniture, ceilings and walls. It is commonly known as "stucco," and is a mixture of whiting, glue, linseed oil and resin. It might be supposed that a composition of this character would deteriorate and crack, but much original Adam work exists to-day in practically a perfect state. If it is required to make one mirror only, the detail can be obtained from several

to be easily bent. Honduras mahogany is a suitable wood for the framework of this mirror, and gives a suitable surface for painting and enamelling.

The construction of this frame is very simple. Two wide stiles are prepared, as shown in the enlarged sectional detail, and a wide top rail and bottom rail are simply dowelled or tenoned between the stiles. The frame when dry is then levelled down and squared up, and then a thin centre tablet is prepared with a sunk panel to receive the applied ornament, and glued on. After this two pilasters are made with semicircular ends and with sunk panels, as indicated in the enlarged sectional view, these being glued down along the stiles, as shown in the elevation. A length of cornice moulding can then be prepared, and should be mitred round the top part, particular care being taken with the breaks round the pilasters and tablet. An enlarged sectional view of the cornice moulding is shown rebated into the framing (Fig. 65) ; this detail is, of course, stronger than simply planting it in the surface, but necessarily takes longer. A frieze moulding should next be prepared and mitred round, the piece between the two pilasters having a bigger projection in order to project beyond the fluted moulding round the opening.

The shelf is the next part to be dealt with, a sectional view of this being shown at A (Fig. 66), and when notched to fit over the pilasters it can be glued to the underside of the bottom rail. It will be necessary to make up the pilasters below the shelf, and this can be effected by gluing in small pieces to correspond with B (Fig. 66). It will also be seen from this sectional view that the shelf is grooved to hold the edges of plates, and this detail can easily be effected by gauging and chiselling to the required section.

The next process is that of forming the rebates for the glass, and, as the sectional view (Fig. 67) shows, this is effected by allowing the moulding to overlap the opening. A flat moulding is made by working the small ogee section along one edge, and a wide rebate is then worked to receive the composition ornament. It will be found advantageous in some cases to buy the moulding complete, which then only requires to be fixed in position. As an alternative, the moulding should be mitred round, and then the frame should be sent to have the composition mounted. A detail of the composition ornamentation is shown by Fig. 68.

The finish of a frame of this kind should be white paint or enamel, and it may hardly be necessary to point out that several coats of thin white paint are much better than two or three coats of thicker paint. The latter fills up some of the detail, and considerably reduces the effect. Should a white or cream enamel finish be desired, two or three coats of paint should precede two coats of good enamel. The work should be executed in a warm shop or room, which causes the enamel to run freely, and at the same time prevents unsightly brush marks.

Clock Cases

MODERN INLAID CLOCK CASE

THOSE who delight in delicate veneer and inlay work—subjects which are dealt with in a later section—will find the making of the clock case shown by Figs. 1 and 2 interesting work, and a decorative and useful article of furniture. Clocks of this type usually occupy a prominent position in a room, and, being comparatively small, offer opportunities of using choice veneers and inlays in decorations, which in larger articles of furniture would be prohibitive as regards expense. Moreover, with jobs of this size some of the odd pieces of veneer which accumulate from other work may be utilised.

Before beginning the woodwork it will be necessary to obtain the dial and movement of the clock, and it will be obvious that the dimensions of the illustrations here given will have to be modified to suit the particular works procured. In settling the size of the case due regard must be paid to the diameter of the face, the length of the pendulum, and the distance from back to front.

The constructive part of the case is of the simplest character, consisting of a box of dry, sound yellow pine $\frac{3}{8}$ in. thick dovetailed together, the top piece being 1 in. thick to allow for shaping to the curve shown. The front and back pieces are glued on to the edges ; but before the latter piece is placed in position, the opening for the back door must be cut. On reference to Figs. 3 and 4, it will be seen that the construction is strengthened by gluing small blocks in all the internal angles. A rebate is worked on the front and sides, $\frac{5}{8}$ in. by $\frac{1}{8}$ in. (bare), to receive the inlaid base moulding, as shown in Fig. 3. When the top has been shaped to the correct curve the whole of the " seen " surfaces of the case must be well toothed and given two coats of hot glue-size, to prevent the pine absorbing the glue too rapidly. A light toothing after the second coat of size will leave the surfaces quite ready for the veneer.

Figs. 1, 2, and 5 show the arrangement of the veneers. Kingwood is used for the main portion, with a cross-band of snakewood and a corner edge of ebony and boxwood. The striped character of kingwood and the snakewood gives a distinctly decorative effect when cut and laid, as indicated by Figs. 1 and 2. The patterns for the front and sides are drawn out on stiff paper, after which the kingwood veneers are shot true (preferably with an iron plate), and lightly glued to their respective positions on the paper. When dry, a toothing plane should be used to slightly rough the veneer surface. Care must be taken when gluing the patterns to the case to get the centre joint correctly placed, and before applying the hand-screws to the hot caul a block of wood should be fitted inside the case to resist the pressure. A caul shaped to one-half of the top curve will be necessary when veneering this portion of the case, a small ebony bead being glued to the centre to conceal the joint. The margin for the snakewood cross-band is gauged off few veneer pins. The cross-band is easily laid with a hammer, and when dry the small corner rebate is removed with a sharp cutting gauge, and finished with a

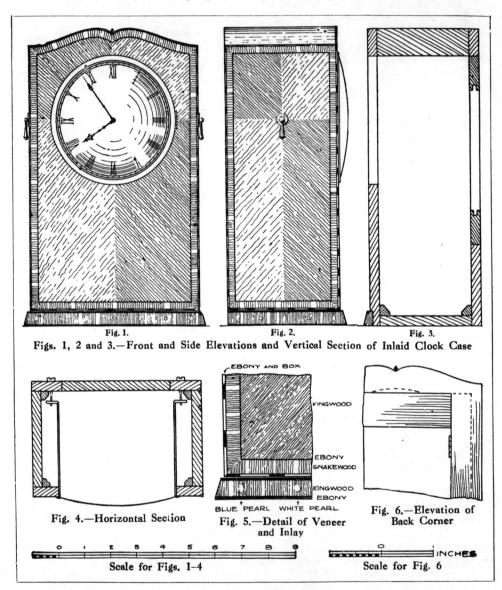

Fig. 1.   Fig. 2.   Fig. 3.

Figs. 1, 2 and 3.—Front and Side Elevations and Vertical Section of Inlaid Clock Case

Fig. 4.—Horizontal Section

EBONY AND BOX
KINGWOOD
EBONY
SNAKEWOOD
KINGWOOD
EBONY
BLUE PEARL   WHITE PEARL

Fig. 5.—Detail of Veneer and Inlay

Fig. 6.—Elevation of Back Corner

Scale for Figs. 1-4

INCHES

Scale for Fig. 6

with a cutting gauge, and the surplus veneer and glue removed with the end of a hot file. The thin ebony line is then glued round and fixed in position with a scratch-stock and cutter. Bind the corner edge with damp tape until dry, and then lightly tooth the surfaces to remove irregularities,

Prepare the base moulding in one piece about 18 in. long, cross veneering the same with kingwood, and inlaying the edges with $\frac{1}{8}$-in. square ebony lines, as indicated in Fig. 5. The small inlays of pearl may be cut and fitted after the moulding has been mitred and glued into the prepared rebate. A fine file should be used to shape the pearl, small chisels and carving gouges being employed to cut the corresponding shape in the moulding. Use a fine file to remove any pearl standing above the surface of the moulding after inlaying, then finish with scraper and glasspaper in the usual manner. A pleasing effect is obtained by using blue pearl for the diamond shapes, and white pearl for the circular shapes. Figs. 3, 4 and 6 indicate the construction and position of a small clamped door hinged to the back. Fig. 4 shows how the clock is attached to the case with small screws passing through the back, and screwed to a metal projection inside, which is drilled and tapped to receive it.

Fig. 7.—Old-style Clock Case

OLD-STYLE CLOCK CASE

The reproduced photographs Figs. 7 and 8 show a clock case of old-style design. The photographs have failed to reproduce the inlay work; but it is shown in Fig. 9. There need be no difficulty about obtaining a movement; but possibly it might have to be a new one. It is advisable to see to this first, as the measurements of the case may have to be altered a little. The case (see Figs. 9, 10 and 11) may be made chiefly in dry soft pine of $\frac{5}{16}$-in. thickness, veneered with saw-cut mahogany veneer, which, besides having a more beautiful " figure " of grain than the solid mahogany, is also better for inlaying. A short study of the sectional illustrations (Figs. 12, 13 and 14) will make all clear as regards the details of construction.

The first thing to do is to make the main body of the case, in the form of a box. For this is required a front, back, bottom, and two side pieces, all of the $\frac{5}{16}$-in. soft pine. The front and back must be the same, the grain to run horizontally, and must measure $8\frac{3}{4}$ in. by $5\frac{5}{8}$ in. With the two sides the grain must run vertically and measure 7 in. by $2\frac{1}{2}$ in. They should be temporarily fixed to the end grain of the front and back with four fine screws to each side, which must be put on quite flush and even at the lower corners. It is then ready for the bottom, which will be $6\frac{1}{4}$ in. by $2\frac{1}{2}$ in. In this condition the front and back may be scribed for the curve at the top edge by means of a pair of compasses set to $3\frac{1}{8}$ in. The scribing will mark off the upper end of the side pieces to a slightly curved bevel. They should be taken apart for cutting to the curves. When this is done they may be

Fig. 8.—Back View of Old-style Clock Case

put together again with extra screws and glue ; then the curves should be trimmed up to receive the top.

The top should be a piece of the soft pine $\frac{3}{16}$ in. in thickness, to measure about 11 in. across the grain by 3 in. with the grain. To ensure it bending correctly without breaking, the inner side may be saw-kerfed $\frac{1}{4}$ in. apart and $\frac{1}{8}$ in. deep. It must be put on as quickly as possible. First, the outer side should be wetted with a rag dipped in very hot water to cause it to curve, then the inner side and the curved edges should be well brushed over with hot glue, and placed quickly together to overhang the front and back about $\frac{1}{4}$ in. It should be fixed at the centre with fine pins, then pressed carefully down and fixed with further pins. It will require to be left over-night to set in a dry place, and it is best to take off the bottom to expose the inner side to the air. When thoroughly set, the bottom may be put on again, and the box trimmed up for veneering on the front, back, and curved top. Before the veneering is done the two side blocks may be prepared. They are of solid mahogany, and measure $8\frac{1}{4}$ in. long by $1\frac{3}{4}$ in. wide by $\frac{3}{4}$ in. thick,

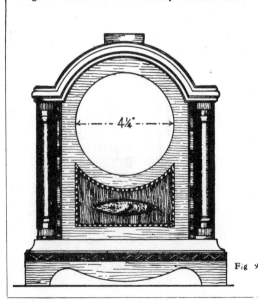

Fig. 9.

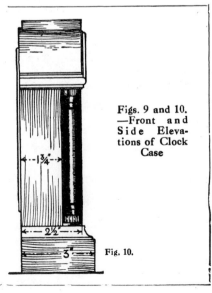

Figs. 9 and 10.—Front and Side Elevations of Clock Case

Fig. 10.

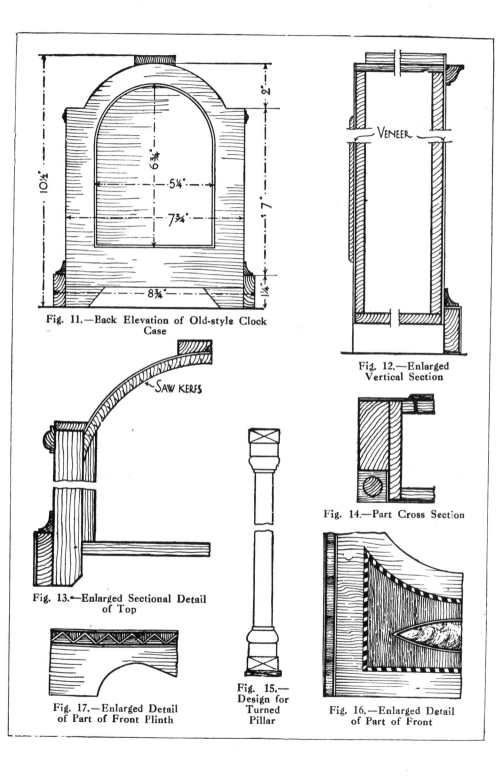

Fig. 11.—Back Elevation of Old-style Clock Case

Fig. 12.—Enlarged Vertical Section

Saw Kerfs

Fig. 13.—Enlarged Sectional Detail of Top

Fig. 14.—Part Cross Section

Fig. 17.—Enlarged Detail of Part of Front Plinth

Fig. 15.—Design for Turned Pillar

Fig. 16.—Enlarged Detail of Part of Front

and are fitted and glued in place flush with the back, but ¾ in. beyond the bottom.

The curved top may then be veneered, and the centre block may be fitted and glued in place flush with the front ; also the two pieces which cover the end grain of the side blocks ; these three pieces are

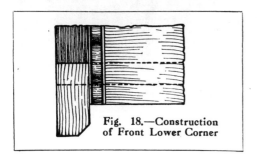

Fig. 18.—Construction of Front Lower Corner

of solid mahogany. When the top is set and trimmed, the front and back can be veneered, and a slip for the plinth, which should measure 1 ft. 3 in. by 1¼ in. by ½ in. finished. This would be best veneered on plain mahogany instead of the pine. Whilst the veneered work is being allowed time to set, the turning and moulding may be made. The two turned pillars will measure about 5⅝ in. in length, and are of solid mahogany. The pattern of these is shown by Fig. 15 ; but the block at the base, ⅛ in. thick, is a separate piece of wood to be glued under for fixing them.

The curved moulding will have to be turned in the form of a ring. Of course only about half of it would be used ; but it is a readier way of making it than by carving or working it out with hand tools. About a foot length of beading to the same section is required to continue round the straight part of the top, which could be worked with a beading plane or a small rebate plane, and the length of scotia moulding for the plinth may be made.

When the veneered front and back are set and trimmed there will be one side of each angle recess uncovered, exposing the deal sides, which must be veneered. The circle for the dial may then be scribed and the position of the inlay set out. Particulars of the inlay work are shown by Fig. 16 ; it consists of a mahogany

veneer, a diamond line of satinwood and ebony, rosewood, a light black line of figured satinwood, a banding of light and black lines and tulipwood. The method of procedure is, first to cut the piece of rosewood veneer to the full size and shape of the space to be inlaid, to be placed accurately in position to scribe the mahogany with the sharp point of a knife. It may be removed to deepen the cut ; then the mahogany veneer must be raised and the rosewood let in. The satinwood is let into the rosewood in the same manner. This part of the work should be allowed to set somewhat before putting in the lines. In the meantime the bandings can be put in, also the banding on the front plinth (see Fig. 17), which is composed of light black lines and greenwood. The light and black line surrounding the satinwood is detached from a piece of inlay banding, and is let in in two pieces neatly joined at the points. The diamond line is the inside part of a narrow banding or stringing. As will be seen, the small sections could not hold together long to stand much handling without breaking ; but they are supported by a light line at each side, which holds the sections firmly. It is often inlaid in its original condition ; but when it is required narrower, or to be used on curved work (as in this case), the

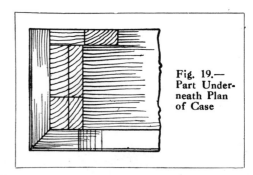

Fig. 19.— Part Underneath Plan of Case

light lines are detached just before being let in. Inlay work and veneering should have plenty of time to set thoroughly before being cleaned off. A fortnight in a dry warm room is usually allowed ; but when time will permit, several weeks or even months. When set it will require cleaning off and levelling with a well-sharpened steel scraper, and smoothing up with No. 2 glasspaper. Then the back can be cut out for the door, the piece that comes out to be used again, as the door. In order to do this it must be cut out very neat, and this may be done with a sharp-pointed knife used after the manner of cutting a picture mount. It is best to cut it on the bevel, and it will require repeated cuts until pierced through. The front may be cut for the dial the same way or with a bow-saw or keyhole saw. Although the door will fit fairly neat, it is better still to face it on the outside with $\frac{1}{8}$-in. stuff, $\frac{1}{8}$ in. larger all round to form a rebate ; fix on with 1-in. brass butt hinges.

The plinth will have to be fitted on $\frac{1}{2}$ in. up from the bottom, and the scotia mould will reach another $\frac{1}{2}$ in. higher. The front and sides should be marked for these, and it will be necessary to fit blocks in the angle recesses to be level with the lower end of the sides and the top edge of the mould, and flush with the front and sides (see Fig. 18). At the back, feet pieces are fitted, of the shape seen in Figs. 8 and 9 ; (see also Fig. 19, in which is shown the mitred plinth). All these are carefully fitted, glued, and pressed close, and when set somewhat firm the plinth mould can be mitred round and glued in place, being further fixed with a few needle points.

In fitting the cornice moulding, the curved piece should be put on first, then the recesses blocked and the straight moulding mitred round. The turned pillars may be fitted in place, but not permanently fixed until the polishing is done. To fit them, in the dead centre of the top end a 1-in. panel pin is driven, with the head nipped off and standing out $\frac{1}{4}$ in. to fit in a hole pierced in the block in the recess. When put in place, the thin block is wedged under the base to fix it. Finally they will be glued at both ends.

The case must be well smoothed up with No. 1 glasspaper, rubbing down all very sharp corners. After being brushed free from dust it should be rubbed over with linseed oil to be french-polished.

A grain filler may be used if the grain of the wood is very open ; but if close, it will be better without. The inside should be stained.

ANOTHER CASE FOR MANTEL CLOCK

Another case for a mantel clock of rather similar design to the preceding one is shown by the half-tone reproduction (Fig. 20). It is of handsome appearance ; and neat, well-finished workmanship is indispensable in its production. A good deal of its beauty depends on the natural colours and "figure" of the woods. Figs. 21, 22 and 23 are drawn to identical scale and give the necessary measurements, but the diameter of the circular opening in the front may be varied up to $4\frac{1}{2}$ in. according to the dial, in which case the inlaid ring need not be put in.

The case may be constructed mostly in dry red deal veneered with mahogany. In this instance it should be of the kind having that peculiar figure of grain known as "fiddle back." The details of construction are fully shown by Figs. 24, 25 and 26. The pieces of wood for the front and back should first be got out in deal, to measure 10 in. by $6\frac{1}{4}$ in. by $\frac{5}{16}$ in., the grain to run horizontally. Two side pieces are next required $8\frac{1}{2}$ in. long by $3\frac{1}{4}$ in. by $\frac{5}{16}$ in. of vertical grain. The front and back pieces must be temporarily screwed to these, the lower edges to be all even to receive the bottom, which will be $6\frac{1}{4}$ in. by $3\frac{3}{8}$ in. The curved top edges are scribed to part of a $6\frac{1}{2}$ in. in diameter circle, and must be taken apart for cutting, the top ends of the side pieces being taken down even to the same curves. This box-work may then be put together permanently (except the bottom) with glue and screws, being then ready for the top to be put on. For this is required a piece of mahogany $\frac{1}{4}$ in. thick to measure about 11 in. wide by $4\frac{1}{2}$ in. long. Saw-kerfs about $\frac{1}{4}$ in. apart and barely $\frac{3}{16}$ in. deep must be cut on the inner side, to enable it to bend with ease. To place in position, the outer side should be sponged over with very hot water, which will cause it

Fig. 20.—Another Mantel-clock Case

to curve, then the inner side may be glued over, also the curved edges, to which it is carefully fixed with fine pins. The bottom may then be taken off to help it the better to set, which will take several hours, before it can be trimmed in order to veneer the front and back, but the centre block can be fixed on. When this is done the veneered work requires further time to set, and the two side blocks may be got out, which are of deal 9 in. wide by $3\frac{1}{8}$ in. long by fully $\frac{3}{4}$ in. thick, to be veneered horizontally on one side and vertically on both end grain edges.

For the plinth is required a slip 1 ft. 6 in. by $1\frac{1}{8}$ in., to be $\frac{1}{2}$ in. thick when veneered on the front side. Whilst this part of the work is resting the turned work, pillars, and moulding may be prepared. The turning consists of the curved part of the ogee moulding in mahogany, the pillars in mahogany, the bases and capitals of the pillars in rosewood. But only half of what is turned will be required for one clock

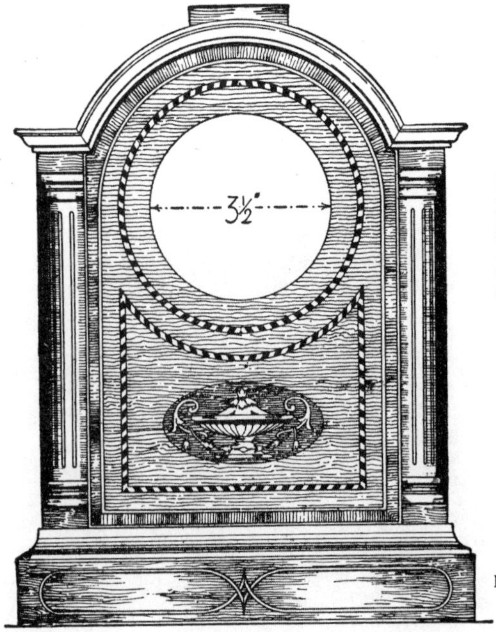

Figs. 21 and 22.—Front and Side Elevations of Mantel-clock Case

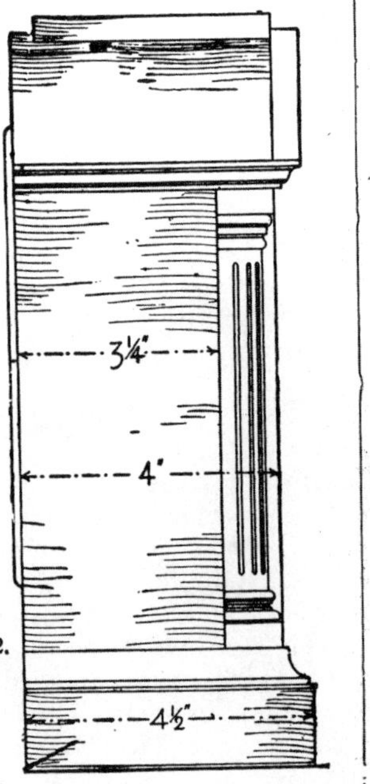

Fig. 21.

Fig. 22.

case, and if carefully cut there will be just sufficient left for another. For instance, the moulding will have to be turned in the form of a ring 7 in. in diameter,

be divided, thus making two quarters. The same is the case with the base and capital turning. The section of these is shown by Fig. 27, in which it will be seen

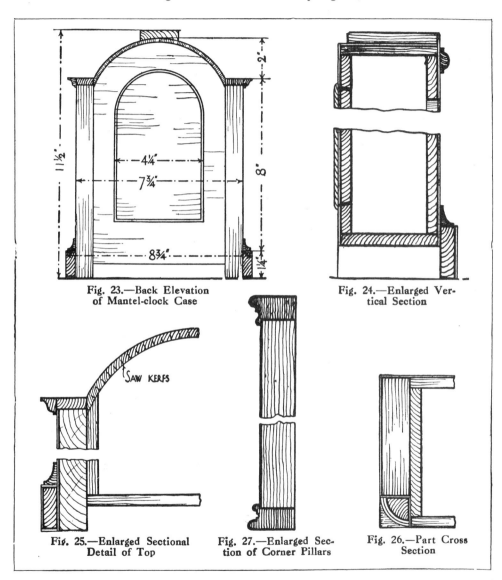

Fig. 23.—Back Elevation of Mantel-clock Case

Fig. 24.—Enlarged Vertical Section

Fig. 25.—Enlarged Sectional Detail of Top

Fig. 27.—Enlarged Section of Corner Pillars

Fig. 26.—Part Cross Section

meter, but less than half of it will be used. For the pillars a piece will need to be turned about 6 in. long by 1¼ in. in diameter, to be equally divided lengthwise, one half only to be used, which must itself

that they are sunk $\frac{1}{16}$ in. to fit the ends of the pillars. The grain of the rosewood should be vertical.

Of the ogee moulding, a straight length of about 1 ft. 2 in. will be required to continue from the curve round the top. Of the scotia moulding for the plinth about 1 ft. 7 in. will be wanted. When these are cut they cannot be applied until the veneered work is trimmed up, and then the first thing should be to veneer the deal exposed on one side of each angle recess, and set out for the front inlay (see Fig. 28). The position of the opening for the dial may be scribed with the compasses, and from that centre the grooving tool may be used for the inlaid circle and the curve just below it. To groove for the straight

the pattern true, which (with ovals) is apt to get a little wrong. To avoid this the face side of the pattern may be marked with a pencil line lengthwise and across the exact centre, then the paper side can be marked the same. Similar lines are made on the surface to be inlaid, and those on the oval should be in line with these when in position. It is important to have the glue in good condition, hot, strong, and not too thick, and the work must be done quickly. The sunk place must be glued first, then the face side of the inlay,

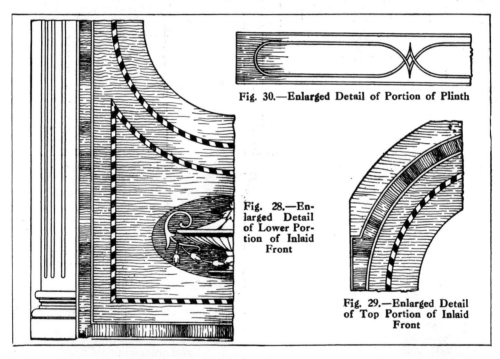

Fig. 30.—Enlarged Detail of Portion of Plinth

Fig. 28.—Enlarged Detail of Lower Portion of Inlaid Front

Fig. 29.—Enlarged Detail of Top Portion of Inlaid Front

diamond lines, the cutter may be gauged from the straight sides of the case. The inlay is stock material, with the outside light lines stripped off. When it is glued and well pressed in, the oval vase ornament may be done next. This also is a stock pattern shaded satinwood in a ground of green sycamore. After straightening the edges by rubbing on a piece of glasspaper, it should be laid in position face downwards and marked round with a sharp-pointed knife, the cut to be deepened to raise the waste veneer. Care must be taken to get

and pressed down close. It has an inclination to curl back at the edges, and should be dabbed over with a rag dipped in hot water, but not too much, or it will swell up. As much as possible of the surplus glue must be forced out by pressing down with the hammer, in doing which the paper gets rubbed off. It should not be left alone until firmly glued down all over.

The margin of the front may next be treated with the banding of tulip-wood between two light lines. The veneer is cut round with the cutting gauge, and taken off with the chisel. The straight lengths are easily laid, the lower corners being neatly mitred ; but to bend it round the curve, one of the lines must be stripped off, and the tulip-wood split with the sharp thin point of a knife at every $\frac{1}{4}$ in. on the outer edge. When it is glued in place the outside line must be glued back as before. Where it meets the top end of the straight length, the tulip-wood of both lengths needs to be joined, which should be done neatly so as not to show ; or a piece of the tulip-wood could be taken out of a wider banding and fitted in. Then there would be no end-grain joints to make, and those with the grain can be made quite invisible (see Fig. 29).

The plinth piece is slipped with green sycamore on both edges, and the front part inlaid with a light line (see Fig. 30), and this may be done next. It must first be marked out true, then the straight lines can be worked out with the grooving gauge. To groove the curves a $\frac{1}{16}$-in. chisel is used, free-hand, steadily scraping the mark until the required depth is reached. If this is found difficult, a piece of thin wood can be cut to the shape of the curve and used as a guide. The line should be wetted with very hot water before gluing, to get it to bend into the curved grooves.

The corner pillars have to be inlaid, each with three lines, and this may be done next if measured for very accurately, but it is safer to wait until they have been fitted. The inlay work, however, should be allowed as much time as possible to set thoroughly before being cleaned up with the scraper and glasspaper. When this is done the door should be cut out of the back, using, as already directed, a sharp-pointed knife held in the same manner as in cutting a picture mount. The piece that comes out may be faced on the back with $\frac{1}{8}$-in. stuff, $\frac{1}{8}$ in. larger all round to form a rebate. The circular opening for the dial may be cut out as may be most convenient, as it is not required for further use on the case.

The plinth may now be fitted. It is to be even with the lower end of the side

blocks, the front corners being mitred ; and here it will be found necessary to glue blocks in the angle recesses to be flush with the front and sides and the edges of the plinth. If the pieces are carefully fitted and thoroughly glued, this should be sufficient, otherwise the side pieces may be secured with a screw through the block and the front piece could be glue-blocked underneath. In putting on the scotia moulding, it should be well fitted and glued to give extra strength. Before fitting the ogee moulding round the top, the deal ends will require to be covered with pieces of mahogany ; then the curved part must be put on first, being secured with a few fine needle points in addition to the glue, and the straight moulding neatly fitted and fixed the same way. In the angle recesses are fitted four small square blocks $\frac{5}{16}$ in. thick of rosewood or mahogany ; then the corner pillars complete with bases and capitals may be fitted, but not fixed. The pillars can now be marked accurately for inlaying the light lines, which are stopped $\frac{1}{4}$ in. from the rosewood.

When the work has had plenty of time to set it should be particularly well trimmed and smoothed up with fine glasspaper, then brushed free from dust, and rubbed over with linseed oil. It is an advantage to allow this several days to dry, when it may be well rubbed with a dry cloth and it is ready for polishing. The pillars are not permanently fixed until the polishing is completed.

The door may be hinged with a pair of 1-in. brass butts, and a simple hook-and-eye put on as a fastening. The set of brass feet and ornaments are stock fittings.

CASE FOR GRANDFATHER CLOCK

The clock case to be described does not follow the lines of the conventional grandfather case, for it is a simple case made of deal and enamelled white. The case stands 6 ft. 8 in. high. In all old clocks the pendulum is hung from a bracket attached to the clock movement, but it is better practice to hang the pendulum from an attachment firmly screwed to the back of the case. In order that this may be done, the back is a board $\frac{7}{8}$ in. thick and measures 6 ft. 6 in. long and 13 in. wide planed all

case with the clock in position, and a side elevation is given by Fig. 32. Fig. 33

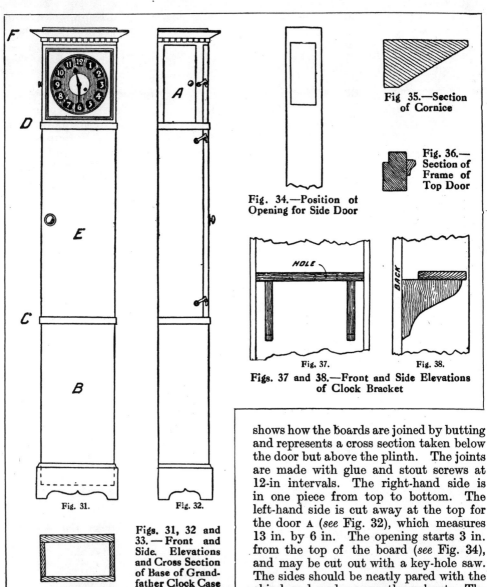

Fig. 35.—Section of Cornice

Fig. 36.—Section of Frame of Top Door

Fig. 34.—Position of Opening for Side Door

Fig. 37.   Fig. 38.

Figs. 37 and 38.—Front and Side Elevations of Clock Bracket

Fig. 31.

Fig. 32.

Figs. 31, 32 and 33. — Front and Side. Elevations and Cross Section of Base of Grandfather Clock Case

Fig. 33.

shows how the boards are joined by butting and represents a cross section taken below the door but above the plinth. The joints are made with glue and stout screws at 12-in. intervals. The right-hand side is in one piece from top to bottom. The left-hand side is cut away at the top for the door A (*see* Fig. 32), which measures 13 in. by 6 in. The opening starts 3 in. from the top of the board (*see* Fig. 34), and may be cut out with a key-hole saw. The sides should be neatly pared with the chisel, and made square throughout. The door should be a close fit in the opening to exclude dust. Secure it with two brass hinges, and add a small brass knob for opening. Add a narrow strip of wood inside as an abutment to prevent the door opening inwards.

over and squared top and bottom and on all edges.

For the sides and front $\frac{5}{8}$-in. boards are suitable. Fig. 31 shows the complete

The next operation is to add the front parts. First work the lower one B, which should measure 29 in. by 13 in. Two boards must be joined together unless stuff sufficiently wide can be obtained. Secure in place with glue and nails, punching in the nail-heads, and subsequently after the first coat of enamel is on, putty up the holes. The plinth is cut from $\frac{5}{8}$-in. stuff and is 6 in. deep. It may be plain bevelled on the top edge, or worked to quadrant section as shown. The lower edges of each piece are cut out in the way shown in Figs. 31 and 32. This gives four feet for the case to stand on, which makes it easier to level the clock and gives it a better appearance. Mitre the three pieces at the corners and glue in place, securing also by screws driven in from the inside. Next add the 1-in. by $\frac{1}{4}$-in. plain fillet C, mitreing the corners.

The door E now may be made, and measures 33 in. by 13 in. Two battens, say 3 in. by $\frac{5}{8}$ in., must be screwed across the inside to stiffen it and prevent warping. Their length should be $11\frac{3}{4}$ in., so as to allow $\frac{5}{8}$ in. at each end to enable them to pass into the shell of the case. Hinge the door on the right-hand side, and add a brass knob for opening the two hook fastenings, as shown in Figs. 31 and 32. At D a piece of 1-in. by 1-in. wood is fitted across between side and side, and glued in place, after which the fillet is added. The door must be made a close fit to exclude dust. Next fix a strip of wood 13 in. by 3 in. by $\frac{5}{8}$ in. across the top at F, taking care to see that the space between its lower edge and the strip at D measures exactly 13 in. This space is to accommodate the glazed door, which is 13 in. square.

The cornice moulding is shown in section by Fig. 35, and measures 2 in. by $1\frac{1}{4}$ in., the bevel being taken off so as to allow $\frac{3}{8}$ in. at the bottom and $\frac{1}{8}$ in. at the outer edge. It is mitred at the corners, glued on, and secured with screws from the inside. It is fixed at a point $\frac{1}{2}$ in. from the top of the case (see Figs. 31 and 32). The interrupted fillet is made by cutting short lengths from $\frac{3}{4}$ in. by $\frac{1}{4}$-in. strip, and gluing them on in the angle below the cornice. The spaces between each piece may be $\frac{1}{4}$ in., and the length of each piece $\frac{7}{8}$ in. Fill in the open space at top of the case with a piece of $\frac{1}{2}$-in. board.

Now make the door which covers the clock face. It is framed up from 1-in. by $\frac{5}{8}$-in. strip, mortised at the corners, as shown in Fig. 36. A rebate $\frac{1}{4}$ in. by $\frac{1}{4}$ in. is run on the inner edge. Make the door a close fit in its seating ; it should measure 13 in. square outside. Add the narrow beading $\frac{1}{4}$ in. from its inner edge on the face which is to be outside, mitreing it neatly at the corners. In the rebate fit a square of 3-ply wood. Find its centre by drawing two diagonals on it, and strike a circle $\frac{1}{4}$ in. less in diameter than the clock face. Cut out the circle, trim its edges true, and put a neat bevel on the outer edge. Then fix this square of wood in its rebate with glue and a few fine pins. The rebate on the face of the door formed by the beading is for the glass, which is puttied in after the first coat of enamel has been applied. Now hinge on the door on the right-hand side, and fix the catch shown in Fig. 32. This completes the structural part of the case so far as the outer shell is concerned.

Next fix inside a bracket to carry the clock movement. This is shown in Figs. 37 and 38, and consists of two vertical supports of triangular form, which should be glued to the back of the case, and further secured with long screws driven in from the back. On these supports rests a horizontal piece, in length the full width of the inside of the case, and in width sufficient to carry the clock movement. It is fixed with screws only, driven into the triangular supports, and sufficient space is left at the back of it to allow free movement of the pendulum. Exact dimensions cannot be given, as they are determined by the dimensions of the clock movement. A hole must be made through this horizontal piece for the cord which carries the clock weight, and must be sufficiently wide from back to front to allow for the travel of the cord as it traverses the barrel of the clock. Small holes also will have to be drilled for the clips that secure the movement in place. The position of this bracket is determined by the distance of the centre of the arbor carrying the clock hands from the base of the movement. When the latter is in position on the bracket, the former allowed between each. Gilding might be applied to the edge of the cornice moulding, the interrupted fillet below it, and to the beading on the door that

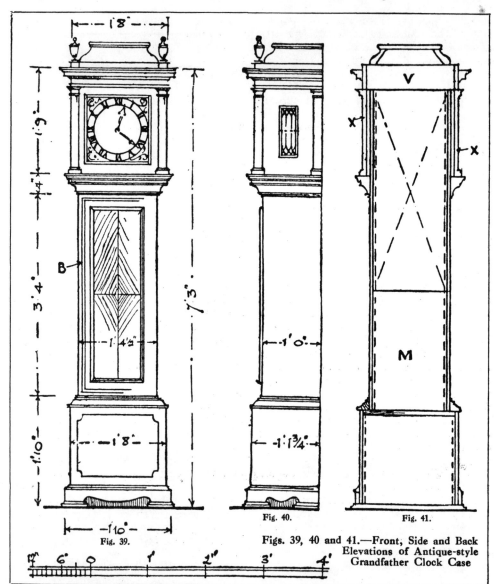

Fig. 39.

Fig. 40.

Fig. 41.

Figs. 39, 40 and 41.—Front, Side and Back Elevations of Antique-style Grandfather Clock Case

should coincide with the centre of the circular opening in the door.

The case should be given three coats of white enamel, ample time for drying being covers the face if desired. The two broad fillets which mark the top and bottom of the large door opening also might be gilded.

ANTIQUE-STYLE GRANDFATHER CLOCK CASE

Three elevations (Figs. 39, 40 and 41)

The case may be made in mahogany, walnut or oak, with equal suitability, of the best type selected for good figuring; parts which are out of sight can be of

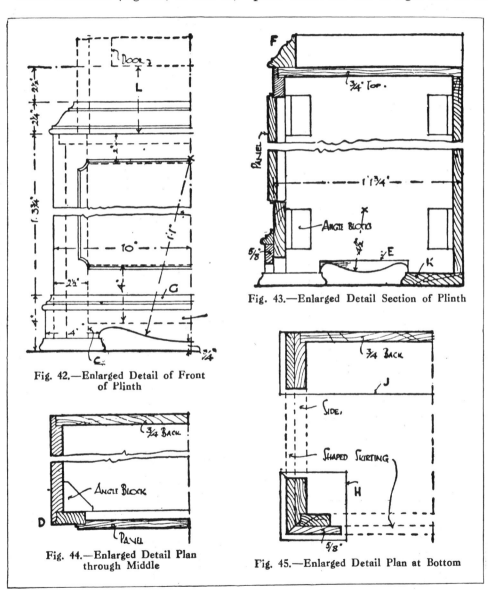

Fig. 42.—Enlarged Detail of Front of Plinth

Fig. 43.—Enlarged Detail Section of Plinth

Fig. 44.—Enlarged Detail Plan through Middle

Fig. 45.—Enlarged Detail Plan at Bottom

are shown of a clock case that is designed upon the lines of the genuine antique article. Such a clock is a very desirable piece of furniture even as a reproduction. cheaper hardwood or well-seasoned pine. The workmanship can be either very simple with plain moulding, etc., or it can be elaborated very considerably.

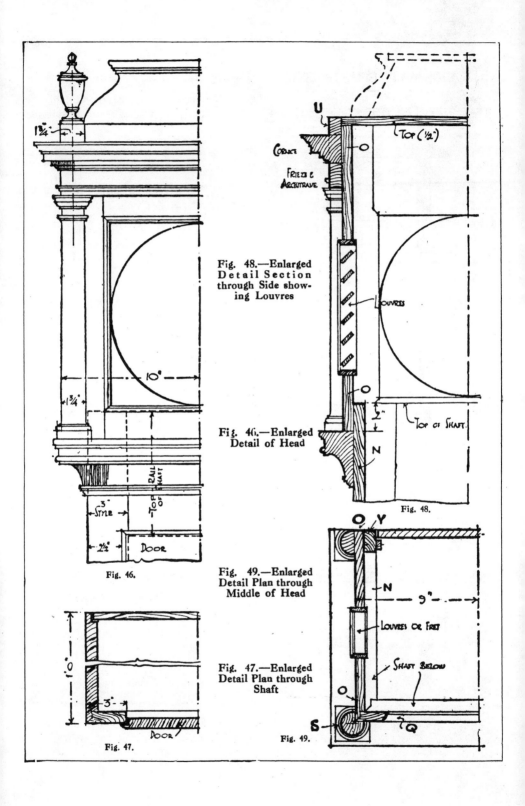

Fig. 48.—Enlarged Detail Section through Side showing Louvres

Fig. 46.—Enlarged Detail of Head

Fig. 49.—Enlarged Detail Plan through Middle of Head

Fig. 47.—Enlarged Detail Plan through Shaft

Fig. 46.

Fig. 47.

Fig. 48.

Fig. 49.

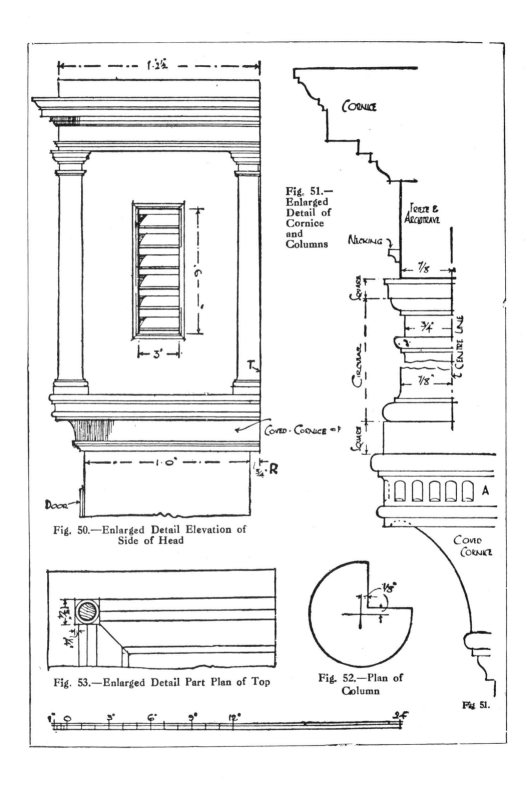

Fig. 51.—
Enlarged
Detail of
Cornice
and
Columns

CORNICE

FRIEZE &
ARCHITRAVE

NICKING

SQUARE

CIRCULAR

SQUARE

⅞"

¾"

⅛"

CENTRE LINE

A

COVED CORNICE

COVED · CORNICE · ⊙ ⅝

DOOR

Fig. 50.—Enlarged Detail Elevation of
Side of Head

⅛°

Fig. 53.—Enlarged Detail Part Plan of Top

Fig. 52.—Plan of
Column

Fig. 51.

In the first instance it will be necessary to procure the actual clock or "movement," which should be fitted with a dial of between 10 in. and 12 in. in diameter, the case being adjusted slightly to the opening required. The dial should be of distinctly old style, if possible, and rather elaborate hands would be quite in keeping. Two stout metal strips will be required securely bolted to the plates of the movement, one at each side, adjusted to suit the exact space, bent at right angles and drilled ready for screwing to the inside faces of the case, in a position accessible for removal on occasion. The weights and pendulum merely work in the boxing or " shaft " of the case.

The present example is constructed in two portions for convenience in moving, the shaft fitting into the capping of the plinth, and being, of course, secured with screws put in on the slope from the inside. The base or plinth is fully shown in Figs. 42 to 45, and has a framed front $\frac{7}{8}$ in. thick, consisting of $2\frac{1}{2}$-in. stiles, 2-in. top rail and 4-in. bottom rail (all seen in Fig. 42), into which a $\frac{3}{8}$-in. panel is rebated $\frac{3}{8}$ in. deep, as in Figs. 43 and 44. This panel has quadrant corners of $\frac{5}{8}$-in. radius and a small hollow (or a carved bead, etc.) worked round its edges. Note that the stiles project 1 in. below the rail at c in Fig. 42. The front is " mitred and rebated " to plain sides 1 ft. $1\frac{1}{4}$ in. by 1 ft. $6\frac{7}{8}$ in. high, as at D (Fig. 44), and secured with angle blocks, which should be used plentifully throughout the job. A rectangle about $6\frac{1}{2}$ in. by 1 in. is cut out of the bottom of the sides E (Fig. 43), and their back edges, together with the top edges of both sides and front, are rebated $\frac{1}{2}$ in. for plain square $\frac{3}{4}$-in. top and back pieces as shown. The top is then completed by the addition of a 2-in. by $2\frac{1}{4}$-in. moulding F (Fig. 43) mitred and screwed along the front and sides. Next a $\frac{5}{8}$-in. by $2\frac{1}{4}$-in. skirting is shaped and fixed to the stiles and rail as in Fig. 42, mitred, returned and shaped on the sides, and finished with a $\frac{7}{8}$-in. by 1-in. moulding as at G. The whole plinth can then be inverted, and completed by the addition of $\frac{7}{8}$-in. feet moulded where shown, the front ones being $4\frac{3}{4}$ in. square (H, Fig. 45), and one continuous piece used at the back J (Fig. 45) and K (Fig. 43). The shaft will be found quite a simple portion of the work, and consists of $\frac{7}{8}$-in. front and sides, the former having 3-in. stiles, $5\frac{1}{4}$-in. bottom rail L (Fig. 42), partially concealed by the plinth moulding, and 9-in. top rail as noted in Fig. 46. Only a 3-in. part of this latter rail is exposed, and it might accordingly be built up with hardwood for the bottom part only.

The door is $\frac{7}{8}$ in. thick, rebated $\frac{3}{8}$ in. by $\frac{1}{2}$ in. to fit the opening, the $\frac{1}{2}$ in. just allowing sufficient space for the hinges. Its edges are moulded as in Fig. 47, and it is quartered on the face and fitted with lock and key. The stiles are mitred and rebated as before to plain sides 12 in. by $\frac{7}{8}$ in. of the same length, rebated to receive a $\frac{5}{8}$-in. back, the lower two feet or so of which (M Fig. 41) can be fixed. At a distance of $2\frac{1}{2}$ in. above the top edge of the door is fixed a $2\frac{3}{8}$-in. by 4-in. coved cornice (see Fig. 48), preparatory to the work on the head of the case. Fig. 48 probably offers the most lucid explanation of the remaining work. In it at N is seen the top of the shaft side, with the coved cornice applied on its face, and at O a $\frac{3}{4}$-in. side measuring 1 ft. $1\frac{1}{4}$ in. by 1 ft. $9\frac{3}{4}$ in. high. This is seen also at O in Fig. 49, where N indicates the side of the shaft on plan at the lower level seen in Fig. 48. In fixing, one piece is lapped against the other for a distance of 2 in. and screwed. In Fig. 49 the side is shown mitred and rebated with a front framing Q $\frac{3}{4}$ in. thick, measuring 1 ft. 6 in. across the front and moulded round the opening, the exact size of which is regulated by the dial.

The top rail of the framing is extended to the same height as O O in Fig. 48, the whole being finished with a $\frac{1}{2}$-in. top as there shown. The finishings of the head (which, it may be pointed out, overhangs $\frac{3}{4}$ in. at the back as at R in Fig. 50) can next be put in hand. First there are four columns turned out of $2\frac{1}{4}$-in. square stuff (unless the caps are turned in separate pieces from the shafts) to the contours in Fig. 51, keeping the ends square as noted and making all the mouldings quite small.

The shafts should be turned to $1\frac{3}{4}$-in. diameter for the bottom third of this

circle should be cut (*see* s, Fig. 49, and plan in Fig. 52), so that they will accurately

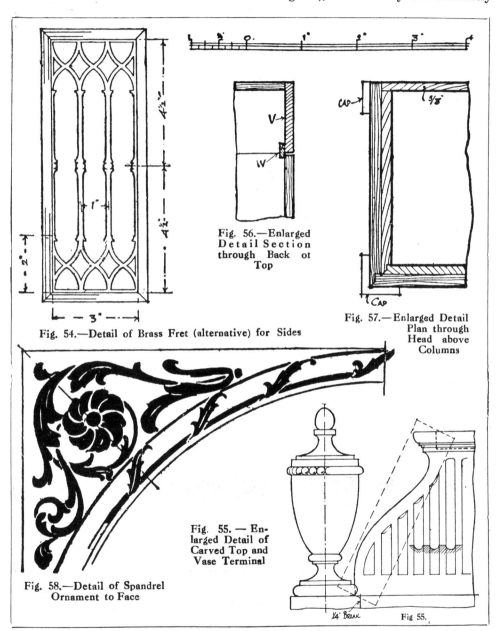

Fig. 54.—Detail of Brass Fret (alternative) for Sides

Fig. 56.—Enlarged Detail Section through Back of Top

Fig. 57.—Enlarged Detail Plan through Head above Columns

Fig. 55.—Enlarged Detail of Carved Top and Vase Terminal

Fig. 58.—Detail of Spandrel Ornament to Face

height, and tapered to $1\frac{1}{2}$ in. at the top in the remaining two-thirds. From two of these columns rather less than a quarter

fit the corners of the head just above the coved cornice, and project immediately above their bases 1 in. from the general face, thus showing as practically complete columns. The two other columns should be cut off flush on one side as at T in Fig. 50, and applied next to the wall, while a 1¾-in. by 1-in. architrave with small necking and a 3-in. by 2-in. cornice, as in Figs. 48 and 51, should be applied and mitred

for the vase (*see* Figs. **46** and **53**). Of course, if it is decided to omit this vase, the break would also disappear.

In the sides of the head, in order that the sound of the gong may not be muffled, perforations are usually provided, and to meet this requirement the sides can

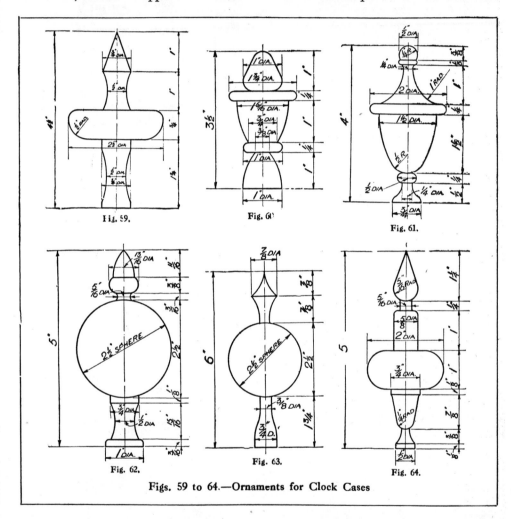

Figs. 59 to 64.—Ornaments for Clock Cases

round the three sides, as shown in the various illustrations. The "blocking course" which surmounts the cornice U (Fig. 48) can then be added, flush with the top and 1 in. thick at the sides, but set back to ¾ in. thick on the front for all except the end 1¾ in. where it forms a base

be fitted with tiny louvres set in a 3-in. by 9-in. opening edged with a beaded strip about 1½ in. by ⅜ in., as in Figs. 49 and 50, or in the more orthodox manner shown in Fig. 54. This is designed for a brass fret backed with deep red silk, bordered with a small moulding not exceeding

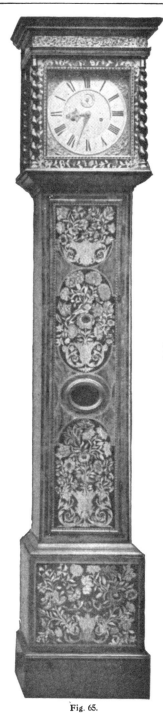

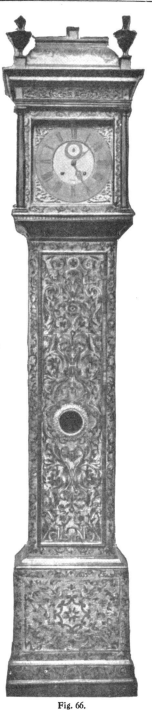

Figs. 65 and 66.—
Two Old English
Clocks

Fig. 65.

Fig. 66.

$\frac{5}{8}$ in. in width and slightly rebated. It can readily be set out with the dimensions given, keeping the tracery $\frac{3}{16}$ in. wide, or it can be adapted for fretwood. If the curved top above the cornice is desired (say for a position where the clock is seen a good deal from above, as, for instance, in a staircase hall), it can be built up with a mitred moulding as dotted in Fig. 48, rebated at the top for a thin cover-board, and filled in flush at the rear. It is shown in detail in Fig. 55, where the dotted rectangle indicates the square piece from which the moulding must be worked. The terminal is also seen, and the optional enrichments shown have previously been mentioned.

The cornice portion of the head can be filled in at the back with a plain fixed board v (Figs. 41 and 56), its ends being covered by the cornice, etc. It will serve to tie the work securely together. The lower portion of the back (marked with a diagonal cross in Fig. 41) should be in one piece, either solid or panelled, fitted into rebates at the sides and against a fillet w (Fig. 56) at the top. The head at x in Fig. 41 will require making out to meet this back by means of small pieces as at y in Fig. 49, turn-buckles being provided at the top and bottom to keep it in position. Small fillets should be provided to cover all joints in order to exclude dust, especially if the clock is a good one. A part plan through the head immediately above the columns is shown by Fig. 57. The glass over the dial can be fixed on the inside by means of a plain rebated strip. In most cases this should also take a mount of some sort to fill in the spaces between the front framing and the dial. This could be of thin wood with a bevelled edge, or might be formed of Bristol board or sheet metal painted to such a design as that in Fig. 58, say in dark steel-grey on a grey ground, or in gold-bronze on grey, in order to get an effect approximating to that of the old models.

ORNAMENTS FOR CLOCK CASES

A range of ornaments suitable for clock cases are shown by Figs. 59 to 64. These are examples of the late seventeenth and early eighteenth centuries. Suitable dimensions are indicated on each, but these could be modified to suit any particular requirement. They may be made of wood and gilded.

TWO OLD ENGLISH CLOCKS

The two clocks shown by Figs. 65 and 66 are very fine examples of old English workmanship which are in the Victoria and Albert Museum, South Kensington, and they are illustrated here merely as a guide to the aspiring worker. Details of these clocks are given in " English Domestic Clocks," by Herbert Cescinsky and Malcolm R. Webster, from which the following particulars are taken. Fig. 65 is described as an eight-day striking clock of the usual type of the period (the date is about 1695), movement by Mansell Bennett, Charing Cross. Its height is 7 ft. and the dial is 11 in. diameter. The base is stated to be an obvious addition, as is probably much of the cornice also.

The clock shown by Fig. 66 is of a very slightly later date, viz. 1710–1715. The movement is by Henry Poisson, London. It is described as an eight-day striking clock, 7 ft. 11½ in. high, and with a 12-in. dial. The case is inlaid with fine scroll marquetry of rosewood and holly in a ground of plane-tree veneer on oak. The fine proportions of these early examples should be found invaluable as a guide for a worker, whether amateur or otherwise, who contemplates the construction of a clock-case for modern use.

Hanging Cupboards and Cabinets

SMOKER'S CABINET

A CERTAIN amount of quaintness of design is shown in the smoker's cabinet illustrated by Fig. 1.

Wainscot oak, left clean without stain or polish, is a suitable wood to use. The sides, shelves, and brackets are of ½-in. stuff. The small inner shelf is of ¼-in. stuff, and the front arch piece and also the back are ⅛-in. fret-wood (all finished thicknesses). As an essential preliminary to the commencement of the job, a full-size setting-out of the front elevation (Fig. 2) should be made, this being drawn accurately to a vertical centre line. From this full-size diagram the exact length of the shelves and also the angle formed by the sloping sides can be taken, and if care is taken at this

Fig. 1.—Smoker's Cabinet

stage of the work it will save possible trouble later on. A side elevation and vertical section are shown by Figs. 3 and 4 on the next page.

The top may be made by gluing two blocks to the ½-in. stuff, as indicated by dotted lines on the front elevation, afterwards cutting and working to shape; or it may be cut from one solid block. The objection to the former method is the possibility of the joints showing, unless the pieces of oak are carefully matched and the joints well made. The second method is therefore recommended, even though it entails rather more work. The sides are housed into the top to a depth of $\frac{3}{16}$ in. and glued and bradded, and the two shelves are similarly fixed to the sides; but in the case of

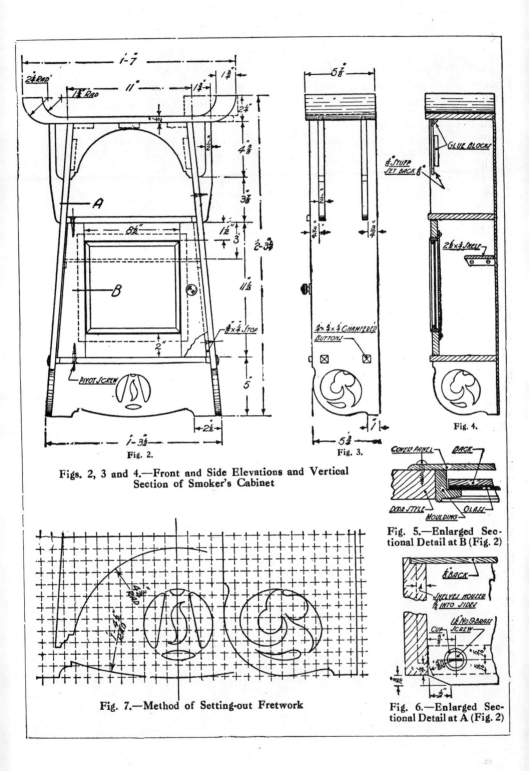

Fig. 2.

Figs. 2, 3 and 4.—Front and Side Elevations and Vertical Section of Smoker's Cabinet

Fig. 3.

Fig. 4.

Fig. 5.—Enlarged Sectional Detail at B (Fig. 2)

Fig. 6.—Enlarged Sectional Detail at A (Fig. 2)

Fig. 7.—Method of Setting-out Fretwork

these members two $1\frac{1}{2}$-in. No. 8 screws are used at each joint. The screw-heads should be well countersunk, and so placed that they are concealed by the brackets at the top and by the "buttons" at the bottom. All the housings should be stopped within $\frac{1}{4}$ in. of the front edges of the sides and glued. The back edges of the sides and top are rebated to receive the $\frac{1}{8}$-in. back, which is secured in position with brads. The upper ends of the four brackets are housed and glued to the top, and the lower parts of these are secured to the sides with 1-in. No. 4 screws, as indicated on the front view. Five angle-blocks are glued behind the front arch-piece, and a little glue is used on the three straight edges of it. This feature is set back $\frac{1}{8}$ in. from the front edges of the sides, and the top projects $\frac{1}{8}$ in. in front of these. The two shelves project $\frac{3}{16}$ in., and are bevelled back flush at their ends (see Fig. 5).

The door, of $\frac{5}{8}$-in. stuff, is framed together with mortise-and-tenon joints, and if no suitable planes are available with which to work the moulding on the stiles and rails, a neat picture moulding may be obtained and mitred and glued into same, as shown in the enlarged detail (Fig. 6). A picture serves as a panel; but if so desired, a mirror or wood panel (carved or plain) may be used. The detail (Fig. 6) shows the method of fixing the picture or mirror, and in any case the $\frac{1}{8}$-in. fret-wood cover-panel ($9\frac{1}{4}$ in. by $9\frac{3}{4}$ in.) should be fixed as a finish. Sixteen $\frac{3}{8}$-in. No. 2 brass round-headed screws are required for this. A plain moulding such as that shown, and not more than $\frac{1}{2}$ in. or $\frac{5}{8}$ in. wide across the face, should be used in preference to an elaborate moulding.

As the door has sloping stiles, it must be pivot hung, this being accomplished by means of two $1\frac{1}{2}$-in. No. 9 brass screws working in the brass cups ordinarily used for screws in hardwood. From the enlarged detail (Fig. 5) it will be seen that the upper pivot screw is $\frac{5}{8}$ in. from the door edge, and the correct position of the lower pivot must be obtained by squaring off the lower shelf, so that a line running through both pivots will be at an

exact right angle with the shelves. The "hanging" stile is planed to a $\frac{5}{8}$-in. radius for clearance when opening, and the "shutting" stile (fitted with a knob) shuts on a $\frac{3}{8}$-in. by $\frac{1}{4}$-in. stop, which is screwed to the inner face of the side.

Two $\frac{1}{2}$-in. diameter holes bored in the back board, about $8\frac{1}{2}$ in. apart and 1 in. below the underside of the top, will provide ready means for hanging the cabinet.

An enlarged setting out of the fretted work is given (Fig. 7), and the central perforation in the lower part of the back should be backed with silk. The inner shelf is optional, but is very useful for the accommodation of small articles. Should it be desired to fit a catch to the door, one of the small bullet pattern would be most suitable.

SIMPLE HANGING SHELVES AND CUPBOARD

The small set of shelves shown by the half-tone reproduction, Fig. 8, and in front elevation by Fig. 9, can be made in a very simple manner from wood $\frac{3}{4}$ in. or even less in thickness. The four shelves are housed $\frac{1}{4}$ in. into the upright sides, which are shaped top and bottom as in Fig. 10, the whole being stiffened by means of a couple of back uprights 2 in. wide, as at A in Figs. 9 and 11. Each of the three lower shelves is notched at the back to receive these uprights, which run up to the underside of the top shelf, and are bradded or screwed to the shelves and sides, and shaped at the bottom as shown.

The pierced and shaped back B (Fig. 9) can easily be added, as can also a thin filling to the back of the cupboard, fixed to small angle fillets as in Fig. 12.

The door of the cupboard can be framed up, or simply made as in Figs. 13 and 14, with thin strips planted on a good piece of three-ply, a method by which a small door can be made quite substantial in appearance, although for anything larger it would be worse than useless. In lieu of a wood panel to the door, it might be preferred to insert a repoussé copper or other form of decorated panel, as shown in the illustration of the finished shelves. The door is hung between a couple of stiles 1½ in. wide, as at c in Figs. 9 and 14, and the whole supported in position by means of four brass wall plates screwed on the back.

and horizontal sections are shown by Figs. 16, 17 and 18. The instructions for making the cupboard just described are equally applicable for this one, and therefore need not be repeated. Details of construction are shown by Figs. 19 to 23.

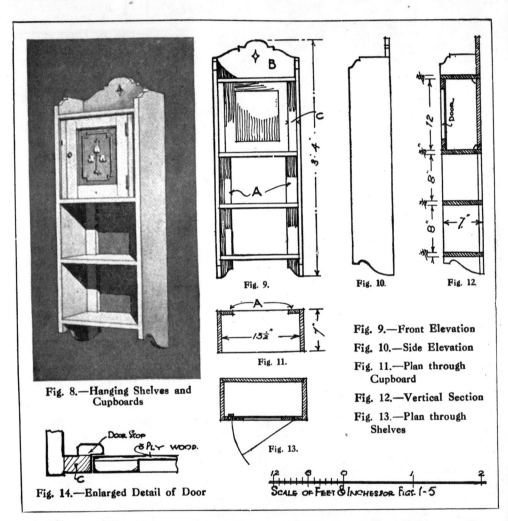

Fig. 8.—Hanging Shelves and Cupboards

Fig. 14.—Enlarged Detail of Door

Fig. 9.

Fig. 10.

Fig. 12.

Fig. 11.

Fig. 13.

Fig. 9.—Front Elevation

Fig. 10.—Side Elevation

Fig. 11.—Plan through Cupboard

Fig. 12.—Vertical Section

Fig. 13.—Plan through Shelves

SCALE OF FEET & INCHES FOR FIGS. 1-5

GLAZED CUPBOARD WITH SIDE SHELF

A cupboard equally as simple as the preceding one, and constructed on practically identical lines, is presented by Fig. 15. A front elevation and vertical

CUPBOARD WITH SHELVES OVER

Fig. 24 shows still another cupboard which is perhaps a little more elaborate than the two former ones. A front elevation and two sections are shown by Figs. 25, 26 and 27 respectively. The

Fig. 15.—Glazed Cupboard with Side Shelf

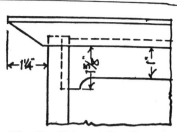

Fig. 19.—Enlarged Detail at A
(Fig. 16)

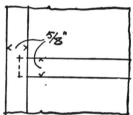

Fig. 20.—Enlarged Detail
at B (Fig. 16)

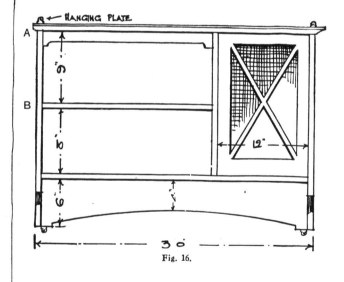

Fig. 16.

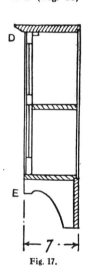

Fig. 17.

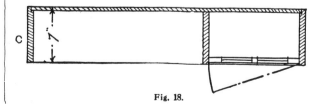

Fig. 18.

Figs. 16, 17 and 18.—
Front Elevation and
Vertical and Hori-
zontal Sections

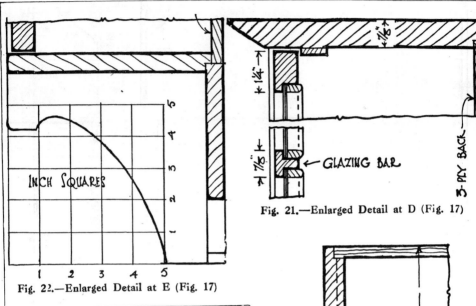

Fig. 21.—Enlarged Detail at D (Fig. 17)

GLAZING BAR

3-PLY BACK

INCH SQUARES

Fig. 22.—Enlarged Detail at E (Fig. 17)

SHELVES STOP HOUSED TO ENDS

Fig. 23.—Enlarged Detail at C (Fig. 18)

reproduced drawings sufficiently reveal the construction, and if studied in conjunction with the instructions given for making the first example of this class of cupboard, the worker will experience no difficulty. The design and method of setting out the ends are shown by Figs.

Fig. 24.—Cupboard with Shelves Over

31 and 32. Fig. 33 is an enlarged horizontal section at one end, and clearly shows the construction of the doors and back of cupboard. A further detail of the doors is shown by Fig. 30. An enlarged sectional elevation at F (Fig. 25) is shown by Fig. 28, and an enlarged plan at G (Fig. 25) by Fig. 29. The finish may be according to the worker's taste.

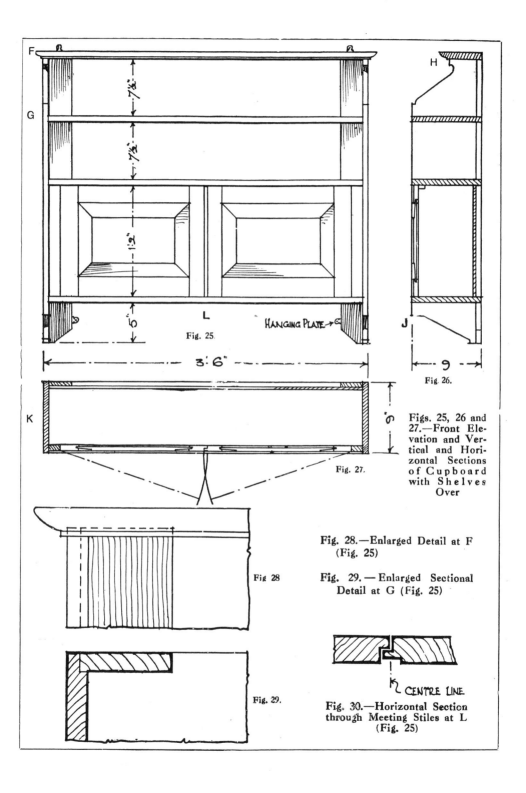

F

G

7½"

7½"

1'2"

5"

L

HANGING PLATE →

Fig. 25.

3' 6"

H

J

9

Fig. 26.

K

6"

Fig. 27.

Figs. 25, 26 and
27.—Front Ele-
vation and Ver-
tical and Hori-
zontal Sections
of Cupboard
with Shelves
Over

Fig. 28.—Enlarged Detail at F
(Fig. 25)

Fig. 29. — Enlarged Sectional
Detail at G (Fig. 25)

Fig 28

Fig. 29.

CENTRE LINE

Fig. 30.—Horizontal Section
through Meeting Stiles at L
(Fig. 25)

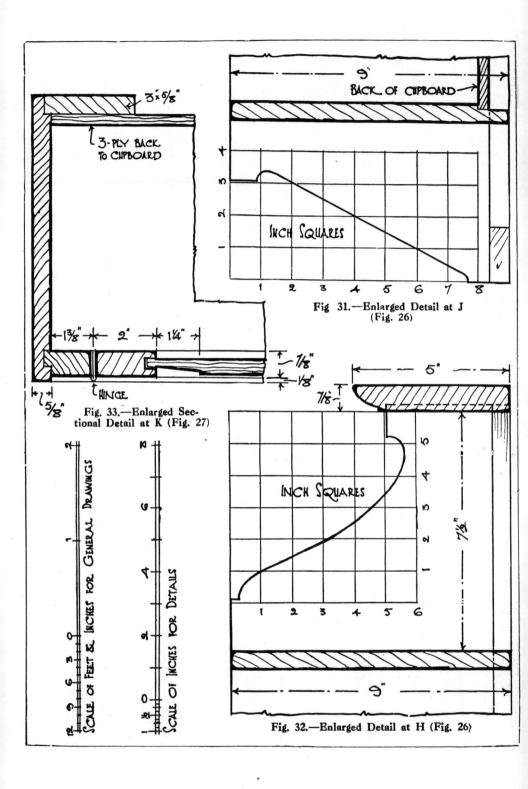

3″ × 5/8″

3-PLY BACK
TO CUPBOARD

BACK OF CUPBOARD

9″

INCH SQUARES

Fig 31.—Enlarged Detail at J
(Fig. 26)

1⅜″   2″   1¼″

7/8″
1/8″

1⅝″
HINGE

Fig. 33.—Enlarged Sectional Detail at K (Fig. 27)

5″

7/8″

7½″

INCH SQUARES

9″

Fig. 32.—Enlarged Detail at H (Fig. 26)

SCALE OF FEET & INCHES FOR GENERAL DRAWINGS

SCALE OF INCHES FOR DETAILS

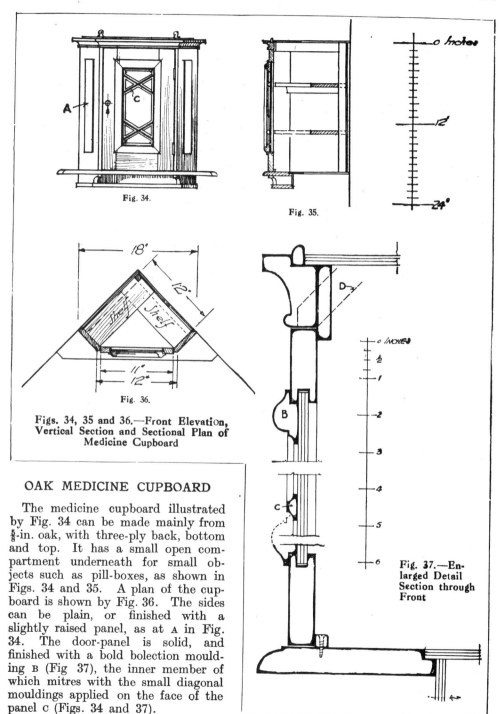

Fig. 34.

Fig. 35.

Fig. 36.

Figs. 34, 35 and 36.—Front Elevation, Vertical Section and Sectional Plan of Medicine Cupboard

Fig. 37.—Enlarged Detail Section through Front

OAK MEDICINE CUPBOARD

The medicine cupboard illustrated by Fig. 34 can be made mainly from ⅝-in. oak, with three-ply back, bottom and top. It has a small open compartment underneath for small objects such as pill-boxes, as shown in Figs. 34 and 35. A plan of the cupboard is shown by Fig. 36. The sides can be plain, or finished with a slightly raised panel, as at A in Fig. 34. The door-panel is solid, and finished with a bold bolection moulding B (Fig 37), the inner member of which mitres with the small diagonal mouldings applied on the face of the panel C (Figs. 34 and 37).

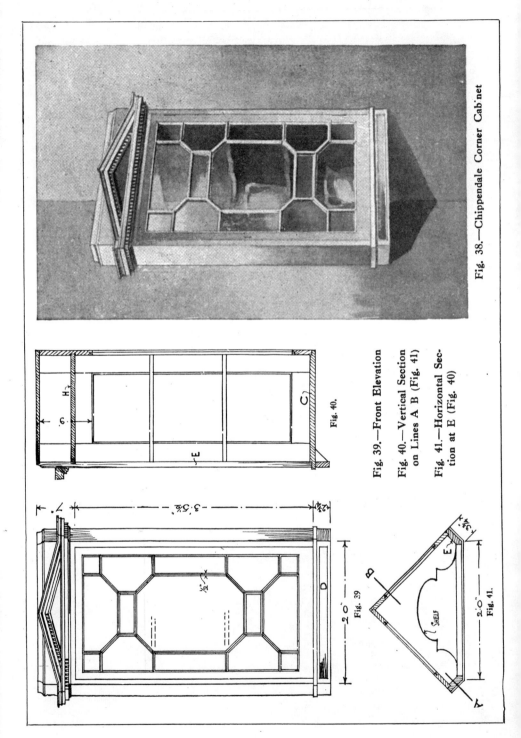

Fig. 38.—Chippendale Corner Cabinet

Fig. 39.—Front Elevation

Fig. 40.—Vertical Section
on Lines A B (Fig. 41)

Fig. 41.—Horizontal Sec-
tion at E (Fig. 40)

Fig. 40.

Fig. 39.

Fig. 41.

SHELF

The dotted lines at D on the latter figure explain the relationship of the sides to the door which is intended to project about ⅛ in. when in the closed position as shown in Fig. 34.

on the geometric pattern of the glazing-bars. Fig. 39 shows a front elevation.

The actual framing of the cupboard starts from a 1-in. bottom shelf C (Fig. 40), rebated ¼ in. deep all round and intended

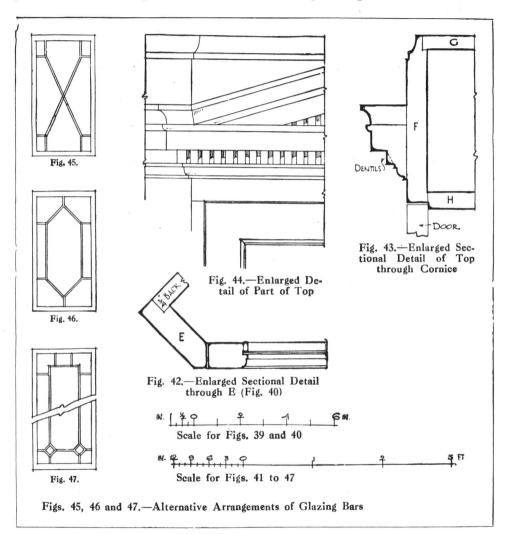

Fig. 45.

Fig. 46.

Fig. 47.

Fig. 44.—Enlarged Detail of Part of Top

Fig. 42.—Enlarged Sectional Detail through E (Fig. 40)

Scale for Figs. 39 and 40

Scale for Figs. 41 to 47

Fig. 43.—Enlarged Sectional Detail of Top through Cornice

Figs. 45, 46 and 47.—Alternative Arrangements of Glazing Bars

CHIPPENDALE CORNER CABINET

The cabinet illustrated by the half-tone reproduction (Fig. 38) is specially designed as a corner fitting, though if desired it could be adapted to a rectangular plan. Its interest depends very largely

to project $\frac{3}{16}$ in. beyond the finished work. It can be of hardwood or merely pine faced along the front edges with strips of mahogany, etc. The 2-in. apron at D in Fig. 39 is not constructional; it is sunk $\frac{1}{16}$ in. on the face, and fixed with angle-blocks as in Fig. 40. The door stiles E (Figs. 40, 41 and 42) extend right up to the extreme top, where they are connected by a rail as at F in Fig. 43, mitred in position and of the same thickness as the door, the whole being moulded as shown, and rebated for a light top board G. An inner top, as at H in Figs. 40 and 43, is desirable, fixed at the necessary level to form a rebate for the door (see Fig. 43), and housed $\frac{1}{4}$ in. to the stiles and the two backs. The latter should be panelled and flush on the inside, rebated at the back corner (see Fig. 41), and having a 9-in. top rail (see Fig. 40), so that they may show an equal margin all round their exposed portions.

Shelves can be fitted as required, but it is suggested that they be made to line with the horizontal glazing bars where dotted on Fig. 39. If shaped on plan as in Fig. 41, they will add to the interest of the whole design.

In order to contrive the pediment in the simplest possible manner consistent with the style, the cornice may be in two sections, as in Fig. 43, the lower portion taken horizontally round the three exposed faces, and also fitted on the rake to form the lower mouldings of the triangular pediment (see Figs. 39 and 44), the top portion being mitred and fitted round last of all. The dentil course will serve to emphasise the cornice, and should be finely cut. The dentils on the raking portion should have their sides vertical (not at right angles to the slope) as shown, and their width measured horizontally (not on the rake) should equal that of the dentils below. Alternative suggestions for the glazing bars are shown by Figs. 45, 46 and 47.

Cabinets and Cupboards

CABINET WITH CUPBOARDS AND SHELVES

ALTHOUGH suited to other positions, the cabinet shown by Fig. 1 would be particularly appropriate in a recess on one side of a fireplace. Practically any kind of wood can be employed in its construction. Various modifications of detail can be introduced to meet special requirements, or the whole thing can be taken as merely a suggestion on the outline of which to fashion some fresh design. The simple inlay on the back can—if constituting a difficulty—be omitted or done professionally, the small oval if adopted forming possibilities for a little quartered veneering. Another way would be to treat this back as a piece of narrow framing enclosing a panel.

Fig. 1.—Cabinet with Cupboards and Shelves

For a painted finish, leaded glazing in the cupboard doors would be most suitable. If, however, hardwood (especially mahogany) be selected, very narrow wooden bars would be more appropriate to the material. In any case, the division of the glass into small panes as shown should be retained, as without this the work loses much of its interest and proportion. Leaded glazing can easily be obtained to order, and should have leads of a flat section, not less than $\frac{1}{4}$ in. wide. The chief dimensions are shown on the elevations, Figs. 2 and 3. Figs. 4 and 5 show a vertical section and a sectional plan respectively.

In order to carry out the work in accordance with the illustrations, the pieces enumerated in the following list will be necessary. The sizes given are those of the various parts when approximately ready for jointing together, and in cutting or ordering the wood small allowances should be made for sawing and planing.

For the uprights and shelves : (1) Two end uprights, 9 in. by $\frac{3}{4}$ in. by 3 ft. $2\frac{5}{8}$ in. ; (2) two intermediate uprights as at A (Fig. 2), $8\frac{1}{4}$ in. by $\frac{3}{4}$ in. by 1 ft. $1\frac{1}{2}$ in. ;

central back piece, 1 ft. $3\frac{1}{2}$ in. by $\frac{3}{4}$ in. by 1 ft. 9 in., made up of two widths dowelled or tongued together, and fixed with grain upright or horizontal, as convenient ; (8) two backs to top cupboards, $9\frac{1}{2}$ in. by $\frac{3}{8}$ in. by 1 ft. 1 in. ; (9) one back to extend across lower cupboards and central division, made up of two

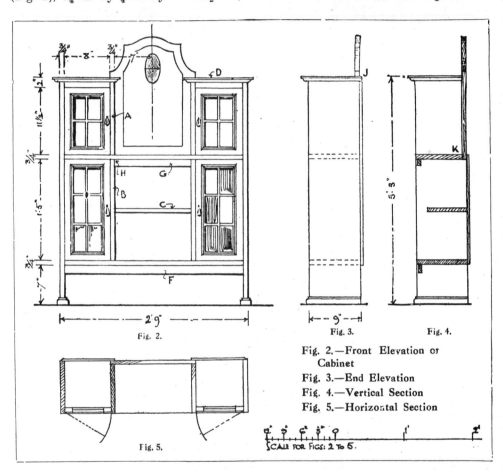

Fig. 2.

Fig. 3.   Fig. 4.

Fig. 5.

Fig. 2.—Front Elevation of Cabinet

Fig. 3.—End Elevation

Fig. 4.—Vertical Section

Fig. 5.—Horizontal Section

SCALE FOR FIGS: 2 TO 5.

(3) two intermediate uprights as at B, 9 in. by $\frac{3}{4}$ in. by 1 ft. $5\frac{3}{8}$ in. ; (4) two main shelves, 9 in. by $\frac{3}{4}$ in. by 2 ft. $8\frac{1}{4}$ in. ; (5) one smaller shelf C (Fig. 2), 7 in. by $\frac{1}{2}$ in. by 1 ft. 2 in. (1 ft. $2\frac{1}{2}$ in. if housed into uprights) ; (6) two top shelves as D (Fig. 2), $10\frac{3}{8}$ in. by $\frac{3}{4}$ in. by $11\frac{1}{4}$ in., moulded as at E (Fig. 6) on three edges.

For the back, doors, etc. : (7) One

or three pieces with grain horizontal, total size, 1 ft. 6 in. by $\frac{3}{8}$ in. by 2 ft. 9 in. ; (10) two doors, 8 in. by $11\frac{1}{4}$ in., composed of 1-in. by $1\frac{1}{4}$-in. stuff, tenoned halved or mitres at the angles, rebated $\frac{3}{8}$ in. for glazing, and either moulded on the outer face in the usual way, or kept square as in Fig. 7 ; (11) two similar doors, 8 in. by 1 ft. 5 in. ; (12) one strip as at F

(Fig. 2), $1\frac{1}{2}$ in. by $\frac{3}{4}$ in. or $\frac{1}{2}$ in. by 2 ft. $1\frac{1}{2}$ in. (or 2 ft. 8 in. if housed into the upright ends) ; (13) two similar strips above doors to top cupboards, but 1 in. deep and 8 in. or $8\frac{1}{2}$ in. long ; (14) one strip, 1 ft. 2 in. or 1 ft. $2\frac{1}{2}$ in. long, as at G (Fig. 2). Alternatively this might be a curved spandrel, as in the illustration of the completed article, in which

joints $\frac{3}{8}$ in. deep, stopped 1 in. back from the front edges as in Fig. 9, the only exception to this being the junction at H (Fig. 2), which can be as in Fig. 10. The fillet there shown will be concealed by the strip or spandrel (No. 14 in list of parts), which together with Nos. 12 and 13 should be fixed, either with or without housed ends as noted, $\frac{1}{8}$ in. back from the

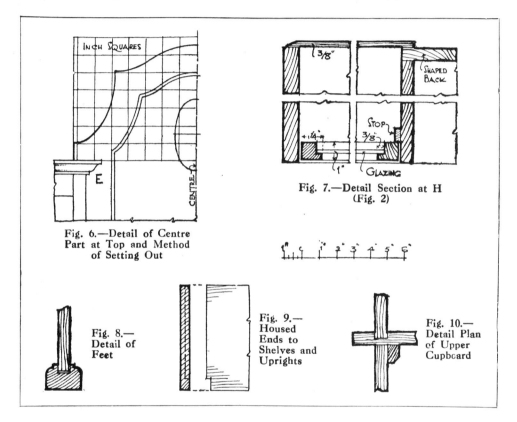

Fig. 6.—Detail of Centre Part at Top and Method of Setting Out

Fig. 7.—Detail Section at H (Fig. 2)

Fig. 8.—Detail of Feet

Fig. 9.—Housed Ends to Shelves and Uprights

Fig. 10.—Detail Plan of Upper Cupboard

case it should be cut to a flat curve from a piece $2\frac{1}{4}$ in. wide ; (15) two feet for the end uprights, 2 in. by $1\frac{1}{2}$ in. by $9\frac{5}{8}$ in., moulded as in Fig. 8, and grooved $\frac{1}{2}$ in. deep to take the housed ends of uprights. In addition to the above parts, there will also be required some small glazing beads for the cupboard doors, and a few small fillets for door-stops, etc.

To construct the cabinet, the uprights and shelves should be put together as shown in Fig. 2, by means of housed

front edges of the shelving. Note that the moulded top shelves overhang $\frac{3}{8}$ in. at the back J (Fig. 3). The back piece No. 7, when shaped as in Fig. 6, is fixed to the intermediate uprights as in Fig. 5, the upper long shelf being cut away in the centre to suit it as at K in Fig. 4, as are also small pieces of the moulded shelves. The $\frac{3}{8}$-in. back pieces (Nos. 8 and 9) can then be applied as in Figs. 4 and 5, and will stiffen the whole work. They may be bevelled off as in Fig. 7, which also shows one of the small doors, these being hinged to fit $\frac{1}{8}$ in. back from the edges of shelving, and fitted with small latches and drop handles. The two feet (No. 15) should be screwed to the uprights from below.

SIXTEENTH-CENTURY CABINET IN OAK

The cabinet shown by the half-tone reproduction (Fig. 11) is based upon the sions so as to work out conveniently in accordance with English lineal measurements, and it might be mentioned that sizes and thicknesses generally may be slightly reduced if economy is desired, work of this type having been executed at a time when oak was more plentiful than at present. Front and end elevations are shown by Figs. 12 and 13, and a vertical section and two sectional plans by Figs. 14, 15 and 16.

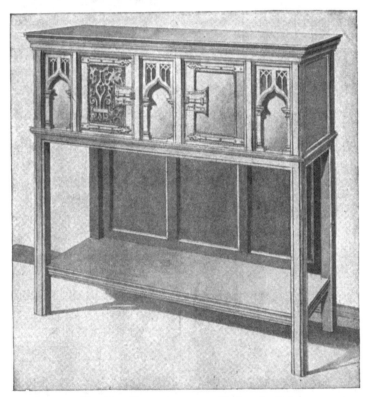

Fig. 11.—Sixteenth-century Cabinet in Oak

design of a fine specimen of sixteenth-century Flemish cabinet-work from the Steen Museum, Antwerp, and has an additional interest for the English crafts-man by reason of the general resemblance which examples of this period bear to those of the Tudor style.

In preparing the drawings, some slight alterations have been made in the dimen-

The cabinet is constructed of oak throughout, the corner uprights being 2 in. square, with a quirked bead worked on three sides (Fig. 17). To these the heads, $2\frac{1}{4}$ in. by $1\frac{1}{4}$ in., and middle bearers, 2 in. by $1\frac{3}{4}$ in., are framed, both the latter having a similar bead worked along the lower angle. The intermediate frames for the cupboard doors are 2 in. by $1\frac{1}{4}$ in.,

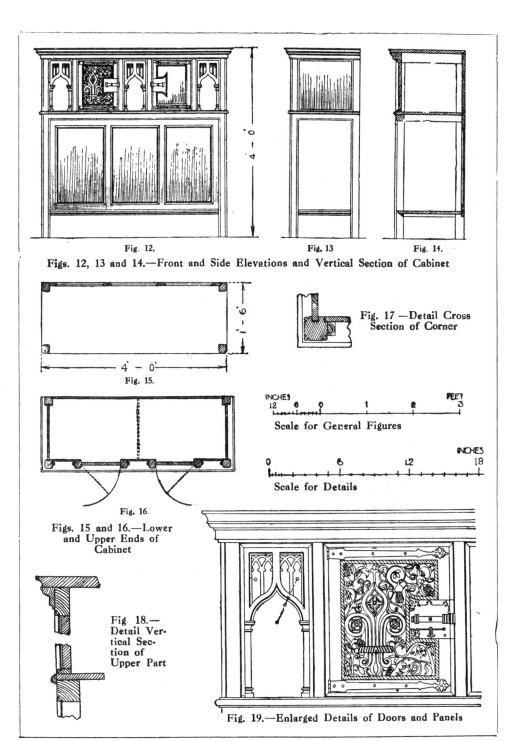

Fig. 12.

Fig. 13

Fig. 14.

Figs. 12, 13 and 14.—Front and Side Elevations and Vertical Section of Cabinet

Fig. 15.

Fig. 17 —Detail Cross Section of Corner

Fig. 16.

Figs. 15 and 16.—Lower and Upper Ends of Cabinet

INCHES 12 6 0 1 2 FEET 3

Scale for General Figures

INCHES 0 6 12 18

Scale for Details

Fig. 18.— Detail Vertical Section of Upper Part

Fig. 19.—Enlarged Details of Doors and Panels

and are rebated to receive the small pierced panels. The panelled back of the lower portion should not be less than ¾ in. thick, with panel moulds worked on the solid. The top is ⅞ in. thick, with a cavetto mould worked on the edge, and under this is planted on a mould out of 2 in. by 1¼ in., completing the cornice effect (Fig. 18). The bottom shelf is constructed in a similar way, except that the shelf is ⅝ in. thick and the small mould

Fig. 20.—Drawing-room China Cabinet

under 1 in. by ¾ in., the shelf being let into the corner posts and mortised to the back. The small traceried panels are made in two distinct parts, the framing of the arch (which is struck from three centres as shown out of ½-in. stuff), and the tracery infilling, which, being fine, might best be cut out of ⅛-in. fretwood or three-ply.

The arch framing has a small quirked bead worked on the angle ; to simplify, a plain chamfer might be substituted. The half columns are, of course, turned, with square top members to the cap and the base. The doors, as shown in the illustration (Fig. 19), are of a somewhat uncommon form of construction. Instead of a framed panel in the manner usual nowadays, they are in one solid piece rather more than ¾ in. thick, probably being made thus to facilitate carving the wood and fitting the lock-plate. This is one reason for the use of the long " cross garnets " in place of ordinary modern butt hinges, as the grain of the wood being all one way (vertical) the doors would have a tendency to split if unsupported by long iron hinges. In the original, only one panel is carved, as shown, and whether one, or both, or neither be so treated is a matter for individual taste. If, however, the carving be attempted, an endeavour should be made to realise the flamboyant character of the work, as indicated on the detailed drawing of the panel. The locks will hardly be possible of reproduction as in the original, so judiciously selected turn-buckles in wrought-iron or copper, with drop handles, might reasonably be substituted.

A small mould, ⅞ in. by ½ in., is planted on below the cupboards, and serves to cover the joint between the shelf and the frame. It need hardly be added that the cupboards may have a vertical division as indicated by dotted lines on the plan, if this be desired.

DRAWING-ROOM CHINA CABINET

The centre cabinet illustrated by Fig. 20 can be made of mahogany inlaid with satinwood, various parts being kept as light as possible in order to produce a graceful effect. It will be noticed that, while each side is the same in appearance, one of them is constructed as a door (Figs. 21 and 22).

Such a cabinet may be made of any required size, the dimensions shown being: total height 4 ft. 9 in., width 1 ft. 9 in. The sides of the glazed cabinet are made

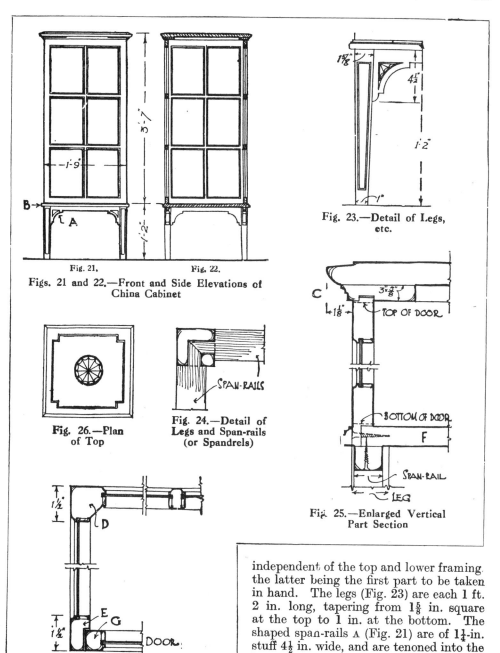

Fig. 21.

Fig. 22.

Figs. 21 and 22.—Front and Side Elevations of China Cabinet

Fig. 23.—Detail of Legs, etc.

Fig. 26.—Plan of Top

Fig. 24.—Detail of Legs and Span-rails (or Spandrels)

Fig. 25.—Enlarged Vertical Part Section

Fig. 27.—Detail Part Plan under Top

independent of the top and lower framing, the latter being the first part to be taken in hand. The legs (Fig. 23) are each 1 ft. 2 in. long, tapering from $1\frac{5}{8}$ in. square at the top to 1 in. at the bottom. The shaped span-rails A (Fig. 21) are of $1\frac{1}{4}$-in. stuff $4\frac{1}{2}$ in. wide, and are tenoned into the legs, the tenons being made as long as possible by mitreing the ends, as in Fig. 24. The moulding B (Fig. 21) is $\frac{3}{4}$ in. wide, and projects $\frac{1}{2}$ in. from the face of the legs ; it is glued on the face of the rails and legs and mitred at the corners. Before finally gluing together, the satinwood stringing on the outer faces of the legs and the fan pattern at the ends of the rails should be inlaid.

The top of the cabinet projects 1⅛ in. all round. It is of 1-in. stuff, and underneath are 3-in. by ⅝-in. strips mitred at the corners, these forming the lower member of the cornice when moulded,

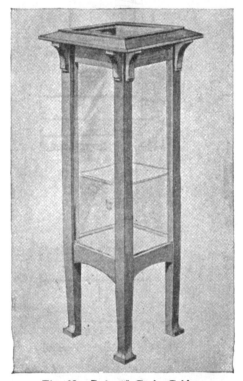

Fig. 28.—Pedestal Curio Cabinet

as at c in Fig. 25. These strips are well screwed to the underside of the top. On the upper face is a line of stringing 1½ in. from the edge, breaking inwards 1½ in. at the corners (see Fig. 26). In the centre is a fan-shaped patera 6 in. in diameter. This ornament is obtainable from inlayers, or it might be omitted.

The carcase now remains to be made, and it will be found that its jointing together requires neat and careful work-

manship. The corner posts on the side opposite the door are 1½ in. square, with the inside corners bevelled off, as at D in Fig. 27. Those right and left of the door are 1½ in. by ⅞ in., as at E (Fig. 27), and the door stiles are 1 in. by ⅞ in. The glazing bars are ¾ in. on the face and ⅞ in. thick. The top rails are 2 in. by ⅞ in. on the three fixed sides, worked as at c in Fig. 25, to fit a rebate on the top. The corresponding bottom rails are the same thickness and 2⅝ in. wide, rebated to fit the pine bottom F (Fig. 25) ⅞ in. thick.

The door has similar rails, but, of course, less by the amount of the rebates at the top and bottom (see the dotted lines in Fig. 25). Its stiles G (Fig. 27) are 1 in. by ⅞ in. To receive the glazing a $\frac{3}{16}$-in. rebate is worked on the bars and framing, the edges next to the glass being hollowed with a quarter-circle moulding, as shown on the details. A line of satinwood stringing would be an improvement in the middle of the bars, and on the stiles, posts, and rails.

Two shelves will be required level with the horizontal glazing bars. They may be of pine covered with a suitable shade of velveteen (the bottom being covered with the same material); or of plate-glass with polished edges, fixed on small brackets at each corner.

The outside glass should be fixed with narrow beads as shown. Three small butt hinges and a very narrow lock will complete the cabinet.

PEDESTAL CURIO CABINET

The pedestal curio cabinet here illustrated might very suitably be executed in mahogany, and will have the general appearance shown in Fig. 28. It consists of a framework about 9 in. square and 3 ft. high, finishing with a top 1 ft. 1 in. square with small curved brackets under. All the sides and the top are glazed, access to the interior being obtained when required by lifting off the top and sliding out one of the glass sides. The intermediate shelves would be spaced at the correct distances to suit the in-

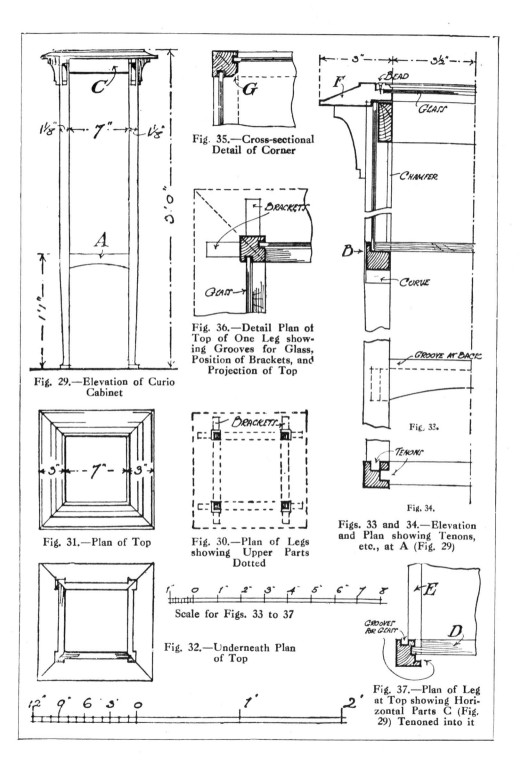

Fig. 35.—Cross-sectional Detail of Corner

Fig. 36.—Detail Plan of Top of One Leg showing Grooves for Glass, Position of Brackets, and Projection of Top

Fig. 29.—Elevation of Curio Cabinet

Fig. 31.—Plan of Top

Fig. 30.—Plan of Legs showing Upper Parts Dotted

Fig. 33.

Fig. 34.

Figs. 33 and 34.—Elevation and Plan showing Tenons, etc., at A (Fig. 29)

Scale for Figs. 33 to 37

Fig. 32.—Underneath Plan of Top

Fig. 37.—Plan of Leg at Top showing Horizontal Parts C (Fig. 29) Tenoned into it

tended contents, and should be of light plate-glass with polished rounded edges.

Fig. 29 is a side elevation, and three plans are shown by Figs. 30, 31 and 32. The elevation shows the main legs, which are intended to be 2 ft. 11¼ in. long, and about 1⅛ in. square finished sizes. From about 12 in. above the floor they are tapered off on their outer faces only to ¾ in. square, being simply finished thus, or curved out again to form feet 1⅛ in. square as shown, at the discretion of the craftsman. Four bearers, as at A (Fig. 29), are then prepared 1¾ in. by 1 in., and 7¾ in. long, being tenoned into the legs ⅜ in. at each end, cut to a slight segmental curve on their undersides, and worked with a rebate ¾ in. wide and ⅜ in. deep along their top back edges. One of these is shown in section in Fig. 33, with the tenons required at each leg. A plan is shown by Fig. 34. The method of supporting the bottom (which can be fitted afterwards, and would be about ⅜ in. thick) is shown in Fig. 33, care being taken that it allows the glass sides to slide right home at B. It will require to be cut to fit closely at the angles, as at G in Fig. 35, the chamfer on the leg at this point being mentioned later.

Before any of the work is fixed together, narrow grooves should be worked up the inner faces of each leg to take the glass, starting from the point B in Fig. 33, and continuing right to the top. These grooves should be about ¼ in. back from the outside faces of the legs, and the glass should fit as closely as possible ; they are shown in Figs. 35, 36 and 37. The other connection between the legs is made by means of four horizontal pieces, as at C (Fig. 29), also shown in section in Fig. 33, from which it will be seen that they are intended to be 1¼ in. deep and sufficiently thin to avoid obstructing the glass. Two of these on opposite sides (that is, parallel to each other) should first be tenoned into the legs as at D on the part plan in Fig. 37, and the two others fixed as at E afterwards. The next step will be to prepare a length of moulding something like that shown at F in Fig. 33, 3 in. wide and 1 in. deep, having a double rebate along the inside top edge. The first or lower rebate is for the glass top, and the second to receive a small moulded bead as shown, either screwed or bradded in position, to secure the glass. The underside has another rebate not more than ¼ in. deep, and just sufficiently wide to take the horizontal pieces below and the top of the glass along each edge.

After the moulding has been mitred together like a picture-frame with an opening 7 in. square, the rebate on the underside should be extended at the corners, as indicated in Fig. 32, in order to fit closely over the top ends of the legs. When this has been done, the eight cut brackets may be prepared out of, say, ⅝-in. or ¾-in. stuff, each 3 in. long, and secured to the legs as closely as possible under the top portion, but, of course, not actually fixed to it, although, if desired, small catches of the hook-and-eye variety can be fixed under the top so that it is held down to a couple of the brackets. But it would not do to attempt carrying the case about by means of the top, unless special precautions are adopted to allow for this. For a very good job it might be worth while to house each of the brackets ¼ in. into the legs.

The intermediate glass shelves can easily be arranged for by slightly chamfering off the inside angle of each of the legs, as at G in Fig. 35, and putting in small brass screw-eyes to support the corners at the required levels.

CROMWELLIAN CABINET AND A MODERN VARIATION

Dating from the first half of the seventeenth century, the massive oaken cabinet shown by the half-tone reproduction (Fig. 38) forms a good example of English work of its period. The elaboration —or, rather, profusion—of its ornament is somewhat too overpowering to be desirable in a modern reproduction ; but in the deep tones of the original they are not at all obtrusive. A careful inspection of the illustration will show that while the construction itself is direct enough, every possible opportunity has been seized to introduce a band of strap-work, a guilloche, or some rather primitive carving, all exhibiting the Jacobean influence. This decoration, it is assumed, would be eliminated in work inspired by study of the cabinet, the result being more restful and, indeed, more refined

drawers below and two shallow ones above, while at the top is a recessed part (as shown by the half plan, Fig. 41) in the shape of three cupboards, in front of which a pair of the characteristic columns or balusters of the time support a frieze, and this in turn a cornice mitreing

Fig. 38.—Cromwellian Cabinet

in consequence. For explanatory purposes rather than as working drawings, Figs. 39 and 40 show the side and half-front elevations respectively of the cabinet almost as it stands, although a certain number of modifications have been introduced. It consists of a large cupboard with a pair of doors, having two deep

round projecting brackets or trusses. The end elevation (Fig. 40) is of interest as showing that the idea of concentrating all the work on the front is of fairly ancient date. The framing is square and perfectly plain; the explanation of the curious appearance of the right-hand stile is that this is the side view of the 4-in. stile showing on the front, this being 4 in. by $1\frac{3}{4}$ in. and substantial enough, although it would scarcely be considered satisfactory in appearance.

The principal modifications introduced in these first figures are as follows : (1) A reduction of the upright division between the large doors A (Fig. 39) to 4 in. wide similar to those at the outsides, instead of as in the original, which is $7\frac{1}{2}$ in. wide and has a carved band down it, and incidentally is really a sham, being actually attached to the left-hand door and opening with it. (2) Altering the bottom drawers to keep them central with the doors above, and not as in the half-tone. (3) Improving the design of the fat balusters and reducing their bulk. (4) Substituting a pair of plain brackets for each of the three in the half-tone, which are of varying widths.

Of course, for modern purposes this piece of furniture is open to criticism, more especially because of its great size and consequent weight, and also on account of the inaccessibility of the upper drawers ; but given such an example as a pattern, there is much to be gathered from it, and many different ways in which it can be varied, retaining, however, the old character. In Figs. 42 and 43 there is such a variation, itself liable to receive similar treatment. This design shows a cabinet of 1-ft. 6-in. projection and 4-ft. $10\frac{1}{2}$-in. width, standing 6 ft. 7 in. over all, as compared with 1 ft. 10 in. by 5 ft. 9 in. by 7 ft. 2 in. in height, as in the first ; and these reduced dimensions (together with the fact that the work can be made in three independent parts) bring it within reasonable limits. Needless to say, four drawers might be substituted for the two shown, and the top cupboards might have larger doors ; or these could be solid, with pieces planted on to form the arrangement first shown (Fig. 39) ; and the extra mitres in the main cornice, as well as the enriched moulding, can be varied to suit. Material is largely a matter of choice, pine or oak being the most suitable, and in the latter case the thicknesses throughout can be reduced.

Reviewing the construction of this second scheme in detail, the lower part (up to the level of B, Fig. 42) is formed at the ends with ordinary square panelled framing tongued into a groove in a 4-in. by $1\frac{1}{4}$-in. upright stile C (Fig. 44), decorated on the face with two sinkings $\frac{1}{16}$ in. deep, separated from the angles and in the centre by plain bands $\frac{5}{8}$ in. wide. This stile is framed up in the usual way with horizontal rails D and E (Figs. 45 and 42) about $2\frac{1}{4}$ in. deep, E having, in addition, a rough continuous piece F (Fig. 45) fixed below to bear on the floor, this applying to the ends also, the whole being finished by the application of a moulded skirting $3\frac{1}{2}$ in. high kept up just clear of the floor as shown. The central upright is $2\frac{1}{2}$ in. wide, and has one sinking similar to those on the ends, and it has a piece of plain stuff fixed on each side G (Fig. 42), which also occurs at the outer ends to keep the moulding to the drawer clear of it. The side framing is rebated at the back H (Fig. 44) to receive a stout back, which should be panelied if possible, and which will serve to make rigid the whole work if properly fixed, a point which is further secured by making the boarded bottom to the cupboard above as a part of this piece of the structure, fitting it partly into a rebate worked on D (Fig. 45), and running the grain from back to front rather than lengthwise.

The drawers will be made in the ordinary way, but with a moulding about 1 in. wide mitred round their fronts. They must slide on grooved runners blocked out to suit, as in Fig. 46. A small moulding J (Fig. 45) is mitred round the top of this part, projecting a little above the top of D.

The next stage of the design is that situated between B and K on Fig. 42, and continues with similar construction to that described for the base, namely, a plain side or end in six panels tongued to C (Fig. 44) as before, and fitted to a stout panelled back ; C is framed up with horizontal pieces L (Fig. 45) in front $1\frac{3}{4}$ in. by $1\frac{1}{4}$ in. below, and 2 in. by $1\frac{1}{4}$ in. at the top M (Fig. 47). The central upright is *fixed* (not as in the old) between

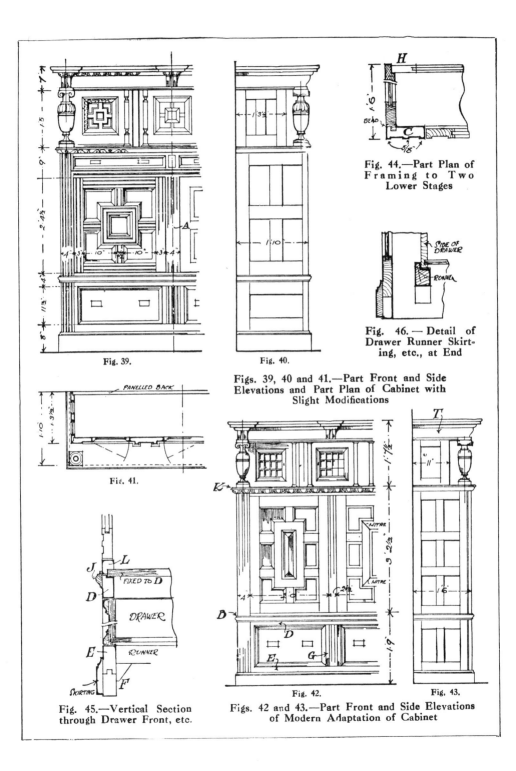

Fig. 39.

Fig. 40.

Fig. 44.—Part Plan of Framing to Two Lower Stages

Fig. 46. — Detail of Drawer Runner Skirting, etc., at End

Figs. 39, 40 and 41.—Part Front and Side Elevations and Part Plan of Cabinet with Slight Modifications

PANELLED BACK

Fig. 41.

Fig. 45.—Vertical Section through Drawer Front, etc.

Fig. 42.

Fig. 43.

Figs. 42 and 43.—Part Front and Side Elevations of Modern Adaptation of Cabinet these, and has strips planted down it on the inside to form stops to the doors. The latter are of 1-in. framing, 3 in. wide next the edges, the inner pieces being 2¼ in. Each door is in seven panels as shown, with small mouldings mitred round, and the middle panel bevelled or raised if desired. The framing surrounding it should be mitred at the angles, as indicated on the right of Fig. 42. This work might be carried out in the manner adopted for the little top doors in the original cabinet, where it is all made up of thin stuff planted on the face of a plain square panel ; and this will simplify the work, which will, however, lose a certain value as regards the sincerity of its construction.

The second stage should be finished with a top cross-tongued together as one piece N (Fig. 47), with a wide shallow rebate and a moulded edge projecting about 1⅜ in. on the three exposed sides, finished as shown with a bold moulding carved if possible, although a plain quadrant section would look well. Probably this part as a whole would seldom be taken off the base, to which it will be seen to fit securely without fear of movement by reference to L (Fig. 45), and would apply at this part equally as a section through the ends.

The top stage still remains to be described, and is shown in detail by Figs. 47, 48 and 49. It has a panelled back rebated into a square end, all as below, except that the end is only 11 in. wide and is mitred into the end of the front O (Fig. 49). In order to make the frieze come properly over the column (which must be kept central with the stile below), the face of the end framing must be set back ½ in. from that below, as noted on Fig. 49 ; but as the stile at O should be kept central with the column, it is consequently reduced to 3 in. in width, and may be plain or sunk on the face as desired. It should be about 1⅜ in. thick, rebated as shown in Fig. 49, to take a piece of ⅞-in. framing P arranged to show a margin of 2 in. all round the small cupboard door. Three of these margins will be required tongued

into uprights 5 in. by 1¼ in., as at Q, sunk on their faces, which will each show 4 in. similarly to the stiles in the lower part of the cabinet. Each upright is finished with a plain piece about 1 in. square, as at R (these are turned balusters in the old work).

The cupboard doors are simply fairly bold mouldings mitred together and rebated for panels or leaded glazing, which latter would be a pleasing introduction. A small stop will be required as at S (Fig. 49), and when completed neat little mouldings as caps and bases should be mitred round the pieces R, as shown in Fig. 49.

The columns, which are 5 in. in diameter and 13½ in. long, can be turned for a distance of 10¾ in., leaving a square base and also a block for the cap. The turned part is finished plain surface or having the upper part of the body carved to the fluted design shown in Fig. 48. It will not be a difficult matter to set out the volutes of the caps 1¼ in. deep, and to carve them to shape, sloping the front decidedly, as on the side view (Fig. 47), and forming alternate wide and narrow ridges, as are there indicated. While the columns are proposed to be made removable, the cornice and fascia should be fixed to the cupboard framing, the end part of which should be connected to a piece T (Fig. 43) 1¼ in. thick and 5 in. deep, its end shaped as at U (Fig. 47), the front fascia being jointed into it as in Fig. 50, which also indicates one of the brackets planted on (V) ; these latter can be plain or sunk on face. An abacus or block 3½ in. square is arranged to come centrally over each column (Fig. 48), and a small bead is planted along the fascia in a line with it. A piece of filling-in is tongued on the top of the framing surrounding the cupboard doors W (Fig. 47) to make it level with the top of the fascia. A thin soffit X (Fig. 47) is fitted in with the aid of angle-blocks and a small bead, and the top boarding is put on with the grain running from back to front overhanging the fascia 2½ in., and broken out farther over the brackets if desired. Its edges are finished with a square slip and moulding as at Y, making the projection about 3½ in., and a good-size bed-mould, which should be returned round the brackets. It will be a simple matter

The fitting up of the interior depends so much on the destined uses of the cabinet, that no suggestions bearing on this work are put forward.

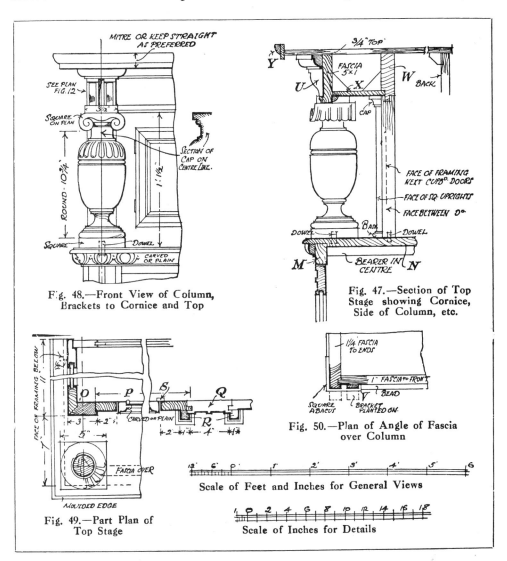

Fig. 48.—Front View of Column, Brackets to Cornice and Top

Fig. 47.—Section of Top Stage showing Cornice, Side of Column, etc.

Fig. 49.—Part Plan of Top Stage

Fig. 50.—Plan of Angle of Fascia over Column

Scale of Feet and Inches for General Views

Scale of Inches for Details

to fix dowels in the top of the middle part of the cabinet, fitting into holes in the bottom of the work just described, to keep same in position, and its own weight will be sufficient to keep it rigid if this is properly done.

CABINET FOR THE DINING-ROOM

The cabinet shown by Fig. 51 would, if executed in mahogany, harmonise quite well with Chippendale furniture, and the design is such that with slight modifications it could be made to match existing inlaid furniture. The shaped edges of the doors could be substituted with inlaid stringing. The particular arrangement of this cabinet is that of glazed cupboards at the sides, with an enclosed cupboard in the centre part. It may be desired to have all the cupboards with glazed doors, in which case the centre door can be

furniture it will be found most economical in the long run to make a full-size drawing on some ceiling or lining paper, and for this purpose the scale drawings will be found invaluable. Two elevations are shown by Figs. 52 and 53. The scale shown should be transferred to a slip of paper, so that the true sizes may be taken off, and then half the whole elevation

Fig. 51.—Dining-room Cabinet

readily adapted to a design harmonising with the side doors. It does not necessarily follow that a centre door with " barred " design should exactly resemble the side doors, because in actual practice it will be found that a simple centre door, designed in good proportion and without curved bars, will give a certain relief to the side ones, and obviate an overcrowded appearance.

When making practically any piece of

should be drawn. A scale sectional elevation (Fig. 54) is given, which should be drawn full size at the side of the half elevation. With such a drawing it should be quite an easy matter to obtain all the sizes required when making. Fig. 55 is a vertical section.

The construction is fairly simple, as the whole piece may be regarded as four separate parts, namely, stand or base, carcase, frieze, and top. After cutting

Fig. 52.　　　　　　　　　　　　　　Fig. 53.

Figs. 52 and 53.—Front and Side Elevations of Dining-room Cabinet

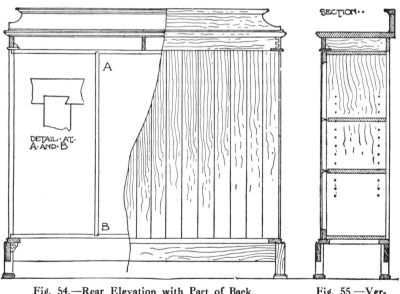

DETAIL · AT ·
A · AND · B

A

B

SECTION · ·

Fig. 54.—Rear Elevation with Part of Back
Removed

Fig. 55.—Ver-
tical Section

SCALE
INCHES
1　　　2　　　3 FEET

out and planing up all the pieces required to make the whole job, it would be best to begin making the stand. The long back and front rails are therefore mortised and tenoned into the outside legs, and this is followed up by tenoning the short end rails into the legs. When this part has been completed the inside legs may be bridled over the front rail. This is effected by cutting away a groove on the front of the rail just the width of the legs, and then the remaining thickness of the rail is cut out of the leg in order to form a prong or fork which fits into the rail. If machinery is employed, all the rails can then be taken out, and the front and end ones shaped. It is inadvisable to cut the shape near

and B (Fig. 54). This is generally called slip-dovetailing, and the partitions should be made ¼ in. longer at each end for the slip dovetail. It is best to cut the slip dovetails in the top and bottom first, stopping them ¼ in. from the front edge, and then shoulders and dovetails should be cut on the partitions to fit the socketed parts. Alternatively the partitions may be pinned or tenoned through the top and bottom, in which case it is customary to wedge the tenons after the job has been glued together. Both the top and the bottom should be lap-dovetailed to the carcase ends. A matched back is indicated in the back view, which is quite good for a strong carcase of this type. The joints would, of course, be grooved

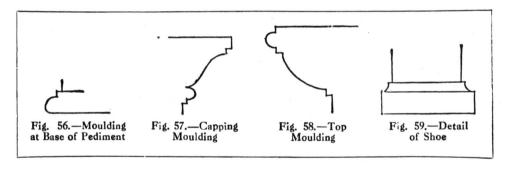

Fig. 56.—Moulding at Base of Pediment   Fig. 57.—Capping Moulding   Fig. 58.—Top Moulding   Fig. 59.—Detail of Shoe

the legs, as this short grain may break away. A little wood should therefore be left on these parts, and finally taken down to the finished shape when the stand has been glued up. If executed by hand, the shapes may be cut with a bow-saw, and then finished as indicated above.

After the stand has been glued up, the legs may be cut off level with the rails and the whole planed perfectly level. A centre cross-rail can be introduced with advantage. The mouldings are then mitred round to the section shown in the sectional view, and the blocks indicated glued to the mouldings and the rails at intervals of about 3 in. in order to strengthen the whole stand.

The construction of the main carcase is fairly straightforward. An enlarged detail is shown of the joints used at A

CUTTING LIST FOR CABINET

No.	For.	Lgth.	Wh.	Th.	Wood	Pcs.	Remarks.
		ft. in.	in.	in.			
1	Legs ..	6½	1½	1½	mahog.	6	Straight grain
2	Front rail ..	4 3	3¼	1¼	"	1	" "
3	End rails ..	1 1¼	3¼	1¼	"	2	" "
4	Back rail ..	4 3	4¼	1¼	"	1	" "
5	Cross rail ..	1 1¼	2¼	¾	wh'w'd	1	" "
6	Moulding ..	7 0	⅞	⅝	mahog.	1	Cuts 3 lengths
7	Carcase ends..	2 9¼	12½	⅞	"	2	Figured stuff
8	Back ..	2 10	3½	⅝	wh'w'd	17	Vee-jointed
9	Top..	4 2	11½	⅝	"	1	
10	Bottom ..	4 2	11½	⅝	"	1	
11	Divisions ..	2 9½	12½	⅞	mahog.	2	Straight grain
12	Door stiles ..	2 10½	1¾	⅞	"	6	" "
13	Rails ..	1 2	1¾	⅞	"	2	" "
14	Centre rails ..	1 4½	1¾	⅞	"	2	" "
15	Panel ..	2 7½	14	⅛	"	1	Pla'n for veneering
16	Frieze front ..	4 3	2½	⅞	"	1	
17	Ends ..	1 1	2½	⅞	"	2	
18	Back ..	4 3	3	⅝	wh'w'd	1	
19	Moulding ..	6 6	2¼	¼	mahog.	1	Cuts 3 lengths
20	Moulded top..	4 3½	14½	⅞	"	1	Figured
21	Pediment ..	4 2½	3½	⅞	"	1	
22	Top moulding	4 0	1⅞	⅞	"	1	
23	Base ..	4 3½	1⅞	⅞	"	1	

and tongued, and the inside parts V'd to give the necessary finish. Two screws

Fig. 60.—Cabinet in Ebony

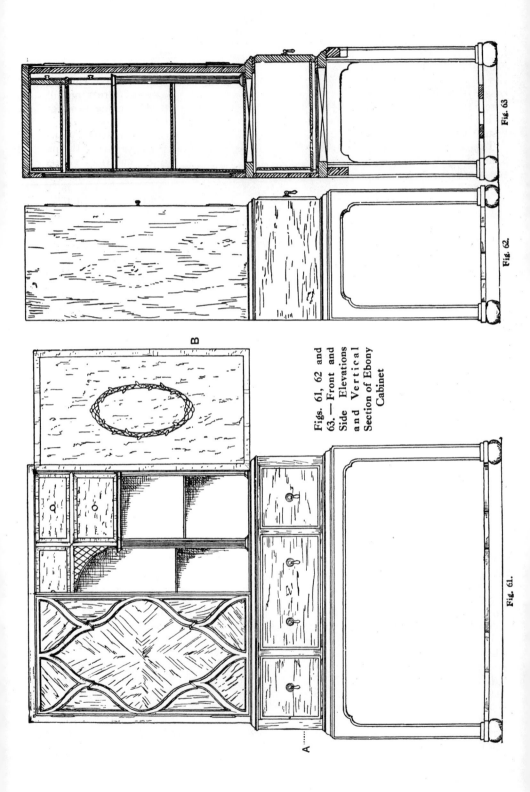

Figs. 61, 62 and 63. — Front and Side Elevations and Vertical Section of Ebony Cabinet

Fig. 61.

Fig. 62.

Fig. 63.

should be used to secure each board at the top and bottom, and particular care must be exercised in order to keep the carcase quite square whilst the matching is being fixed, or an untrue carcase will result.

The frieze box can next be made. This should be of solid mahogany, and the front corners mitre-dovetailed. The back can be lap-dovetailed, as indicated in the back view. It will be seen that the back rail is made rather wider, so that the bottom edge will be level when the mouldings are mitred round. The moulded top is next made and secured to the frieze by pocket-screwing from the inside. The pediment does not present any special difficulty, it being simply shaped as shown with base and capping mouldings attached. Details of the various moulds, etc., are shown by Figs. 56 to 59.

The doors should be mortised and tenoned together, then rebated, and the slats fitted to receive the bar mouldings. Each door should have the slats first fitted in all straight lengths, stub-tenoning the ends into the doors, and halving the slats where they cross. Separate curved diamond centres should then be prepared by fitting curved pieces round a diamond shape, and keying the corners with veneer. When these are dry they can be taken off the blocks, and cut into the straight bars with V'd joints. For additional strength small slips of silk or linen should be glued into the angles, and the bars can be mitred over the slats. The usual bar is astragal ; but with this design a plain rectangular one can be introduced, with the front corners slightly rounded. The curved edges can be cut and finished after the bars have been glued on. The shelves for this bookcase should rest on fillets, so that the front edges coincide with the second and third bar from the bottom.

The veneering of the centre door should be effected by fitting and gluing the pieces down to stiff paper, and then veneering the panel with a caul, the paper being removed after the veneering is dry. Bullet or French catches should be used

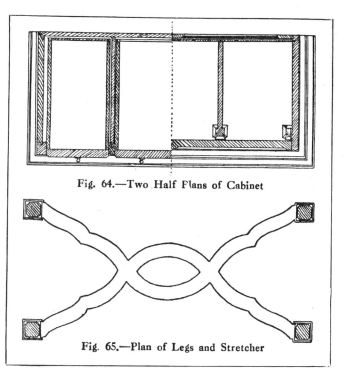

Fig. 64.—Two Half Plans of Cabinet

Fig. 65.—Plan of Legs and Stretcher

for the doors in preference to locks and keys.

CABINET IN EBONY

In the cabinet shown by Fig. 60 the same idea has been followed as used in the Queen Anne periods and in a good deal of Spanish work, namely, a closed cabinet with drawers, etc., inside, the whole on a stand. The woods used are ebony and an uncommon coromandel of a rich brown colour, and a broad figure something like walnut, the whole having a rich though perhaps a quiet effect. On opening the doors an interesting change is obtained by the interior being lined with satinwood, inlaid with ivory. Front and end elevations are shown by Figs. 61 and 62, and two half plans by Fig. 64. A vertical section is presented by Fig. 63, and a plan of the legs stretcher by Fig. 65. The two half plans are on the levels A and B (Fig. 61). The reproduced drawings are to a scale of 1 in. to 1 ft.

The constructional part is in mahogany. The top carcase is secret dovetailed at the angles, the inside fittings (the drawers are made in cedar) being worked in with the carcase. It is perhaps worthy of note that the doors are of one plain piece, with no clamps; this has stood perfectly.

The shaped mouldings are applied. Though on the drawing the ends, etc., appear to be bare, actually the figure of the wood overcomes that. The three deep drawers in the lower carcase project with a simple moulding on the corners. All the large mouldings are frames faced with ebony. The stand is on plain ebony legs, with an ovolo moulding worked on each edge, and is held at the bottom with a shaped stretcher, the four diagonals of which are framed into the centre piece. The whole stands on ball feet. All arrises are protected by small ebony corners. The handles and hinges are oxidised, and the interior knobs are of ivory.

The outside sizes are: height 5 ft. 1½ in., extreme width 3 ft. 1 in., extreme depth 1 ft. 4 in.

Collectors' Cabinets

SMALL EGG CABINET

THE eggs of British birds vary from about $\frac{3}{8}$ in. in diameter to as much as 2 in. (as about $1\frac{1}{2}$ in., and it is for sizes ranging between these limits that the cabinet shown in front elevation by Fig. 1 has been planned. Large drawers are not suitable

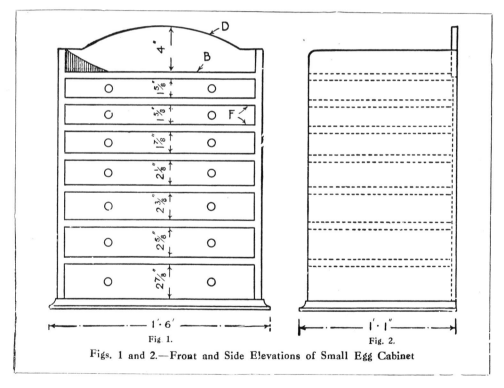

Fig. 1.

Fig. 2.

Figs. 1 and 2.—Front and Side Elevations of Small Egg Cabinet

in the case of those of the golden eagle), while those of the gull or heron average for this class of collection. Divisions in the drawers are not recommended, a better plan being to line each drawer thickly with sheets of good cotton-wool, in which the eggs can be securely bedded, the whole being covered with a sheet of thin plate-glass with polished edges. Thoroughly seasoned mahogany or oak should be used throughout, and all thicknesses kept as light as possible. A section of the cabinet is shown by Fig. 2.

The sides can finish $\frac{3}{8}$ in. thick, and are housed $\frac{1}{4}$ in. into a $\frac{5}{8}$-in. moulded base (Fig. 3), and screwed from below. A $\frac{3}{8}$-in. top shelf B (Fig. 1) is dovetailed into them as at C in Fig. 3, the joint stopping $\frac{3}{8}$ in. back from the front. A curved back rail D (Fig. 1) can be let into rebates at the top of the sides, and should itself be re-

Were it not for the fact that occasional complete removal may be necessary, the drawers could be secured from this danger by means of pins in their sides sliding in stopped grooves in the main carcase-sides. Fig. 4 also shows a sheet of glass resting in slight rebates at the top of the drawer. For dust-excluding reasons these rebates should be worked on all four edges of each drawer.

CABINET FOR COINS

The cabinet for storing coins shown in front elevation by Fig. 5 should be constructed of mahogany or other wood, and will hold about 800 coins. It is 1 ft. 3 in.

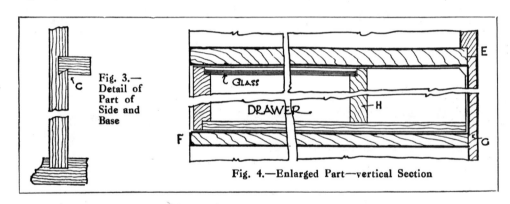

Fig. 3.—Detail of Part of Side and Base

Fig. 4.—Enlarged Part—vertical Section

bated to suit the top shelf, as at E in Fig. 4. The drawer divisions F (Figs. 1 and 4) should be solid from front to back, in order to avoid any possible obstruction or jarring. If desired, they can be of pine faced with hardwood, and they need be little more than $\frac{1}{4}$ in thick. They can be stop-housed or dowelled to the sides. A thin back G (Fig. 4) fitting in rebates in the side and base will complete the carcase.

The drawers should have $\frac{3}{8}$-in. sides, front and back, dovetailed, etc., in the usual manner, and a $\frac{3}{16}$-in. or three-ply bottom. The latter should be let into rebates in the front and sides, and finished quite flush on the underside as in Fig. 4. This figure shows how the drawer-back H is kept forward at least 2 in. from the ends of the sides, in order to guard against any inadvertent pulling of the drawer too far.

long, 12 in. high, and $8\frac{1}{2}$ in. deep. The top and bottom are lap-dovetailed into the sides, with the fronts mitred so as to conceal the dovetails. The two sides are rebated out on the front edge to receive the sash ; the back edge is also grooved to receive the tongue on the back board (see Fig. 6).

The drawers, twenty-four in number (see Figs. 5 and 7), containing sunk holes for the coins as shown (see Fig. 6), are a series of shelves $\frac{1}{2}$ in. thick ; these are prepared with grooves in the ends, stopped from the front edge (see Fig. 8), which fits on the runners (see Figs. 9 and 10). The shelves are gauged to an equal thickness on the front edges, but are slightly bevelled off towards the back on the underside, to give a lead or clearance, so that the slides may pass each other without touching. Two small ivory knobs are screwed in each drawer. The cabinet and is secured in the same manner. The sash is framed together with dovetails,

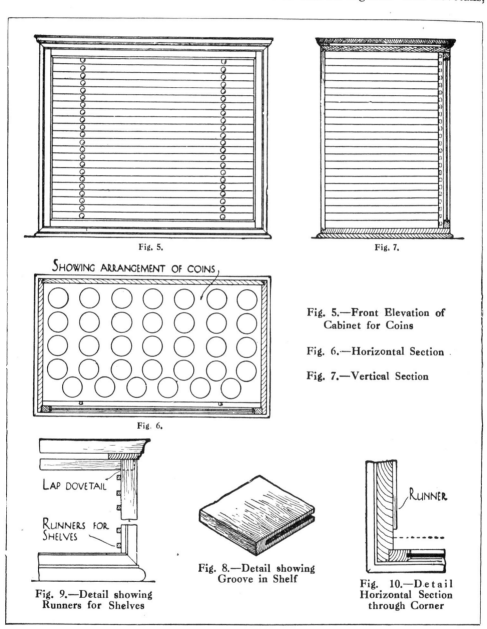

Fig. 5.

Fig. 7.

SHOWING ARRANGEMENT OF COINS

Fig. 6.

Fig. 5.—Front Elevation of Cabinet for Coins

Fig. 6.—Horizontal Section

Fig. 7.—Vertical Section

LAP DOVETAIL

RUNNERS FOR SHELVES

RUNNER

Fig. 8.—Detail showing Groove in Shelf

Fig. 9.—Detail showing Runners for Shelves

Fig. 10.—Detail Horizontal Section through Corner

stands on a base moulded on four sides, and screwed from the underside ; the cornice is thicknessed up, as in Fig. 7, the glass being glued up in the sash, fitting into the grooves prepared to receive it. It is hinged on the right-hand side with small brass butt hinges, and is kept closed by a small steel spring fixed in the rebate, or by fitting small bullet catches.

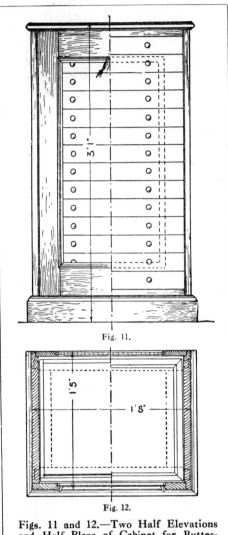

Fig. 11.

Fig. 12.

Figs. 11 and 12.—Two Half Elevations and Half Plans of Cabinet for Butterflies, etc.

CABINET FOR BUTTERFLIES, MOTHS, BEETLES, ETC.

The cabinet shown by Fig. 11 is suitable for storing butterflies, moths, beetles, etc., the method of construction being

that applied to the cabinets of public museums.

Fig. 11 shows the cabinet, one half having the door removed. In the plan (Fig. 12), the right half shows the cover of a drawer ; on the left this is removed, and the dotted lines indicate the skeleton top. Fig. 13 is a broken vertical section on the centre line, one-third full size. Fig. 14 is a section through the top corner of the case, the lettering being the same as in Fig. 13. Fig. 15 is a plan of the same parts, with the moulded top removed ; the dotted line indicates the drawer beneath, T being the door tenon. Fig. 16 is a section at the lower corner of the case, and shows the method of fixing the plinth, runners, etc. Fig. 17, a horizontal section of the same parts, illustrates the hanging of the door, the dotted lines showing the housing of the various parts. Fig. 18 is an isometric view of a corner of the framed bottom, showing how the front rail is fixed, and the shape of the rebate bottom. Similarly, Fig. 19 shows one corner of a drawer, Fig. 20 illustrates a method of joining the corners of the cover frames, and Fig. 21 an isometric view of the joint used in framing up the door (without the moulding).

The cabinet contains fourteen drawers, and these are sufficient for a fairly large collection ; but the size may be varied to requirements, although it is advisable not to reduce the depth of the drawers, but rather their number. Also the interior height of the case should be a multiple of $2\frac{1}{4}$ in., the standard depth of the drawers, which are interchangeable. Each drawer contains a sheet of cork O (Fig. 13) glued to the bottom, and fitting closely all round ; to it the specimens are pinned. Each drawer, besides being covered with a dust-tight glazed frame, is also furnished with a cell C to contain camphor, which drives off destructive insects. The drawers slide on thin oak runners K grooved into the sides of the case, the overlapping edges of the drawer fronts being stopped against their ends.

The containing case has two solid sides, with a framed and panelled back and bottom F ; a skeleton top, to which is fixed

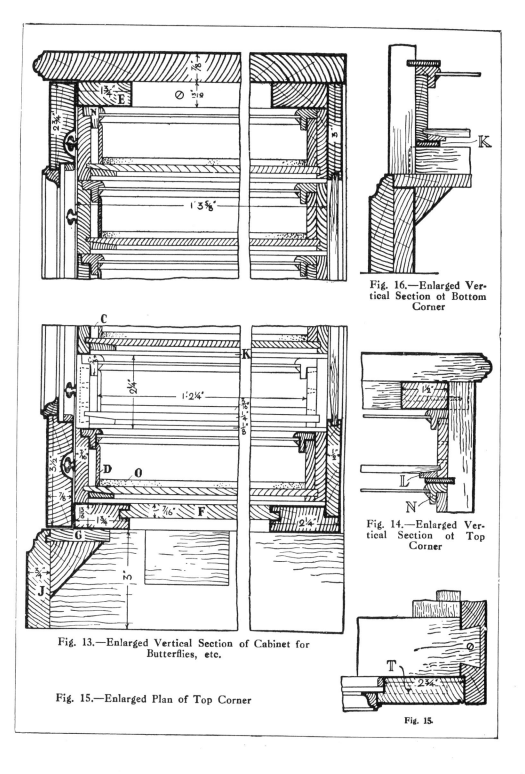

Fig. 16.—Enlarged Vertical Section ot Bottom Corner

Fig. 14.—Enlarged Vertical Section of Top Corner

Fig. 13.—Enlarged Vertical Section of Cabinet for Butterflies, etc.

Fig. 15.—Enlarged Plan of Top Corner

Fig. 15.

a solid top, with overhanging and moulded edges ; a solid plinth J, fixed to the base ; and a glazed and moulded door. The door is carried over the side of the case on the hanging side, and is hinged at the back so that the drawers may be opened without throwing the door right back ; on the striking side it is rebated into the side for the purpose of obtaining a hold for the lock bolt. A false bead is sunk in the face of the hanging stile to make it correspond with the opposite side. The outer case, with the exception of the back, should be made of dry, sound hardwood, free from knots, and straight-grained ; baywood, black walnut, or wainscot oak are the woods most suitable. Of the interior parts, the front rails of the top and bottom, the rebate piece G (Figs. 13 and 17), and the drawer fronts, should be of the same wood as the case ; the drawer runners, blocking pieces L (Fig. 14), and the top glazed frames should be of straight-grained oak. The remainder of the cabinet may be of American or kauri pine ; no yellow or white deal must be used, as the gums and resins are injurious to some specimens.

To proceed with the construction first prepare the stuff carefully, with the faces out of wind, the edges shot straightly, and the material gauged to proper thicknesses. Then make a template $2\frac{1}{4}$ in. wide $\frac{1}{8}$ in. thick, and 6 in. long, for spacing the runners accurately. Square over on the inside face of one of the sides a line 4 in. from the bottom end ; this will be the top side of the housing groove of the framed bottom. Ascertain the thickness to which this will hold when finished, which should be $\frac{13}{16}$ in., and set this amount off below the line. Next with the thickness of the template mark off the face line of the bottom runner, which is not grooved in (see K, Fig. 16). The line just drawn will be the starting point for all the grooves, the face lines of which will be obtained by successive applications of the flat side of the template to the line last drawn, until the top is reached ; the width of the grooves will then be set off with the thickness of the template below the face lines. The last line marked at the top will show the

bottom of the rail E (Fig. 13) and the bed of the dovetails thereon ; the thickness of this rail must be marked beyond, and the side cut off $\frac{1}{16}$ in. longer. All the groove lines must be knife-cut from the front edge as far as the gauge line ; this line, which represents the inside of the drawer fronts, will be $\frac{1}{2}$ in. from the edge on the left side and $\frac{1}{2}$ in. plus the door rebate from the edge of the right side. Turn the lines on the edge in pencil, pair the other side, and square over.

Then set off on the outsides for the plinth a line level with the underside of the bottom, and gauge it $\frac{3}{16}$ in. deep ; gauge also the rebate for the door, and for the framed back, from the front edges. Make two stops in the bottom groove, one at $\frac{1}{4}$ in. the other at $1\frac{3}{4}$ in., from the front edge for the dovetail shown in Fig. 18. All the grooves are $\frac{1}{4}$ in. deep, they may be cut absolutely square with the sides by planing straight and square a piece of 1-in. stuff, long enough to reach across the side, fixing it to the lines with clips, and running the tenon saw against it, first cutting a notch with the chisel at the front end, to make a play for the saw ; finish the grooves with the router. Cut the socket for the dovetail in the bottom first ; then, when the front rail is cut to length, fit it in the groove and mark the dovetail—the size marked will be that at the back, and must be transferred (see Fig. 18). Set out the width of the case on the top rail from the plan, where it is shown by dotted lines. The shoulder lines will be of the same length at top and bottom, the dovetail at the top going through the side to within $\frac{1}{4}$ in. of the face.

When the housings, etc., are worked, begin fitting up. First glue in the drawer runners at the bottom ; these are cut cross grain, the grain being parallel with the front of the case. Having driven in the first one, run a shoulder plane across the face to make it square with the side, and proceed in the same way to the top. The framed bottom F (Fig. 13) should have been glued up and faced over previously, and may be inserted in one piece ; then cramp up and fix the top rails, square the case and block it underneath, leaving it to dry whilst the back is prepared. Set out the back, its width from the plan and height from Fig. 13, these being drawn full size on a rod. The tenons will be $1\frac{1}{2}$ in. by $\frac{3}{16}$ in., and the panel grooves $\frac{1}{4}$ in. by $\frac{5}{16}$ in. When the back is finished, screw it in position to dry.

the front rail will be fixtures ; all the other must be slotted, as shown in Fig. 13.

The drawer fronts may be prepared in one length ; gauge them $2\frac{1}{4}$ in. full in width, plough the bottom groove $\frac{1}{2}$ in. up, $\frac{1}{8}$ in. wide, and $\frac{3}{16}$ in. deep, and rebate the top edge a full $\frac{1}{4}$ in. deep to Fig. 13.

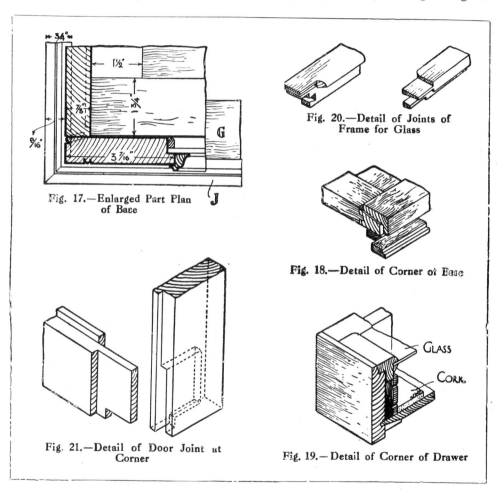

Fig. 17.—Enlarged Part Plan of Base

Fig. 20.—Detail of Joints of Frame for Glass

Fig. 18.—Detail of Corner of Base

Fig. 21.—Detail of Door Joint at Corner

Fig. 19.—Detail of Corner of Drawer

The case may now be cleaned off and the plinth fixed ; the rebate piece must run over the edge of the left side as shown in Fig. 18, and the side rails J (Fig. 13), after being slotted for the top screws, can be screwed in as shown in Fig. 14. Next clean off the top edges flush with the rails and fix the moulded top. The screws in

Cut off the fronts and fit in the openings. Begin at the bottom and work up, fitting them tight one above another ; the last one will not go in, in consequence of all being of slightly full width, to allow of subsequent cleaning off, however, it may be fitted by removing the bottom one and driving the tier down. **Prepare the sides** and backs in lengths, the first $1\frac{7}{8}$ in., the latter $1\frac{1}{2}$ in. wide ; plough the sides $\frac{1}{8}$ in. deep, $\frac{3}{8}$ in. up. Cut them roughly to length, set off two in pairs from Fig. 13, and place them on the outside of the others also arranged in pairs ; hand-screw them up, and cut and plane the ends to the length. Set off the dovetail sockets, cutting with a dovetail saw ; then separate and mark the fronts and backs, keeping the top edge of the side flush with the rebate in the front, and the top side of the plough groove flush with the lower edge of the back. A groove $\frac{1}{8}$ in. wide and $\frac{3}{16}$ in deep must be sunk in each side $\frac{1}{4}$ in. from the front dovetail line to receive the partition D (Fig. 13), which is put in from the bottom after the drawer is glued up, the grooves being stopped $\frac{3}{8}$ in. down from the top. Chamfer the bottom equally at the sides and front, slot the back for a screw to allow of shrinkage, gauge the blockings L (Fig. 14), and glue them in, in 2-in. lengths, before cleaning off and fitting the drawers. Then prepare the cover frames N (Figs. 13 and 14), which are dovetailed at the angles, as shown in Fig. 20. The lower pin on the side piece is shown full length as left from setting out ; when the frame is glued up this will be cut back flush with the back of the tongue. The bevel of this tongue is shown exaggerated ; take off a couple of shavings after gluing up the frame. Set each frame out separately to its own drawer. Cut the lengths

off slightly long, lay the back and front pieces in place, and press the ends of the side pieces against them, marking the sight line with a knife. Repeat the process with the sides and set out therefrom. The frames should be glued up with their top sides resting on a true surface ; then clean off the drawers, when the latter may be finally fitted in the case.

The rebate for the glass of the door is $\frac{3}{16}$ in. deep, and is carried up square behind the quadrant corners of the top rail. A $\frac{1}{4}$-in. tenon is used in the middle of the thickness. The shoulder in the top rail is made as shown in Fig. 21, sinking in to the moulding line at the springing, and tapering off to the sight line at the top ; this prevents the wood breaking away when the shoulder is cut. The hanging stile needs to be fox-wedged, as the edge is seen.

The door is hung, as shown in Fig. 17, with a pair of $2\frac{1}{2}$ in. brass butts sunk flush in the bead on its back edge, and housed to the depth of the flap at the front edge ; the housing in the case is from the thickness of the flap inside to nothing at the back of the knuckle. The lock should be let in flush with the inside of the door, at the middle of the height of the stile.

The whole of the outside of the cabinet and the drawer fronts should be french-polished ; and the knobs, preferably of bone or vegetable ivory, being inserted. the cabinet is finished.

Music Cabinets

SHERATON MUSIC CABINET

To make the Sheraton music cabinet shown by the half-tone reproduction, Fig. 1, and by the reproduced drawings, Figs. 2 to 5, the following material will be required. Mahogany: 2 ft. of 1-in. stuff, 10 ft. of $\frac{3}{4}$-in., 2$\frac{1}{2}$ ft. of $\frac{5}{8}$-in., 6 ft. of $\frac{1}{2}$-in., and 6 ft. of $\frac{1}{4}$-in. Deal: 6 ft. of $\frac{3}{4}$-in. Moulding: 4 ft. of top moulding A (Fig. 6), 6 ft. of astragal (Fig. 7), and 12 ft. of $\frac{1}{4}$-in. ovolo (Fig. 8). Satinwood band: 24 ft. of $\frac{1}{2}$-in. (Fig. 9). There will also be required: one left-hand cupboard lock, one 2$\frac{1}{2}$-in. drawer lock, one pair of 2-in. hinges, 3 ft. of coppered steel wire, and $\frac{3}{4}$ yd. of green pongee silk. For the stool there will be required 1$\frac{1}{2}$ ft. of 1$\frac{1}{4}$-in. mahogany, and two 1$\frac{3}{4}$-in. squares of mahogany 3 ft. long.

To begin the making of the cabinet, cut off the stuff, allowing sufficient for working, and joints where necessary.

Fig. 1.—Sheraton Music Cabinet

Rough it over with a coarse smoothing plane, and square up the carcase ends to size, as in Fig. 10, also the deal top and bottom, and dovetail them as illustrated. Groove the ends at x (Fig. 10) $\frac{3}{8}$ in. deep, stopping the groove $\frac{3}{4}$ in. from the front as shown, to receive the fixed shelf or cupboard bottom. Finish the inside ends with a fine plane, and then scrape and glass-paper. Glue in the deal top and bottom, and cut a shoulder on the cupboard bottom, $\frac{3}{4}$ in. from the front, to agree with the groove x. Glue the dovetails only, then push in the shelf and cramp it.

Square the drawer sides and front and back, and plough a $\frac{1}{8}$-in. groove inside the drawer front at the bottom, the top of the groove to be $\frac{1}{2}$ in. from the bottom edge. Dovetail the drawer and fix the drawer back $\frac{1}{2}$ in. up, level with the top of the groove in the drawer front. Then get out two $\frac{7}{8}$-in. slips of $\frac{1}{2}$-in. stuff, as in Fig. 11.

and groove the same as the drawer front. Clean up inside of the drawer, and glue up the dovetails. Then glue in the slips as shown, so that the grooves in same are in a line with the groove in the front. Clean up the drawer bottom to size, and bevel it to fit the groove A (Fig. 11). Let the bottom overhang the back of the drawer by $\frac{3}{4}$ in., to allow for shrinkage. Screw the bottom to the back of the drawer with two $\frac{5}{8}$-in. screws.

Plough a $\frac{1}{8}$-in. groove in the muntings, cut a shoulder at top and bottom, and groove to receive shelves. Then heat the edges and glue flush to the ends. Allow them to dry, clean up the $\frac{1}{4}$-in. mahogany back panel, and bevel the outside edges to fit the groove in the muntings. Push it in, cramp the carcase top and bottom at the back, and screw the muntings and panel to the shelves. Fit the drawer exactly to the aperture, slightly bevelling inwards the top front edge.

Now make the deal frame (Fig. 12) to receive the top moulding, gauge the material ($\frac{3}{4}$-in. deal) to $1\frac{3}{4}$ in. wide, and nail together the exact size of the top of the carcase. Let the front and ends overhang. Now hand-screw the frame at the front and back to the top shelf, and glue in blocks as shown, and allow to dry. Then cut off the overhanging pieces, and mitre and glue the moulding round as at A in Fig. 6.

The top of the cabinet should be moulded, and should be $20\frac{1}{2}$ in. by $14\frac{1}{4}$ in., finished. The pediment B (Fig. 6) is screwed behind it. Plane the top part, and glue the bottom edge of the front and half-way on the ends, and hand-screw down.

Square the inner edges of the door stiles, gauge and mortise, and cut tenons on the rails. Glue up and cramp the door squarely. When dry, fit the door as follows : From the inside edge at the bottom, gauge $1\frac{1}{2}$ in., and plane down to this line. Then place the door firmly on the shelf, and fit the back to the end, also reducing the stile to $1\frac{1}{2}$ in. in width. The top rail and front stile will, of course, be

fitted to the opening. Bevel all the edges slightly inwards. Now mitre the $\frac{1}{4}$-in. ovolo moulding (Fig. 8) round the inside of the door, so that it recedes $\frac{1}{16}$ in. from the front surface. Place the door on its face, get out three strips of beading $\frac{3}{32}$ in. thick and $\frac{5}{8}$ in. wide, and cut them into the back of the door as in Fig. 13. Put the upright in first, then the cross-pieces, and bevel the front edge with a sharp chisel to fit the groove in the astragal moulding (Fig. 7), and finish as in Fig. 14.

Now push in the drawer as level as possible with the front of the carcase, nail temporarily two blocks at the back to retain it in position, and level the whole front with a trying plane. Then pull out the drawer, glue two stops and place them $\frac{1}{4}$ in. in on the shelf X. Gently push in the drawer, so that it recedes $\frac{1}{16}$ in. from the front edge, pull it out, and pin the stops in position.

The stool or stand of the cabinet will now be dealt with. Cut a cardboard shape as at A (Fig. 4), take the $1\frac{3}{4}$-in. square pieces, and cut four pieces $13\frac{1}{2}$ in. long. Square them up on the two front sides of each, mark the outline of the cardboard shape, and fret them out. Then fasten them in a bench screw, round the toes and half-way up (leave the back edge square) with a spokeshave, and rasp and glasspaper. Then cut off to 13 in. long. The rails should be fret cut, first marking with a cardboard mould. Cut the front rails $16\frac{1}{4}$ in. long, and frame up as in Fig. 15 ; the end rails are 11 in. long. The back of the stool will be flush with the carcase back. The back rail will be $16\frac{1}{4}$ in. long and $2\frac{1}{2}$ in. wide. Dowel and frame up flush with the front of the legs ; then cramp it. Fit in corner ties with glue and screws.

Stand the carcase on the stool, and, placing a piece of $\frac{1}{4}$-in. ovolo moulding, mark round the outside edge of the moulding. Round off the top edge of the stool to this line, and clean up. Then get out two $\frac{1}{2}$-in. stuff shelves and two $\frac{1}{4}$-in. slips $1\frac{1}{4}$ in. wide for the shelf rests, and fit them.

To insert the banding, it is required to

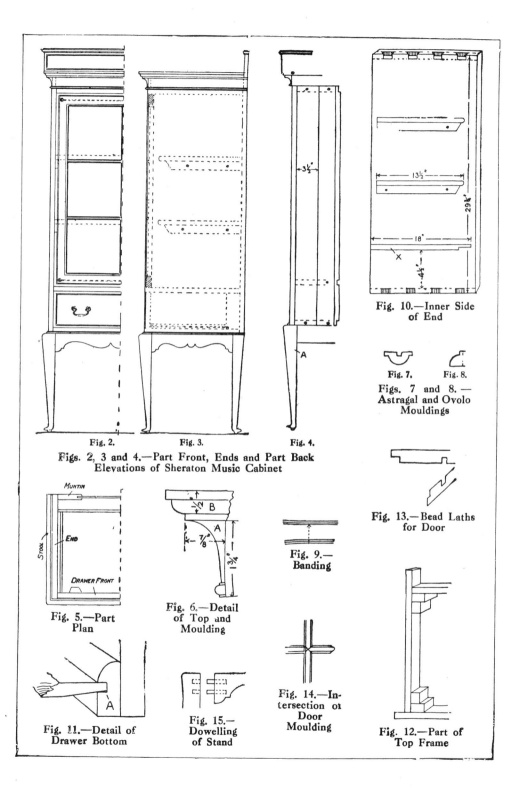

Fig. 2.

Fig. 3.

Fig. 4.

Figs. 2, 3 and 4.—Part Front, Ends and Part Back
Elevations of Sheraton Music Cabinet

Fig. 10.—Inner Side
of End

Fig. 7.   Fig. 8.

Figs. 7 and 8. —
Astragal and Ovolo
Mouldings

Fig. 13.—Bead Laths
for Door

MUNTIN

STOOL

END

DRAWER FRONT

Fig. 5.—Part
Plan

Fig. 6.—Detail
of Top and
Moulding

Fig. 9.—
Banding

Fig. 11.—Detail of
Drawer Bottom

Fig. 15.—
Dowelling
of Stand

Fig. 14.—In-
tersection of
Door
Moulding

Fig. 12.—Part of
Top Frame

retain only the crossband and one set of lines. Therefore set the gauge as in Fig. 9, and gauge round the edges of the door top, drawer, and pediment; the latter should be $2\frac{1}{4}$ in. wide of $\frac{5}{8}$-in. stuff. Rebate not quite the thickness of the band, mitre the banding, and well wet with a swab; glue down, rubbing the glue out with the narrow edge of a hammer. Wipe off with a swab, and when dry clean up with a scraper. Keep the scraper well on the horizontal surface, in order that the band should be flat, and draw it towards you, or the banding will chip.

To fit the lock, first gauge from the top of the lock to the centre of the pin. Mark this on the drawer front, and through this mark in the centre of the front bore a $\frac{3}{8}$-in. hole. Now gauge the depth of the plate on the inside of the front, cut with a dovetail saw two or three kerfs, and chop out for the lockbox. Insert the lock, mark round the plate, cut in level, and screw down. Then fix on the hinges. Two inches down from the top of the back of the door, mark the length of the hinge. Then gauge the width of the plate on the door edge (leave the round part of the hinge protruding), and cut the folded hinge in flush.

After polishing, the work will be ready for fitting together. Mitre and glue astragal mouldings on the laths in the door as Fig. 14. Then fit 21-oz. glass in the door, and mitre the beads in with pins or needle points. Make a hem in the top and bottom of the silk curtain, and pass through the wire, bending the ends in the form of an eye with pincers. Screw on with round-headed screws. Fix the stool with one screw to each angle piece. The shelf rests should be screwed on the inside, and loose shelves placed thereon. Screw the hinges to the carcase, allowing the closed door to recede $\frac{1}{16}$ in. from the surface. Fix on the top with a screw in each corner of the deal top, and finally screw the pediment to the back of the top. At the bottom of the pediment should be jointed a piece of $\frac{1}{2}$-in. mahogany, in order to raise the inlaid band level with the top. Handles should be fixed on the front of the drawer as shown.

MUSIC CABINET WITH DRAWERS AND CUPBOARD

The half-tone illustration (Fig. 16) shows a music cabinet that might very readily be modified to suit the degree of elaboration or simplicity required in any given case. The cabinet consists of three drawers intended to have swing or drop fronts for readier access to the contents, and below, a cupboard fitted with folding doors. It is proposed to be made in mahogany, and either treated with inlaid lines and banding and quartered panels as shown, or with plain polished surfaces. The legs, also, instead of being worked as shown, could, if desired, be made to a plain square section and merely tapered downwards. For a third possible simplification, the swing fronts to the drawers might give place to the older form of fixed fronts, although the others are far more convenient and not really difficult to contrive. Front and side elevations of the cabinet are shown by Figs. 17 and 18.

The cabinet, it will be seen, has four legs, each about $1\frac{1}{4}$ in. square, but breaking out $\frac{1}{16}$ in. all round for a piece $1\frac{1}{2}$ in. high, as at A (Fig. 17), below which it tapers inwards to $\frac{3}{4}$ in. square $1\frac{1}{2}$ in. above the floor, where it is worked to the form shown at B in Fig. 19, the whole being kept square on plan. Should the suggested lines of inlay be decided on, all the outer faces may be treated, or it can suitably be reserved for the two outer faces of the front legs only. When the legs are in hand, pieces for bearers at the level of C (Fig. 17) can then be prepared for framing between the legs on all four sides, $\frac{7}{8}$ in. deep and $1\frac{1}{4}$ in. wide, rebated to take a board to form the bottom of the cupboard, as in Fig. 19, where D indicates the front bearer and E the back one, the latter being grooved to take the back filling-in piece F. The side bearers will also need grooving to receive the side panels, the grooves coinciding with those shown at G in Fig. 20. A top bearer H

Fig. 16.—Music Cabinet with Drawers and Cupboard

spaces of about $3\frac{1}{4}$ in. deep each. At the same level neat strips to act as runners should be fixed on the insides, while below the third drawer should be fitted a similar bearer, but rebated to take a thin division to form a top to the cupboard, across the middle of which a small shelf might also suitably be fixed.

Fig. 21 will serve to explain the method of fixing the cupboard doors, which are intended to be hung with ordinary brass butt hinges to pieces as at N, grooved into the legs for preference, and having a small strip planted on at O to form a bar to dust. A similar strip might be run along the top and bottom of the cupboard on the inside if thought desirable. The doors have rebated meeting stiles as at P ; but one is made $\frac{1}{4}$ in. wider than the other, so that although it projects behind its fellow, yet the line of their meeting as seen from the outside is kept in the centre. The door framings might be about $\frac{7}{8}$ in. thick, ovolo moulded on the solid externally and rebated for the panels, the latter being secured in position by small beads, all as at R in Fig. 19, and either plain, bevelled, or quartered and inlaid at discretion. A stop at top and bottom should be provided (unless the strips previously mentioned are

(Fig. 17) and J (Fig. 19), $\frac{5}{8}$ in. by $1\frac{1}{4}$ in., is framed between the front legs, and similar ones at the sides, but grooved in the same way as the lower bearers. At the back at this level all that will be necessary is to fix a small piece as at K (Fig. 19), against which the back piece L (which fits into grooves in the bottom bearer as described, and in the back legs as at M, Fig. 20), can be fixed. The side panels also, whether inlaid or plain, will fit into grooves in the legs G (Fig. 20) and bearers. A similar bearer to H (Fig. 17), and also measuring $\frac{7}{8}$ in. by $1\frac{1}{4}$ in., will be required under each of the two top drawers, tenoned into the legs, and leaving drawer

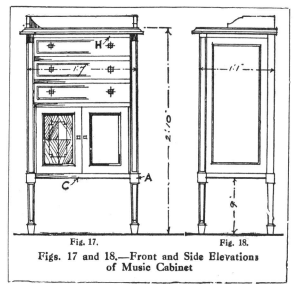

Fig. 17.

Fig. 18.

Figs. 17 and 18.—Front and Side Elevations of Music Cabinet

adopted) for the doors, which might suitably be fitted in such a way that their outside faces when closed would be just a shade behind the various bearers. These in their turn might be recessed $\frac{1}{16}$ in. behind the face of the legs. The top might be about $\frac{3}{4}$ in. thick, finished with a moulded edge on three sides, as in Fig. 19, and made up of two pieces cross-tongued together. The small skirting, $2\frac{1}{4}$ in. by $\frac{3}{8}$ in., to back and part sides, and cut to the curved ends shown, are

able, than the orthodox, except in such cases as the present, where the sides have not sufficient thickness to admit of much grooving. The drawer fronts are then prepared about $\frac{5}{8}$ in. thick and rather more than the full size of the openings, in order to allow of their being adjusted exactly as required at the last. At each end they have a small strip of brass bent to a right angle and screwed on as at v (Fig. 20), so that it will project into a wide saw-cut made in the centre of the

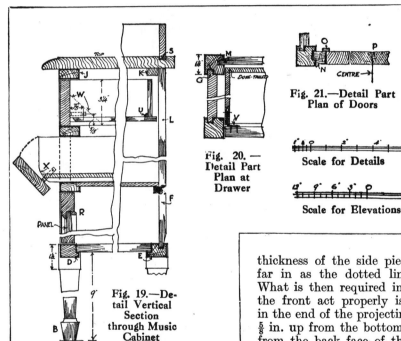

Fig. 21.—Detail Part Plan of Doors

Fig. 22.—Detail Section through Side of Drawer

Fig. 20.—Detail Part Plan at Drawer

Scale for Details

Scale for Elevations

Fig. 19.—Detail Vertical Section through Music Cabinet

let into grooves cut to receive it as at s in Fig. 19. It will be sufficient to mitre this skirting at its angles.

The drawers should be fairly light in build, and may be made on quite the usual lines, or in accordance with the following particulars. The sides, $3\frac{1}{4}$ in. by $\frac{1}{4}$ in., and back $2\frac{3}{4}$ in. by $\frac{1}{4}$ in., are dovetailed together, and the bottom fixed to them by means of small strips as at T (Fig. 22) and U (Fig. 19). This method is simpler, but less commend-

thickness of the side piece, to about as far in as the dotted line w (Fig. 19). What is then required in order to make the front act properly is a hole drilled in the end of the projecting strip to come $\frac{5}{8}$ in. up from the bottom edge and $\frac{7}{8}$ in. from the back face of the drawer front. And when this has been effected, a screw should be put through the side, on which screw, and in the space afforded by the saw-cut, the brass strip is threaded, to work fairly loosely, the projecting end of the screw being, of course, filed off smooth. By these means it will be found that when the bottom corner of the side has been cut off to the curve x (Fig. 19), the front will drop as the drawer is pulled out, as shown in the case of the second drawer in Fig. 19. The third drawer is omitted in this detail in order to economise space.

MUSIC CABINET IN OAK

The music cabinet shown by the half-tone reproduction (Fig. 23) is not difficult to make. Two elevations, two sectional plans and a vertical section are given by Figs. 24 to 28.

The sides, top, and back are ¾ in. thick (finished size), as are also the door and surrounding frame. At each angle is a post 1¾ in. square, rebated to receive the angle of the carcase. This rebate facilitates the construction of the corners, as the meeting pieces need only be butt-jointed, since the joint itself will be covered by the post, and the necessity for complicated joints is dispensed with. The top should be cut to receive the ends of the posts, and, if properly housed great strength and rigidity are thereby ensured.

On the lower parts of the corner posts is introduced a little turning of Jacobean character, while in the square blocks just above the turned feet, mortises are cut to receive a shelf, which may be ½ in. to ⅝ in. thick. This shelf will be found useful in practice for such pieces of music as are in more constant use than the rest, and which are often left on the top of the piano.

The sides are framed and panelled, the panels being "stuck moulded," though, if preferred, the mouldings can be planted on instead of being worked out of the solid. As it is improbable that the back will be seen much, it can be left plain.

Fig. 23.—Music Cabinet in Oak

The lower part of the cabinet is finished with a small moulding planted on the sides and back, and in the case of the front, on the lowermost interior shelf.

The door is, of course, framed with mortise-and-tenon joints, and has a rebated panel for glass, with shifting beads to secure the lead lights in position (see Fig. 29). Lead cams about ⅜ in. or ½ in. wide give a good effect. The shelves are ½ in. thick, and may be secured to battens on the sides and back.

The details shown of the panel moulds (Fig. 30), turned legs (Fig. 31), top mould (Fig. 32), and lower mould (Fig. 33) should be drawn out full-size at the beginning of the work. This may easily be done by means of the scale reproduced.

The inlay shown on the front of the corner posts and on the side panels is of holly and ebony. Of course, if it is desired to simplify the work these may be omitted, and as a further simplification the sides might be plain instead of panelled as shown; but the enhanced effect which the panels give to the appearance generally will amply repay the time and labour expended in working them. The door is hung with small brass butts, and a turn-buckle fastening with swivel drop handle is shown. The latter would look best in oxidised bronze. A lock may be added if desired. Finally, as to finishing the surface, this will depend to some extent on the surroundings in which the cabinet is to be placed; but in the

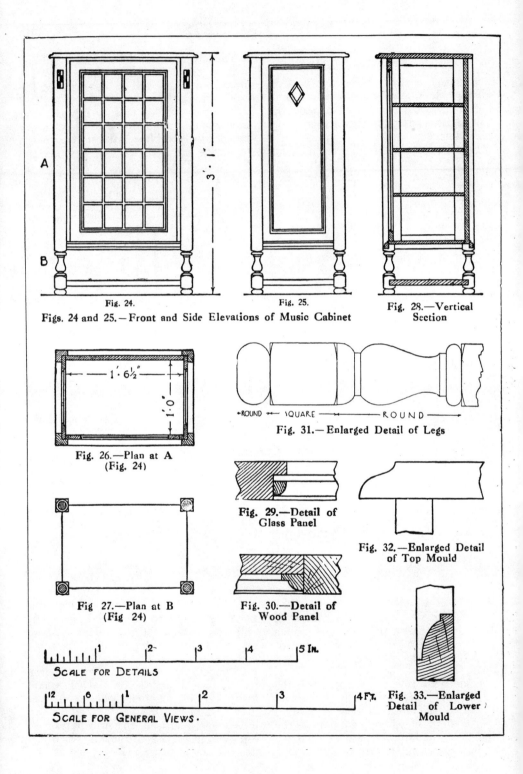

Fig. 24.

Fig. 25.

Fig. 28.—Vertical Section

Figs. 24 and 25.—Front and Side Elevations of Music Cabinet

Fig. 26.—Plan at A (Fig. 24)

←ROUND → ↠SQUARE ——→ ← R O U N D →

Fig. 31.—Enlarged Detail of Legs

Fig. 27.—Plan at B (Fig 24)

Fig. 29.—Detail of Glass Panel

Fig. 30.—Detail of Wood Panel

Fig. 32.—Enlarged Detail of Top Mould

Fig. 33.—Enlarged Detail of Lower Mould

SCALE FOR DETAILS

SCALE FOR GENERAL VIEWS.

absence of any special circumstances of this nature, the wood might be darkened by fuming, depth according to taste, and then wax-polished.

MAHOGANY MUSIC CABINET

The music cabinet shown by Figs. 34 to 38 is designed for execution in mahogany, and all the dimensions given indicate finished sizes. The carving introduced adds to the attractiveness of the piece, but may be omitted if a simpler effect is sought ; or it may be replaced by a scheme of quartered veneering. Similarly the number of the drawers may be increased or decreased to some extent to meet individual requirements, the depth being varied so as to retain as far as possible the overall height of the cabinet as shown in Fig. 38.

As regards construction, the first members to be taken in hand are the four $1\frac{1}{4}$-in. by $1\frac{1}{4}$-in. corner posts all of which are tapered and shaped at the lower end to form the legs. They are also recessed on all four sides for the small cocked bead, housings being formed immediately below these to receive the ends of front and side spandrel pieces. The front pair of posts are chamfered on the external angles, and mortised for the front top and bottom carved rails and also for the drawer rails, the back pair of posts being mortised for a top rail only. All the posts are grooved to receive the sides, the preparation of which should be proceeded with when the posts have been prepared.

The sides each consist of an inner frame of $2\frac{1}{4}$-in. by $\frac{1}{2}$-in. moulded stiles and rails with a $\frac{1}{4}$-in. panel. To this frame the $3\frac{1}{8}$-in. by $\frac{5}{8}$-in. top and bottom carved rails are glued with tongued-and-grooved joints, and a tongue is then worked on the complete side ready for assembly to the corner posts (already grooved), sufficient allowance being made in the width of the stuff for this tongue. The side spandrel pieces should next be prepared, so that they may be fixed in place in their housings when the sides and posts are assembled. Fig. 39 is a part section through the side of the cabinet, and it

will be seen that the inner frame is set back $\frac{1}{8}$ in. from the carved rail, which is flush with the post. The spandrel pieces both side and front are set back $\frac{1}{4}$ in. from the leg face.

With the sides of the carcase complete, the front carved rails and the drawer rails and runners should next be taken in hand and fixed to unite the sides, the front spandrel piece being secured at the same time. Fig. 40 gives a general view of the carcase, in which it will be seen that a $\frac{5}{8}$-in. by $\frac{5}{8}$-in. fillet glued and nailed to each of the back legs affords a fixing for the back ends of the drawer runners, they being notched and screwed to these fillets. The bottom of the cabinet is formed of a drawer rail and runners with the addition of a back rail, all being grooved for a ply-wood dust-board. Another pair of fillets are fixed to the back legs to form a rebate for the panelled back, which is screwed in place along its sides and tongued to the top rail at its upper end, holding the carcase rigid.

A detail of the pediment and side brackets is given by Fig. 41. The top is secured in place by pocket screwing through the top rails (see Figs. 38 and 39), the pediment and side brackets having previously been fixed to the top by screwing through the underside of same. It will be seen by reference to Fig. 38 that the moulding is glued to the face of the pediment, but the brackets have the capping fixed on their tops.

The construction of the drawers is shown by Figs. 42, 43 and 44. For convenience in use these have fronts which fall automatically on the drawers being pulled out, making the contents of same more accessible. The arrangement is quite a simple one, and consists of brass plates, which are let in and screwed to the ends of the drawer fronts and pivoted on screws fixed in the drawer sides. These latter must be set in about $\frac{1}{4}$ in., so that the heads of the pivot screws will run clear when the drawer slides in or out (see Fig. 44). The bottom is held by grooved oak slips along the sides, and supported at its front edge by the 3-in.

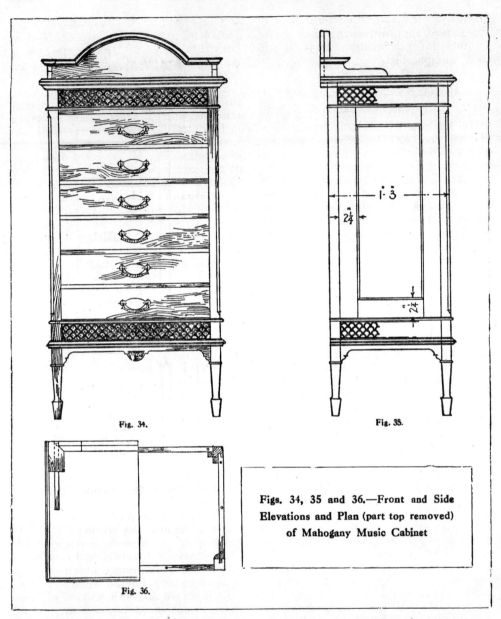

Fig. 34.

Fig. 35.

Fig. 36.

Figs. 34, 35 and 36.—Front and Side
Elevations and Plan (part top removed)
of Mahogany Music Cabinet

by $\frac{1}{2}$-in. rail let in and screwed to the
bottom edge of the sides as indicated in
the details, and the back and sides are
dovetailed together in the usual way.
The dotted lines in Fig. 43 show the
position of the front when it falls. Guide
clips are fitted to the drawer runners, and

for the top drawer a pair of top guides
are also necessary. These are shown in
Fig. 39. In Fig. 38 it will be seen that
the front edges of the drawer rails are
set back $\frac{1}{8}$ in., and, of course, the drawer
fronts should be similarly set back, the
carved rails and bottom drawer rail

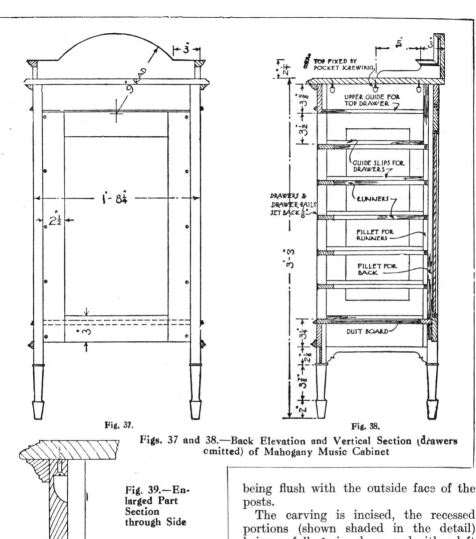

Fig. 37.

Fig. 38.

Figs. 37 and 38.—Back Elevation and Vertical Section (drawers omitted) of Mahogany Music Cabinet

Fig. 39.—Enlarged Part Section through Side

being flush with the outside face of the posts.

The carving is incised, the recessed portions (shown shaded in the detail) being a full $\frac{1}{16}$ in. deep, and either left plain or punched, according to taste.

An alternative design is given for the rails (Fig. 45); but no attempt should be made to employ both, and so far as the rails are concerned, the design may be fretted out in some fretwood and applied as an overlay, the thickness of the rail being reduced accordingly. The designs are set out on $1\frac{3}{4}$-in. by $1\frac{1}{4}$-in. squares with a $\frac{1}{8}$-in. margin, and will repeat ten times on the front rails and seven times on the side rails. In Fig. 45 will be found details of the mouldings which with

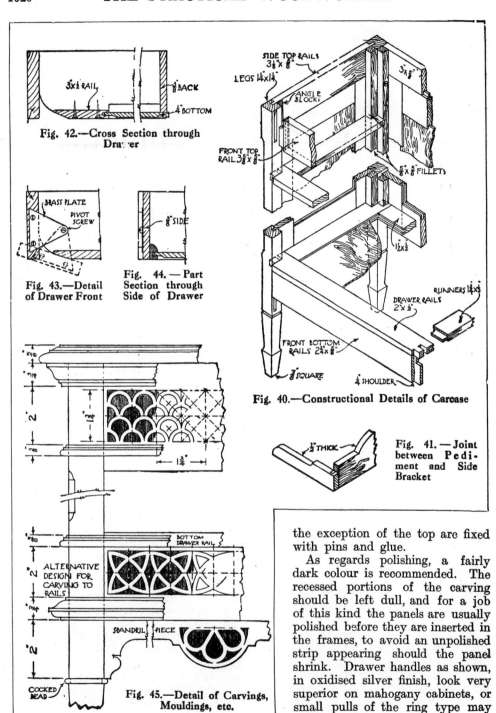

Fig. 42.—Cross Section through Drawer

Fig. 43.—Detail of Drawer Front

Fig. 44.—Part Section through Side of Drawer

Fig. 40.—Constructional Details of Carcase

Fig. 41.—Joint between Pediment and Side Bracket

Fig. 45.—Detail of Carvings, Mouldings, etc.

the exception of the top are fixed with pins and glue.

As regards polishing, a fairly dark colour is recommended. The recessed portions of the carving should be left dull, and for a job of this kind the panels are usually polished before they are inserted in the frames, to avoid an unpolished strip appearing should the panel shrink. Drawer handles as shown, in oxidised silver finish, look very superior on mahogany cabinets, or small pulls of the ring type may be used with good effect.

Gramophone Cabinets

TABLE-TYPE GRAMOPHONE CABINET

THERE is nothing to limit the quality and tastefulness that may be embodied in the cases or cabinets for gramophones, and as a consequence gramophones are available which may be installed in drawing-rooms as permanent features, so there is no excuse for those who banish their instruments to the lumber-room, whence often it is too much trouble to fetch them. The instrument to be described, though restrained in the matter of decoration, if well made and finished, should be beyond reproach. It depends for its decorative effect mainly on the fretwork front, designed to take the place of the usual louvre boards that are used to conceal the mouth of the horn in most hornless instruments. There are no special difficulties in the construction of this instrument. Oak or mahogany is suggested as the best material, the latter for preference, as it is easier to work and has better resonance than oak. The instrument is quite separate from the tripod support on which it rests. This is not an essential matter, but facilitates transport as, for instance, when it is desired to take it into the garden.

Fig. 1 is a front elevation of the cabinet. The higher central portion is the gramophone proper. It is flanked on each side by cupboards capable of holding a good supply of 10-in. records. Fig. 2 is a plan view showing also by means of dotted lines the position of the supporting tripod.

With the exception of the baseboard, which should be $\frac{1}{2}$ in. to $\frac{5}{8}$ in. thick, the wood employed is $\frac{3}{8}$ in. thick. First make the baseboard to the dimensions given in Fig. 3. The grain of the wood should run in the direction of the 26$\frac{1}{2}$ in. dimension. The simplest plan is to work a board 26$\frac{1}{2}$ in. by 11 in., and to glue on the back extension (13$\frac{1}{2}$ in. by 6$\frac{1}{2}$ in.) as well as the $\frac{1}{2}$-in. strip in front. Considerable accuracy in the working of this baseboard is desirable, as it forms the foundation of the whole structure. Fig. 4 is a sectional view, back to front, of the gramophone part of the instrument, and shows the relative positions of the various parts. The box measures 18 in. long by 13$\frac{1}{2}$ in. wide externally, the internal dimensions being $\frac{3}{4}$ in. less, if wood of the thickness specified above is used. No bottom is made to the box, as it is attached direct to the baseboard (Fig. 3), and the front has the lower part absent for a width equal to the height of the mouth of the horn (see Fig. 4). The corners may be dovetailed; but a joint made as shown in Fig. 5 is quite satisfactory, involves less trouble, and looks better when all is finished.

Before gluing up, see that the four sides of the box when held together at the corner joints stand fair on the central part of the baseboard. After gluing, bring the joints together and secure by winding tape or other flat material round the box, drawing it as tightly as possible. If the rebates have been accurately made and fitted, this should be sufficient to ensure close glue joints ; but if otherwise, it may be necessary to use a few fine pins to hold the joints together until the glue sets. Subsequently they may be withdrawn, and the holes plugged with wooden pegs put in with glue.

Next see that the four sides of the box stand square with each other. Tes with the square and adjust if necessary. When the joints are firm, prepare the top of the box and glue it on, weighting it heavily to ensure a close joint all round. This done, strike a gauge line all round $2\frac{3}{4}$ in. from the top, and cut through with the tenon saw. This gives the lid. Note specially that the board which forms the top of the lid overhangs at the front $\frac{3}{16}$ in. (see H, Fig. 4). Now prepare a piece of $\frac{3}{16}$-in. wood for the fretted front, planing it to a good surface. It should measure $13\frac{1}{2}$ in. wide by $14\frac{5}{8}$ in. deep, the grain of the wood running across the width (see Fig. 1). Detach a strip $13\frac{1}{2}$ in. by $2\frac{3}{8}$ in. and glue it to the front face of the lid. It will sit under the $\frac{3}{16}$ in. projection of the top board above-mentioned, making the front fair. The sectional view (Fig. 4) shows how the parts go together.

The fretwork panel should next be marked out. The open-work should measure, say, $12\frac{1}{4}$ in. wide and $8\frac{5}{8}$ in. deep, allowing 1 in. below the lid joint and 1 in. above the plinth, plain. The design in Fig. 1 may be enlarged or some other design may be preferred. If the latter, bear in mind that the pattern should be an open one, otherwise the voice of the instrument will be throttled. Lay aside this panel until the metal horn has been fixed in place.

Prepare a board to form the support for the motor and other parts of the mechanism, cutting it to exact dimensions of the box inside. The grain of the wood should run across the width of the box. Detach a strip A (Fig. 4) 3 in. wide and attach it across the back of the box as shown, that is, 2 in. below the lid joint. A firm attachment can be made by using a fillet of wood x (Fig. 4) glued along the two sides and

back of the box at the correct height. To make assurance doubly sure, put in a few fine brass screws, being careful that their points do not show on the outside of the box. Glue in the strip A and screw it neatly to the fillets. It would be well, however, to first make the hole for the tone-arm, the size of which will be determined by the diameter of the latter at its base.

The portion carrying the motor and which has to be hinged to A, as shown at B, must now be dealt with. It will measure $9\frac{3}{4}$ in. by $12\frac{3}{4}$ in., and will require some stiffening. The most workmanlike way of effecting this would have been to cut it narrower by 3 in., and to add two $1\frac{1}{2}$-in. strips, one on each side, tongued, grooved and glued on, as shown in section in Fig. 6. Another way would be to add two strips, crossing the grain, one on each side below, set in sufficiently to clear the fillets E (see also Fig. 6). Fix by measurement the position for the motor spindle, determined by the length cf the tone-arm (usually about 8 in.), and central in the width of the box, and bore the hole an easy fit for it. Then temporarily connect this piece with the strip A, using neat brass or nickeled hinges, and see that it works freely when raised and lowered. The purpose of making this piece movable, of course, is to give access to the motor for oiling and repairs.

The filleting is continued along the inside front of the box by a strip shown in section at c. This is made deep enough to permit of the keyhole passing through it, and it is so shaped at its bottom edge as to conform to the curve of the metal horn, permitting the latter to be screwed to it. The box lid may be finished by adding the moulding H (Fig. 4), of any section, neatly mitreing it at the corners, and securing it with glue. The lid is to be hinged at its left-hand side. Sink the hinges in its lower edge, and prepare corresponding seatings in the edge of the box. It will be better to defer attaching the lid until the whole of the work is completed.

The construction of the horn may now be considered. It may be made of sheet metal ; tinplate is as good as anything.

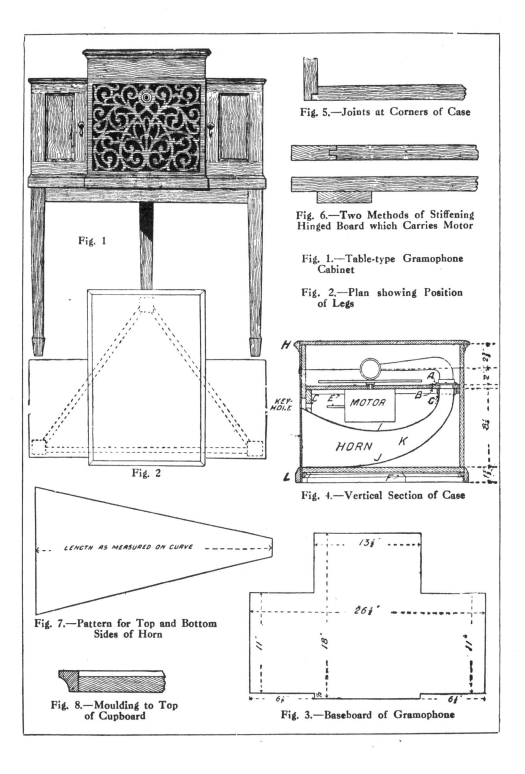

Fig. 5.—Joints at Corners of Case

Fig. 6.—Two Methods of Stiffening Hinged Board which Carries Motor

Fig. 1.—Table-type Gramophone Cabinet

Fig. 2.—Plan showing Position of Legs

Fig. 1

Fig. 2

Fig. 4.—Vertical Section of Case

Fig. 7.—Pattern for Top and Bottom Sides of Horn

Fig. 8.—Moulding to Top of Cupboard

Fig. 3.—Baseboard of Gramophone

The curved top and bottom are first cut from the sheet. These will be of equal width at their wide and narrow ends, but that marked J will necessarily be of greater length than I. Draw the curves full-size on paper and measure their respective lengths. Then on paper construct the shapes as shown in Fig. 7, the width at the wide end being the full width of the box inside, and the width at the narrow end being slightly greater than the internal diameter of the base of the tone-arm. These paper shapes may then be used as templates for cutting out the top and bottom of the horn. This done, bend the metal pieces to suit the curves already drawn. The shapes for the sides K may be determined by taking an impression with paper of the edges of the two curved pieces, having first arranged the latter in proper relation to each other. From the paper impression cut the two sides of the horn. It only remains to unite the edges of the four pieces with tinman's solder. If the curves have been neatly cut and well-fitted, no overlap is necessary, and it may be remarked that as the horn is hidden, small blemishes in the soldering may be ignored. On the other hand, the horn may be made of thin wood, say $\frac{1}{8}$ in. thick ; it will be quite satisfactory. Holes must be drilled along the edges of the openings at both ends for fixing. It should be noted that any looseness of fit inevitably will result in jarring sounds, caused by the loose parts vibrating sympathetically with certain notes.

The small end of the horn is shown entering a socket at G (Fig. 4), which is made by gluing on four strips of wood to the underside of the strip A, best done before A is fixed. Screws driven into these strips from the inside of the end of the horn constitute a sufficiently good means of attachment. The large end of the horn is similarly secured, the sides to the sides of the box, the top to the strip C, and the bottom to the baseboard. When fixed the inner surface of the horn should be blackened by coating it with a mixture of french-polish and lampblack.

The assembling of the mechanism is best deferred until the whole of the cabinet-work is completed, but may be here mentioned as the box in which it is housed is being dealt with.

The motor will be provided with suitable means for attaching it to the board that is to carry it. The speed-regulator will be fixed separately, and care must be taken to place it in correct relation to the motor so that the two may be properly connected. As generally arranged, it will come in the near left-hand corner clear of the table. The brake may be fixed in the far left-hand or near right-hand corner, at the option of the constructor. The tone-arm is fixed by screwing its flange to the strip A.

The two cupboards will each require two sides and a top. The height inside should be sufficient to permit a 10-in. record to enter with something to spare, say $10\frac{1}{2}$ in. Fig. 3 furnishes the width and depth (outside dimensions). The back and side may be joined by rebating, as described in connection with the case, and united to the baseboard and the side of the case with glue, screws being used in addition to make a firm job. The top is then glued on, and when the glue has set the moulding may be added. The latter butts against the box and is mitred at its outer angles. In Fig. 8 is shown how this moulding may be attached so as to form a raised edge to the tops of the cupboard, very useful for restraining needles.

The doors are framed and panelled, and a small mitred beading is run round the panel. They are hinged on the outer side. A neat drop handle on the other side adds to the good appearance of the cabinet. The plinth, shown in section at L (Fig. 4), must be applied after the rest of the work is completed. It follows the outline given in Fig. 3, and provides a recess 1 in. deep into which the tripod head passes. It is glued on, mitred at all angles, and further secured by a small fillet, shown at F (Fig. 4).

The construction of the tripod support is sufficiently indicated in Figs. 1 and 2 and calls for little description. The three legs, which may be $1\frac{3}{4}$ in. square in section at the top, taper down to the shaped feet from a point some 5 in. from the top. They are connected by strips 3 in. by ¾ in. mortised into their tops. A study of Fig. 2 will show how the legs are spaced so that their tops sit loosely in the recess of the cabinet formed by its plinth.

The whole of the woodwork should be french-polished before screwing on the

PEDESTAL CABINET FOR GRAMOPHONE

The illustrations, Figs. 9 to 14, show how a gramophone of the hornless and enclosed turn-table class can be fitted with a pedestal forming a cupboard for records. As a rule the cases of these instruments

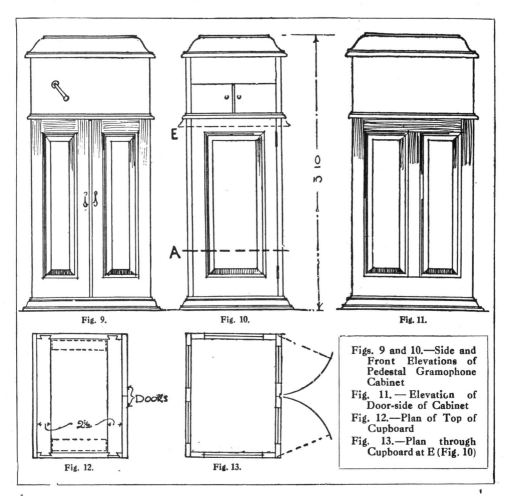

Fig. 9.   Fig. 10.   Fig. 11.

Fig. 12.   Fig. 13.

Figs. 9 and 10.—Side and Front Elevations of Pedestal Gramophone Cabinet
Fig. 11. — Elevation of Door-side of Cabinet
Fig. 12.—Plan of Top of Cupboard
Fig. 13.—Plan through Cupboard at E (Fig. 10)

various hinges and attaching the parts of the mechanism. The woodwork that comes immediately behind the fretted panel above the mouth of the horn should be blackened, and this may be done with the same mixture as suggested for the inside of the horn.

are of considerably greater depth than width, and on this account the doors of the cupboard have been placed at one side, but this is a matter that is optional.

The sides of the cupboard consist of moulded and raised-panel framing, flush on the inside, finished ⅞ in. thick, and tongued at the fixed angles. The doors are hinged, as at c in Fig. 15, in order to offer no obstruction to the interior when open. At the bottom they are fixed to a solid shelf D (Fig. 14), while at the top

phone (wnere shown by dotted lines at E in Fig. 10).

In order that the gramophone can be readily removed from the pedestal if necessary, it should not be fixed in any

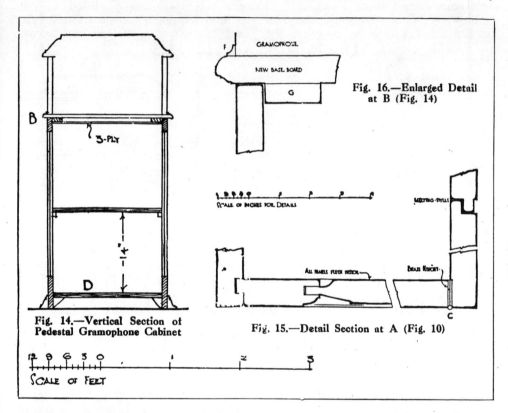

Fig. 16.—Enlarged Detail at B (Fig. 14)

Fig. 14.—Vertical Section of Pedestal Gramophone Cabinet

Fig. 15.—Detail Section at A (Fig. 10)

SCALE OF FEET

they are secured by means of a couple of dovetailed rails (where marked 2½ in. in Fig. 12). A piece of three-ply fixed on their undersides serves to fill the space between these rails (see Fig. 14). One shelf is fitted, serving to divide the cupboard into two tiers of the requisite height to suit record albums. Next to the floor the cupboard is finished with the moulded base removed from its original position on the gramo-

way. Instead, it should be fitted with a new moulded baseboard and small cover-mould F (Fig. 16), and a couple of rails (as at G in Fig. 16) added in the position shown dotted in Fig. 12. By this means the instrument can be dropped into its proper position with the rails between those already mentioned as dovetailed, and once there is prevented by its own weight from any possibility of lateral movement.

Music Stools

LOOSE-SEAT MUSIC STOOL

THE particular style of music stool illustrated by Fig. 1 makes it most suitable for production in mahogany. finished by fuming and wax-polishing. It is fairly simple in construction, involving only the simplest joints. The carving on the rails should come well within the scope of comparatively inexperienced workers. In Figs. 2 and 3 are shown front and side elevations. The stool is fitted with a loose " drop-in " seat, which would look well if covered with a light patterned tapestry.

Work should be begun by preparing the four legs, which are of 1⅜-in. square mahogany. The four rails, 3½ in. by ⅞ in., can also be cut out. The rails are tenoned into the legs in the usual way, and are rebated to receive the loose seat, the outer edge being shaped with a rebate plane and glasspaper, as in the section (Fig. 4). The tops of the legs must also be worked so as to continue both the moulding and the rebate for the seat. The stool may now be temporarily cramped up, and the stretchers

Fig. 1.—Music Stool with Loose Seat

made and fitted. The cross section of these is shown by Fig. 5; the shape shown can be worked with a steel scratch. The two stretchers are, of course, halved together and tenoned into the legs.

The strapwork carving on the rails, of which a detail is given by Fig. 6, should be carefully set out. It is in quite low relief, and requires but few tools in its execution. Care should be taken to see that the interlacing of the pattern is correct, as it is on this that it depends a great deal for its effect. The portion which comes on the rails should be carved first ; the short ends of the stool are then glued up, and the carving on these finished. The whole should then be glued up, and the carving on the back and front of the stool completed. Triangular pieces of wood A (Fig. 3) are glued in the corners between the rails and the legs, and then worked to the shape shown with gouge and file.

The stool can now be cleaned up, darkened if necessary, and polished. The mahogany can be darkened either by fuming with ammonia or by means of a weak solution of bichromate of potash. Wax-polishing will prove to be the most satisfactory, as the carving prohibits a glossy finish being given to the wood.

The frame for the seat should be made from fairly thick stuff tenoned or halved at the corners. This should be made of a cheaper wood, such as birch or white-wood. In upholstering the seat the following method could be used: The webbing should first be tacked tautly to

part section by Fig. 7 are well-seasoned mahogany and rosewood; for the legs and the moulding round the seat, solid rosewood, the boxing and other parts being of mahogany, veneered with rose-wood wherever the surfaces are visible.

The mechanism for raising and lowering the seat is made of brass, and is of the simplest possible construction, so that there should be little likelihood of it getting out of order. At the same time

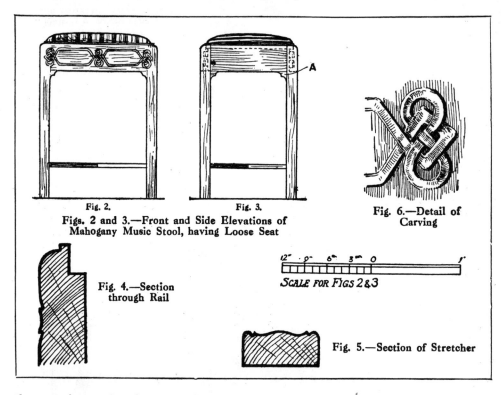

Fig. 2.   Fig. 3.

Figs. 2 and 3.—Front and Side Elevations of Mahogany Music Stool, having Loose Seat

Fig. 6.—Detail of Carving

Fig. 4.—Section through Rail

SCALE FOR FIGS 2 & 3

Fig. 5.—Section of Stretcher

the seat frame (interlacing in the usual way), and then covered with a layer of good stout canvas. Over this is spread a layer of horsehair or wadding, which is covered with calico. Then the final covering of tapestry (or whatever takes the worker's fancy) is put over this.

ADJUSTABLE MUSIC STOOL

The woods suitable for the adjustable music stool shown in part elevation and

it is necessary to have a means of adjust-ment that can be operated rapidly. The boxing is made deep to ensure stability and smooth working. Fig. 7 shows the stool, half in elevation and half in section, and a sectional plan is shown by Fig. 8. For clearness, the raising and lowering mechanism has been omitted, but it is illustrated and described in detail later.

The legs are cut from 2-in. by 2-in. rosewood and are 19¼ in. long. When

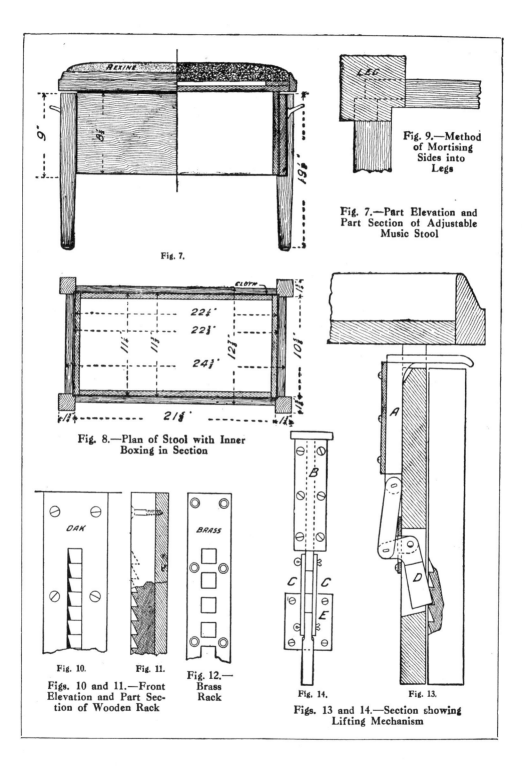

Fig. 7.

Fig. 9.—Method of Mortising Sides into Legs

Fig. 7.—Part Elevation and Part Section of Adjustable Music Stool

Fig. 8.—Plan of Stool with Inner Boxing in Section

Figs. 10 and 11.—Front Elevation and Part Section of Wooden Rack

Fig. 12.—Brass Rack

Figs. 13 and 14.—Section showing Lifting Mechanism

planed and squared the net size is $1\frac{3}{4}$ in. by $1\frac{1}{4}$ in. From a point 9 in. from the top they are tapered on all four sides to $1\frac{1}{4}$ in. by $1\frac{1}{4}$ in. at the bottom. Rosewood in one respect resembles mahogany —the grain is apt to dip in one part and to rise in another, on the same surface. Therefore it is necessary to have a sharp plane-iron finely set, or difficulty may be experienced in getting the surfaces fair.

The outer boxing is 1 in. thick for the ends and $\frac{3}{4}$ in. for the sides. The greater thickness at the ends is important, as they have to carry the rack-work by which the movement of the seat is checked, and consequently also they carry the whole weight of the sitter. Fig. 9 shows how the four sides of the boxing are mortised into their respective legs. It will be seen that a corner of the leg is cut away to the extent of $\frac{3}{8}$ in. each way to give a clear run to the inside boxing. This, of course, is only done so far down as the boxing extends. By removing the corner in this way the tenons can be made longer and therefore stronger ; also the legs have a better appearance, as there is less recess between them. The tenons do not extend across the full width of the side and end boards, but are stopped 1 in. from the top edge. Having made these four boards and fitted the tenons to the mortises so that all close up truly, veneer the front sides of them and their top edges with rosewood. In the centre of the end pieces inside cut a vertical channel $1\frac{3}{4}$ in. wide and $\frac{5}{8}$ in. deep to accommodate the rack-work shown in detail in Figs. 10, 11 and 12.

Now trim the edges of the veneer, and glue up the mortise joints all round. After gluing the mortises and driving them well home, test the framework for squareness, and adjust if necessary. The veneering of the sides is stopped at the point where the tenon enters the leg. It is better to run it on to the tenon, and afterwards to cut away along a line squared off from the inside rebate. This ensures the veneer making a close joint with the leg.

The inner boxing may now be made, and is built of four pieces of mahogany joined by dovetailing. The boards need not be more than $\frac{1}{2}$ in. thick. Some degree of accuracy is necessary, as this boxing when veneered must fit the outer boxing with just so much play as to admit of a packing $\frac{1}{16}$ in. thick being interposed between the two all round. If made truly square and worked so that after veneering it measures accurately $\frac{1}{8}$ in. less in width and length than the inside measurements of the outer boxing, it will be satisfactory. The object of introducing packing material is twofold : to ensure smooth working and to protect the surfaces of the inner boxing, which come into view when the seat is raised, and therefore would look unsightly if scored by rubbing against the sides of the outer boxing. It is well to allow some days to elapse after the dovetailing before veneering, otherwise the dovetails will show up through the veneer, owing to the end-grain wood shrinking less than the other. No dimensions have been mentioned for the principal pieces, as they appear in Figs. 7 and 8.

Next make the seat, which consists of a $\frac{3}{4}$-in. board, and might be of deal, as it is not seen. This board should measure 24 in. by 13 in., and should have all edges carefully squared, as well as all the corners. The very simple moulding is worked from 2-in. by $\frac{7}{8}$-in. rosewood to the section shown in Fig. 13, mitred and attached with glue. A strengthening fillet might be added round the inner angle if desired, but is unnecessary if the moulding has been well fitted and glued. The top, which now has the form of a tray, is glued to the top of the inner boxing and further secured with screws. Before this is done, however, it is well to cut away the spaces at the tops of the two ends to accommodate the heads of the lifters, and also to cut the slots for the cranked pawl. In fact, it is better to complete and fit all the lifting mechanism before securing the seat top.

The seat is upholstered on a stretcher made to fit loosely inside the top. This is a plain rectangular deal frame halved at the corners and glued together. It may be made from 3-in. by $\frac{5}{8}$-in. stuff. Allowance has to be made for the two thicknesses of covering material. Send the stretcher to the upholsterer, and instruct him to put on a horsehair stuffed cushion. He will support this on a base-work of tapes (indicated in Fig. 8). It should be covered with any strong material like ticking or stout sheeting. The outer cover may be fixed by the worker. Use upholstery pins—not tin-tacks—and work from the centres of the sides and ends towards the corners, putting on all the tension possible. If the measurements for the stretcher have been right, and the work neat, the cushion should drop into the tray top without side or end play, and will require no further securing.

The lifting mechanism is shown in detail in Figs. 13 and 14. The rack is made of oak, but possibly a metal rack would have a longer life. Figs. 10 and 11 show the form of the teeth, and how the rack is secured to the inside of the boxing. It is well to glue as well as screw. The section of the rack is $1\frac{1}{4}$ in. by $\frac{5}{8}$ in., and the teeth are pitched $\frac{3}{8}$ in. apart. They commence $1\frac{1}{2}$ in. from the top, and stop at the point reached by the pawl when the seat is at its lowermost position. They should be chiselled out neatly, the points being kept rather blunt, and when finished the rack may be rubbed over with a mixture of vaseline and plumbago to act as a lubricant. If a metal rack is preferred, the construction may be as shown in Fig. 12. It consists of a brass plate, say $\frac{3}{32}$ in. thick, pierced with a series of rectangular holes and a channel is cut away in the wood behind it to allow for the nose of the pawl.

Refer now to Figs. 13 and 14. A is an L-shaped piece of brass $\frac{7}{16}$ in. by $\frac{3}{16}$ in. in the vertical member, but splayed out in width at the top, as shown, where it enters and is secured to the horizontal member. The latter is $1\frac{1}{8}$ in. by $\frac{7}{16}$ in. in section. Its back end is slotted and the vertical piece fitted and secured by soft soldering. Its front end is bent downwards as shown to give a grip for the fingers. The lower end of A is

rounded and drilled for the through-pin. B is a brass plate which is screwed to two parallel strips of mahogany, the whole forming a guide in which A works freely up and down. The plain brass links C (Fig. 14) are $\frac{7}{16}$ in. by $\frac{3}{32}$ in. in section, drilled at each end, the holes being pitched $1\frac{1}{4}$ in. apart. D (Fig. 13) is a cranked pawl made from a casting. Its lower end is thickened to $\frac{5}{16}$ in. It is pivoted to a brass bracket E, which is slotted centrally where the cranked part works. Exact dimensions are not material, but ample strength is desirable, as the weight of the sitter comes on the pawl and bracket. The weight of A and the two links together is sufficient to keep the nose of D pressed against the rack, when all joints work freely. This mechanism is made in duplicate, one set being fitted at each end of the stool. It will be seen that when the two pieces A are lifted simultaneously the pawls D are drawn clear of the rack, and the whole inner part of the stool may be raised to any desired height. On releasing the pieces A the pawls at once engage the racks, and the seat remains fixed at the desired height. Actually there is no need to lift by the pieces A, as the same action takes place if the stool top is lifted by the hands gripping the moulding at the ends. In lowering, however, the pieces A must be gripped to free the pawls.

The packing between the two boxings consists of ten strips of billiard cloth $1\frac{1}{2}$ in. wide glued on to the inside of the outer boxing. These strips are arranged vertically, three along each side and two at each end. They secure a very smooth action, and, as already pointed out, prevent marking the polished outer surface of the inner boxing. A dusting with french chalk further diminishes the friction. The spacing of the strips is indicated in black in Fig. 8.

It only remains to french-polish the stool and add the two brass handles. Castors are not advised for the legs, as a music stool should stand firmly. If, however, it is decided to fit them it is advisable to use balls running in sockets, so that the carpet is not damaged.

MUSIC STOOL WITH BOX SEAT

The music stool with box seat shown by Fig. 15 should be made of mahogany,

Fig. 15.—Music Stool with Box Seat

hard straight-grained stuff being necessary for the legs, which must be free from

of their length being simply turned as shown, or tapered. Their tops are cut out to the scroll form set out from Fig. 19, where the squares representing inches will facilitate enlargement. This scroll termination of the top represents a certain amount of cutting to waste; but if two legs are set out, and one of them reversed and put close up to the other, it will be found quite simple to make the two from one piece of 1¾-in. or 1½-in. wood, 6 in. by 2 ft. 1 in.

Seat rails 5 in. by 1 in. and of the lengths shown should be tenoned into the legs, as at A in Figs. 16 and 20, and by the addition of a piece of three-ply B (Fig. 18) will form a box of the required size to take sheet music. Fig. 20 shows the rails $\frac{1}{10}$ in. back from the leg faces, and the internal angle of the leg chamfered off. Before the framework is finally put together, two circular-turned rails C (Figs. 17 19 and 21) should be fitted between the scroll ends of the legs, by means of small stubs turned on their ends

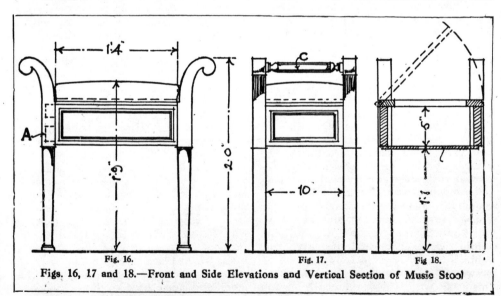

Figs. 16, 17 and 18.—Front and Side Elevations and Vertical Section of Music Stool

shakes. Two elevations and a section are shown by Figs. 16, 17 and 18.

The legs in the middle are finished about 1½ in. square. the bottom 12¾ in.

and fitted tightly into sockets bored in the legs.

A small bearer for the seat should be fixed at each end, as at D in Fig. 19, and its joint with the rail covered with a $\frac{1}{4}$-in. strip of mahogany E, with its front edge flush with the legs. The seat frame F is next made, and should have a small rebate as shown worked all round the outer edges to take the edge of the upholstering. The narrow strip left exposed below this should line with the strip E. Wood 2 in. by $\frac{3}{4}$ in. will serve for the seat frame, the joints of which are halved, glued, and screwed. English webbing should be

needle, using a suitable twine. The hair is covered with strong calico or canvas, tacked to the edges of the frame, a sheet of wadding laid over, and the final covering put on. Silk plush or Utrecht velvet is suitable for this. The tack heads are covered with a gimp to match, small-headed gimp pins being used. The underside of the seat should be covered with a twill lining material stretched lightly and tacked on.

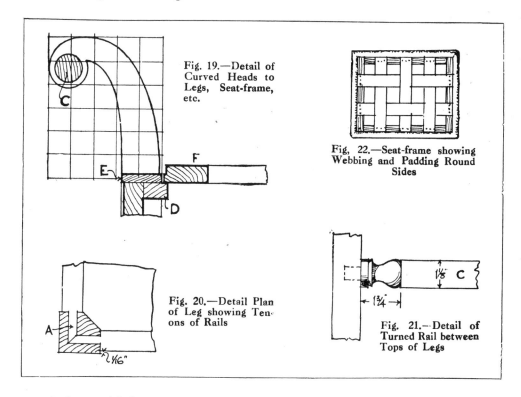

Fig. 19.—Detail of Curved Heads to Legs, Seat-frame, etc.

Fig. 22.—Seat-frame showing Webbing and Padding Round Sides

Fig. 20.—Detail Plan of Leg showing Tenons of Rails

Fig. 21.—Detail of Turned Rail between Tops of Legs

stretched as tightly as possible, and tacked on the upper side, as shown in Fig. 22. A good-quality canvas is then tightly stretched and tacked over the webbing, and a rib of 1-in. square wood screwed on all round for the padding. This is done by tacking a strip of canvas 4 in. wide round the outside of the frame, putting flocks on the rib, and covering with the canvas. This should be tacked to the inside of the rib, and stitched round with a 6-in. double-pointed upholsterer's

The seat should be fitted with brass hinges to one of the long rails, and should have a rule-joint stay inside. Lines of simple inlaid banding, as shown on the rails in Figs. 16 and 17, would be an improvement to the appearance of the stool.

ANOTHER MUSIC STOOL WITH BOX SEAT

Another box-seat music stool of a more refined design than the one just described.

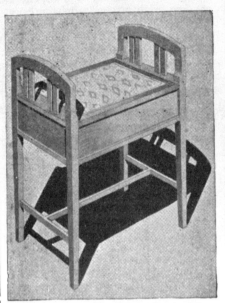

Fig. 23.—Another Music Stool with Box Seat

though of not quite such simple construction, is shown by the half-tone reproduction Fig. 23. It will not be necessary to detail the making of this stool for the working drawings and the preceding instructions will be found quite a sufficient guide. Fig. 24 shows a half elevation and half vertical section on the line A B

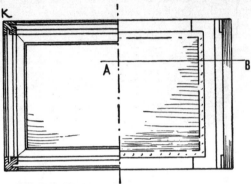

Fig. 25.—Half Horizontal Section and Half Plan of Music Stool

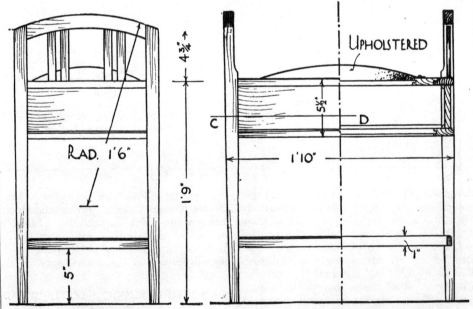

Fig. 26.—End Elevation of Music Stool

Fig. 24.—Part Elevation and Part Vertical Section of Music Stool

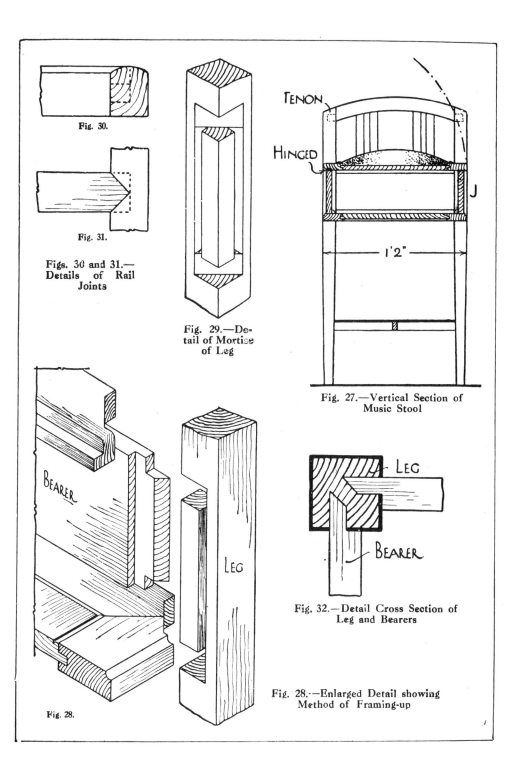

Fig. 30.

Fig. 31.

Figs. 30 and 31.—
Details of Rail
Joints

Fig. 29.—De=
tail of Mortise
of Leg

TENON

HINGED

J

1'2"

Fig. 27.—Vertical Section of
Music Stool

BEARER

LEG

Fig. 28.

LEG

BEARER

Fig. 32.—Detail Cross Section of
Leg and Bearers

Fig. 28.—Enlarged Detail showing
Method of Framing-up

of the plan (Fig. 25). This latter figure presents a half plan of the top, and a sectional half plan on the line C D of Fig. 24. An end elevation and a vertical cross section are shown by Figs. 26 and 27 respectively. Fig. 28 is an enlarged detail showing the method of framing up, whilst the method of mortising, etc., for the legs is shown by Fig. 29. Figs. 30 and 31 show in elevation and plan the joint of the rails at C (Fig. 24). An enlarged detail of the post K (Fig. 25) is shown by Fig. 32.

bench and the cheeks of the pedal board ; also allow 2½-in. projection at each end of the top outside the legs.

Set out the underside of the top for the legs, which may be trenched in to a depth of ⅛ in., glued, and nailed through from the upper side, or mortised and tenoned. The height of the seat also will be ruled to some extent by the make of pedal board ; about 1 ft. 10 in. will be found a convenient height, measuring from the centre " natural " of the pedals to the top of the bench, and allowing

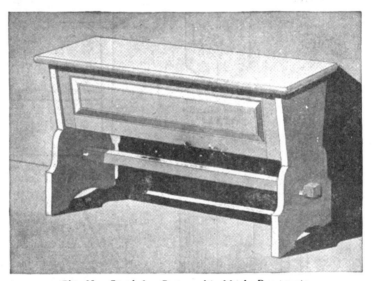

Fig. 33.—Stool for Organ with Music Receptacle

BENCH OR STOOL FOR ORGAN WITH MUSIC RECEPTACLE

An organ bench should be made of material to match the organ case or the surrounding furniture.

For the bench shown by Fig. 33. and in cross section by Fig. 34, first prepare the top, or seat, from 11-in. by 1¼-in. stuff, and the legs from 12-in. by 1¼-in. stuff. No length is given, as the measurement between the legs will vary according to the compass of the pedals and the style of pedal board ; but when the bench is placed in position there should be a clearance of ½ in. between the legs of the

extra length of leg from the top of the pedals to the floor. Mortise and tenon a rail. 2½ in. by 1½ in., to be fixed between the legs, the lower edge of the rail being 1 in. clear above the heel board of the pedals. The tenons of this rail may project through the legs and be pinned on the outside, as shown in Fig. 34. each edge of the rail should be slightly chamfered. The edges of the legs may be left square, chamfered, or moulded as desired.

The top or seat of the bench should be well rounded, especially at the edge facing the instrument, otherwise the edge of the seat would be an obstacle to the player whilst pedalling ; also round off each corner of the seat to a radius of about 1 in. Some players like the seat to be level, others prefer it to be slightly sloped to the instrument ; the slope, however, should not exceed $\frac{1}{2}$ in.

The music receptacle may be made as shown in Fig. 34, which is a cross section complete. The back and bottom of the receptacle may be of 9-in. by $\frac{1}{2}$-in. stuff, and the ends of 11-in. by $\frac{3}{4}$-in. stuff ; the front may be a plain 12-in by $\frac{3}{4}$-in.

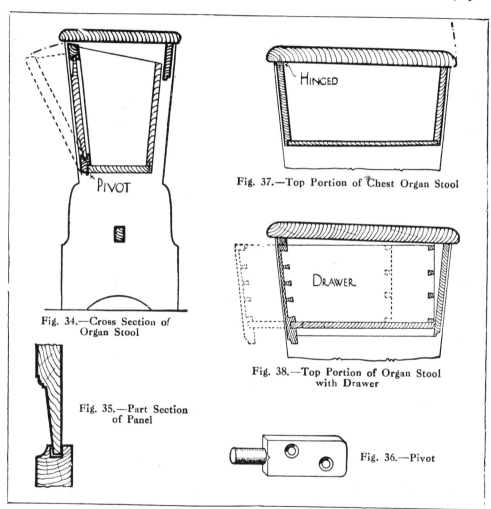

Fig. 34.—Cross Section of Organ Stool

Fig. 35.—Part Section of Panel

Fig. 37.—Top Portion of Chest Organ Stool

Fig. 38.—Top Portion of Organ Stool with Drawer

Fig. 36.—Pivot

from back to front. A board of $\frac{3}{4}$-in. stuff, moulded on the lower edge, should be trenched and glued between the legs on the side facing the instrument, as shown in Fig. 34 ; this board keeps the seat from sagging, and also prevents the bench from racking out of square.

board, or may be framed out of 1-in. stuff with a $\frac{3}{4}$-in. raised panel, as shown in detail in Fig. 35, the joints of the framing being mortised and tenoned or dowelled together. The front, back, and ends of the receptacle should be dovetailed together to make a strong job, the lower inside of the front being re-bated $\frac{1}{2}$ in. by $\frac{1}{2}$ in. to receive the bottom, which is screwed on from underneath. A division may also be put between the front and back of the receptacle in a position to suit the size of music books ; the division will also prevent the thin $\frac{1}{2}$-in. back bending or warping. Two metal pivots (Fig. 36) are fixed on the lower edge of the front, one at each end, holes being bored in the legs, on the inside, to receive the pivots. When fixing the receptacle in position, allow the front to set back $\frac{1}{4}$ in. from the edge of the bench legs. If preferred, between the legs of the bench a rail 2 in. by $1\frac{1}{4}$ in. may be fixed, to which the music re-ceptacle may be hinged with a pair of $2\frac{1}{2}$-in. brass butt hinges, and a spring catch or lock may be used as a fastening if desired.

Another plan for a music receptacle is shown by Fig. 37, and needs a wider seat, as the width inside the receptacle should be sufficient to accommodate full-size organ music when laid flat down-wards. For the sides between the legs of the bench, fix two 6-in. by $\frac{3}{4}$-in. boards, their lower edges being rebated to receive the bottom, which is of $\frac{1}{2}$-in. stuff. Also fix a bearer 1 in. thick between the back and front boards ; this bearer acts as a division for the music, and also supports the seat, which is cut in two at the centre, each half of the seat being hinged to the backboard with a pair of 2-in. brass butts.

Fig 38 shows an arrangement in which the bench is made with fast seat as in Fig. 33, but containing a drawer for the music underneath the seat. On the side of the bench farthest from the instrument, fix a frame to receive the drawer (which may be about 5 in. deep), the top rail of the frame being $1\frac{1}{4}$ in. deep and the bottom rail $1\frac{3}{4}$ in. deep. A small mould should be worked on the lower edge of the bottom rail. If two drawers are desired, a division 1 in. thick will be required. the division being brought flush

with the front of the drawer frame. The runners for the drawers may be screwed to the inside of the legs and to the division, the latter extending across the seat and being joined up to a board of 6-in. by $\frac{3}{4}$-in. stuff, which is fixed between the legs, as shown in Fig. 38. The drawers should be dovetailed together, and, if desired, the drawer fronts may be worked similar to the raised panel that is shown in Fig. 33.

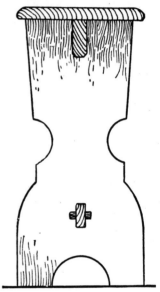

Fig. 39.—End Elevation of Organ Stool without Receptacle

ORGAN STOOL WITHOUT RECEPTACLE

Fig. 39 shows an end elevation of an organ stool constructed without any receptacle for music. This may be made on practically the same lines as the pre-ceding ones, but it should be provided with a centre rail of 4-in. by $1\frac{1}{2}$-in. stuff, fixed under the centre of the seat in place of the two undersides of the former examples. This rail is clearly shown in the figure.

Fancy Boxes

INLAID TRIPLE WORK-BOX

AN effective triple work-box inlaid in mother-of-pearl with ornamental brass hinges at the sides that enable it to

A very simple method of jointing together the corners of the trays is suggested, a skilled worker, however, being quite at liberty to adopt a more elaborate system.

A convenient size for the work-box

Fig. 1.—Inlaid Triple Work-box

open out into three trays is shown by Fig. 1. The box is shown open by Fig. 2, this illustration rendering clearly the working of the hinges, there being nothing in the construction of the box and hinges that an amateur could not undertake.

would be 10½ in. by 8½ in. by 7 in. deep, the trays measuring 2 in. deep in each case and the lid 1 in. deep. Mahogany or satin walnut would be the most suitable material for making the box, a thickness of ⅜ in. being required for the sides, and thinner material serving for the top of the box and the bottom of the trays.

Begin by preparing the material for the sides of the trays and lids. Cut six pieces measuring $8\frac{1}{2}$ in. by 2 in., six pieces $10\frac{1}{2}$ in. by 2 in., two pieces $8\frac{1}{2}$ in. by 1 in., and two $10\frac{1}{2}$ in. by 1 in., and plane up all carefully to the exact measurements. The corners are mitred together, the next item being therefore to plane them all to an angle of 45°, as shown by A (Fig. 3). Mark a line $\frac{3}{8}$ in. from one edge, and then carefully plane away the corner up to that line as indicated by B. Before joining together the corners it will be necessary to cut a rebate in the top and bottom of each piece forming the sides of the trays, so that they nicely fit into one another. Fig. 4 shows how the sides of the three trays are cut. A rebate is made in the top edge of each, measuring $\frac{1}{4}$ in. by $\frac{1}{4}$ in., and at the bottom on the inner face measuring $\frac{3}{8}$ in. by $\frac{1}{4}$ in., this being made a little deeper to allow for fitting in a bottom $\frac{1}{8}$ in. thick. An ordinary marking gauge, with the point substituted by a sharp cutter, will serve for cutting the rebates if one does not happen to possess a rebate plane. Clean up with a glass-paper block, slightly rounding off the tops as indicated. A similar rebate is cut in the sides of the lid, omitting, of course, to cut one round the top edges.

A simple method of jointing, and one that yields a good appearance if neatly done, is by keying the corners together (see Fig. 5). Two saw-cuts are made in each corner as indicated, then a strip of $\frac{1}{16}$-in. beech, coated with glue, is hammered in. In order to obtain a good fit of the trays, the complete article should be carefully squared up and tied together with strong string before the saw-cuts are made, the glued strips being then driven in and the work allowed to dry.

For the bottom of the trays prepare three pieces of $\frac{1}{8}$-in. fretwood measuring $10\frac{1}{4}$ in. by $8\frac{1}{4}$ in., and glue into the rebate at the bottom of each tray. A nice piece measuring $10\frac{1}{2}$ in. by $8\frac{1}{2}$ in. by $\frac{1}{4}$ in. should be prepared for the top, this not being glued in place until the small amount of inlaying has been done.

Fig. 6 gives the patterns of the hinges on an enlarged scale, the three parts being next drawn out to the required size. These are sawn out of brass of about the thickness of a sixpence, the little engraved work included in the design being done afterwards. Care must be taken that the screw-holes for fixing the hinge are set out in line (see Fig. 7) to ensure it working properly, it being observed that the greater the slope given to the plates the wider the trays will open. Having obtained a pattern on thin paper, paste on to the metal, and saw out with a fret-saw with fine teeth, truing up with a needle file on completion. When the engraving is completed run a little sealing-wax into the lines, and then clean up with fine emery-cloth and oil. The hinges are then fixed with $\frac{1}{4}$-in. large-headed screws, leaving enough play for the plates to easily move.

Fig. 8 gives the pattern of the mother-of-pearl fish which is inlaid in a piece of brass of elliptical form in the centre of the lid. Obtain a piece of brass about 3 in. by 2 in., and a piece of mother-of-pearl slightly smaller of the same thickness, and gum together with a piece of paper in between. The two materials are cut out at the same time, the pattern being pasted on the upper one. Thus, after sawing out, one will fit into the other when separated, if a vertical cut has been made all round. Mark out the form of the ellipse on the lid, and then cut to the same depth as the thickness of the brass, taking care, in chiselling out, to obtain a level bottom and a recess no deeper than the brass. Cement in with glue and whiting, then when dry level off. The two fish on the front of the trays are inlaid similarly, the patterns being given by Figs. 9 and 10.

Fig. 11 gives the pattern of the hinged clasp, the design of which is based on seaweed. For making this, a piece of metal measuring $4\frac{1}{2}$ in. by $1\frac{1}{2}$ in. will be necessary for the lower part, and a piece 4 in. by $\frac{3}{4}$ in. for the upper. For the hinge obtain a $1\frac{1}{4}$-in. length of small brass tubing, and solder to the edge of the upper half (Fig. 12). Divide this

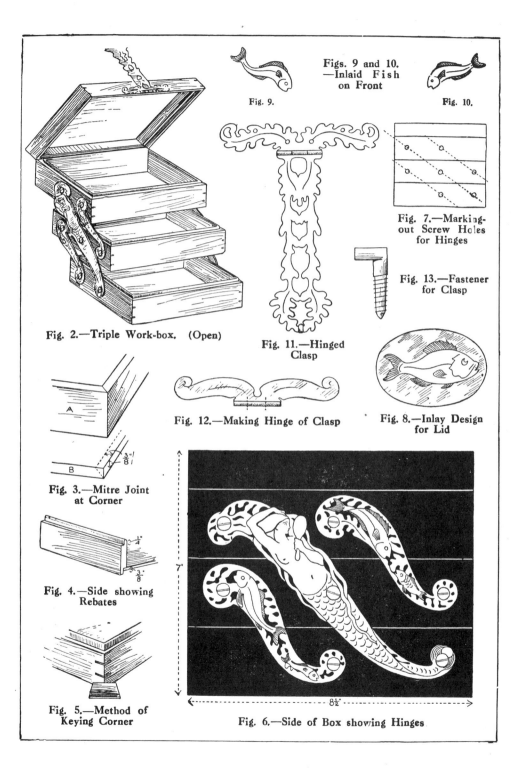

Figs. 9 and 10.
—Inlaid Fish
on Front

Fig. 9.

Fig. 10.

Fig. 7.—Marking-out Screw Holes for Hinges

Fig. 13.—Fastener for Clasp

Fig. 2.—Triple Work-box. (Open)

Fig. 11.—Hinged Clasp

Fig. 3.—Mitre Joint at Corner

Fig. 12.—Making Hinge of Clasp

Fig. 8.—Inlay Design for Lid

Fig. 4.—Side showing Rebates

Fig. 5.—Method of Keying Corner

Fig. 6.—Side of Box showing Hinges

into three, and then saw away the middle section as shown. This being soldered to the edge of the other section of the clasp and a pin put through the whole, the hinge is complete. Screw the upper plate to the lid with ¼-in. screws, and then file a screw, as shown by Fig. 13, for fastening the clasp, the screw being turned upwards when it is required to unfasten it.

Glue on the top of the lid, which is hinged with a pair of ¾-in. brass hinges, then the work-box is complete and ready for polishing.

VENEERED MAHOGANY WORK-BOX

The work-box illustrated by Fig. 14 has been designed with a view to showing a good application of veneering. It depends for its decoration on well-arranged figured veneers of contrasting colours. The interior of the box is shown in Fig. 15. A section and interior plan are given by Figs. 16 and 17.

As is indicated in the diagrams showing the arrangement of the top and sides (Figs. 18 and 19), the three veneers selected are : " well-figured Cuba mahogany " veneer, " curl " veneer, and " fiddle back." The curl veneer should be the darkest in colour, and the fiddle back the lightest. The various veneers vary in colour according to the age of the wood, and care must be exercised in the preliminary selection to ensure the necessary contrasts of colour. It is usual in first-class work of this character to accentuate or diminish the colours of the various veneers by slightly staining some before polishing the whole. To obtain a successful result, however, this must be done by an experienced polisher, as otherwise the sharpness of the design is likely to be spoiled. If the veneers are well chosen in the first instance, the finished job can be stained all over with bichromate of potash stain, which darkens all the veneers without making the lightest of them very dark in colour. As the effect so much depends on the relative colour values of the various veneers, it will be found a good plan to make up a small piece of veneering together with the box, which may be usefully experimented on before the box is stained and polished.

The interior of the box is fitted with a tray containing two spaces, one being fitted with a lid. The inside of the lid is intended to be padded with silk, the necessary thickness being made up with wadding, with the silk buttoned down at intervals to produce the cushioned effect. The main box or groundwork for the veneering is made with secret dovetailed corners, as is indicated in Fig. 20. It will be seen from A and B in Fig. 20 that a wide pin is introduced near the top. This is made larger, so that when the lid is cut away from the bottom part, the proper shoulder or half-pin is left on each part. The box sides, back, and front should be rebated at the bottom as indicated, in order to receive the bottom. This feature can also be introduced to advantage at the top in order to obviate the end grain for veneering on. When the parts have been dovetailed together and the insides cleaned up, the top and bottom should be fitted and glued in position. When thoroughly dry the whole is planed up perfectly square and true, and then toothed sized before veneering. The sizing can be done with weak glue well rubbed into the grain of the wood, using a short-haired glue-brush. When the size has quite dried, any excess should be removed by toothing down with a very fine toothing plane.

The next step is the preparation of the veneer (*see also* section on veneering), and it must be emphasised that veneers should be well shrunk before they are worked up and laid. Veneer is usually cut from solid wood in a more or less moist condition, in order to reduce the risk of splitting. Should the veneer not be well dried before laying, shrinkage takes place and shows itself by frequent cracks on the surface. This is particularly the case in regard to curl veneers, this particular kind shrinking a good deal. Many otherwise excellent pieces of furniture veneered with " curl " show cracks in the surface after a few months, and to prevent this shrinking before laying is absolutely essential. Curl and other figured veneers also require flatting, which is done at the same time as shrinking. It

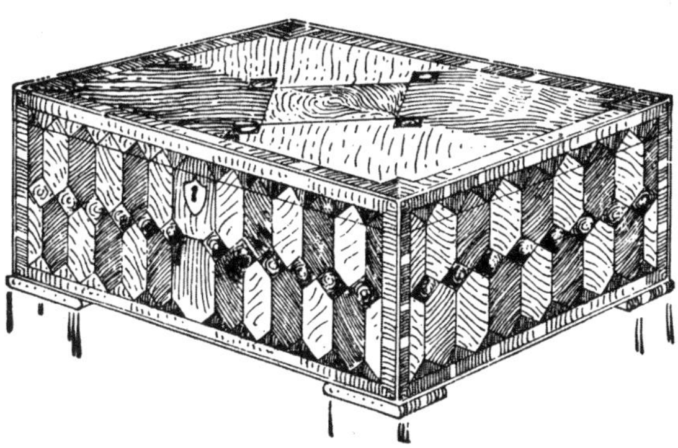

Fig. 14.—Veneered Mahogany Work-box

is a good plan to moisten the veneer first if it is very buckled in order to prevent splitting it when pressed flat. After the veneer is moistened in small sheets, $\frac{1}{2}$-in. pinewood pieces are made very hot on a plate or over a shaving blaze. The veneers are then placed between them, and the whole lightly hand-screwed together. This is repeated three or four times until all the moisture has been drawn out of the veneer, and it will be readily understood that the pressure and heat, in addition to properly shrinking the wood, will have made the veneer leaves absolutely flat. If the veneers are exposed to the air again they will have a tendency to buckle. To obviate this they should be laid on the bench with a covering board and a weight.

The veneers being properly prepared, the next step is to take the veneering in hand. Cartridge paper should first be damp-stretched on an old drawing or other flat board, a margin

about $\frac{1}{2}$ in. wide only being glued. When the paper has thoroughly dried, a line-drawing should be made of the top, sides, and front. A sharp, hard pencil should be used in order to ensure absolute accuracy. All the lines indicated in the parts should be shown with the exception of the $\frac{1}{8}$-in. edging. The crossbanding, it should be noted, should run to the extreme edges in the first instance. The line-drawings having been prepared, the lozenge-shaped pieces can be partly prepared by gauging off strips as indicated in B^1 in Fig. 21. A small mitre cut is then prepared as indicated in diagram D^1 in order to facilitate cutting the ends. The procedure necessary to complete the veneering is almost identical with the various parts.

As an example, the front will first be

Fig 15.—Box Open)

considered. A length of cross-banding should first be gauged off the fiddle-back veneer, mitred at each end, and then lightly glued down to the drawing.

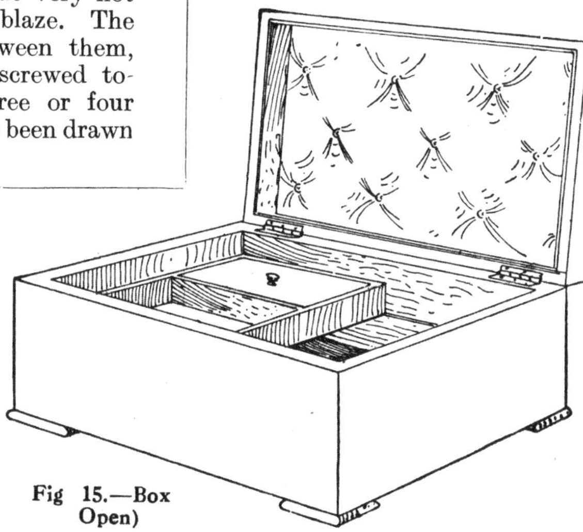

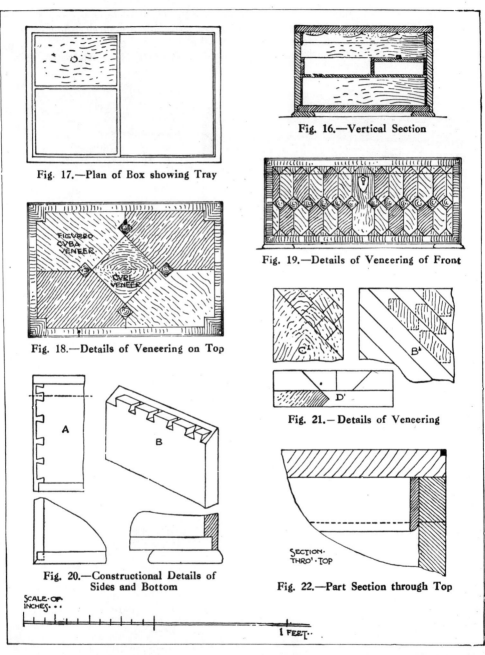

Fig. 17.—Plan of Box showing Tray

Fig. 16.—Vertical Section

Fig. 18.—Details of Veneering on Top

Fig. 19.—Details of Veneering of Front

Fig. 21.—Details of Veneering

Fig. 20.—Constructional Details of
Sides and Bottom

Fig. 22.—Part Section through Top

SCALE·OF·
INCHES· · ·

1 FEET·

Should it not be possible to obtain each length in one piece, butt-joints between various short pieces should be made with a very sharp chisel. Each piece is then glued down to the paper, and if the joints have been carefully made they will hardly show. Diagram c¹ in Fig. 21 indicates the preliminary step with regard to the small curl squares. The strips should be gauged off at an angle of 80° with the centre line of the curl, and then the squares can be gauged off to the exact size required. These pieces should all be marked, so that when glued down they will be in the same relative position as when in the leaf. A mixture of shades and colour is thus avoided. A half square is then prepared and glued in the corner. Then a half lozenge shape is fitted, if necessary, with a shoulder plane and shooting board to the exact shape. A whole square of curl is then glued down, and so on piece by piece until each side, etc., is finished. The work takes some time to complete, and when stood aside a board should be placed on the veneer in order to prevent possible buckling. When quite dry the paper is cut round and each design shows complete with paper on one side.

To veneer the box, one side is well glued, and after the glue has chilled, the veneer is pinned in position with the paper uppermost. A wooden caul is then heated and then cramped and hand-screwed down. Each veneered surface is treated in this way, and then all the paper is toothed off the veneer. The square edges are next inlaid by cutting small rebates to receive $\frac{1}{8}$-in. square lines. These should be glued in, and the box bound round with tape until the glue is dry.

After the box is thoroughly dry it should be scraped and properly glass-papered up prior to gauging and sawing off the lid. The edges are then planed to fit, and beads are fitted inside the lid as shown in the section through the top (Fig. 22), which ensures the surface of the box remaining exactly level when the lid is down.

Special hinges should be used to attach the lid. They are called box hinges, and allow the lid to fall back a little beyond the perpendicular. A box lock is next fitted, and then the feet. The escutcheon is intended to be cut out of either mother-of-pearl or ivory with a fret-saw, and then inlaid. The tray is quite simple in character, and may be slid from side to side on the thin fillets shown.

JEWEL-BOX AND HAND-MIRROR

The two half-tone reproductions (Figs. 23 and 24) show a jewel-box made in mahogany, inlaid with satinwood. Later the making of a hand-mirror to match this box is described.

The finished measurements of the box are $7\frac{1}{2}$ in. by $4\frac{1}{2}$ in. and $3\frac{1}{2}$ in. high. A part elevation and section of the box are shown by Fig. 25, and a plan by Fig. 26. The four sides are of $\frac{3}{8}$-in. thick mahogany and the top and bottom of $\frac{1}{4}$ in. For the sides, a piece is prepared in one length 2 ft. by $2\frac{1}{4}$ in., and on each long edge a slip of the sycamore is glued, to be finished to $\frac{1}{8}$ in., which will make the sides $2\frac{1}{2}$ in. wide. When the piece is cleaned up on both sides and evenly thicknessed and the edges planed straight to the correct width it may be marked across square for the four box sides, which may then be cut. They are to be dovetailed together in the way known as " mitre-dovetail " or " secret-dovetail." In this case, it is as if the wood box sides were of $\frac{1}{4}$ in. thickness, ordinary dovetailed and covered on the outside with wood of $\frac{1}{8}$ in. thickness, mitred at the corners. But it is worked in the solid as in making lap dovetails, with the laps $\frac{1}{8}$ in. over to be mitred. If the setting out is done correctly, there need be little chance of failure ; but, of course, neat fitting is indispensable. The cross marks shown in Fig. 28A (p. 1047) indicate waste, and the dotted lines show where the box will have to be cut through to form the lid, which it is necessary to consider in setting out the dovetail pins.

When the joints are all made, they may be glued up, and after observing that it is quite square and true, may be left in a very dry place to set. In the meantime the bottom and top of $\frac{1}{4}$-in. thick mahogany must be prepared. They are glued in place and secured with screws ($\frac{3}{4}$-in. No. 4), three to each edge, the heads being countersunk flush with the bottom ; but sunk $\frac{1}{16}$ in. below the surface of the top, in view of the satin-wood banding which has to be inlaid round the margin, and covers the screws.

The centre of the lid is inlaid with a

Fig. 23.—Jewel-box (Closed)

fan-oval ornament of satinwood and green sycamore. This and the banding are stock patterns, which can be bought for so small a sum that it would not pay to make one. It is shown in Fig. 26. The banding is inlaid first, by making a cut with the cutting gauge $\frac{1}{8}$ in. on the margin and $\frac{1}{16}$ in. deep, and another $\frac{3}{8}$ in. (the width of the banding) inside it. The waste between is then pared out and scraped level with a $\frac{1}{4}$-in. chisel, to allow the banding to lie in quite neatly and nearly level, the corners being cut to a mitre. For inlay work it is essential to have the glue in good working condition ; it should be hot, strong and thin enough to run freely. It is also an advantage to warm the work. The glue is run plentifully into the groove, and the banding laid in quickly and pressed down with a suitable flat iron or other weight to squeeze out the glue. It is advisable to keep going over it until no part shows any tendency to rise.

The fan-oval may then be inlaid. It has paper glued over it at one side to keep it together and this must be the outside. To get it true in position, the lid should be pencil-lined lengthwise and across the centre, to correspond with the lines on the oval, as shown in Fig. 26, therefore it must be marked on the paper

side. Whilst being held in position, it is marked round with the sharp point of a knife, then cut to about $\frac{1}{16}$ in. deep, and the waste pared away as was done for the banding. When it is ready for gluing in, the place for it should be warmed and glued, and the paper side of the oval wetted with hot water and immediately placed in and pressed with the hammer to work out the superfluous glue. In doing this the paper gets rubbed off. and sometimes some of the sections have an inclination to rise ; but it must be persevered with, and it might be necessary to place over it a piece of paper, then a well-heated flat piece of wood cramped or weighted down. After about ten hours' rest in a dry, warm place to set, the wood may be removed ; but the inlay should be allowed as much time as convenient to set—at least several days—before being cleaned up with the steel scraper and glasspaper.

When this is done the square corners should be rounded off with the glass-paper wrapped over a cork rubber ; then the sides may be marked $\frac{5}{8}$ in. from the top surface, and cut through square and

Fig. 24.—Jewel-box (Open)

true with a fine saw, to form the lid. The sawn edges will require lightly plan-ing, and the lid can be hinged with box-hinges, so that it can only open upright and cannot fall back. The lock also can be put on, and an oval of satinwood is let in at the key-hole.

Under the bottom, slips are put on, to stand forward about ⅛ in. as a beading.

They are of 1-in. by $\frac{3}{16}$-in. section, mitred at the corner and fixed in place with glue and screws. Under these at each corner ball feet of brass are screwed on (*see* Fig. 25). The box should now be rubbed

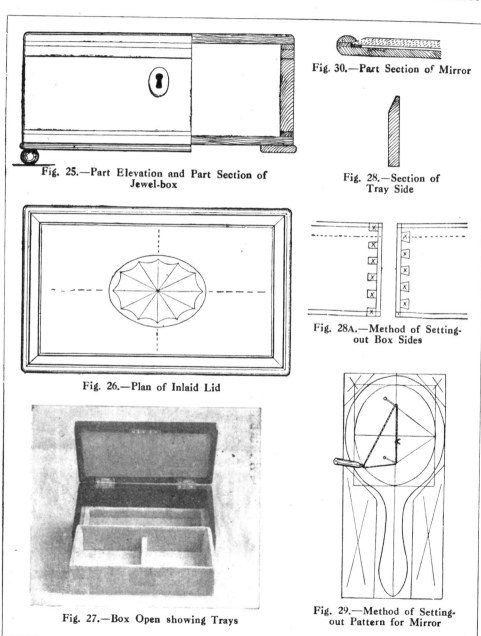

Fig. 25.—Part Elevation and Part Section of Jewel-box

Fig. 30.—Part Section of Mirror

Fig. 28.—Section of Tray Side

Fig. 26.—Plan of Inlaid Lid

Fig. 28A.—Method of Setting-out Box Sides

Fig. 27.—Box Open showing Trays

Fig. 29.—Method of Setting-out Pattern for Mirror

all over with linseed oil, and left a few days to dry in, when it can be french-polished.

The box is fitted with two trays, as shown in Fig. 27, lined with a good quality grey velvet. The bottom tray is $\frac{1}{2}$ in. deep, and the other one rests on it, and of accurate depth so that the velvet-covered sides stand up about $\frac{1}{4}$ in. higher than the mahogany box sides to go up into the lid, which also is to be lined on the underside. The upper tray is made to fit fairly close so as to seem permanent and keep the lower place secret; but by a steady pull gripping the centre division piece it can be lifted out (see Fig. 27). It cannot be pulled out hurriedly on account of the vacuum. The velvet inside the lid when closed presses over the edges of the tray, keeping it dustproof and practically airtight. The bottom tray is composed of four slips of wood, $\frac{3}{8}$ in. by $\frac{1}{4}$ in. in section, for the sides and a bottom of thin stiff cardboard. The velvet is glued on before they are fixed together with fine wire nails. The method is to cut the cardboard for the bottom, and fit in the slips of wood, allowing for the thickness of the velvet, which may then be cut for each piece. For the slips it must be cut about $1\frac{1}{4}$ in. wide and about 1 in. over long. To fix it, the slips should be glued on the under edge and inner side, and the velvet put on; then they may be fixed together with the fine pins or nails. The velvet must be glued on the cardboard bottom the net size, and it may be fixed on with $\frac{3}{8}$-in. fine wire nails. The outer sides of the slips may then be glued and the velvet drawn over, neatly fitting it at the corners and clipping off the surplus, except the over-width, which must be glued under the bottom. It should fit in place fairly tight, unless it is intended for lifting out. In that case it should be slightly loose, and would require a silk-ribbon loop at the centre of each end by which to raise it; the loop may be fixed by gluing on the bottom. To give a finished appearance to the bottom, it may be covered with velvet or paper.

With the other tray, the short sides are $\frac{1}{4}$ in. thick, with the top edge bevelled on the inner side to $\frac{1}{8}$ in. (see Fig. 28). The long sides are $\frac{1}{8}$ in. thick, and the bottom of cardboard. The method of making the tray is the same as for the bottom one, the division piece being put in and fixed just before the outer sides are glued for drawing over the velvet. For the lid a piece of cardboard is cut, allowing for the velvet to turn over the edges, to be glued on the back about $\frac{1}{2}$ in., and it is glued in place. The trays should be allowed plenty of time in a dry place for the glue to dry thoroughly and the box may have the fittings put on and the polishing finished.

To make the mirror, first a piece of cardboard should be obtained and cut to a true oblong 12 in. by $5\frac{1}{2}$ in., to make a pattern. On this, a pencil line is made lengthwise and one across, dividing the space into four equal parts. A true oval (ellipse, strictly speaking) is then struck out on one half of the cardboard, the diameters being $5\frac{1}{2}$ in. by $4\frac{1}{2}$ in. To do this, an oblong that size should be first marked out, with lines across dividing it into four smaller ones to find the centres. The best way to describe the ellipse is by means of three pins, a piece of string and a pencil (see Fig. 29). To ascertain the exact points for the two pins shown, take half of the length-wise diameter line, which will be $2\frac{1}{4}$ in., and two lines that length may be ruled from the end of the short diameter line as shown. At that point a third pin may be inserted for the purpose of tying the piece of string so as to bring it to the right tension. Another oval is made $\frac{1}{2}$ in outside, which is to be the outline of the frame; and the handle may be drawn freehand or with the compasses. The other lines shown mark the waste (indicated by cross marks), which may be cut away. With a sharp-pointed knife, the inner oval should be cut out clean and true, the waste piece to be given as a template in ordering the bevelled silvered plate to be made to it.

The other part is the pattern for the woodwork, but is not yet cut to the

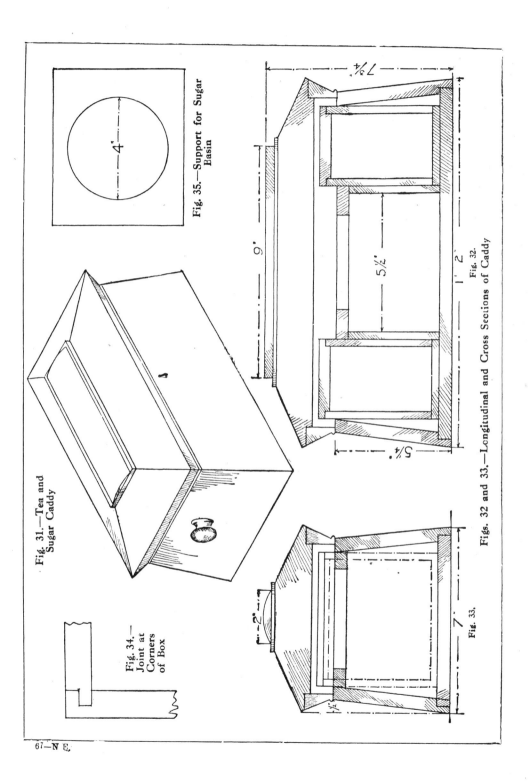

Fig. 35.—Support for Sugar Basin

Fig. 31.—Tea and Sugar Caddy

Fig. 34.—Joint at Corners of Box

Figs. 32 and 33.—Longitudinal and Cross Sections of Caddy

Fig. 32.

Fig. 33.

true outline. Three pieces of wood are now required to be cut to the roughed-out outline of the pattern. Two of them must be of mahogany fully $\frac{3}{16}$ in. in thickness, and one of sycamore $\frac{1}{8}$ in. thick, all to be planed straight and even to lie together as close as possible. The sycamore may then have the oval cut out with a fret-saw, neatly to take the glass. It is then glued to one of the pieces of mahogany, and it is advisable to cramp it well to a level piece of board.

The other piece of mahogany must have the oval cut out $\frac{1}{8}$ in. inside the line, as it has to be glued on the front of the sycamore when the glass is in place to cover the edge of the bevel all round. When it is cut, it must be trimmed and neatly rounded with the spokeshave and glasspaper, and the rounded edge should be rubbed with a linseed-oil rag, and polished, as it is much easier to do now than when in place on the front of the glass.

The cardboard pattern for the glass should be taken and $\frac{1}{4}$-in. strip cut off all round the edge in one piece. This is to be placed in behind the glass to form an air space and keep it from the wood, to prevent any chance of rubbing. The mahogany front may then be tried in place to see that it fits quite well, and is glued and cramped as before.

Several days in a dry place should be allowed to set, and the cardboard pattern may be cut to the correct outline from which to mark, the wood being then cut out with the fret-saw and nicely rounded with the spokeshave to the section shown by Fig. 30. When smoothed up with No. 2 and No. 1 glasspaper it is ready for polishing.

TEA AND SUGAR CADDY

The caddy shown by Figs. 31 to 33 should be made either of oak, mahogany, or black walnut.

The box is made of $\frac{1}{2}$-in. material, with the sides sloping inwards, as shown in Fig. 32. The corner joints are tongued and grooved as in Fig. 34. The sides are rebated to take the bottom board,

which is fitted between. Before the box is glued together, two small stop grooves are cut in the front and in the back pieces. These grooves are for the two $\frac{1}{4}$-in. partitions, between which the tea boxes slide (see Fig. 32). Allowance of $\frac{3}{8}$ in. is made on the top of these partitions for the piece into which the sugar basin fits (see Fig. 35). The corners of the box should be glued and cramped, then the partitions slid in from underneath. The bottom should then be glued and bradded.

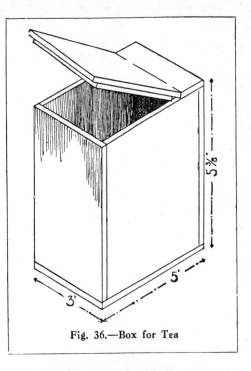

Fig. 36.—Box for Tea

When the glue is dry the sides should be smoothed and glasspapered.

A cross section of the lid is shown in Fig. 33. The mounted top is made with the rebate plane, the rounded piece being glued upon the top. The lid is also bevelled and rebated underneath to take the framed fillet that fits over the inner boxes. This framed fillet is first mitred, then beaded and bevelled with the bead and rebate planes ; it is then glued and bradded. The lid is fixed with brass butt hinges.

The boxes for the tea and sugar are shown in Fig. 36. They are made of ¼-in. material, and are made to slide in. The corners are neatly bradded, the lids being fixed with very small brass hinges. If a lock is required, it should be fixed before the piece (Fig. 35) is fixed. A turned knob is screwed on each of the simply as antiques ; but something better than a mere box can be made of them. They vary in style and are well made, the workmanship far surpassing the present-day machine production, and in most cases are worth restoring. The bands and lines of those that are veneered can often be matched, and if the veneer

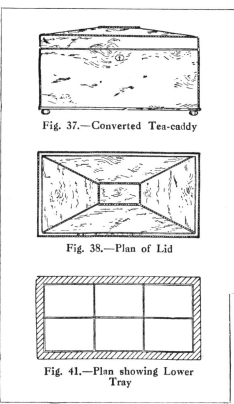

Fig. 37.—Converted Tea-caddy

Fig. 38.—Plan of Lid

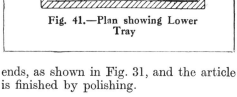

Fig. 41.—Plan showing Lower Tray

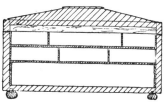

Fig. 39.—Vertical Section showing Partitions

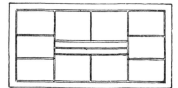

Fig. 40.—Plan showing Upper Tray

ends, as shown in Fig. 31, and the article is finished by polishing.

CONVERTING OLD TEA-CADDY INTO JEWEL-CASE

Old tea-caddies such as that shown in elevation and plan by Figs. 37 and 38 are now more often kept as ornaments than used for the purpose for which they were originally intended. Where the interiors are damaged, or the cut-glass sugar basin is missing, they are not worth preserving

is not worth patching, a whole side is a small matter to renew. No attempt should be made to add feet where the original had none, or an extra bead to "improve" it.

The work of restoring a veneered caddy is far easier than one would anticipate. Sometimes they are found covered with dirt, and not even the kind of wood can be recognised ; but a judicious use of soap and water will often bring to light a piece of workmanship that very little beyond furniture cream is required to revive. At other times perhaps a coat of varnish has to be removed before the grain of the wood is discovered. Generally the french-polish must be cleaned off, and this may be done with a pad of calico soaked in methylated spirit. Having removed the polish, go over all the angle bands and remove any that are loose, scraping off the old glue before re-gluing. Cut lengths to fit in the spaces where any are missing. These joints should be cut slightly on the bevel to make a neat joint. Any veneer that is loose should be re-glued, and small damaged places cut out and re-instated with wood to match as nearly as possible. Should the wood be dark mahogany, a solution of permanganate of potash and water will often produce the required tint. Both the bands and the veneer with which the restoration is done will be thicker than the old work, and will no doubt appear to be a very patch-work job at first; but after the glue has been left to harden for a day, the use of a steel scraper will soon produce an even surface, which can be finished with fine glasspaper, and prepared for repolishing.

Some caddies have an interlining and partitions mitred at the corners and just slipped in. This is most useful when it is to be converted into a jewel-case, for two pieces 1 in. wide cut off all round form the sides for the two trays (see Figs. 39, 40 and 41). These should be reduced sufficiently to allow the trays to slip in with ease. For the bottom of the trays, thicker wood should be used; that sold for fretwork is very suitable. The partitions for the trays are of the thin wood, and fitted with a V-joint and glued. When the tray is completed the top edges should be rounded with fine glasspaper, and then french-polished. The outsides of the tray should also receive a few coats of polish. Make another lining of the thicker wood, and fit into the bottom to support the trays. The top tray will rest on the lower one. Treat the lower lining and bottom in a similar way to the outside of the trays before putting in. It is better than lining with material, and makes a neater finish.

The lining for the compartments of the trays should be of velvet; dark green is one of the best colours for the purpose. First cut out pieces of brown paper as shown, and these should be slightly smaller than will cover the space, as the velvet takes up some of the room. Cut the velvet in squares slightly larger than the paper. Glue the paper, and press the velvet on it. When dry cut out the pieces not required, and glue down the edge that is turned over. At the same time they may be creased to form little boxes, slightly glued round the top edges, and put into position. The compartments for rings are made with similar paper. Two rolls are covered with velvet, and pressed into each space; these should be just firm enough to hold the rings securely. Keep the velvet slightly below the top of each space, so that a small edge of wood is visible.

THREE SMALL FANCY BOXES

The three small boxes illustrated in the photographic reproductions (Figs. 42, 43 and 44) are made up from scraps of mahogany $\frac{1}{4}$ in. thick. They are just the kind of receptacles ladies delight in for stowing away their trinkets and the other small objects—hairpins, hat-pins, etc.

The oblong box (Fig. 42) measures $10\frac{1}{2}$ in. long by $3\frac{1}{4}$ in. wide, and its height is $3\frac{3}{8}$ in. As it is covered with fabric there is no need for dovetailing the angles. They are put together with glue and long brass pins. Iron pins are a mistake for work of this kind, because in time their heads rust, and rusty marks are communicated to the fabric. The lid, which overhangs some $\frac{3}{16}$ in. all round, has the edges bevelled. The covering fabric is old brocade in pink and silver. Owing to the thickness of the material it is rather intractable, but the difficulty may be got over in the following way: A length of material is cut in one piece to cover all four sides, with an overlap of $\frac{1}{4}$ in. at the top and bottom. This is glued on, the glue being used sparingly, so as to preclude the possibility of any of it coming through the silk. The one vertical joint is at one of the back angles, where the overlapping piece is turned in and glued down, thus making it safe against fraying.

The overlap at the bottom is glued down, pieces being taken out at each corner to make it sit snugly, and over all is glued a piece of billiard cloth. The overlap at the top is dealt with as follows : Along the centre of each edge of the side boards a saw-cut ¼ in. deep is made, as shown in Figs. 45 and 46. Glue is worked

Fig. 42.—Box Covered with Silk Brocade

into these saw-cuts with a knife, and the material is then forced down into them, using the blade of a penknife. The result is as shown in Fig. 46. Before covering the lid, a piece of springy wool serge, as used for curtains is cut to the size defined by the inner edges of the bevels and glued in place, after which the brocade covering is applied and stretched over the serge and bevels, and carried under the lid, where it is glued down, ½-in. overlap having been allowed for the purpose. The underside of the lid is then lined with white silk, the edges of the latter being turned under. The best way to manage this lining is to paste the silk to a piece of thin card or stout paper, cut to the desired size, and to turn the margin over all round and paste it down to the other side of the backing. When the paste is dry the lining may be glued in place.

The box and lid having been covered with brocade, the latter is secured to the former with two small brass hinges. A clasp fastening is made from stout brass wire in the form shown by Fig. 47, and a small plate with central stud is fixed to the front of the box and adjusted so that the clasp will snap over it. The wires are soft-soldered together.

The inside of the box is left with the mahogany surface untreated ; but if desired it might be enamelled white. In decorating boxes with applied fabric, the great point is to see that there are no loose ends or edges that may become frayed, otherwise with very little use they develop into unsightly wrecks.

The box (Fig. 43) is made in the following manner : The bottom is cut to shape, the front and back edges being arcs of a circle (see Fig. 48). The sides are cut so that the grain of the wood should run vertically, which facilitates the bending of the two which form back and front. These are soaked in hot water, and then glued and nailed in place. The ends are then added, and lastly the top, so that at this stage the box is entirely closed. All surfaces are made smooth with glass-paper, the corners being rounded. The top is pared away

Fig. 43.—Box with Inlaid Miniature

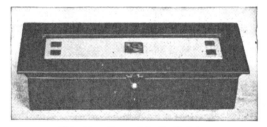

Fig. 44.—Box with Shell Inlay

with the chisel to give it a certain amount of convexity, a central space being left flat for the miniature and its frame (see Fig. 49). Then a gauge line is run round at a point where the lid is to be separated from the box proper, and the line cut through with the dovetail saw.

As the lid is not to be hinged, it is necessary to add a lining to the box part, which should stand up above the line of separation of the box and lid.

The measurements of the box are 6½ in. long by 3¼ in. wide at the widest part,

put in in four pieces, those conforming to the curved sides first, and those for the two ends afterwards. Fig. 48 shows these details.

At this stage the polishing of the box may be undertaken. It only remains to add the miniature. The frame is turned from a ring of ivory. Miniature and glass are secured to the frame by

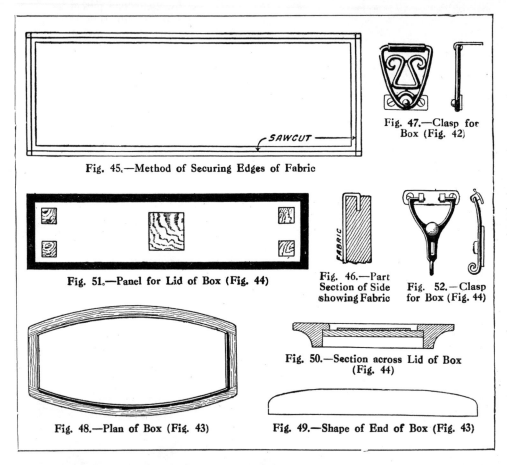

Fig. 47.—Clasp for Box (Fig. 42)

Fig. 45.—Method of Securing Edges of Fabric

Fig. 51.—Panel for Lid of Box (Fig. 44)

Fig. 46.—Part Section of Side showing Fabric

Fig. 52.—Clasp for Box (Fig. 44)

Fig. 50.—Section across Lid of Box (Fig. 44)

Fig. 48.—Plan of Box (Fig. 43)

Fig. 49.—Shape of End of Box (Fig. 43)

the ends narrowing down to 2⅜ in. The depth of the box is 2 in. Sizes, however, are not material, as dimensions can be adopted which may suit the purpose for which the box is intended. The lining stands ¼ in. above the top edge of the box, and is made of two thicknesses of stout mahogany veneer glued together. The grain runs vertically. The lining is

gluing a circle of Bristol board over the back of the frame, the rebate of which is made of such a depth as to ensure the back of the miniature standing flush with the back of the frame. The frame then is sunk in the cavity already made for it and secured with glue. It will always be found that the lid fits the box best when it is put on in the way it stood when the box and lid were in one piece. It is well, therefore, to add some little mark to the box and the lid as a guide to their proper relationship. Two small black dots would suffice, or a small ornamental device might be painted on the front of the box and the lid, say in gold-size, and gold-leaf applied.

The bottom of the box should be covered with billiard cloth. It gives a good finish and prevents scratches to table tops.

The box shown by Fig. 44 is $8\frac{3}{8}$ in. by $2\frac{3}{8}$ in. by $1\frac{5}{8}$ in. deep externally, exclusive of the lid, which, it will be seen, overhangs considerably. The box and lid in this case are made separately. The former is put together with glue and pins, and all four sides are brought to a fair surface. The lid is framed together by mitreing. A length of mahogany strip $\frac{13}{16}$ in. by $\frac{1}{2}$ in. is prepared to the section shown in Fig. 50. This is cut to the proper lengths, and the mitres are joined with glue without nails. Then a panel is prepared. This measures 8 in. by $2\frac{1}{4}$ in. (the inside dimensions of the box). The opening left after mitreing the four pieces of the lid measures $7\frac{1}{2}$ in. by $1\frac{11}{16}$ in. A piece of stout mahogany veneer is cut $\frac{1}{4}$ in. less in length and width than this opening, and glued down on the prepared panel. This is shown in Figs. 50 and 51.

The decoration of this panel consists in inlaying five squares of polished shell. The pieces of shell are rubbed flat on a Washita stone, and to the same thickness as the veneer. They are then shaped with the file until truly square, after which their outlines are scribed out on the surface of the veneer, the pattern being as shown in Fig. 51, and the shapes so defined are cut away, the veneer only

being removed. The further treatment of the panel consists in french-polishing the veneered portion to a dull silvery lustre, by using aluminium powder with the polish in the manner already described, but using white polish. This does not work quite so well as the ordinary french-polish, and some degree of practice is required to get a good surface with the aluminium powder. The process is facilitated, however, by dusting the surface of the panel with the powder after applying the polish, removing all loose powder, and then polishing it over a second time. When a satisfactory result is attained the squares of shell may be glued into their respective cavities.

The lid is secured with two small brass hinges. The catch employed is shown by Fig. 52. It is cut from sheet brass, and a bead of silver is soldered in.

There is an infinite amount of scope for the tasteful treatment of these little boxes. The coloured lacquer effect can be varied as regards tint by using various dry pigments with the french-polish, and designs in gold or aluminium leaf may be added to the polished surfaces. If Japanese patterns be used, the resemblance to actual lacquer work may be made very close. There are many classes of objects which may be applied by way of decoration, amongst which may be mentioned cameos, carvings in ivory, small oil paintings, pierced metal-work (watch clocks and the like), semi-precious stones like onyx, agate, cornelian and jade, with or without metal settings. Also such objects as butterflies' wings, snake and lizard skins, amber, tortoise-shell and even fancy hardwoods may be worked in.

Screens

ANCIENT AND MODERN SCREENS

THE study of screens from an historic standpoint is an interesting one, especially with regard to those of Eastern origin, notably those of China and Japan. Fine examples of the latter are much sought after and command high prices.

The origin of Chinese lacquer is veiled in an obscure antiquity. It differs essentially from European or American systems of lacquering, which consist really of varnishing, a copal varnish being made of resin, oils and turpentine. Chinese lac is the natural product of the lac tree, which was, and still is, cultivated to a great extent in China for this particular purpose. The processes connected with lacquering of the best kind are really combinations of "gesso" work and coach painting by the

Fig. 1.—Example of Japanese Lacquered Screen

old method, when several coats of paint and varnish were applied and frequently rubbed down in order to produce a beautifully smooth and glossy surface. The groundwork of lacquer work is usually cypress wood. This wood is particularly suitable for this class of work; being free from knots and shakes, it stands well and is fairly even grained. In preparing the groundwork, any small cracks or interstices are filled in with a preparation, and then rubbed down smooth. Then the lacquer is coloured in order to give it rather more body. Paper was usually then applied and coated with a mixture of burnt clay and varnish which was rubbed down with a whetstone and effectually "filled," the groundwork providing a suitable non-absorbent basis for the application of the several succeeding coats of lacquer.

A design is then prepared by the artist, who transfers it in outline to the groundwork. This design is usually intended to be a slight relief similarly to ordinary "gesso" work, and the processes involved are almost identical to those employed by ordinary "gesso" workers. For lacquer work, a preparation is made of lacquer with added ingredients to give it still more body, and this is carefully coated on to the parts requiring relief. Several coats have to be applied according to the modelled effect desired, and the several coats are, of course, allowed to dry before another is proceeded with.

With real lacquer work a rather laborious process is then proceeded with, namely, the preparation of a suitably hard and smooth surface for the reception of the painting or gilding, which is usually such a fine feature of lacquered work. One coat of lacquer is applied, and when quite dry and hard it is carefully rubbed down with fine powder and rags until but little remains. Another coat is then applied and treated similarly. It will be understood that this part of the work is on exactly the same lines as fine carriage painting, or french-polishing, and like both of these processes, a successful result depends largely on the amount of rubbing down practised. Whilst Chinese lac is the oldest and preceded the Japanese lac, the latter is considered the finer of the two.

One such example of modern work is shown by Fig. 1. This was shown in the last Japan-British exhibition, and may be considered a representative example of modern Japanese craftsmanship in lacquer work. The framing and groundwork are made of a kind of cedar wood (jindai-sugi), and the surfaces of the faults are rubbed down with wet straw and fine sand, so as to leave the harder parts of the grain standing in relief. One side only of the screen is decorated. A cock and hen, chickens, chrysanthemums and other flowers enter into the composition, all being in relief and beautifully executed. The majority of the decorations is composed of gold, silver and other metals, mother-of-pearl, coral and

richly gilt lacquer. The chief feature is, of course, the incrustations; but it should be mentioned that lacquer work forms a part of the decoration, and in addition the whole is finished with transparent lacquer finely applied.

A modern screen based on the Louis XVI. period is shown by Fig. 2. It is intended to be executed either in carved mahogany or enamelled white. The construction in both cases is identical, and does not call for any very special comment. To take the centre frame, it may be said that the middle rail is rebated on both edges to receive the glass and wood panels. The sectional view at A (Fig. 3) shows the section of the fluting. A recessing is also indicated at B, which would run along all the stiles and rails, this detail considerably lightening the appearance of the work. At the top an elliptical panel is introduced, which should be executed in two-ply wood in order to obviate shrinkage. The side panels are fairly simple, and in this connection it should be said that the curved top rails should be cut from the solid and tenoned into the stiles in the same way as the bottom rails. In the top parts of the side frames are introduced decorative bars, which should be cut out from a previously prepared cross shape, and then carved up to the design shown. A good plan is to fix two slats or bars into the top opening of the frame, showing about $\frac{1}{2}$ in. on the front, and set back a sufficient distance from the front face to allow the carved cross shape to be inserted. All the top panels are intended to be of glass, and the latter should preferably be patent rolled plate, about $\frac{1}{8}$ in. thick.

A section of the bead is given at C (Fig. 3). The straight ones would, of course, be worked in lengths, and the best plan for the curved ones would be to cut them out of the solid and mould on the spindle machine. This would also apply to the elliptical-shape bead necessary for the centre frame, and to facilitate fitting the ellipse should be made in two parts, and joined at the top and bottom. The head-piece of the centre frame could be fretcut in three parts, and secured to the rail by means of very small dowels. In the case of white enamelled work, this head-piece could be made of compo., which would be much more economical and easier to fix. All the bottom panels are intended to be of silk, and if these were required in any quantity they could be specially made to any design. Plain and then attached. Composition patera could, of course, be employed in the case of white enamelled work.

Gilt screens are a special feature of the Louis XVI. period, and the design indicated would prove effective if finished in gold leaf. The usual thing is to execute the flat parts in dull gold leaf,

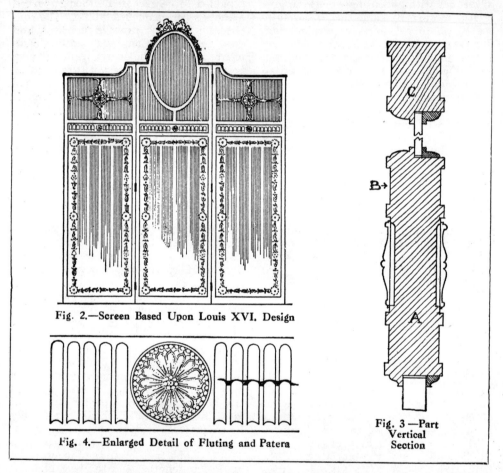

Fig. 2.—Screen Based Upon Louis XVI. Design

Fig. 4.—Enlarged Detail of Fluting and Patera

Fig. 3 —Part Vertical Section

silk or taffeta could be used, but for Louis XVI. work, it is thought that a special design should be prepared based upon the bordered example shown by Fig. 3.

Fig. 4 shows a detail of the fluting and the patera, the former of which should be carved out of the solid. and the latter should be turned and carved separately and the high parts are burnished to produce a necessary contrast.

Fig. 5 illustrates a three-fold screen based on work of the Louis XV. period. More curves are introduced into this example, and a little ingenuity will suggest additional frames to extend the screen if necessary to four or more frames.

The best method of connecting the top rail of the centre frame is shown in Fig. 6. The rails and stiles should be mortised and tenoned together, and when glued up and dry, the proper curves can be transferred to the top and bottoms and the shapes cut out. Moulding the inside round should next be proceeded with, care being taken that the moulding is stopped to allow for the necessary carvings at intervals. The joint neces-

out that their beads can be built up with veneer, which may be made fairly flexible by slightly warming ; or as an alternative cane beads, which are capable of being easily fixed to the curves, can be introduced.

The silk panels in this example are intended to be of ordinary material, and if a striped pattern of good colouring and design, as indicated, can be obtained, a good effect is produced whether the frames

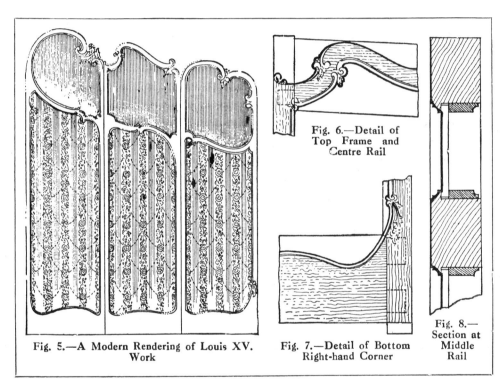

Fig. 5.—A Modern Rendering of Louis XV. Work

Fig. 6.—Detail of Top Frame and Centre Rail

Fig. 7.—Detail of Bottom Right-hand Corner

Fig. 8.— Section at Middle Rail

sary for the bottom right-hand corner of the outside frame is shown in Fig. 7. The curve at the bottom necessitates a mitre joint inside to the shoulder. If nicely executed, it will be found that the inside edge can then be moulded and carved without any danger of the cross grain chipping out. The section shown by Fig. 8 indicates the middle rail, and the bead indicated is intended to be cut from the solid similarly to the earlier example. It should, however, be pointed

are of mahogany or white enamelled wood or wood gilt. Each of these treatments would be quite suitable, and is, of course, decided by the intended environment of the finished screens. All the screens now in question should be hinged together with the proper knuckle - joint screen hinges. These may be obtained in various sizes, and, of course, they are reversible. Ordinary hinges cannot be employed, as these types will only act in one direction. It is a good plan to buy the hinges before the screens are made, so that the frames can be made to the correct thickness, thus ensuring their effective hinging.

A three-fold screen suitably designed for use in conjunction with Sheraton or similar furniture is shown by Fig. 9. With this particular type any number of extra frames can be introduced, it being only necessary to vary the inlaid designs for the top panels. A section of the stiles and also the top and bottom rails is shown at A (Fig. 10). A simple treatment of

difficulty, if the mortised-and-tenoned joints are properly made. Should winding occur, it is a difficult matter to rectify, as the frames stand quite alone and cannot be adjusted as with doors hinged to carcases, and secured at the centre. The top panels are intended to be executed in finely figured mahogany veneers, with a back line outlining the centre ellipse and also round the hollow-sided diamond shapes. Fine curls are intended for the centre, with a good splash-figured Cuba

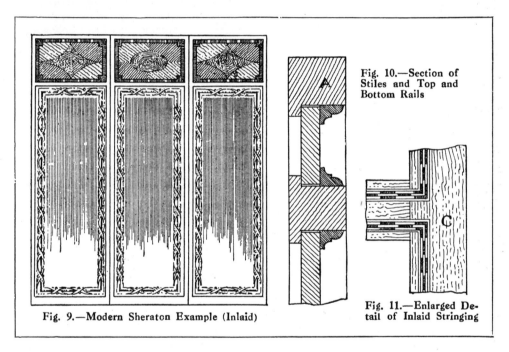

Fig. 10.—Section of Stiles and Top and Bottom Rails

Fig. 9.—Modern Sheraton Example (Inlaid)

Fig. 11.—Enlarged Detail of Inlaid Stringing

the frame only is required for a screen of this character, where the ornament is essentially surface decoration and does not project. If mouldings are introduced at all they need only be small, as otherwise they have a tendency to detract from the finely veneered surfaces. Fig. 11 gives an enlarged detail of the inlaid stringing.

The construction of the frames is quite straightforward, the rebates, of course, being worked before the frames are glued up. Great care must be taken to ensure that the frames are made quite true and free from winding, a matter of no great

mahogany for the quartering, and strongly marked fiddle-back figured veneer for the cross-banding. The patterns should be built up in damp-stretched paper and veneered by means of cauls. In the bottom panels a suitable green colour should be employed for the silk panels, these being stretched over the thin panels shown, or three-ply substitutes. The latter are quite suitable, and possess the additional qualification of being unshrinkable.

The sections of the rails show mouldings mitred round in place of ordinary beads.

The latter are rather wider than ordinary beads, and they serve to conceal the lap of the silk at the back. Well-figured

and a rebate. The latter is carved up, and recesses or grooves are introduced along the stiles and rails, which gives a fine appearance for so simple a detail. This grooving can be done before the frame is put together by moulding the rails right through, and stopping the grooves on the stiles where necessary, so that they can be properly finished as at B, where the frames have been put together. The carving can also be done whilst the frames are in pieces, it being only necessary to have the corners for completion after gluing up. Carved wood mouldings are much better in appearance then the composition variety, the former having a crispness or sharpness which

Fig. 12.—Another Rendering of Louis XVI. Screen

satinwood would look excellent in a screen of this design, with the top panels executed in East and West Indian satinwood. and curl veneers of satinwood. Pale blue silk is suitable for use with satinwood, and acts as an antidote to the yellow colour of the satinwood framing.

The example of screen shown by Fig. 12 is a modern rendering of the Louis XVI. style. Silk panels can in this case be introduced in the top panels if desired ; but if the white is finished with white enamel and gilt reliefs, rolled plate glasses at the top are more usual.

Fig. 13 shows the sectional view of the top rail, which is moulded with an ovolo

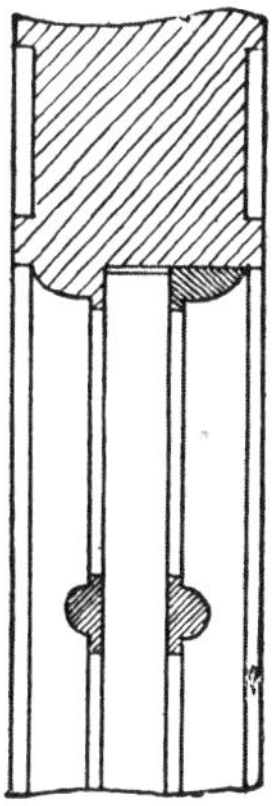

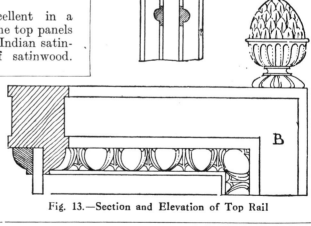

Fig. 14. — Section of Bottom Panel and Astragal Moulding

B

Fig. 13.—Section and Elevation of Top Rail

cannot be properly reproduced in composition ; but if the composition is desired for purpose of economy it can be introduced into rebated framing.

The section (Fig. 14) illustrates the

arrangement of the bottom panels, and also shows a section of the astragal moulding, which is simply mitred and glued down to three-ply panels. To execute the hollow corners in the design, it will be found the best plan to have circles turned to the desired section, and then not more than three hollow corners can be cut out of each one. The patera are made either of carved wood or "compo.," and are attached by gluing ing, as the case may be, after which the carvings are carefully detached from the board and glued down to the polished or enamelled surface. At the top of the centre frame the ribbon, torch, etc., should be executed separately, and preferably carved both sides. It should be attached to the frame by dowelling and gluing.

With regard to the gilding of this screen and the other examples, it should be mentioned that for first-class work

Fig. 17.—Detail of Border Design

Fig. 15.—Stencilled Screen

Fig. 16.—Design for Centre

or pinning in the position shown. In the bottom panels carved reliefs are introduced, and these are best executed by first tracing the outline of the carving from the drawing, and then gluing it down to wood of the required thickness. Fret-cutting can then be proceeded with, and then the shapes should be glued down to a board of pine or white wood with paper between the joints. After the glue is dry, the carving can be completely finished, and also the polishing or gild- nothing but good English gold-leaf should be employed. An inferior and less satisfactory material is metal or bronze powder, which does not retain its brightness for so long a period. Bronze powder has always a hard appearance, which is unsuitable for dull gilding and tarnishes fairly easily.

STENCILLED SCREENS

A convenient and very suitable method of decorating screens is by stencilling, a simple suggestion for treatment of a three-fold screen being given by Fig. 15. This design consists of a centre decoration in the case of the middle leaf, shown separately by Fig. 16, a top and bottom border being carried right along the three folds, one repeat of which is given by Fig. 17.

The construction of the framing of a suitable screen is clearly shown in Fig. 18, which gives the structure of one of the outside leaves. It consists of a light framing A that is tenoned together at the corners, and strengthened by cross pieces set at distances of 8 in. or so, which are halved where they cross. The frames are usually covered with

in the way described. The dark portions of the design shown by Fig. 15 could then be suitably stencilled in a deep brown on it, the leaves in a darker green than the ground, and the stems and acorns in a yellow-brown colour.

Two alternative methods of hinging that involve only slight expenditure and are quite serviceable for light screens are given in Figs. 19 and 20. The hinge (Fig. 19) consists of two laths of the full length of the uprights of the screen, laced together in the manner shown, one of each being screwed to the adjoining frames. The laths can conveniently be of the full width of the framing and about $\frac{3}{8}$ in. thick. The edges are then slightly

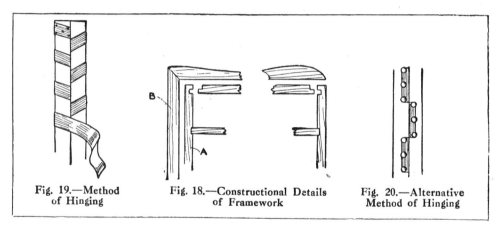

Fig. 19.—Method of Hinging

Fig. 18.—Constructional Details of Framework

Fig. 20.—Alternative Method of Hinging

paper first, pasted to the woodwork, and the fabric is tightly stretched over by gluing it round the edges, the leaves being hinged together by the fabric in a similar manner to that which will be described. The light frames over which the fabric is stretched are strengthened by stouter outside pieces B (Fig. 18) in the case of the outer leaves, and a top and bottom piece in the case of the middle one, these being nailed to the inner frames, and thus covering up the glued edges of the fabric.

A cheap and artistic screen may be made by constructing a simple framing of pine, say of 2-in. by 1-in. material, staining it a green colour, and then covering with material of a similar shade

rounded off with glasspaper, so that they will not cut the tapes with which they are bound, and they are then stained the colour of the screen frame. The tape used for binding should be in some colour to harmonise, although not necessarily to match. It should be about $\frac{3}{4}$ in. to 1 in. wide. The manner of binding is clearly shown in Fig. 19. Begin by securing, at a slight angle, with tacks at the top to one lath, and then bring round behind the adjoining one ; pass between the two and round the first, so repeat until the bottom is reached, and then secure with tacks as at the beginning. When screwed to the frames they will be found to hinge both ways. Fig. 20 is a somewhat simpler type of hinge of not quite so good appearance. Strips of strong fabric are tacked on alternately back and front close up to one another the whole length of the frames, the result being not only a double-action hinge, but one that is draughtproof.

tenoned. The decoration, which is stencilled, could either be executed on a painted three-ply panel that is grooved into the frames, or on a fabric stretched over a light frame, held in place with a narrow beading all round. A not too

Fig. 21.—Stencilled Folding-screen

A rather elaborate screen is shown by Fig. 21, the measurements for one of the leaves being given in Fig. 22. Use 1½-in. square material for the uprights, into which the top and bottom rails are

coarse textured canvas is a good material to employ, and this is procurable in a large variety of shades. The ornamental detail on the top and bottom of the outside leaves is shown by Fig. 23. A full-size enlargement of the figure in Fig. 21, with all the details included, should be made. A good colour effect would be produced by employing a cream or a pale buff ground, dress and hat in pink, purplish-blue shadows, red flowers and fan, and light brown hair. Four separate cutting can be best executed with a penknife ground to a fine point, a piece of glass being the best on which to cut. When each sheet has been fully cut out it is necessary to coat the paper with some preservative, which will give it additional toughness, and render it waterproof, and

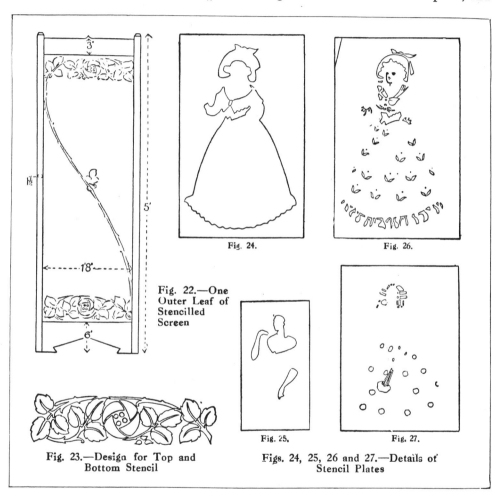

Fig. 22.—One Outer Leaf of Stencilled Screen

Fig. 23.—Design for Top and Bottom Stencil

Fig. 24.

Fig. 26.

Fig. 25.

Fig. 27.

Figs. 24, 25, 26 and 27.—Details of Stencil Plates

plates will be necessary, the parts that are in one colour being each traced off and transferred to a separate sheet. The four plates are shown respectively by Figs. 24 to 27, Fig. 24 being in stencilled pink, Fig. 25 a similar colour but slightly yellower, Fig. 26 purplish blue, and Fig. 27 in brown and red. The tor this purpose french-polish is as good as anything. Ordinary oil paint is used for stencilling. It should be employed thick, but well ground up before starting. The brush to use in stencilling should be short and stumpy, and is worked with a dabbing action, from the edge to the centre of all openings. By keeping it tolerably dry, and applying only just a little colour at a time, one is able to obviate the tendency of the paint to work under the stencil plate.

FIRE-SCREEN WITH SILK PANELS

The fire-screen of which a general view is given in the half-tone reproduction (Fig. 28) can be made of almost any kind of wood ; but as it is intended to be filled with pleated silk, a dark colour will probably be most suitable as well as

lower one $\frac{5}{8}$ in. by $\frac{1}{4}$ in. as at B. These rebates will regulate the width of the tenons by which the parts are connected, as at C, D, and E in Fig. 29. The tenons should be $\frac{7}{8}$ in. long and $\frac{3}{8}$ in. thick.

A fretted panel about $\frac{1}{4}$ in. thick, set out from the geometric basis in Fig. 31, is used to fill the bottom opening. The diagonal lines in this are at angles of 30° with the horizontal. The larger panel is filled in with a rectangular lattice composed of strips $\frac{5}{8}$ in. or $\frac{3}{4}$ in. wide and $\frac{1}{4}$ in. thick, halved where they cross (*see*

Fig. 28.—Fire-screen with Silk Panels

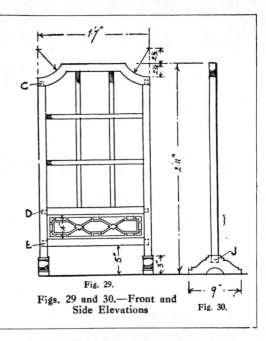

Fig. 29.

Figs. 29 and 30.—Front and Side Elevations   Fig. 30.

serviceable. Front and side elevations are shown by Figs. 29 and 30. The two uprights and three rails are all finished $1\frac{1}{4}$ in. by 1 in. square in section ; but as the top rail is curved at the ends as shown, this part should be cut out of a piece $3\frac{1}{2}$ in. by 1 in., in order to avoid awkward joints where the curves meet the horizontal portion. As put together, it will be observed that these stiles and rails form two panels, a large one above a narrow bottom one. The back edges of these should be rebated, the top one $\frac{3}{8}$ in. by $\frac{1}{4}$ in. as at A (Fig. 32), and the

F, Fig. 33), and neatly fitted into position. To take their ends the rebate $\frac{3}{8}$ in. wide already mentioned should be widened as at G (Fig. 33) to the exact size required to fit them, keeping their faces in the same plane with the front of the fretwork below. The rebate proper (H) will then be left to receive the silk or other backing.

For stability a moderately heavy base is necessary, and this takes the form of two shaped feet (Fig. 34), 9 in. by 3 in. by about $1\frac{1}{2}$ in., into which the stiles can be well tenoned. as at J in Fig. 30.

ORNAMENTAL SCREEN FOR NEEDLEWORK

The screen shown by Fig. 35 is designed to take a piece of needlework. The picture is worked in silk threads of various colours on a satin ground, the faces and arms of the figures and the sky being painted (*see* Fig. 36). To show the being made more or less to represent a lance supporting a banner, on which some insignia is worked. In some cases when the banner has become worn and shabby the best part bearing the insignia (often in the form of a crest, coronet, or motto) is preserved by framing somewhat similar to this one, but in the shape of a shield. As a piece of furniture they are to be

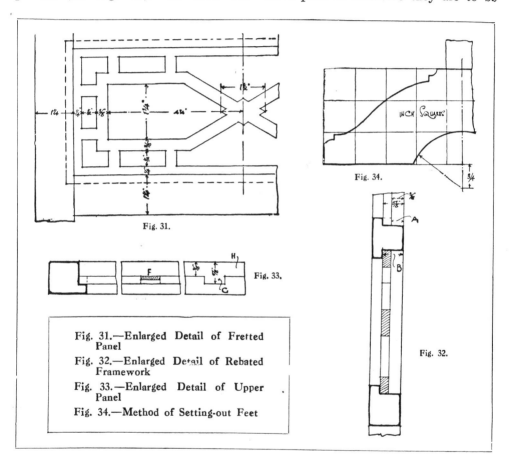

Fig. 31.

Fig. 33.

Fig. 34.

Fig. 32.

Fig. 31.—Enlarged Detail of Fretted Panel

Fig. 32.—Enlarged Detail of Rebated Framework

Fig. 33.—Enlarged Detail of Upper Panel

Fig. 34.—Method of Setting-out Feet

finished article in full length, as in Fig. 35, the parts naturally appear small; so a separate photograph of the stand is shown by Fig. 37. Fig. 38 shows how the back of the framed picture is made adjustable on the staff. This style of screen is antique, and is often called a " banner screen." Some of them really are banner screens, the pillar or staff found in well-furnished drawing-rooms, used as a fire-screen or sun-screen, but chiefly for the display of choice examples of needlework.

The screen is of mahogany inlaid with banding and stringing. The full height is 4 ft., the base 10 in. square, and the oval frame 1 ft. 1½ in. by 10 in.

The base may be made first. There

is no need to use solid mahogany for this, as it will be much better to make it in dry soft pine veneered. Two pieces of

Fig. 35.—Ornamental Screen for Needlework

the pine are required 10½ in. square, to be faced straight and level to lie together quite close. Then they should be toothed and glued across each other, being well cramped and left to set for several days. When it is set it can be marked out to the shape, which is simply a matter of scribing with the compasses, care being taken, of course, that it is true. The corner curves are got by scribing 2-in. diameter circles. The concave outline is a segment of a 9-in. diameter circle.

It must be cut to the shape very true and square on the edges, which must be toothed for veneering. The top side also will require to be planed level and toothed. The edges are to be cross-veneered, allowing about ⅛ in. over at each side for trimming off (*see* Fig. 39).

This may be put on in many pieces neatly joined, and will require several hours to set sufficiently to be trimmed for veneering the top side, which has also to be inlaid, as shown in Fig. 40. In the illustration various particulars are given. The true shape of the base is shown in relation to the square of soft pine, of which the lines A indicate the outline. The other lines B and those connected with them signify the rough outline of the veneer as it is laid on in four quarters. The crossed lines C are the fine joints of the veneer, and the dotted circles mark the diameter of the hole to receive the pin of the turned pillar, and the outline of the turned collar for same.

The veneer also will require several hours to set before it can be trimmed.

Fig. 36.—Frame and Top of Pillar

When this is done the margin may be gauged round ½ in. on with the cutting gauge, the veneer being then removed with a chisel to be replaced with the banding of tulipwood. This is $\frac{3}{8}$ in. wide, being the inside part of the stock pattern material with the light lines stripped off. It will need to be put on in many small pieces, the edges of which must be cut slant to fit as they are put on. On the large curves the pieces can only be about $\frac{3}{4}$ in. where they fit against the edge of the veneer, and $\frac{1}{16}$ in. less on the outer edge. In going round the small curves, the pieces may be about $\frac{1}{4}$ in. on the outer edge, slanting in to $\frac{1}{8}$ in. The black and light diamond line is the inside part of another stock material. To get it on one of the outside lines only must be stripped off. The other one is to remain on the outer side to keep the sections together in getting it glued on,

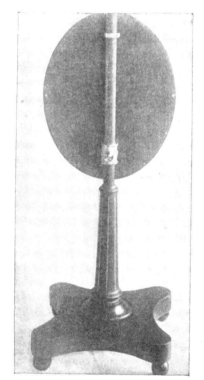

Fig. 38.—Back View with Frame Lowered

to be trimmed off when set, which will not be for a few days.

The frame may next be made. It

might seem to be a difficult matter to make so light a frame to be sufficiently strong. To cut it out of solid board a

Fig. 37.—Base and Bottom of Pillar

good deal of very short grain would unavoidably occur, which might be very apt to bend and break. To avoid having any short grain it would have to be jointed together in several segments, which does not seem practicable owing to the small section of wood. A method which some cabinet-makers adopt is to make a wood template of the oval, and build up the frame round it with several layers of veneer, taking care that the ends of each layer meet at a different position.

In this particular instance, however, another method is used. Upon a piece of hard five-ply board the oval frame should be struck out in pencil, and cut out with a fret-saw, when a frame of $\frac{3}{8}$-in. section, having equal strength all over, and likely to keep its shape permanently, is the result ; it is naturally a little supple, due to thinness of stuff, until the backboard of $\frac{3}{16}$ in. mahogany is put on with fine brass screws. The front is then cross-banded with tulipwood $\frac{5}{8}$ in. wide. It is put on in small pieces,

out with the sharp cutting gauge, like a small rebate to take the diamond line, which is put in the same as was done with the base.

Whilst this part of the work is left to set the turned work may be got ready.

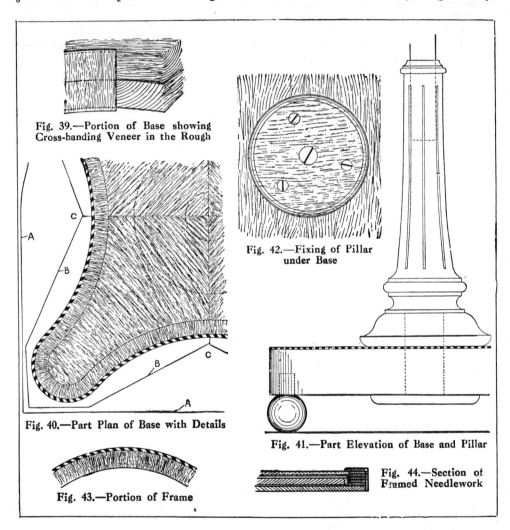

Fig. 39.—Portion of Base showing Cross-banding Veneer in the Rough

Fig. 40.—Part Plan of Base with Details

Fig. 43.—Portion of Frame

Fig. 42.—Fixing of Pillar under Base

Fig. 41.—Part Elevation of Base and Pillar

Fig. 44.—Section of Framed Needlework

kept even with the outside, which when moderately set is veneered right round in one length ; the backboard has to be taken out to keep it from getting stuck with the glue. When set the frame is considerably stronger and more rigid. The front outside corner has to be worked

This comprises four ball feet 1¼ in. in diameter, with pins for fixing about ¾ in. long by ½ in. ; a base collar 4¼ in. in diameter by 1 in., with a 1¼ in. hole in the centre ; lower part of pillar 8 in. long by 2¾ in. at thickest point, with pin 2¼ in. by 1¼ in. ; plain pole 3 ft. 1 in.

long by $\frac{7}{8}$ in. in diameter. The patterns of these and method of fixing is shown in Fig. 41. The plain pole is fitted into a hole made in the base turning. The pin fits through the collar and main base, to be fixed as shown by Fig. 42. These joints are usually turned to screw together, which is an advantage when they have to be taken to pieces ; but that is so seldom that it is hardly worth doing. With the method shown by Fig. 42 the pin should fit tight, and it will be quite firm without being glued ; so it can be taken apart by withdrawing the centre screw. The other joint may be glued, also the ball feet ; but not until the polishing is done. All the turned work, of course, should be of solid mahogany, and it will be seen that the pillar is inlaid with vertical light lines.

When the veneered and inlaid work is quite set it will require to be cleaned off with a well-sharpened scraper. The front of the frame should be as shown by Fig. 43. Furniture of this kind should be trimmed and cleaned up particularly well, and given a high-grade french-polish finish.

The frame must be fitted with a piece of glass, also a piece of white picture mount and a thin board on which to stretch the silk. The cardboard is fixed to the wood board with a touch of glue, for the silk to be stretched over and fixed at the back with $\frac{1}{4}$-in. tacks. It should fill the frame up so that when the mahogany back is screwed in it keeps the needlework firm against the glass (*see* Fig. 44). The brass fittings for adjusting the frame on the pole and the vase ornament are stock goods, to be obtained from dealers in cabinet-makers' metal fittings.

Work-tables

INLAID WORK-TABLE

THE table shown by Fig. 1 would, in these days of expensive furniture, be well worth reproducing. The construction involved demands no more than an average skill in woodworking, and the cost of

Work may be commenced with the four legs out of stuff $1\frac{1}{2}$ in. square, finishing $1\frac{1}{4}$ in. square for the box portion, and tapering to $\frac{5}{8}$ in. square at the bottom. The four sides are then prepared and jointed to the legs in the usual manner of table construction, the mitred tenon,

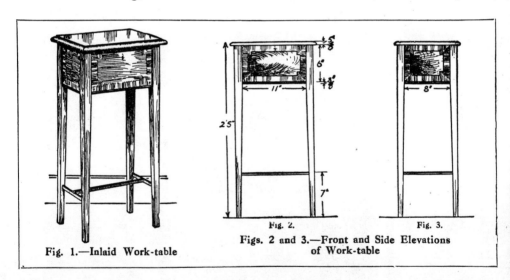

Fig. 1.—Inlaid Work-table

Fig. 2.

Fig. 3.

Figs. 2 and 3.—Front and Side Elevations of Work-table

materials is comparatively small. It could be made of Cuban mahogany, the sides and top decorated by the use of figured veneers, and the whole darkened to a deep plum colour and french-polished. The elevations shown in Figs. 2 and 3 give all the necessary measurements, while in Figs. 4, 5 and 6 are shown working details.

shown in Figs. 4 and 5. It may be mentioned that such wide tenons as these are best cut with a rebate plane. Before gluing up, however, the veneering or the inlaying must be carried out. These subjects are fully dealt with in a later section.

The illustrations show a method of

decoration by veneering and the use of bandings. If this is carried out, the following procedure will be the best. Draw the patterns full-size on stout drawing-paper which has previously been " stretched " on a board. Build up the veneer on this, cutting it roughly to shape with a fine dovetail saw, and finishing with a fine shoulder or rebate plane, and gluing the various pieces in place, keeping them in position with veneer pins until the whole has set. After this they may be levelled and roughened with the toothing plane (failing this, a fine saw will serve), and then glued to the sides, using hand-screws and hot wooden cauls. After

that the bandings are not cleaned off until they are thoroughly set, otherwise they will sink below the surface of the surrounding wood, owing to the shrinkage of the glue in drying.

With the completion of the inlay, the lower stretchers may be made and fitted. The scratch stock mentioned above is also useful here in working the moulding. The ends can then be glued up and finally the whole. The method of fixing the bottom is shown clearly in Fig. 6, and also the method of hinging the top. The top is veneered or inlaid similarly to the sides, and the moulding round its edge is one which can easily be worked by means

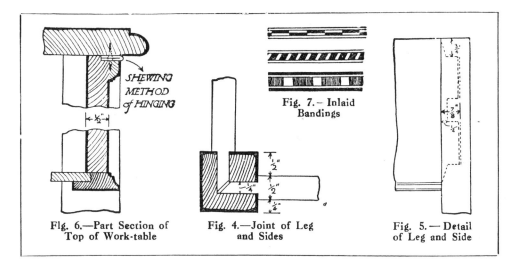

Fig. 7. – Inlaid Bandings

Fig. 6.—Part Section of Top of Work-table

Fig. 4.—Joint of Leg and Sides

Fig. 5. — Detail of Leg and Side

allowing a day or night for the veneer thoroughly to set, they may then be cleaned up with a sharp scraper and fine glasspaper.

An alternative and much easier form of decoration would be to simply inlay a banding. These bandings, of which some typical examples are shown in Fig. 7, can be obtained at any veneer shop. In cutting the channel for the banding, a cutting gauge with two cutters should be used for the outside edges ; the inside can then be " routed " out with a thin piece of steel fixed in a scratch stock. The more intricate parts of the channel can be cut with fine chisels. Care must be taken

of a rebate plane and glasspaper. The fitting of a lock and a hinged brass stay to prevent the top from falling back too far completes the actual construction. The table can now be cleaned up with fine glasspaper, darkened with a solution of potassium bichromate, filled and finally polished.

WORK-TABLE WITH SLIDING BODY

A work-table which has a top 3 ft. by 1 ft. 4 in. is shown partly in elevation and partly in section by Fig. 8. Under the frame is a sliding body or well, the interior of which is fitted as a lady's work-box, with additional accommodation for small pieces of unfinished work. A tray, furnished with the usual assorted com-partments for needles, cotton, etc., rests in the top of the well (*see* Fig. 9), and may

diately over the sliding body is a drawer working between solid guides D (Fig. 8) framed into the rails of the table, as shown in Figs. 10 and 11. A shaped stretcher is framed between the legs, and carries a small oval shelf, as shown in Fig. 12.

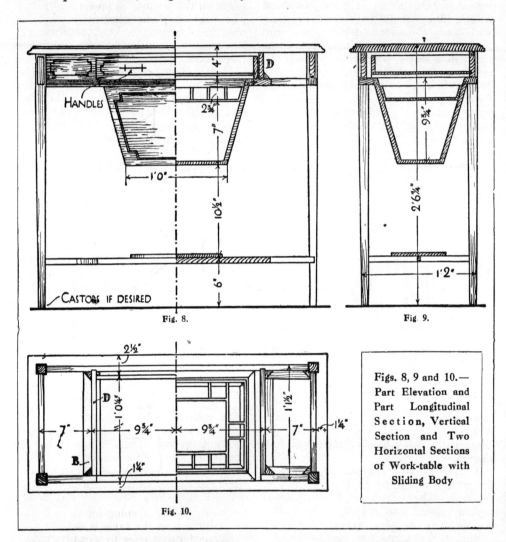

Fig. 8.

Fig 9.

Fig. 10.

Figs. 8, 9 and 10.— Part Elevation and Part Longitudinal Section, Vertical Section and Two Horizontal Sections of Work-table with Sliding Body

be removed bodily. Access to the interior of the well can also be obtained through the central compartment, which is bottom-less, but which may, if preferred, be covered with a lid, stuffed outside with cotton-wool to form a pincushion. Imme-

The top and drawer rails, and the rails of the framing, are of $\frac{3}{4}$-in. stuff, and the legs are $1\frac{1}{4}$ in., tapering to $\frac{3}{4}$ in., the joints connecting them to the rails being shown in elevation in Figs. 11 and 13, and in plan in Fig. 14. The well is of $\frac{1}{2}$-in.

pine, square-jointed and bradded, and afterwards veneered with wood to match the remainder, which could be of mahogany or walnut, inlaid with mosaic bandings of ebony and box. Fig. 15 shows the sliding body.

A wide rail is framed between the sides of the table, and a hardwood tongue, oak for preference, is grooved and glued in it; this is stopped back 1 in. from the front edge. A similar but slightly thinner rail is tongued and grooved to the well, as shown in Fig. 11, and a plough groove made in its edge, in which works the hardwood tongue. This must be fitted so that there is no side play. It is best to fit it first rather stiffly, and then rub powdered

french chalk over the tongue. The rim of the well should be dowelled at the mitres, as shown in Fig. 16. The tray, which is 2 in. deep, is made of $\frac{5}{16}$-in. stuff bradded together and glued, and lined with silk. It is an advantage to glue a piece of green baize on the bottom to prevent scratches on the table top when the tray is taken out.

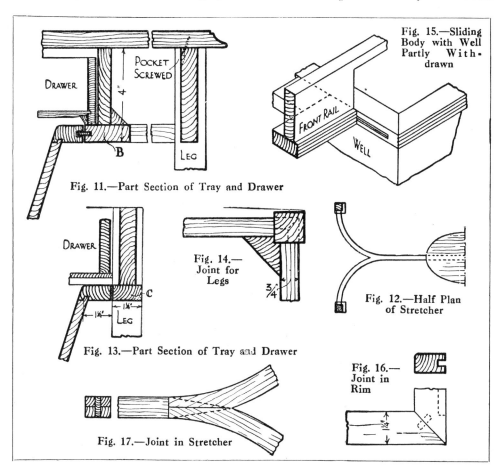

Fig. 15.—Sliding Body with Well Partly With-drawn

Fig. 11.—Part Section of Tray and Drawer

Fig. 14.—Joint for Legs

Fig. 12.—Half Plan of Stretcher

Fig. 13.—Part Section of Tray and Drawer

Fig. 16.—Joint in Rim

Fig. 17.—Joint in Stretcher

To provide an opening for the drawer, the front rail of the table is cut through from the bottom edge to within $\frac{1}{2}$ in. of the top, and the cross guides D (Fig. 10) are kept flush with the ends of the opening. These guides must be well fitted and fixed with glued angle-blocks, and screwed to the top, as shown in Fig. 11, the bearers B (Figs. 10 and 11) being screwed to them. The table top, not being very wide, may be solid, and screwed to the framing, as shown in Fig. 11. The moulded rails c (Fig. 13) should be cut in tight between the legs, and fixed after the framework is glued up. It will be noticed that there is no opening at the back, neither the drawer nor the sliding body passing out on that side, and the groove

the curved portions being tenoned into the legs.

WORK-TABLE WITH FITTED TRAY

The perspective reproduced drawing (Fig. 18) shows a lady's work-table, which combines two essentials—usefulness and good appearance. The advan-

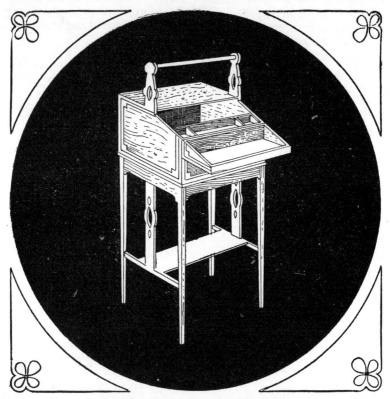

Fig. 18.—Work-table with Fitted Tray

in the sliding rim must be taken through at the back, but stopped in the front to prevent disfigurement of the moulded rail (see Fig. 15). The joint in the shaped stretcher is shown in Fig. 17. The two curved ends are first jointed together square, and then grooved diagonally through the middle. They are then glued up and bradded, thus forming a tapering mortise into which the tenon on the straight rail is fitted, the opposite ends of

tages of a small table such as is illustrated will be appreciated, as a fitted tray gives all the required space for storing small articles, and the roomy box part gives ample storage space for work in hand. The hinged lid can be used as a tray, and as all these points are embodied in one piece, its advantages will be apparent. From the point of view of design, the table can be readily adapted to match other pieces of furniture in a room. If dark oak predominates, a suitable treatment would be to introduce twisted or turned legs, and small overlaid mouldings to panel out the top part. If made in walnut, overlaid mouldings or inlays as indicated would look equally well. The table as drawn is intended to be executed in mahogany inlaid with boxwood lines, and dull finished. A cutting list is given below, divided into top and bottom parts.

For	*Lgth.*	*Wh.*	*Th.*	*Pcs.*	*Wood.*	*Notes.*
STAND—	*ft. in.*	*in.*	*in.*			
Legs	1 8	1 1/8	1 1/8	4	mahog.	
End rails ...	1 2 1/2	1 7/8	5/8	2	"	
Bottom rails ...	1 2 1/2	3/4	1/2	2	"	
Back & front rails	1 7 1/2	1 7/8	5/8	2	"	
Shelf	1 7	4 1/2	3/8	1	"	
End uprights ...	1 1 1/4	2 3/4	3/8	2	"	
TOP PART—						
Ends	1 2	8 1/2	7/16	2	"	
Back	1 7 1/2	8 1/2	7/16	1	"	
Front	1 7 1/2	8 3/4	7/16	1	"	
Top	1 7 1/2	14 1/4	7/16	1	"	
Bottom	1 7 1/2	14	5/16	1	3 ply mahog.	
Moulding ...	2 8	1/2	1/4	2		Each length cuts 2
Fillets	1 2 1/2	1/2	3/16	2	"	
Uprights ...	7	2 5/8	5/8	2	"	
Handle	1 7	3/4	3/4	1	"	Round section
TRAY—						
Ends	6 0	2 1/4	1/4	1	"	1 cuts 2 ends
Front	1 6	1 1/4	1/4	1	"	
Back	1 6	2 1/4	1/4	1	"	
Bottom	1 6	2 7/8	3/16	1	"	1 cuts 5 divisions
Divisions ...	6	2 1/4	1/4	1	"	

The illustrations show the necessary working details, and also a small sketch is given showing the table closed (Fig. 19). Front and end elevations are shown by Figs. 20 and 21. A sectional view of the table when open is shown by Fig. 22, and, as will be seen, the work-table is made with the top and bottom part separate. The tray divisions are shown in plan (Fig. 23), and if simply placed on two thin fillets screwed inside the ends, it may be pushed backwards or forwards. This enables either the back or front of the box part to be easily reached if required. This tray should be dovetailed together at the corners, and the divisional mitre notched in, as indicated in Fig. 24. The two small divisions may be enclosed with lids as indicated, with small ivory or bone knobs, and prove quite useful for thimbles, needles, etc. These small compartments could be lined with silk or velvet packed out with cotton-wool to the lines shown in Fig. 23. Very thin wood fillets are first glued round to receive the lids, and then small pieces of card are cut slightly smaller than each side and bottom. Cotton-wool is then carefully pulled and placed on each to form pads, which are covered with thin silk. The silk should be turned over the backs of the cards, and can then be glued at the back. When prepared in this way the bottom pad can be secured with a touch of glue, the side pads being added and secured in the same way.

The stand should be made by first planing up all the pieces, and tapering the legs to the size shown. The top and bottom rails of the ends are then mortised and tenoned together, the bottom rails having bevelled shoulders. These should be fitted together and tested, and the centre slat may be tenoned between the rails, the shaping being done after the tenoning has been completed. After shaping the slats and fitting up dry, the whole should be separated and all inside surfaces scraped and glasspapered. Then the ends may be glued and clamped up. When quite dry the rails are tenoned in between the ends and also the bottom shelf, this part being followed by gluing up the whole bottom part.

To make the top part it should be considered as a simple dovetailed box, with the corners through-dovetailed. The top is simply glued on to the exact width required after the dovetails are glued up. Fig. 22 shows the end shapes for the dovetailed box, the fall-over part being made separately and fitted in to the main box, as indicated in the small perspective sketch of the work-table. Great care must be taken with the fitting, and then the parts may be separated prior to toothing and veneering. The surfaces should be sized after toothing, and if knife-cut veneers are used, they can be laid with a veneering hammer (*see* later section). When quite dry all the edges are cleanly trimmed, and the falling part fitted again.

The hinges can now be fitted. It will, of course, be necessary to let them in flush on each of the edges.

No mention has so far been made of the

inlaying. This has been intentionally postponed until after the hinging, which enables the lines to be all gauged off

be used for this part of the work if a proper inlaying gauge is not available.

Before the surfaces are scraped and glasspapered, it will be necessary to fix the pierced handle pieces indicated by means of three $\frac{1}{4}$-in. dowels bored about 1 in. deep in the box and the handle. A $\frac{3}{4}$-in. round rail is then prepared and bored into each handle, and the rail is inserted prior to gluing in the dowelled handle pieces. The cleaning-up of the box should be done before unhinging the top part prior to polishing it.

PLAIN WORK-TABLE

The work-table shown by Fig. 25 is constructed upon the simplest possible lines consistent with good appearance. Fig. 26 shows a front elevation.

The legs are 2 ft. 5$\frac{1}{4}$ in. long, 1$\frac{1}{8}$ in. square at the tops tapering down to $\frac{3}{4}$ in.

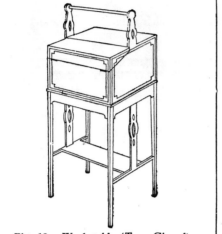

Fig. 19.—Work-table (Tray Closed)

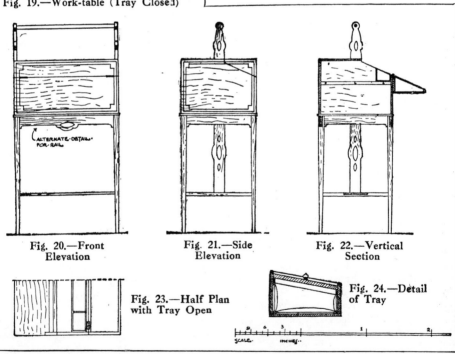

Fig. 20.—Front Elevation

Fig. 21.—Side Elevation

Fig. 22.—Vertical Section

Fig. 23.—Half Plan with Tray Open

Fig. 24.—Detail of Tray

straight-edges, and ensures their accuracy and straightness. An ordinary gauge with a small square cutter can quite well

at the bottom, where they are merely finished off square. They are connected by three rails, as in Fig. 27, of 4-in. by $\frac{3}{4}$-in.

stuff curved along its under edges as at A in Fig. 26, which shows a segment of a circle of 2 ft. 2 in. radius, that for the shorter sides being proportionately less. At the points B and C in Fig. 27 the rails should be tenoned into the legs with the adjoining mortises and tenons at different levels in order to avoid cutting away the leg too much at any one point. The joints at the other two angles are ordinary tenons. Four rails 1¼ in. by ⅜ in. are introduced 6 in. above the floor, tenoned

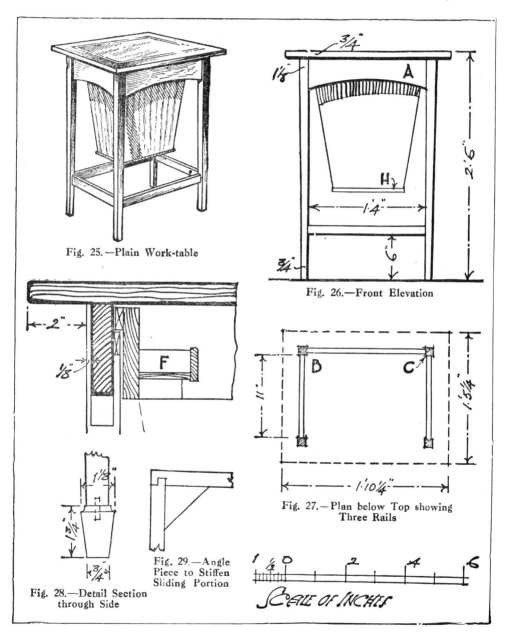

Fig. 25.—Plain Work-table

Fig. 26.—Front Elevation

Fig. 28.—Detail Section through Side

Fig. 29.—Angle Piece to Stiffen Sliding Portion

Fig. 27.—Plan below Top showing Three Rails

SCALE OF INCHES

slightly into each leg in order to tie the four together. A top, 1 ft. 10¼ in. by 1 ft. 5¼ in. and ¾ in. thick, out of one piece

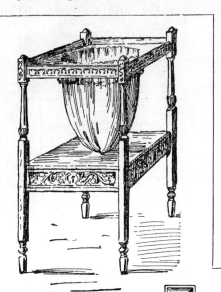

Fig. 30.—Carved Work-table with Open Silk Pocket

of well seasoned and nicely marked wood will be required; it should have square edges with the angles just taken off, and it can be fixed with small oak dowels let into the top of each leg. Alternatively it can be easily secured by screwing in a slanting direction through the top inner edges of the rails.

For the sliding top from which the workbag is intended to swing, a front similar in thickness and outline to A in Fig. 26 (but without any tenons) will be needed; this it is intended to fix to the other pieces, which are of 3-in. by ½-in. stuff put together in the simplest manner; strictly the joints should be dovetailed, but considering the lightness and loose work-

ing of the whole, perhaps this is not necessary. When completed the arrangement has the appearance of a drawer without a bottom. Along the top edges at each end of this sliding portion should be fixed oak strips about ¾ in. by ¼ in., as runners to work upon similar strips on the side rails, marked with diagonal crosses in Fig. 28. Along either end of the sliding part also it will be useful to fit a ledge for pins, scissors, cotton, etc. As shown in section in Fig. 28, this can be done with ¼-in. stuff throughout, first planting a piece as at F 1¾ in. by ¾ in. on the inside of the front and back portions, this serving as fixing for a bottom and side piece, the top angle of the latter being rounded as shown, these ledges would be fitted along the two short sides, while under them at all four angles it will probably be advisable to fix a triangular block (Fig. 29) to stiffen them and preserve the rectangular

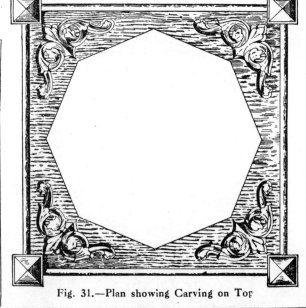

Fig. 31.—Plan showing Carving on Top

outline. These triangles will be concealed by the ledges, and should be fixed flush on the underside; they help to ease the pleated silk of the bag round the corners.

Drawer

Fig. 32.—Corner Elevation of Carved Work-table showing Details of Carving

The silk can be of any desired length and degree of fullness, and should be carefully tacked round where indicated by a dotted line in Fig. 28, and similarly

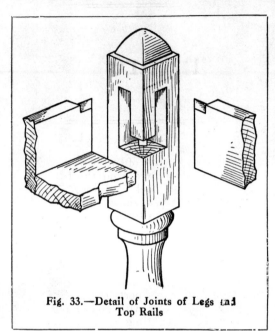

Fig. 33.—Detail of Joints of Legs and Top Rails

attached to a thin wooden bottom H (Fig. 26) measuring about 10 in. by 5 in.

CARVED WORK-TABLE WITH OPEN SILK POCKET

The construction of the work-table shown in perspective by Fig. 30 is so apparent that it would be superfluous to detail it. The top portion consists of four rails tenoned into the uprights. The rails are ploughed at the bottom of their inner faces to receive the framing that supports the silk bag. This framing is shown in plan by Fig. 31 (*see* p. 1080), while Fig. 32 (p. 1081) is a corner elevation showing the carved work on the rails and tops of the corner posts. Alternatively thin fillets could be glued to the inner faces of the rails, and a panel or framing of thicker stuff supported on them, but the former method would obviate the risk of the panel warping, in addition to making the whole construction more substantial generally. In either case the uprights should be notched for the corners of the panel. This is clearly shown in Fig. 33, from which it will be seen that a solid support is thus provided for the panel. The most satisfactory method of securing the silk bag would be by means of a circle (or sectors) of thin wood screwed on underneath, and clamping the bag between itself and the underside of the panel or framing. In the design shown the bag is tacked on to the inner edge of the opening, a silk cord being used to protect the silk from the heads of the tacks. The drawer shown fitted into the lower platform is optional, for, if desired, the lower portion could consist of the rails only. The design is in the nature of an artistic suggestion which is capable of being modified in many different ways to suit the craftsman's own ideas. The height may be 30 in. and width of side 14 in., but any other reasonable dimensions may be adopted.

The wood is a matter of personal choice, but probably the most suitable for the nature of the design would be oak.

Writing Furniture

SMALL MAHOGANY WRITING-TABLE

THE design of the small mahogany writing-table shown by Fig 1 is of the late Georgian period. Its attractive appearance is apparent in the photographic reproduction. Front and side elevations are shown by Figs. 2 and 3, whilst Fig. 4 represents a section at c (Fig. 2) and shows the division of the top drawer. It will be noticed that the drawers can be opened from each end, a feature seldom met with in present-day furniture.

Supporting the body of the desk are four tapering square legs cut out of 1¼-in. material, shaped as shown in Fig. 5, and connected at the top by pieces ¾ in. thick cut according to sizes given. The desk sides are of ¾-in. material,

Fig. 1.—Small Mahogany Writing-table

having a bottom ¼ in. thick. It is again divided by a ⅛-in. piece of mahogany forming a runner for the top drawer. This member, together with the bottom, is moulded with a half-round bead on three sides only, the back being square.

The top is made of two pieces, the lower portion being fixed, and the top hinged so as to fall back and form one flush writing-surface, as shown in Figs. 3 and 5. Fixed along the top edge of the hinged part is a cock bead moulded and cut, as shown in Figs. 6 and 7. The top sides of the fixed part and the under side of the hinged portion are covered with green baize, leaving a margin of 1 in. round the four sides of the whole top when open. Both the hinged and fixed portions of the top are moulded on three sides, as in Fig. 5.

The top drawer is made of ¾-in. ends, with small half-round bead running round the outside edges, the side being of ¼-in. material and the bottom ⅛ in. thick. The fittings are uncommon, as will readily be seen by reference to the illustrations. The lower drawer has no fittings or handles, and forms a secret drawer, access to the same being obtained by pressure from each end. It is made of the same thickness material, and finished with half-round bead at the ends similar to the top drawer.

OAK WRITING-DESK

The most suitable wood for the desk shown by Fig. 8 (p. 1086) is oak. Figs. 9 and 10 show front and side elevations, and in Fig 13. The handle and escutcheon plates are of polished brass, and give a striking contrast to the dark colour of the oak.

The legs are of 2-in.-square material

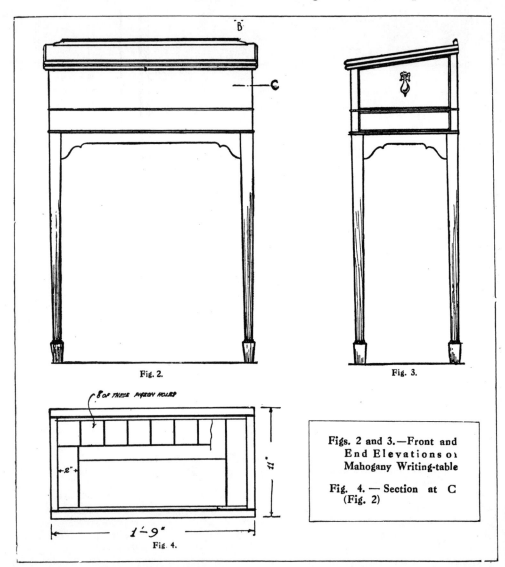

Fig. 2.

Fig. 3.

Fig. 4.

Figs. 2 and 3.—Front and End Elevations of Mahogany Writing-table

Fig. 4. — Section at C (Fig. 2)

two half-plans and a part back elevation are shown by Figs. 11 and 12.

The top is of $\frac{3}{4}$-in. material ($\frac{5}{8}$-in. finished thickness) in two pieces, and moulded at the front and sides as shown

(finished), and turned as shown in Fig. 13. The axis of the circular portion not being vertical, but at an angle pointing inwards, the outside edge, which corresponds with the outside corner of the square portion,

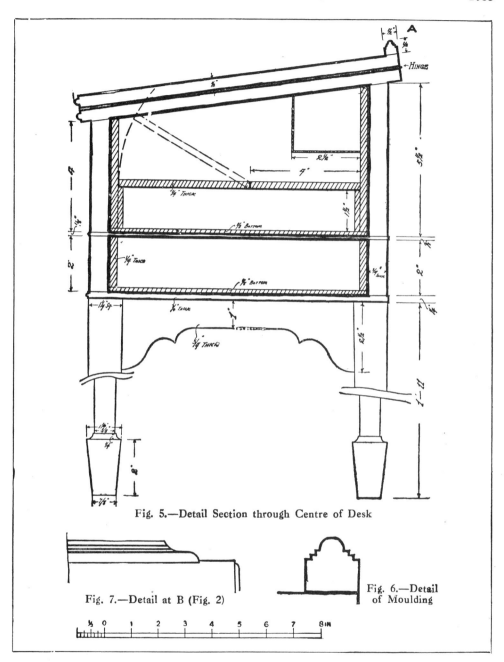

Fig. 5.—Detail Section through Centre of Desk

Fig. 7.—Detail at B (Fig. 2)

Fig. 6.—Detail of Moulding

is vertical and parallel to the square portion (*see* Fig. 13).

The front is composed of two rails of $\frac{7}{8}$-in. by $\frac{3}{4}$-in. material (finished), and a shaped portion $\frac{3}{4}$ in. thick (finished size), both tenoned and dowelled into the legs and flush with the outside surface of the legs. The sides and back are of $\frac{3}{4}$-in.

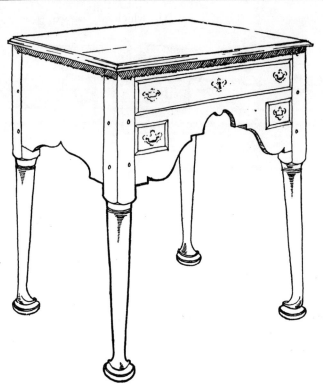

Fig. 8.—Oak Writing-desk

thick material (finished) tenoned and dowelled into the sides, shaped as shown in Figs. 9, 10 and 12, and finished flush with the outside surfaces of the legs.

Fig. 11 gives a section through the drawers. The top one, which occupies the whole length between the front legs, is 3 in. deep overall, and the small ones at each side are $2\frac{1}{2}$ in. The fronts are of $\frac{3}{4}$-in. material (finished), and the ends, sides and bottom of $\frac{1}{4}$-in. stuff. The surface of the drawers when shut is flush with the remainder of the front, with a $\frac{1}{8}$-in. half-round moulded bead running round the drawer at the front and projecting beyond

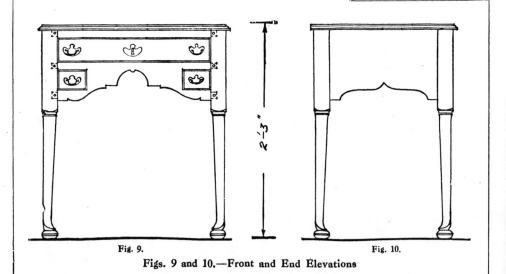

Fig. 9.

2'-3"

Fig. 10.

Figs. 9 and 10.—Front and End Elevations

the main surface. The drawer runners are of soft wood, and four are tenoned are tenoned into the front and back. In Fig. 11, which gives two half plans

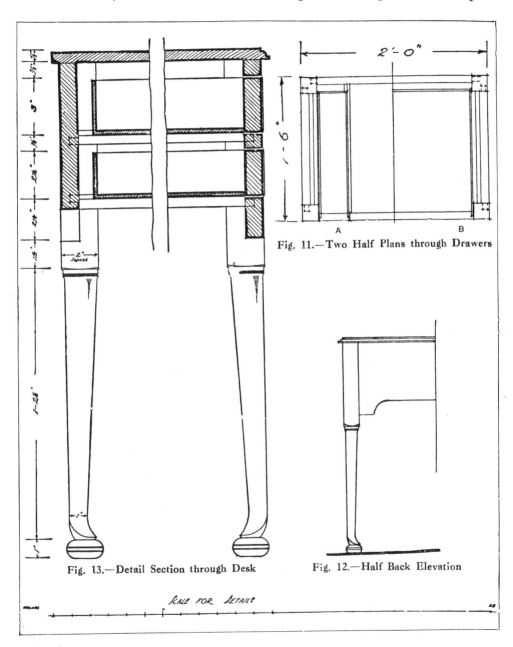

Fig. 11.—Two Half Plans through Drawers

A B

Fig. 13.—Detail Section through Desk

Fig. 12.—Half Back Elevation

SCALE FOR DETAILS

into the legs, and the remaining two for the interior edges of the lower drawers through the drawer line, A is top drawer and B is bottom drawer.

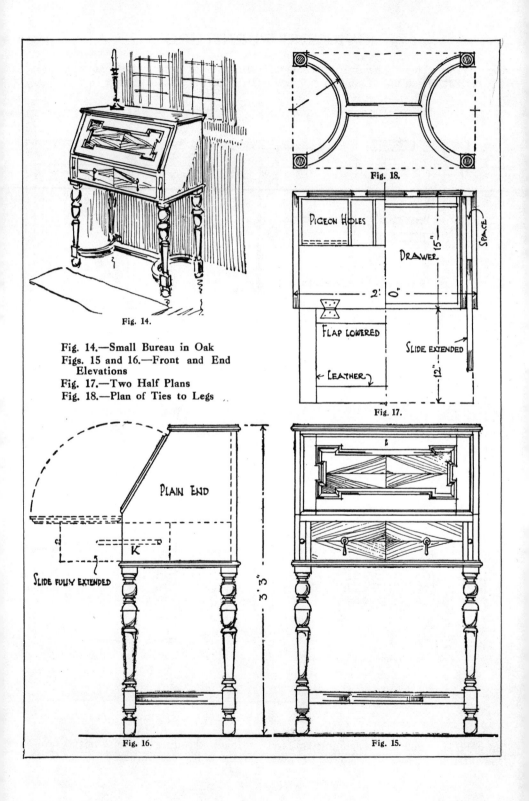

Fig. 14.

Fig. 18.

PICEON HOLES

DRAWER

15"

SPACE

FLAP LOWERED

SLIDE EXTENDED

2' 0"

2"

LEATHER

Fig. 17.

Fig. 14.—Small Bureau in Oak
Figs. 15 and 16.—Front and End
  Elevations
Fig. 17.—Two Half Plans
Fig. 18.—Plan of Ties to Legs

PLAIN END

K

SLIDE FULLY EXTENDED

3' 3"

Fig. 16.

Fig. 15.

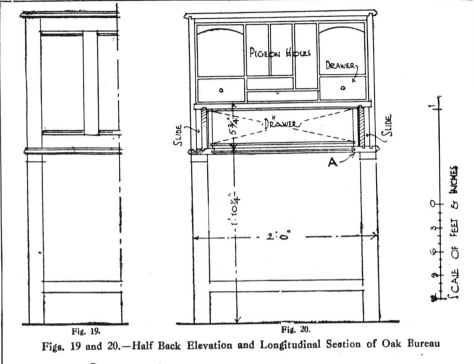

Fig. 19.   Fig. 20.

Figs. 19 and 20.—Half Back Elevation and Longitudinal Section of Oak Bureau

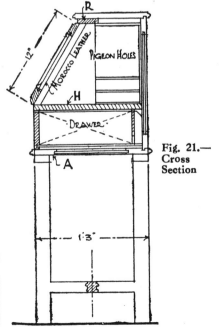

Fig. 21.—
Cross
Section

SMALL BUREAU IN OAK

Designed for a dining-room, the bureau shown by Fig. 14 (p. 1088) may be carried out in oak, selected for the best possible figure and grain. At the same time it would look extremely well executed in dull-polished Italian walnut, and its small proportions might be increased consistently throughout, in the event of a larger article being required. In addition to the general illustrations (Figs. 15 to 19), reduced reproductions of the full-size working details are given.

What may perhaps be termed the key to the whole construction is a piece of horizontal framing, shown in section at A in Figs. 20 and 21, and also at B in Fig. 22. This consists of 4-in. by 1-in. oak mortised and tenoned together and grooved for a thin panel, the whole measuring 2 ft. by 1 ft. 3 in. overall, and serving as a base to the upper half of the work. Below and sub-tenoned into it there are four legs, round-turned to a very carefully considered profile (as in Fig. 22) out of $2\frac{3}{4}$-in. square oak. The widest portion is intentionally arranged at c, and the small portions remaining square should be very accurately reduced, the upper one to $2\frac{1}{8}$ in. on each face, and the lower one to $1\frac{3}{4}$ in. The ties near the floor are set out as in Fig. 18, and worked to the section given at D in Fig. 22, the sunk top surface being very effective in such a position. As the size is small, each curved portion might be worked out of one solid piece ; or it might be preferred to build them up, each in two lengths, halved accurately in the middle and tenoned into the legs at the ends. The straight central rail could be dovetailed from below into the curved portions, the sunk top being worked when the whole tie has been put together.

The shell or carcase of the upper part of the bureau is composed of the following parts : First, two plain ends as in Fig. 16, mitred as in Fig. 23, to a simple back framed up in three panels (Figs. 19 and 24), the whole being tongued into grooves in the horizontal framing already referred to as the key to the situation, as at J in Fig. 22. Similarly they are tongued into the underside of a top piece 1 in. thick, and moulded on all four edges (Fig. 25). Next, with its upper surface 2 ft. 4 in. above floor level, there should be arranged a shelf as at H (Fig. 21), $\frac{7}{8}$ in. thick, stop-housed slightly into the ends, and butted against the inside of the back.

At each end of the drawer space now formed there should be contrived a cavity for a pull-out slide, by means of a piece as at J (Fig. 22), secured by means of tongues and grooves as shown, except on the actual face of the work. Each slide should be arranged to pull out 8 in. only, by means of a groove worked in it, as at K in Fig. 16, and a peg fixed on the inner face of the end and projecting into the groove. The width overall of the slide compartment should equal that of the top of the leg. The slide should close quite flush on the face, be fitted with a tiny turned-oak knob, and covered on its top edge with felt or soft leather. The

bottom edge should be ultimately finished by means of a moulded strip as at L (Fig. 22), mitred all round, and the drawer can be made in the usual manner, but with a piece of oak applied as at M, to reduce the friction and wear on the framing below. The drawer front is intended to be veneered in quarters, and to be rebated for and finished with a narrow bead mitred round, as in Fig. 26.

Like the rest of the work, the flap should be carefully set out on paper as a preliminary to the actual work. It must finish the same thickness as H (Fig. 21), in order to bear properly upon the slides, and consists of framing $2\frac{3}{4}$ in. wide and having a small moulding worked round its outer edges, as at O in Fig. 25, from which all its particulars can be gleaned. The framing is cut away on the face to suit the mitred arrangement of the panel moulding, but on the inside remains a simple rectangle. The panel is almost flush on the inside, allowing for a morocco-leather lining to be glued in place, while on the outside it is finished with another quartered arrangement of selected veneer (Fig. 27). The flap is fixed with small best-quality brass counter-flap hinges, in the position shown in Fig. 26, which gives its position in relation to the sloping top of the end-piece. Under the front edge of the top it should meet a small splayed piece, as shown by Fig. 28 (seen also at R in Fig. 21), and it should be supported in its closed position by moulded strips housed into the end pieces as at S (Fig. 25), these making a good finish to the appearance when open.

The pigeon-holes and small drawers incorporated with them can be in very thin oak, holly, or satinwood, set out as indicated in Figs. 20 and 21. In the best work they are built up separately and inserted complete. Antique oxidised drawer-handles and a good lock will complete the work.

OAK JACOBEAN WRITING-BUREAU

The oak Jacobean writing-bureau shown by Fig. 29 (p. 1092) is made up with three drawers, above which are pigeon-holes

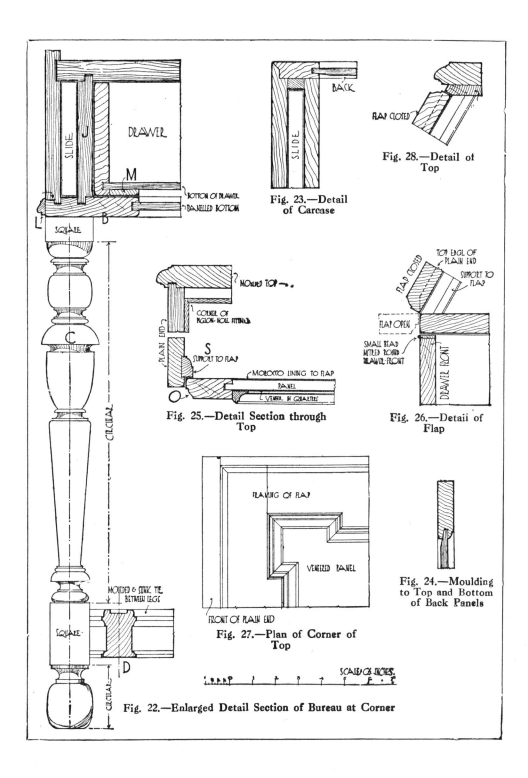

SLIDE

J

DRAWER

M

L

SQUARE

B

BOTTOM OF DRAWER

PANELLED BOTTOM

Fig. 23.—Detail
of Carcase

BACK

SLIDE

FLAP CLOSED

Fig. 28.—Detail of
Top

CIRCULAR

C

MOULDED TOP

CORNER OF
PIGION-HOLE FITTINGS

PLAIN END

S

SUPPORT TO FLAP

O

MOROCCO LINING TO FLAP

PANEL

VENEER IN QUARTERS

Fig. 25.—Detail Section through
Top

TOP EDGE OF
PLAIN END

SUPPORT TO
FLAP

FLAP CLOSED

FLAP OPEN

SMALL BEAD
MITRED ROUND
DRAWER FRONT

DRAWER FRONT

Fig. 26.—Detail of
Flap

FRAMING OF FLAP

VENEERED PANEL

FRONT OF PLAIN END

Fig. 27.—Plan of Corner of
Top

MOULDED & SUNK TIE
BETWEEN LEGS

SQUARE

D

CIRCULAR

Fig. 24.—Moulding
to Top and Bottom
of Back Panels

SCALE OF INCHES.

Fig. 22.—Enlarged Detail Section of Bureau at Corner

Fig. 29.—Oak Jacobean Writing Bureau

enclosed by a hinged flap. The latter, when opened and supported on two slides, forms a writing space. Front and side elevations are given by Figs. 30 and 31.

The main features of construction are apparent in the section (Fig. 32). The sides are prepared out of 1-in. stuff and finished $\frac{7}{8}$ in., the rails being $2\frac{1}{4}$ in. by $\frac{7}{8}$ in., dovetailed and grooved into the sides. The drawer bearers are of 1-in. stuff and $\frac{7}{8}$ in. finished. The back is framed and panelled, framing $2\frac{1}{4}$ in. by $\frac{7}{8}$ in. with a panel $\frac{5}{8}$ in. thick, grooved. The framing is grooved and tongued into the top and bottom rail. The drawers have $\frac{7}{8}$-in. thick fronts, moulded on the edge,

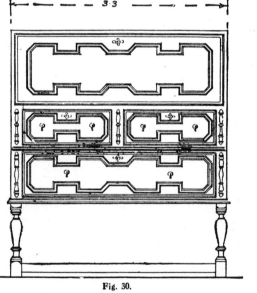

Fig. 30.

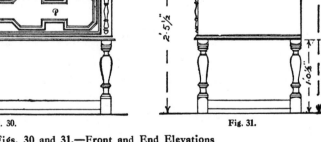

Fig. 31.

Figs. 30 and 31.—Front and End Elevations

SCALE OF FEET

and rebated over the rails and stiles, with a moulding planted on to form the raised and shaped panels. The sides of the drawer are dovetailed to the front, and the usual construction of a well-made drawer as shown gives the necessary finish. The top is mitred and rebated to suitable sinking to take it, but this would be a matter of taste. The flap would be fixed by brass counter-flap hinges sunk. The handles should be of a good pattern. Those suggested are drop handles and are a little later in style than Jacobean, but, nevertheless, are very suitable. The lock-

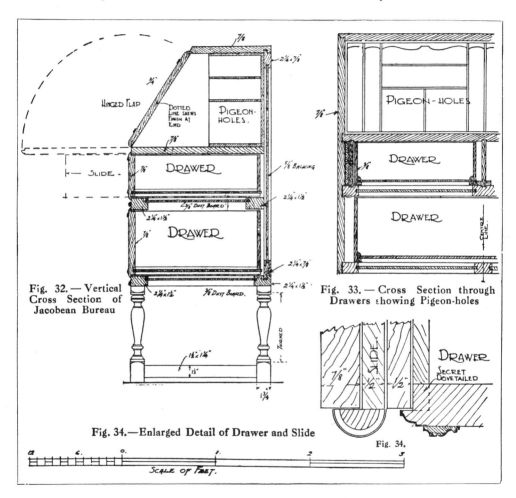

Fig. 32. — Vertical Cross Section of Jacobean Bureau

Fig. 33. — Cross Section through Drawers showing Pigeon-holes

Fig. 34.—Enlarged Detail of Drawer and Slide

Fig. 34.

SCALE OF FEET.

sides as shown. Details of the drawers are shown by Figs. 33 and 34.

The slides to support the flap are masked by the turning to which they are fixed. The flap is solid, but could be framed if wished, the panel mouldings covering the joints, and also, if desired, it can have a leather cover inside with plates should be open strap-work or fretted ; a number of suitable designs can always be selected from at a good iron-monger's shop.

The pigeon-holes are formed of $\frac{1}{4}$-in. wood, and can be built up to meet requirements. Those shown are of useful dimensions for stationery. Small drawers can also be introduced ; but these should be raised 2 in. or 3 in. above the writing surface to clear all loose papers.

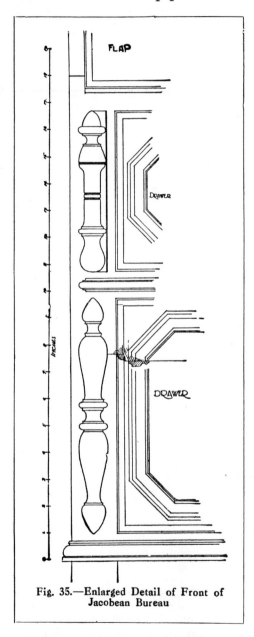

Fig. 35.—Enlarged Detail of Front of Jacobean Bureau

The legs supporting the whole should be carefully turned to a simple pattern,

the mouldings small, in keeping with the period, and the struts slightly rounded on the top corners. An enlarged detail of the front is given by Fig. 35.

The most suitable finish would be to stain and wax-polish.

COMBINED WRITING-TABLE AND CABINET

The combined writing-table and cabinet shown by Fig. 36 is 4 ft. 6 in. high, 2 ft. 2 in. wide, and 1 ft. 3 in. deep. The top portion serves as a china cabinet, the doors having leaded lights and copper fittings. Below the cabinet is a nest of pigeon-holes, and under this is a drawer, which, when partly drawn out, forms a rest for the writing flap above. The lower portion is fitted with two shelves for books.

Oak would be the best material to use, but the nest of pigeon-holes would look better in satinwood or holly. The leading dimensions are given in the drawings (Figs. 37 and 38). Fig. 37 shows alternative designs for the leaded lights of the cabinet. A full-size section of the whole cabinet should be prepared before beginning the construction.

First get out the two ends, which are 1 ft. 3 in. in the widest part, and therefore would probably have to be jointed up. As the upper portion of the ends is 8 in. wide, the best position for the joint would be in continuation of this width. Shoot the back and top and bottom edges, and mark the outline and the positions of the housings. Work a rebate on the inside back edges, as shown at A (Fig. 39), for a length of 2 ft. $4\frac{1}{4}$ in. from the top. Next cut out the housings for B, C, D, and the two shelves E (Fig. 38), B, C, and E being dovetailed, as shown by Fig. 40, and B and D plain-housed. The frame D is mortised and tenoned together, as shown by Fig. 41. The back edge is rebated, and a hollow is worked on the front edge (see also F and G, Fig. 42). Having prepared the shelves B, C, E, and the framework D (Figs. 38 and 42), cut their ends to fit into the corresponding housings, and work a scotia moulding on the front edge of the shelf B.

The top of the cabinet should now be prepared, and housings cut to enable it to fit over the ends. A rebate is worked on the back under edge, as shown at H in Fig. 42. The top is afterwards moulded. Care should be taken, when preparing the ends, not to chip off the wood between the housings and the outer edges. The two ends are housed into the feet or bearers J (Figs. 37 and 38), which are of 3½-in. by 1½-in. stuff, shaped as shown.

Next to be taken in hand are the doors of the cabinet, the writing flap, and the drawer. The doors are mortised and tenoned together in the usual way, and are rebated on the inside to receive the leaded-glass panels, which are held in position by small beading sprigged to the frame. The two meeting-stiles are rebated, and a bead is run along the face of one, as shown in section at Fig. 43. A small bead is secured round the cabinet, as shown at M (Fig. 42), to form a stop for the doors. The correct width for the writing flap should be ascertained by measurement; this would come out at about 1 ft. 0¼ in. The frame is mortised and tenoned together. A tongue is worked on the panel edges, fitting into corresponding grooves on the inside of the frame (*see* Fig. 42). The inner surface of the panel should be a trifle below that of the frame, as it has to be covered with green baize, which is glued over the panel. This covering may be dispensed with if desired, in which case the panel should be flush, as shown. A thumb moulding is worked on the edges as shown. The flap, when closed, rests on two strips screwed to the ends (*see* Figs. 36 and 42). The drawer is constructed in the ordinary way, and does not require any special description. A narrow strip of baize should be glued along the top edge of the front, to prevent the surface of the flap from being scratched when it is resting on the drawer, and two drawer stops o (Fig. 42), 1½ in. long, should be screwed to the framework D to prevent the drawer being pushed too far back. The span rail K is got out of 3-in. by ⅝-in. stuff, and should be shaped as shown in Fig. 37;

this may be secured by simply butting against the ends, but it would be better to let it in.

The framework D (Fig. 42) and the shaped span rail K should be blocked at the angle, as shown in Figs. 38 and 42. The back, which should be screwed to the shelves, sides, etc., is made up of ½-in.

Fig. 36.—Combined Writing-table and Cabinet

boards grooved and tongued together. The doors are hung with ordinary 1½-in. brass butt hinges. One keyplate only is necessary, but two look better. Suitable drawer handles should be fixed, and a keyplate should be screwed both to the drawer front and to the face of the flap.

The nest of pigeon-holes, shown in elevation by Fig. 44, is made separately

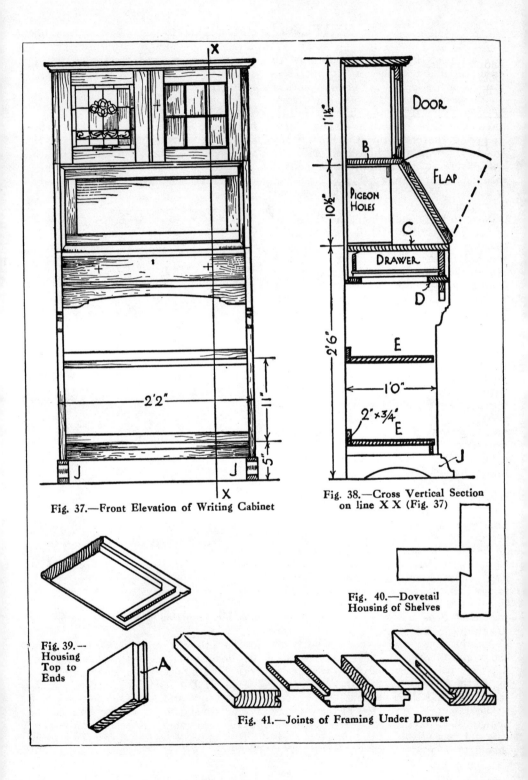

X

DOOR

1'1½"

B

FLAP

PIGEON
HOLES

10½"

C

DRAWER

D

2'6"

E

1'0"

2" × ¾"

E

J

X

Fig. 37.—Front Elevation of Writing Cabinet

2'2"

11"

5"

J   J

Fig. 38.—Cross Vertical Section
on line X X (Fig. 37)

Fig. 39.—
Housing
Top to
Ends

A

Fig. 40.—Dovetail
Housing of Shelves

Fig. 41.—Joints of Framing Under Drawer

and slipped in from behind, the depth from back to front being 6 in. Material ¼ in. thick should be used for this. The bottom corners are fitted with drawers, as shown in Fig. 44. The arched pieces L should be well glued in last of all.

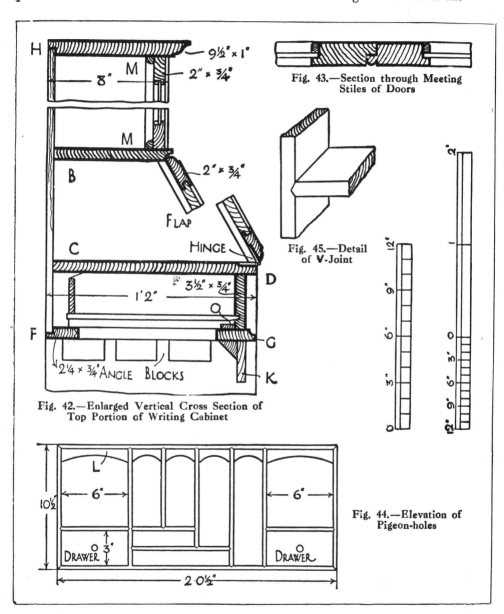

Fig. 43.—Section through Meeting Stiles of Doors

Fig. 45.—Detail of V-Joint

Fig. 42.—Enlarged Vertical Cross Section of Top Portion of Writing Cabinet

Fig. 44.—Elevation of Pigeon-holes

corners are mitred together, the V-ends of the division pieces fitting tight into corresponding grooves (*see* also Fig. 45). The

The cabinet may be fumigated and wax-polished, or stained, the former method being the more suitable.

RECESSED BOOKCASE-SECRETAIRE

The use of a recess for a fitted bookcase which has an escritoire or writing attachment is a feature which will no doubt be appreciated in many dining-rooms. In most small houses and flats there is hardly room for a bookcase, if the sideboard, dining-table, and dinner-wagon receive the space they deserve for appearance and comfort. In such circumstances a bureau-bookcase is really desirable, and, fitted as suggested in a recess at the side of the fireplace, it has the considerable advantage of being in a fairly warm part of the room, a feature which should not be ignored.

A secretaire of the type shown in the perspective drawing (Fig. 46) not only economises space, but considerably reduces the cost, as only narrow ends are

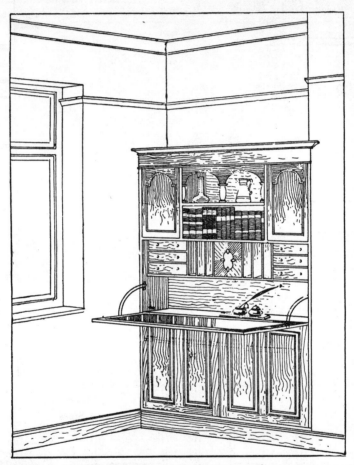

Fig. 46.—Recessed Bookcase-secretaire

required, and a back can be dispensed with if the wall is moderately level and in good condition. As will be seen from the illustration, the most is made of the available space. The two side cupboards are invaluable for ink, spare pens, extra stock of stationery, and old correspondence, which is usually untidy if not

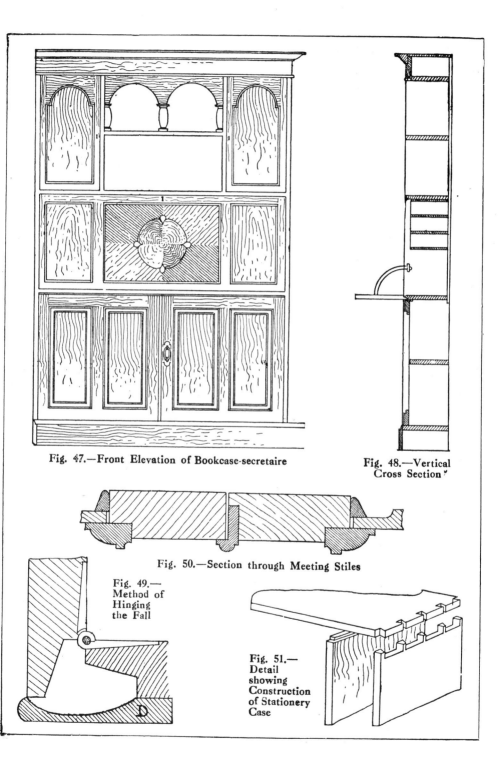

Fig. 47.—Front Elevation of Bookcase-secretaire

Fig. 48.—Vertical Cross Section

Fig. 50.—Section through Meeting Stiles

Fig. 49.— Method of Hinging the Fall

Fig. 51.— Detail showing Construction of Stationery Case

definitely provided for, whilst the centre part is fitted up for a few necessary works of reference or much-used volumes. The arched cupboard part is quite a decorative feature if furnished with one or two pieces of pottery or pewter.

But the main feature, and the one most appreciated, is the secretaire writing-part fitted with drawers and pigeon-holes, and provided with a fall-down writing-flap. This flap is certainly the most difficult part of the job, but the exercise of ordinary care and accuracy should ensure success. The large cupboards underneath the writing part are invaluable for the storage of small portfolios, part numbers, and general impedimenta. In this instance the carcase ends should extend from underneath the dustboard at the top right down to the floor, and, as will be seen in the elevation (Fig. 47), all the main divisions can be fixed between the carcase ends, so as to form the necessary divisions. An important point to bear in mind is that the cornice rail runs right through, it being necessary to cut away the carcase ends just the thickness of the rail for this purpose. The top of the carcase is set back for this reason, as indicated in the sectional view (Fig. 48).

The table shelf must be shaped on the front edge, as shown in Fig. 49. Ordinary brass back-flap hinges are used to connect the flap with the table shelf, and if the edges are shaped as shown, the flap will fall level with the shelf. Having prepared the cornice board to the section indicated, and also the table shelf, these parts and also the three other main horizontal divisions can be slip-dovetailed in between the carcase ends. Both the main vertical divisions can next be slip-dovetailed in position. Should the total width of the whole job exceed, say, 3 ft., it is a good plan to introduce a vertical division in the bottom part. This should be arranged to fit behind the doors, so that rebated action of the fall and shelf can be arranged.

After the main carcase has been glued up and set, the doors and flap should be proceeded with. The top doors should be made with a small stuck moulding

forming a rebate to receive the panel, and the bottom doors should be made as shown by Fig. 50. Long and short shouldered joints are necessary. The mouldings are then fitted in as shown to receive the panel.

The flap or fall should be made rather like an ordinary three-panelled door, which means that the framing should be mortised and tenoned together with the panels grooved in with bare-faced tongues. These should be carefully fitted so that they come flush on the inside. The panels should, of course, be veneered and cleaned up on the outside before being glued in, and in this connection it should be mentioned that if ordinary oak is used for the framing and nicely-figured oak for the side panels, the centre quartered device should be made from some well-marked pieces of pollard-oak veneer. The small pieces are intended to be of either rosewood or ebony.

The inside of the fall should have a veneer lipping about 1 in. wide glued round in order to receive the leather lining. This can easily be laid with a hammer, and should be cut to the exact width required with a cutting gauge after it is dry, the superfluous veneer being removed with a chisel.

The cornice rail and frieze moulding should next be attached, and the carcase may then be fitted and fixed in the recess. The cornice moulding may then be attached, one end of the moulding being returned on itself, as shown in the perspective view. This gives the necessary rebate to receive the dustboard, which can next be fitted and glued down.

In the sectional view (Fig. 48), a back to the upper part is shown, but the introduction of this part is quite optional. Should it be decided on, three-ply wood ⅜ in. thick is quite suitable. The arch should now be fitted with the columns as shown, with small square caps and vases to finish off the latter.

To complete the fall part, the frame should be fitted in the opening, and the small curved piece D (Fig. 49) attached as shown. Then the bottom edge of the fall is rebated, and the hinges cut in. It is important to note that the centre of the back flap-pin should coincide exactly with the corners of the flap and the shelf, in which case the former is bound to turn correctly, as on an axis, and, more important still, the inside surface will be level when the flap is lowered. The skirting should next be fitted, and then the bottom doors. Quadrant stays are used to support the falling flap.

The construction of one corner of the stationery case is shown by Fig. 51. All the vertical and horizontal divisions should be slip-dovetailed. This part should be completed by making the small centre door and the small drawers.

An open-grained finish to oak is desirable, this being effected by means of stain and slightly french-polishing. This should have a final rubbing with wax, which imparts a desirable tone to the work.

COMBINED WRITING-DESK AND BOOKCASE

The combination of a writing-desk and bookcase, both of which are desirable features in every home, are means by which economy of space is attained.

A design for a piece of furniture of this description is shown by Fig. 52. The lower portion is designed for the writing-desk, and the upper portion that of the bookcase. Drawers, trays, and cupboards are fitted in the two arms of the writing-desk; the drawers to accommodate small books, while the trays can be utilised for the indexing of catalogues, letters, or the storage of loose papers, as required. These trays are a saving on ordinary drawers, both in labour and material, their construction being very simple and light. The long cupboards will conveniently take rolls, etc. Between these two arms immediately below the writing-desk a rack is fitted, which can be utilised for keeping ledgers or other ponderous books.

The desk itself is provided with a slightly sloping top, and forms the cover to a large shallow drawer suitable for the storage of large papers which require to be kept flat. A locker comes directly

behind this desk, and can be used for storing documents of a private nature, so that they are always close at hand if wanted. A flap is provided to close the locker. The desk could be easily fitted up as a roll-top desk, if desired, by securing runners to the panels at the side of the desk; and the roll cover could be fixed inside the locker just mentioned, the flap being omitted.

Fig. 52.—Combined Writing-desk and Bookcase

The end compartments of the bookcase are provided with shelves, adjustable to any desired position. This is effected by fixing to the framing strips of brass which are holed to receive small hardwood pegs. These pegs are removed to the required place, and the shelves are rested on them. In these end compartments can be stored books which are not often in use, while the centre portion is for books more frequently wanted. This

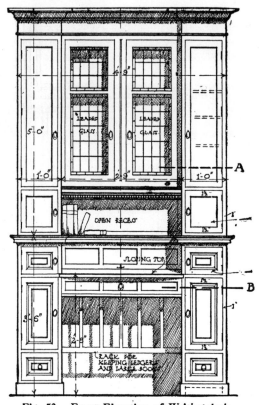

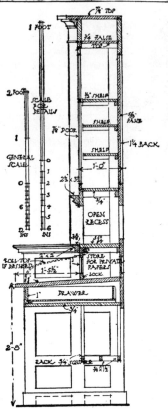

Fig. 53.—Front Elevation of Writing-desk
and Bookcase

Fig. 57.—Vertical Cross
Section through Centre

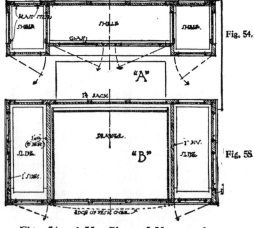

Figs. 54 and 55.—Plans of Upper and
Lower Parts

Fig. 56.—End Elevation
of Lower Part

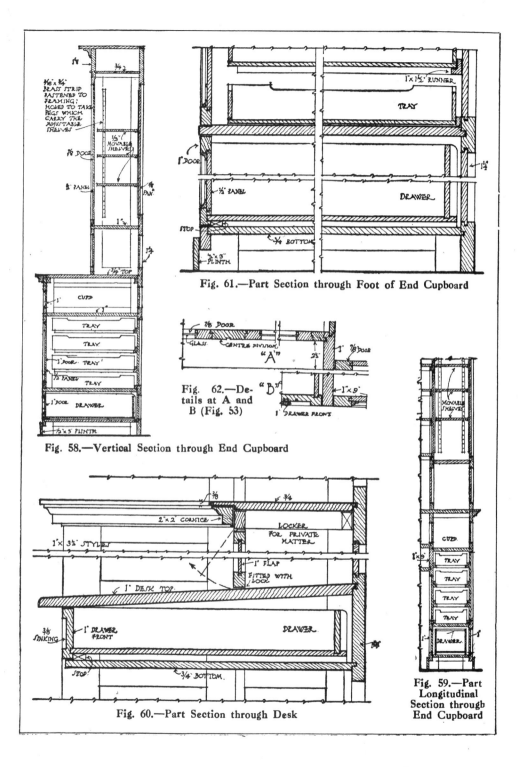

Fig. 61.—Part Section through Foot of End Cupboard

Fig. 62.—Details at A and B (Fig. 53)

Fig. 58.—Vertical Section through End Cupboard

Fig. 60.—Part Section through Desk

Fig. 59.—Part Longitudinal Section through End Cupboard

centre cupboard is fitted with ordinary shelving, and the doors are glazed with plain, clear leaded-glass in small squares.

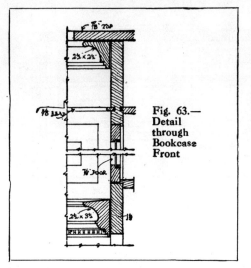

Fig. 63.—
Detail
through
Bookcase
Front

Below this centre cupboard and over the locker previously mentioned is an open recess, meant for putting books which are in everyday use. The recess is left open at the back, the coloured wall showing

through, lending relief to the whole. This design, of course, is meant to be executed in hardwood, and would look exceedingly well in polished mahogany, while the cornice and plain leaded glazing are very pleasing. If variety is desirable, inlaid panels may be fixed, and the small bead shown in the panels omitted.

The illustrations may be described as follows : Fig. 52 a perspective sketch, Fig. 53 a front elevation, Fig. 54 a plan at A (Fig. 53) and Fig. 55 a plan at B (Fig. 53), Fig. 56 a part side elevation, Fig. 57 a vertical section through the centre, Fig. 58 a vertical section through the end cupboard, Fig. 59 a part longitudinal section through the end cupboard, Fig. 60 a part section through the writing-desk, Fig. 61 a part section through the foot of the end cupboard, Fig. 62 details at A and B (Fig. 53), and Fig. 63 a detail through the bookcase front (Fig. 57).

OFFICE FURNITURE

Writing furniture and fitments possessing a characteristic style pertaining to the office are dealt with in a later section under the title of Office Furniture.

Plant Stands, etc.

OCTAGONAL STOOL FOR JARDINIÈRE

THE stool illustrated by Fig. 1 is intended to be finished with white paint and enamel.

Regarding the wood, dry yellow pine or American whitewood would be suitable, that is, if it is to be finished with paint and enamel. For the dining-room, hall, or study the stool would perhaps be more suitably made in one of the furniture hardwoods (figured oak for choice), and finished with a wax polish.

The working drawings (Figs. 2, 3, 4 and 5) give all necessary dimensions, and the method of construction is shown in the sectional views (Figs. 3 and 5), where it will be seen that the body of the stool is built up on two octagonal moulds, each cut from 1-in. stuff, and these should be prepared first. The lower mould is perforated with a 6-in. diameter hole for access to the inside of the stool when assembling and painting, and the upper mould has four holes bored, through which 1¾-in. (No. 14) screws pass to secure the top of the body.

The plan view (Fig. 4) indicates the method of striking out the octagonal top, and in marking out the two moulds by the same method great accuracy should be secured, as otherwise the eight sides of the octagon will not be all of the same length, and consequently the eight planks forming the sides of the body will have to be of varying widths, which will bring extra trouble with doubtful results. The best way to ensure accuracy and similarity in the moulds is carefully to set out the top mould and bore the four screw-holes already referred to, and through these holes screw the two pieces together, cutting and planing them both to shape and size at the one operation.

Fig. 6 shows the setting-out of the sides. The 6-in diameter hole in the lower mould should be fret-sawn out, as are also the ornamental perforations and shapings to the eight planks of ⅜-in. stuff forming the sides of the stool.

If the dimensions given in the diagrams are adhered to, the *inside* width of the planks will be approximately $4\frac{1}{16}$ in. ; but the actual width must be taken from the moulds when these are finished. Hence the advice to cut these first ; and bearing in mind the fact that the *outside* width is greater, the first thing to do on the planks, after they have been planed up, is to mark the inside width off on the inside faces with a marking gauge, leaving about ¼ in. on the outside of each mark. Then follows the shooting of the bevelled edges of these members, and to ensure the accuracy which is essential to good joints, it is advisable to do this part of the job on the donkey-ear shooting-board shown by Fig. 7, a trying plane being used in the same manner as for square-edge shooting. The illustration shows one of the planks (dotted) in position ready for shooting. Of course the

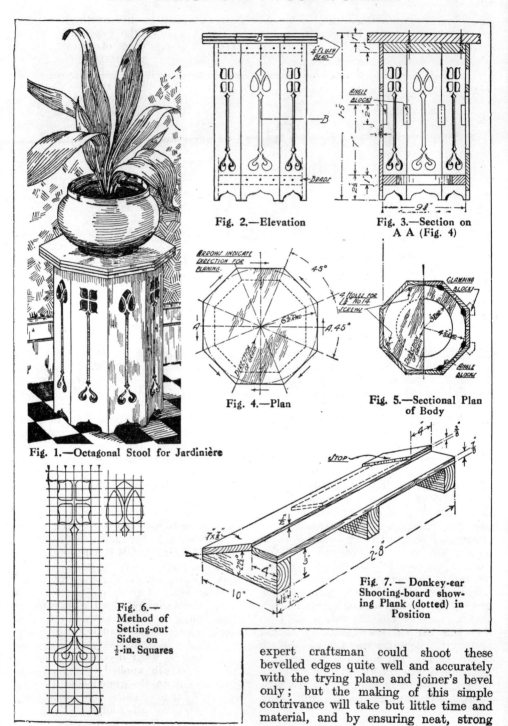

Fig. 2.—Elevation

Fig. 3.—Section on A A (Fig. 4)

Fig. 4.—Plan

Fig. 5.—Sectional Plan of Body

Fig. 1.—Octagonal Stool for Jardinière

Fig. 6.— Method of Setting-out Sides on ½-in. Squares

Fig. 7. — Donkey-ear Shooting-board showing Plank (dotted) in Position

expert craftsman could shoot these bevelled edges quite well and accurately with the trying plane and joiner's bevel only; but the making of this simple contrivance will take but little time and material, and by ensuring neat, strong joints would amply repay the less competent woodworker for the extra trouble that would be necessitated.

Each plank is secured in place with glue and six 1¼-in. brads, three in each mould (*see* the elevation). When the body has been glued and nailed together, and before the glue has had time to set, some strong cord (venetian-blind cord would do) should be tightly bound round it midway between the two moulds to cramp the joints of the planks together, the angles formed by these being protected from bruising under the cord by means of the clamping blocks shown in the sectional plan. Whilst the body is thus cramped up, angle blocks are glued into the internal angles; they should be planed up to fit those angles to secure strength at these points. After the glue has set, the cord and clamping blocks may be removed. The brads should be punched about ⅛ in. below the surface, and the exterior of the body cleaned up with a fine-set smoothing-plane.

The top of the stool can now be taken in hand. It is shown with its edges ornamented with a ¼-in. flush bead, and this should be worked exactly in the middle of the thickness of the stuff, for the reason that adjacent sides of the octagon have in some cases to be worked from opposite directions to avoid working against the grain (*see* arrows and direction of grain on the plan), and if the bead is not central on the edges it will not intersect correctly at the angles. This done, the job should be rubbed down with fine glasspaper, in preparation for painting or wax-polishing; but in this operation go gently at the angles, otherwise they will soon lose their sharp-cut appearance.

In the case of an enamel finish, a coat of priming should first be given, then the brad holes should be stopped and two coats of paint applied. The paint should be made so that it will dry " flat," that is, without gloss; and this is accomplished by using more turpentine and less linseed oil than for ordinary paint. Each coat of paint should be lightly rubbed down when quite dry and hard, and here

again care must be taken with the angles, or bare wood will be exposed at these points. The two coats of enamel should be evenly laid on, and the stool is finished. For the convenience of painting or polishing, it is advisable to remove the top, which can be refixed when the wax polish or last coat of enamel is hard. The inside of the stool should be given at least the priming and two coats of paint.

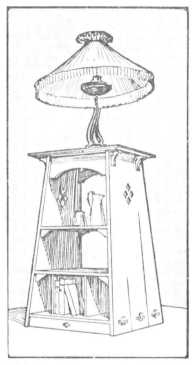

Fig. 8.—Pedestal Lamp-stand with Bookshelves

PEDESTAL LAMP-STAND OR FLOWER-STAND WITH BOOK-SHELVES

The pedestal shown by Fig. 8 is made in the simplest manner possible, namely, that in which the construction forms the decoration or, more properly speaking, the design, as the word decoration suggests rather too much applied ornamentation not essential to the construction. The working drawings show the sizes most likely to give all-round satisfactory

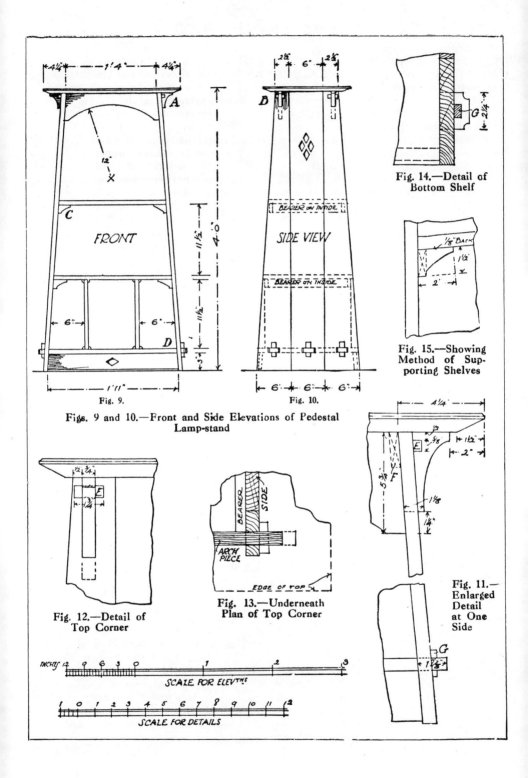

Fig. 14.—Detail of Bottom Shelf

Fig. 15.—Showing Method of Supporting Shelves

FRONT

SIDE VIEW

Fig. 9.

Fig. 10.

Figs. 9 and 10.—Front and Side Elevations of Pedestal Lamp-stand

Fig. 12.—Detail of Top Corner

Fig. 13.—Underneath Plan of Top Corner

Fig. 11.—Enlarged Detail at One Side

INCHES

SCALE FOR ELEV^TNS

SCALE FOR DETAILS

results; but they can be varied somewhat if desired in order to produce a more elongated appearance, by increasing the height anything up to 5 ft., and perhaps reducing the width and depth, these being matters for individual adjustment, although it is not advisable to increase the bulk beyond the widths given, or a ponderous effect may be produced.

The illustrations consist of front and side elevations (Figs. 9 and 10) and six details of small parts to a larger scale, and from these it will be seen that the main supports are the sloping sides shown on edge in the front view and broadside on in the other. These sides are composed of three 6-in. by $\frac{3}{4}$-in. (less thick if oak is the material) boards laid edge to edge, tapered upwards to a total width of 11 in. at the top, and simply ornamented with a pattern of four diamonds set out on a centre line 3 ft. 3 in. up from the floor level, pierced right through the middle. The three boards are held together by bearers on the inside for the shelves, as will be described later, and two shaped pieces to go at the top should be cut out, following the dimensions shown on the front view and the detail (Fig. 11), including the radius of 12 in. for the curved lower edge. The ends are cut out with pieces $4\frac{1}{2}$ in. deep, projecting $2\frac{1}{4}$ in., and shaped to the hollow curve shown, each projection being fitted through a $4\frac{1}{2}$-in. by $\frac{3}{4}$-in. slot cut in the top of the sides, and secured by a $\frac{5}{8}$-in. wedge 2 in. long fixed through a small slot cut to receive it, as at E (Figs. 11 and 12). Inside at the top, where indicated on the former detail by dotted lines at F, is a ledge or stiffener similar to the bearers required for the shelves below, about 2 in. by $\frac{1}{2}$ in. butting against the shaped arch-pieces at each end.

The enlarged plan (Fig. 13) shows one of the arch-pieces passing through a side and a wedge pushed through the projecting end of the arch, also the position of the bearer on the inside out of sight. The top will subsequently be completed by a good overhanging shelf as dimensioned, having a wide bevel below and a small one to take off the top edge as shown. The widths forming this will have to be dowelled together where they butt, or else have ledges on the underside between the arches, similar to the bearer previously described. When the whole stand has been completed and the top is nailed or screwed downwards on to its supports, the upper part will be found quite secure and rigid.

Dealing next with the bottom, this has a shelf in three widths 3 in. above the floor, and each width has a piece $2\frac{1}{4}$ in. wide projecting $1\frac{7}{8}$ in., with its angles hollowed out all as on the detail (Fig. 14). Each of these projections is secured by a wedge (G on detail; see also Fig. 11) very similar to those used at the top. Under the front and back edges of this bottom shelf are fitted thin skirtings just clear of the floor, and a diamond $1\frac{3}{4}$ in. long is cut out of the centre of each as shown. At a height of $11\frac{1}{2}$ in. above this shelf is fitted another similar one, but with the difference that as the sides are already tied in sufficiently top and bottom by the construction adopted (which is, of course, an old craftsman's method), it will only require to be supported by two 2-in. by $\frac{1}{2}$-in. ledges or bearers, one along each side, the ends of which are concealed by thin brackets 2 in. by $1\frac{1}{2}$ in. shaped as in Fig. 15 (where the ledge behind is shown by dotted lines), and fixed $\frac{1}{8}$ in. back from the edge of the shelf. The bottom space can be subdivided by two upright pieces into three compartments, these uprights being grooved into the shelves at top and bottom, or fixed with small angle fillets as indicated on the front view.

Another shelf is fixed $11\frac{1}{2}$ in. or so above the last, precisely similar, except that in consequence of the slope of the design its length and width are rather less. All the slopes will need careful setting out before cutting the stuff, and the number of angles just slightly out of the square will be found to be rather greater than usual, and while not presenting any degree of difficulty, will call for care and forethought in the work to ensure the best results.

The stand would constitute a useful

fitting by itself, or would form a very effective pedestal for a large shaded lamp, for which purpose a few books arranged in the lower part would give sufficient

the inside of one end to the enclosed space under the bottom shelf, and so into the floor or to a wall plug on the skirting.

Fig. 16.—Plant Stand

stability, while the electrician would have a good opportunity to fit up some type of table lamp to stand on the top, for which the wire might be taken down on

PLANT STAND

The work entailed in the construction of the plant stand shown by the photographic reproduction (Fig. 16) is of quite a simple character.

First prepare the four legs, which are to be 1 in. square and 3 ft. 5⅝ in. long. The diagonal rails marked A and B in the elevation (Fig. 17) are to be tenoned into the legs as shown at C in the plan (Fig. 18). A detail of these rails and their joints is shown by Fig. 19. The joint between rail

ported a flat shelf ½ in. thick and 9⅞ in. square, slightly rounded off on all four sides and notched out at each corner, as shown in Fig. 20, in order to fit round the legs. It will be necessary to double-rebate the legs, as shown in Figs. 21 and 22, for a height of 11¾ in. above the top of the shelf before any parts of the work are fixed together. This will leave room

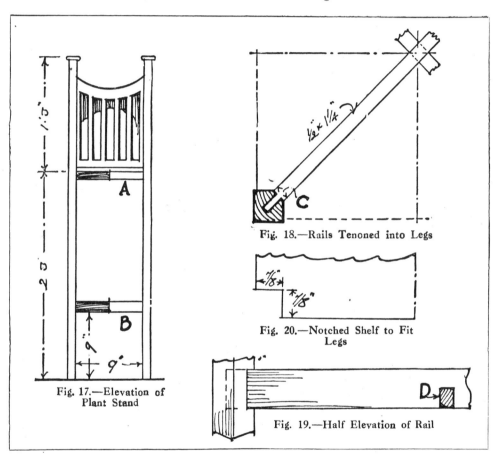

Fig. 18.—Rails Tenoned into Legs

Fig. 20.—Notched Shelf to Fit Legs

Fig. 17.—Elevation of Plant Stand

Fig. 19.—Half Elevation of Rail

and leg is made by first taking off the inner angle of the leg to a width of ½ in., as at C (Fig. 18), for a height of 1¼ in., at the correct level, and then working a mortise 3/16 in. wide and about ¾ in. long in the middle of the angle as indicated. The rails are halved together where they cross in the centre, as shown at D (Fig. 19). On the upper pair of rails there is sup-

for the four fretwork sides of which the dimensions are given in Fig. 23. Wood of ¼ in. thickness should be used for these. Fig. 23 also shows the method of setting these sides out. The top edge should be curved concavely to a radius of 7¼ in.

In fitting the sides into the ¼-in. rebates it will be sufficient to butt them against the top of the flat shelf, after which they can be glued in position and further secured by means of small fillets splayed as necessary to fit into position as at E (Fig. 24). As a finish to the legs small caps are secured to the tops of the legs. These should be 1⅝ in. square and ⅜ in. thick with rounded edges.

others are small packing-cases which have been reduced to the requirements of the case.

The box shown by the half-tone reproduction (Fig. 25) is a step beyond these primitive forms, but still very simple. It may be made of teak or oak, left natural

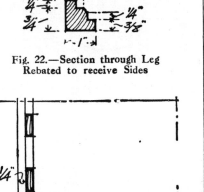

Fig. 22.—Section through Leg Rebated to receive Sides

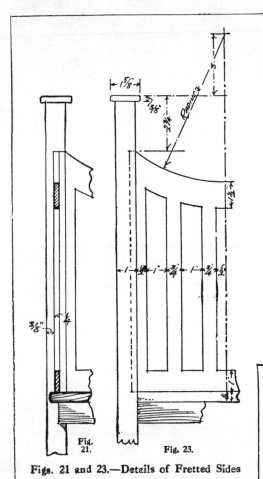

Figs. 21 and 23.—Details of Fretted Sides

Fig. 24.—Quarter Plan through Sides

surface, or in pine finished with paint or stain.

In making the box (of which Fig. 26 is a dimensioned elevation and Figs. 27 and 28 plan and section respectively), first prepare all the material by planing it to the sizes given in the following material list: For the sides, two pieces 15 in. long, 13 in. wide and ½ in. thick, and two similar pieces only 12 in. wide; for the bottom, four pieces 13 in. long, 2 in. wide and ½ in. thick; for the posts, four pieces 20¼ in. long and 1½ in. square; for the top rails, four pieces 11 in. long, 1¼ in. wide, and ⅞ in. thick; for the bottom rails, four pieces 11 in. long, 1¼ in. wide, and ⅜ in. thick;

SHRUB BOX FOR PORCH OR GARDEN

The appearance of a garden or porch is very often much improved by the introduction in simple and convenient positions of a few shrub boxes. While some of the more primitive are simply small barrels,

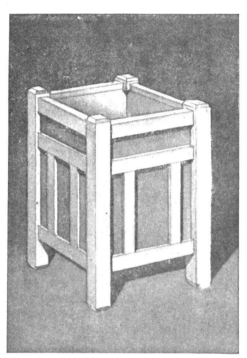

Fig. 25.—Shrub Box for Porch

and for the panelled effect on the sides four pieces 11 in. long and eight others $8\frac{3}{4}$ in. long, all being $1\frac{1}{4}$ in. by $\frac{3}{8}$ in. thick.

The sides of the box are then set out, two 15 in. by 13 in. wide, and two 15 in. by 12 in. wide. The first pair is then marked off for the notches of the bottom strips, which are cut out before the sides are put together. Cut

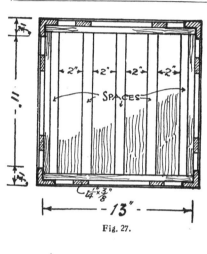

Fig. 27.

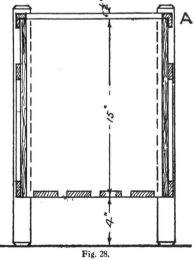

Fig. 28.

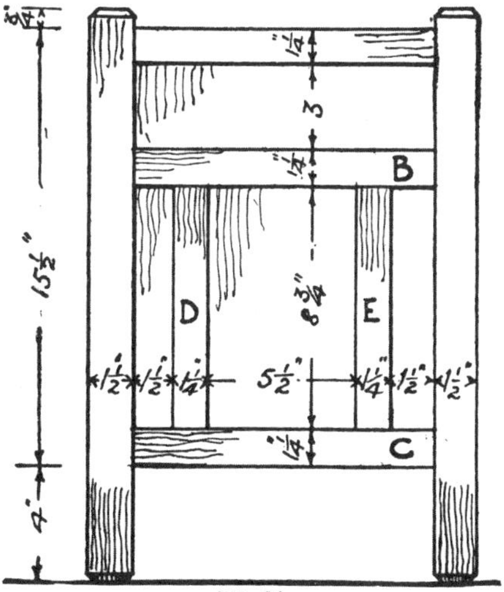

Fig. 26.

Figs. 26, 27 and 28.—Elevation, Plan and Vertical Section

the notches by sawing in the sides and chiselling out from the inner and outer face. Nail the box together as shown in Fig. 29, and fit the bottom strips in position as shown in Fig. 30, well securing them by means of nails. The corner posts are then cut to length, and checked

bottom as shown, and then fitted in position, and are fixed by screwing from the inside of the box.

The top rails are now prepared, and rebated as shown at A in Fig. 28. If a rebate plane is available, this part can be quickly done. If not, use a small saw

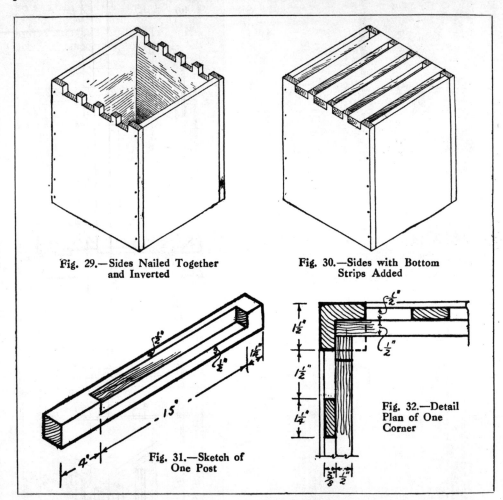

Fig. 29.—Sides Nailed Together
and Inverted

Fig. 30.—Sides with Bottom
Strips Added

Fig. 31.—Sketch of
One Post

Fig. 32.—Detail
Plan of One
Corner

out or stop-rebated as in Fig. 31, so as to fit the corners of the box. Careful work is required at this part, the posts being set out with the square and scratching gauge. Proceed with the cutting out of the notches, and see that they are cleaned out to form a right angle. These posts are slightly chamfered at top and

along marks on both edges, and cut out with the chisel. The horizontal rails are fitted in as shown at B and C in Fig. 26. Each of these pieces should be well screwed from the inside, as should also the uprights D and E, which are fitted last of all. A detail plan of one corner is shown by Fig. 32.

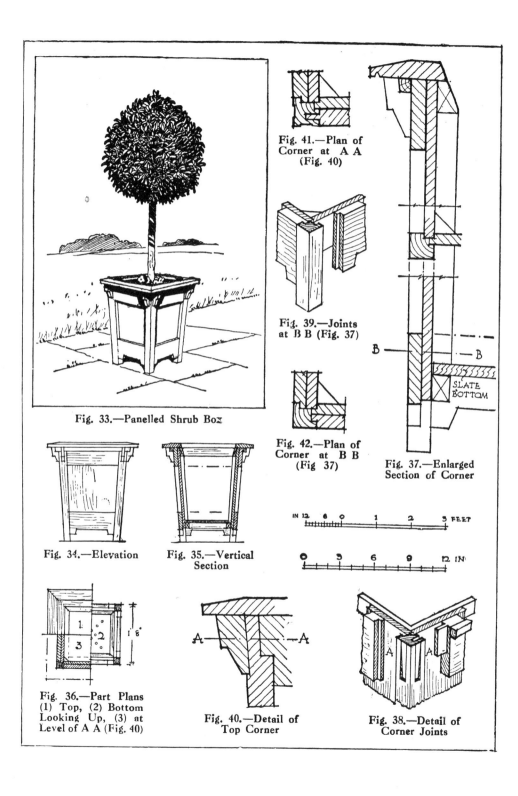

Fig. 41.—Plan of Corner at A A (Fig. 40)

Fig. 39.—Joints at B B (Fig. 37)

Fig. 42.—Plan of Corner at B B (Fig 37)

Fig. 37.—Enlarged Section of Corner

Fig. 33.—Panelled Shrub Box

Fig. 34.—Elevation

Fig. 35.—Vertical Section

Fig. 36.—Part Plans (1) Top, (2) Bottom Looking Up, (3) at Level of A A (Fig. 40)

Fig. 40.—Detail of Top Corner

Fig. 38.—Detail of Corner Joints

SLATE BOTTOM

IN 12 6 0   1   2   3 FEET

0   3   6   9   12 IN

The shrub box is then ready to be finished. Plane the joints smooth and glasspaper well, each member being glasspapered in the direction of the grain of the wood.

PANELLED SHRUB BOX

Fig. 33 (p. 1115) shows a rectangular panelled palm or shrub box of a more elaborate nature than the last. An elevation and vertical and horizontal sections are shown by Figs. 34, 35 and 36.

The carcase is held together by the grooving of the top and bottom rails of the respective sides of the angle posts, and made further secure by the application of the rebated and grooved jointing, angle blocks, and ledged treatment of the solid filling pieces at the back of the framing, so arranged to form sunk panels. The legs are 2 ft. 7½ in. long, 2½ in. square at the top, and diminished in length to finish 2¼ in. square at the bottom. The total height of the box, including the capping, is 2 ft. 9 in. The width at the top, exclusive of the capping, is 2 ft., and at the bottom 1 ft. 8 in.

The capping projects 3¼ in. beyond the face of the legs and top rail all round, and is made up in four pieces each 2 ft. 7 in. long, 6¾ in. wide, and 1½ in. deep, all splayed and grooved and mitred at the angles (*see* Figs. 36 and 37).

The top rails are 6 in. deep and the bottom rails 8 in. deep, and shaped as shown. Details of the jointing of the rails are shown by Figs. 38 and 39. The panel filling is 1 in. thick, and does not diminish in thickness. Therefore there will be a slight difference in the depth of the sunk panel from the face of the legs downwards, which will necessitate the bottom rail being slightly narrower than the top rail, and both planed off so as to diminish accordingly.

The respective sides would be framed up complete with legs, rails, and panels firmly secured and fitted together, the brackets, capping, small fillet under, and angle blocks being fixed afterwards.

The sectional drawings (Figs. 40, 41, and 42) are self-explanatory so far as the actual jointing of the different members is concerned, and are only to be taken as a guide in this respect, as it is obvious that a careful full-size setting out of the tapering sides and legs, etc., will be necessary before cutting the rebates, tenons, and grooves, in order that these may coincide and meet all round in a proper manner.

The box is shown as being provided with a perforated slate bottom supported on small bearers secured to the sides and mitred at the angles, but this could be replaced with strips spaced about ¾ in. apart, as in the preceding example.

FLOWER VASE WITH REPOUSSÉ PANELS

The vase shown by Fig. 43 is designed with the idea of using finger-plates in copper repoussé for ornamentation, but, of course, these could be omitted if desired.

Finger-plates of excellent design are purchasable from furnishing ironmongers in various styles of finish—dull and bright brass, copper, bronzing in various shades, and electro-plate. The standard size is 12 in. by 3 in., and four are required.

The vase itself, apart from the decoration, is entirely of wood with the exception of the water vessel, which is best made of zinc. Tinplate, however, may be used if coated inside with bath enamel, at least three thin coats being given.

The construction of the woodwork presents few difficulties except as regards the trumpet-mouthed head. The scale of inches will serve to fix all dimensions. The joints are made with glue and reinforced with thin brass pins, their heads being filed fair with the wood surface. Fig. 44 shows an elevation and Fig. 45 a half vertical section, whilst a plan of the base portion is shown by Fig. 46.

The trumpet mouth is made in the manner shown in Fig. 47. A piece of soft wood is planed accurately to a rectangular section measuring 2⅜ in. by 1⅞ in. and mitred into a square frame 8⅜ in. by 8⅜ in. externally. On the upper surface is laid down four strips of ¼-in. mahogany 1⅝ in. wide, mitred at the corners and securely glued together and to the soft-wood frame, to form the lip of the case, as shown in Figs. 45 and 47. The central opening in the frame must correspond accurately with that of the tube. Before joining the softwood pieces a light gauge line is run along the inside lower edge $\frac{1}{4}$ in. in. When the pieces are joined this

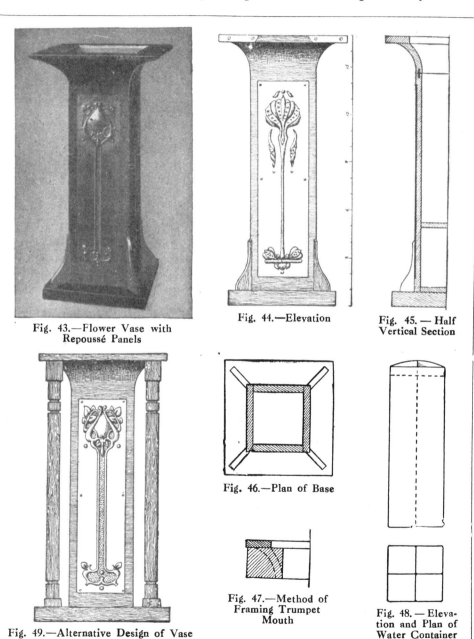

Fig. 43.—Flower Vase with Repoussé Panels

Fig. 44.—Elevation

Fig. 45. — Half Vertical Section

Fig. 46.—Plan of Base

Fig. 47.—Method of Framing Trumpet Mouth

Fig. 48. — Elevation and Plan of Water Container

Fig. 49.—Alternative Design of Vase

forms a starting-point for the carving of the external curve, which is of $1\frac{7}{8}$-in. radius. It is best to make a template to this radius, and it will be found convenient to make one of saw-blade, which can be used as a scraper to finish the surfaces after they have been cut to the approximate radius with the gouge. It will be seen that by using a mitred frame instead of a solid block, all work on the curved surfaces can be done lengthwise of the grain. Moreover, the mitre joints are useful guides in carving away the second pair of sides. It should be noted that the external radius ends $\frac{1}{4}$ in. inside the edge of the lip, as shown in Fig. 47. The trumpet mouth is attached to the tube with glue and small dowels of hardwood, eight of the latter being used (*see* Fig. 45).

The whole tube may next be veneered with mahogany, or such other wood as may be fancied, the grain of the veneer being laid across the length of the tube, thus allowing the veneer better to conform to the curve at the top. When the glue has set, the finger-plates may be laid in place and their outlines scribed on the veneer surface, after which the lines may be incised with a sharp knife, and the veneer within them removed with the chisel, so as to provide a sunk seating for each plate.

The base is a plain square $\frac{3}{4}$ in. thick, to which the tube is glued and screwed centrally ; but before assembling it is well to remove the angles of the tube for $3\frac{1}{2}$ in. from the bottom, so as to make a seating for each of the four buttress pieces. Fig. 46 shows the base in plan view, the tube being in section. The buttress pieces are cut from $\frac{1}{4}$-in. stuff, shaped as shown, and are secured with glue and fine pins.

Before assembling it is well to complete the glasspapering of all surfaces. French-polishing, either glossy or dull, gives the best result, but the kind of finish adopted will be determined by the class of wood used and the character of the finger-plates.

The finger-plates may be attached with brass pins or screws, the latter being preferable, as the thickness of wood is barely $\frac{1}{4}$ in.

The water vessel (Fig. 48) should be a loose fit in the wooden tube. It is best made with a lap joint at one corner and a turn-over to the inside at the top. The bottom should be attached in such a way as to avoid any projection outwards. A cross-piece made from strips of zinc $\frac{1}{2}$ in. deep is inserted at the top for the double purpose of giving a finger-hold and of better supporting the flower stems. The depth is 10 in.

The inside of the wooden tube should be finished with a thoroughly waterproof coating, as water is sure to be spilt on it from time to time. Either enamel or aluminium paint is suitable, and should be worked well into all the angles.

If a piece of fine cloth be glued to the base of the vase it will safeguard the polish of any surface on which it may be stood.

As the size of the vase is governed by that of the finger-plates, necessarily it comes out rather large ; but that is no drawback for large rooms. For a smaller vase the panels may be repoussé to a smaller size, or marquetrie decoration or such other form of enrichment as may appeal to the maker may be substituted.

On the other hand, if a more ambitious result be desired, the alternative design shown in Fig. 49 might be adopted, the construction of which will be obvious, it only differing from the one described in its larger base and the substitution of four square columns for the buttress pieces. The appearance of the vase is improved by adding four corner pieces to the trumpet lip, as shown in Fig. 44. These are strips of metal finished to match the finger-plates, each being secured with four screws.

Oak Bedroom Suite

THE bedroom suite illustrated and described in this section has been designed primarily for construction in oak, to be finished either a fumed colour or the dark Jacobean shade so much in vogue at the present time. For those workers who can afford to spend more time on the work an excellent result would be obtained (with but slight modification and the judicious use of mosaic bandings) in mahogany.

The Wardrobe.—Dealing first with the wardrobe, which is shown by the half-tone reproduction (Fig. 1), the over-all height of this is 6 ft. 6 in., carcase width 3 ft. 6 in., and depth 1 ft. 6 in. Front and side elevations are shown in Figs. 2 and 3 and a plan by Fig. 4.

It will be noted that in the photographic reproduction the upper panels of the two side pilasters enclose leaded lights, which may appeal to some workers as an alternative suggestion to the plain wooden panels shown in Fig. 2.

The construction follows the usual method, that is, the wardrobe is built up in four sections (*see* diagram, Fig. 5)—base or plinth, drawer carcase, hanging carcase and cornice, and the making of each will be dealt with in this order. The plinth frame is built up as shown at Fig. 6. The front and ends are mitred together, tongued and glue blocked ; a better method, but more tedious, would be to use secret dovetails at the front corners. The ends are connected at the

back by means of a stretcher, dovetail housed into them. This stretcher is wider than the rest of the frame by 1 in., the thickness of the moulded slip A (Fig. 7), to receive which it is notched as at B (Fig. 6). This slip is mitred at the corners, glued to the plinth frame, and strengthened by glue blocks. The section at Fig. 7 should make the construction clear, while the necessary sizes for the shaping of the front and ends are given in Fig. 8. The finished height of the plinth frame is 5¼ in. Care should be taken that when dry the frame is absolutely true and out of winding, as any twist would seriously hinder the successful fitting cf the upper carcases.

The drawer carcase has a solid bottom (which may, for the sake of economy, be of pine or whitewood faced with oak) lap-dovetailed into the ends, the grain of which runs vertically. The top, however, need not be solid, but may consist of front and back rails 3 in. wide, bracketed, as shown in Fig. 4, to obtain a greater width for dovetailing. The back for this carcase should be solid, clamped at the end with stiles 3½ in. wide (*see* Fig. 9) and screwed into a bevelled rebate in the ends as in Fig. 10. Before leaving the construction of this portion the worker is reminded that drawer carcases should be made slightly wider at the back in order to facilitate the smooth running of the drawers. The moulded slip capping this carcase is then mitred round and secured with glue and screws. The drawer itself is constructed in the usual manner, the front of $\frac{7}{8}$-in. wood, while the sides and back are $\frac{1}{2}$ in. and the bottom $\frac{1}{4}$ in.

The hanging carcase is constructed

Fig. 1.—Wardrobe of Suite

is framed up with stiles $3\frac{1}{2}$ in. wide and rails 3 in. wide, screwed into rebates as in Fig. 10. The interior fitting of the wardrobe is a matter for the individual. If the usual shelf, carrying triple swivel hooks, is fitted about 1 ft. from the top, it may be housed into the sides, or may rest upon fillets screwed to them. Ordinary coat hooks can then be fitted to rails screwed to the framed back and to the sides.

The two framed pilasters enclosing the door are mortised and tenoned together, with the panels fitted into ploughed grooves if the upper panels are of wood, while if a leaded light is used a rebated framing should be made. These pilasters are dowelled and glued to the carcase front. The door itself is a quite simple framing, into which the glass is fitted, as in Fig. 11, by small triangular blocks glued and pinned at intervals in the rebate. The inside of the rebate should be well blacked with a mixture of lamp-black and french polish to avoid unsightly reflections. A light framed back is fitted as in Fig. 12, a vertical stile running through with two rails mortised into it, with grooves ploughed into them for the reception of $\frac{1}{4}$-in. panels. The stile and rails are notched, so that the panels fit against the door frame; the whole back is attached to this with round-headed brass screws.

The height of the cornice is 6 in., and is commenced by making a plain dovetailed framing of pine, to which is glued a facing slip $\frac{1}{4}$ in. thick forming the frieze. The cornice moulding, which is built up in three sections as shown (Fig. 13), is mitred round and glued into

along similar lines, except that it will be more convenient to reverse the usual order in dovetailing, i.e. to cut the pins first and to mark the dovetails from them, supporting the ends vertically while this is being done. The back, shown in Fig. 9,

Fig. 2.

Fig. 3.

Figs. 2 and 3.—Front and Side Elevations of Wardrobe

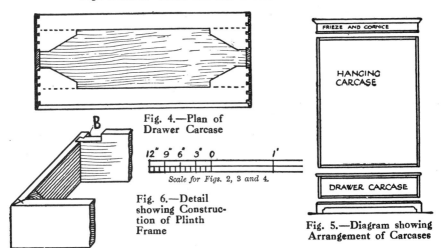

Fig. 4.—Plan of
Drawer Carcase

B

12" 9" 6" 3" 0   1'

Scale for Figs. 2, 3 and 4.

Fig. 6.—Detail
showing Construc-
tion of Plinth
Frame

FRIEZE AND CORNICE

HANGING
CARCASE

DRAWER CARCASE

Fig. 5.—Diagram showing
Arrangement of Carcases

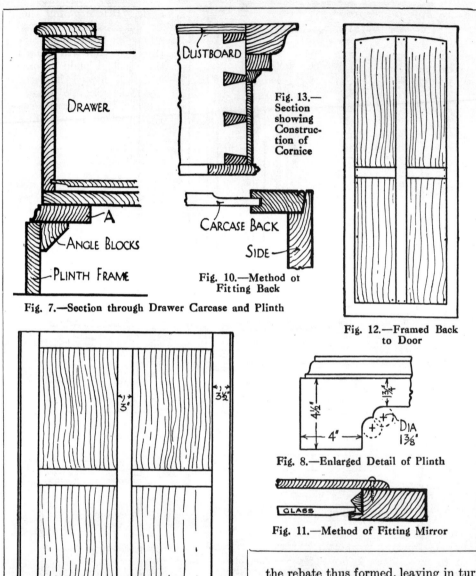

Fig. 13.—Section showing Construction of Cornice

Fig. 7.—Section through Drawer Carcase and Plinth

Fig. 10.—Method of Fitting Back

Fig. 12.—Framed Back to Door

Fig. 8.—Enlarged Detail of Plinth

Fig. 11.—Method of Fitting Mirror

Fig. 9.—Back Elevation

the rebate thus formed, leaving in turn another rebate for the reception of the dustboard. A frieze moulding mitred round, screwed and glued to the underside, completes this portion.

In assembling the four sections, the plinth frame can be secured to the drawer carcase with screws, while blocks are glued to the top and bottom of the hanging carcase fitting into the corners of the cornice frame and of the top moulding of the drawer carcase. In finishing, the parts of pine should be darkened to match the rest and finished by "dry-shining."

The Dressing Chest.—This is shown in half-tone by Fig. 14, and two elevations and the plan are shown in Figs. 15, 16 and 17. Ample drawer space is provided, but if a chest of drawers is included in the suite the piece might well be converted into a dressing-table proper, containing only the two top drawers. The construction of the ends is shown by Fig. 18. The legs are first planed to $1\frac{5}{8}$ in. square, tapering at the bottom to $1\frac{1}{8}$ in. No casters are shown in the illustrations, where these are desired it will be necessary to shorten the legs by $1\frac{1}{4}$ in. The ends, the grain of which runs vertically, are dowelled between the legs as shown. The position of the dowel holes must be carefully marked on both ends and legs, those on the latter being arranged so that the carcase ends are set back from the legs about $\frac{1}{4}$ in. A wooden depth gauge should be fixed to the twist bit used, in order to obtain the correct depth for each dowel hole. The next step is to cut the grooves B (Fig. 19) into which the drawer runners are housed, and also the stopped rebates on the rear legs which take the panelled back. The ends can then be cleaned up and glued between the legs. Fig. 19 (on p. 1125) shows the ends completed.

When quite dry the tops of the ends should be planed level and the rails and bottom prepared. The rails, bottom, and ends are then marked out for the mortise-and-tenon joints connecting them (*see* Fig. 19 and the detail in Fig. 20). The latter figure also shows the dovetailed joint between the top rail and the ends, and the arrangement of drawer runners

and dustboards. Before gluing the carcase together the drawer guides G (Figs. 21 and 22) should be screwed to the ends, being of a thickness that will bring them flush with the legs. A plain apron piece C (Fig. 15) is fitted between the legs, after which the carcase can be glued and cramped together. The drawer runners and dustboards, which may well be of

Fig. 14.—Dressing Chest of Suite

three-ply material, can then be fitted and inserted from the back. The panelled back, shown in Fig. 21, can now be constructed, fitted, and screwed in position. The whole carcase can then be cleaned up and glasspapered.

The drawer fronts should then be prepared and planed to a close fit into their respective apertures, after which the construction of each drawer framework can be taken in hand separately. The slips taking the drawer bottoms should next be glued in, and when dry the bottoms themselves fitted in and screwed. Each drawer can then be carefully planed till it slides smoothly, but is by no means loose. The drawer fronts having been cleaned up,

probably three pieces will have to be jointed together to obtain sufficient width. These joints should be dowelled, glued, and well cramped together. The moulding shown in Fig. 23 can then be worked on the front and ends, and the top after-

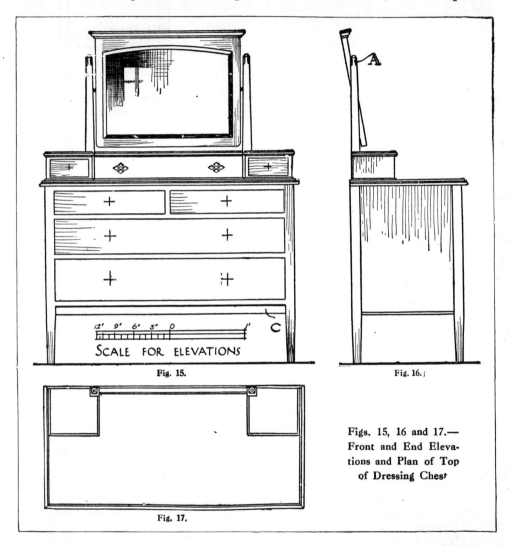

Fig. 15.

SCALE FOR ELEVATIONS

Fig. 16.

Fig. 17.

Figs. 15, 16 and 17.— Front and End Elevations and Plan of Top of Dressing Chest

small stops must be glued to each rail, and before the glue is set each drawer must be carefully pushed back to its desired position, in this case about ⅛ in. from the carcase front.

Next, the top can be proceeded with;

wards secured to the carcase by screwing through the front and rear top rails. After cleaning up and glasspapering the top, the upper portion of the chest can be taken in hand.

Here a beginning should be made with

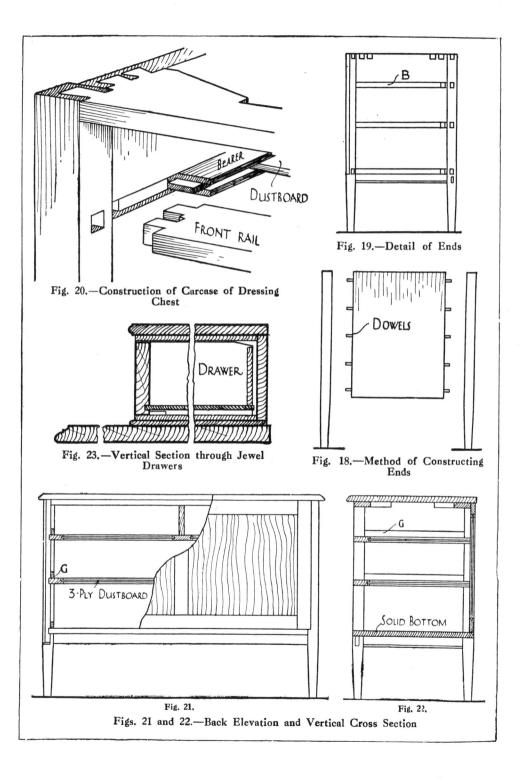

Fig. 20.—Construction of Carcase of Dressing Chest

Fig. 19.—Detail of Ends

Fig. 23.—Vertical Section through Jewel Drawers

Fig. 18.—Method of Constructing Ends

Fig. 21.

Fig. 22.

Figs. 21 and 22.—Back Elevation and Vertical Cross Section

the jewel boxes, a section through which is shown in Fig. 23. Each is a miniature drawer carcase, lap-dovetailed at top and

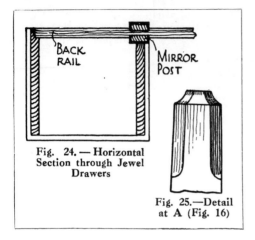

Fig. 24. — Horizontal Section through Jewel Drawers

Fig. 25.—Detail at A (Fig. 16)

bottom and with a moulded top and bottom secured with glue and small screws. The back of each outside end

Fig. 26.—Washstand of Suite

should have a rebate cut to receive the back rail, which runs the whole length of the table, connecting the two jewel

boxes and supporting the mirror posts and mirror (Fig. 24). The mirror posts, the upper ends of which are shaped as in Fig. 25, are fitted to the back rail by means of a bridle joint (Fig. 24). The diamond shape decoration on the back rail is intended to be recessed about $\frac{1}{8}$ in. The inside corners of the jewel boxes are then cut away to receive the posts, and the back rail and posts secured to the boxes with screws, long ones being used to fix the mirror posts to the inner ends of the jewel boxes. The whole superstructure can then be screwed to the top from underneath, and the jewel drawers made and fitted. The mirror frame can then be framed up and a length of ovolo moulding secured to the top edge with dowels. The frame should be fitted between the posts with good cast brass movements and a thin back cut to shape and screwed on.

The Washstand. — The washstand, illustrated by Fig. 26, is 2 ft. 5 in. high, including casters, and is designed to take a standard size marble top 3 ft. 6 in. by 1 ft. 6 in. Figs. 27, 28 and 29 show the necessary working drawings, while Fig. 30 shows a vertical section through the carcase. The construction of this is very similar to that of the dressing chest, the ends being dowelled between the legs and a solid bottom tenoned into the legs and trenched into the carcase ends (Fig. 31). The top rails are lap-dovetailed into the ends as in the dressing chest, while a central pilaster is tenoned between the bottom and the top rail, lying flush with the carcase front and being recessed as in the section (Fig. 32). The back should be framed together and screwed into rebates cut in the back legs, while the back rails are set in the thickness of it. An apron piece is fitted below the carcase bottom as in the dressing chest.

A section of the door frame is shown in Fig. 33, stiles and rails are 2 in. wide and are quite plain, enclosing a panel, the grain of which runs vertically. If possible, two well-figured panels of wainscot oak should be used for these, secured in position by a bead mitred round and pinned into the rebate. The doors are then hinged to the legs, being set back

side of the marble, in order to retain it in the correct position.

The upper part of the washstand is quite straightforward, consisting of a plain rebated frame into which are fitted vertically 6 in. by 2 in. white glazed tiles. The upper edge is shaped as shown, and

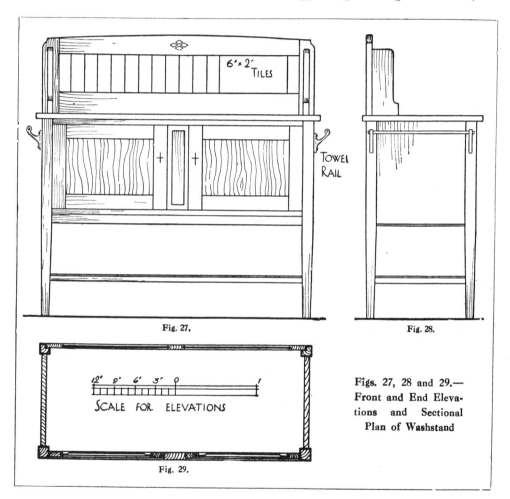

Fig. 27.

Fig. 28.

6"× 2" TILES

TOWEL RAIL

SCALE FOR ELEVATIONS

Fig. 29.

Figs. 27, 28 and 29.— Front and End Elevations and Sectional Plan of Washstand

slightly, as were the drawer fronts of the dressing chest, and bullet catches fitted in the edges of the meeting stiles. A door stop should then be glued and pinned in position. The marble top will be found to be so heavy that it will need no fastening to the carcase, but, if desired, blocks of soft wood may be glued to the under-

the diamond-shaped decoration recessed to a depth of about $\frac{1}{8}$ in. Brackets of the shape shown and $\frac{5}{8}$ in. thick are then prepared and secured to the back with stout screws. The whole is then screwed to the marble top; a sketch showing the positions of the screw-holes in the latter should be given when ordering the marble.

An alternative suggestion to the tiled back, and one in vogue at present, is that This substitution would in no way affect the method of construction. The piece

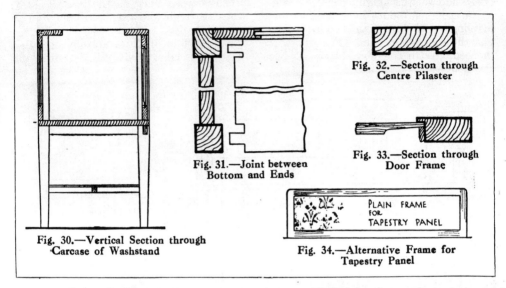

Fig. 32.—Section through Centre Pilaster

Fig. 33.—Section through Door Frame

Fig. 31.—Joint between Bottom and Ends

PLAIN FRAME FOR TAPESTRY PANEL

Fig. 30.—Vertical Section through Carcase of Washstand

Fig. 34.—Alternative Frame for Tapestry Panel

shown in Fig. 34, that is, a plain frame enclosing a glazed panel of good tapestry. can now be cleaned up and glasspapered, and towel rails screwed to the ends.

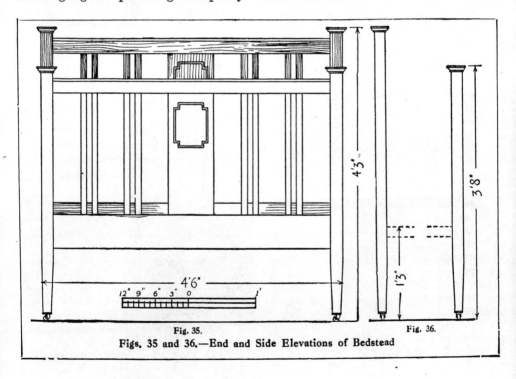

Fig. 35.

Fig. 36.

Figs. 35 and 36.—End and Side Elevations of Bedstead

Wooden Bedstead. — The woodwork in connection with the bedstead consists of the head and foot, which are connected by a pair of light angle-iron bearers carrying the mattress. These bearers, and the necessary brackets for fixing to the bedposts, should be obtained before commencing the construction of the bedstead. An excellent fitting is the "Vono" bedstead fitting, which has the advantage of rendering the whole affair rigid.

moulding. A moulding of the section shown in Fig. 38 is worked along the upper edges of the top rails; this will most easily be executed with the aid of a scratch stock and a suitably shaped cutter.

The upper panel on the central splats is obtained by pinning on a small moulding of suitable section, forming the shape shown in Fig. 35. Before gluing together, the whole should be well cleaned up, and

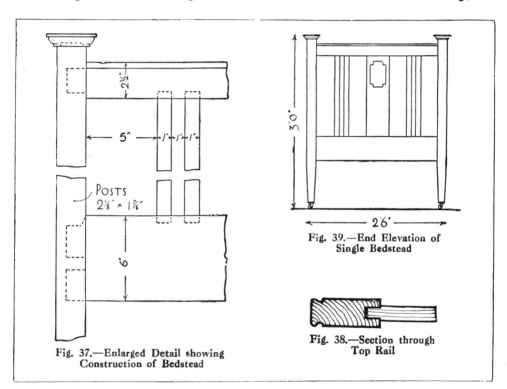

Fig. 37.—Enlarged Detail showing Construction of Bedstead

Fig. 39.—End Elevation of Single Bedstead

Fig. 38.—Section through Top Rail

Figs. 35 and 36 give the main dimensions and the general proportions of the head and foot. They are both straightforward pieces of joinery, details of the construction being shown in Fig. 37. The posts are planed to $2\frac{1}{8}$ in. by $1\frac{7}{8}$ in., while the thickness of the rails is 1 in. and that of the central splat $\frac{1}{2}$ in. The narrow vertical slats, arranged in pairs, are 1 in. by $\frac{1}{2}$ in. The tops of the posts are finished off by planting on a capping on which has been worked a plain ovolo

the sharp arris taken off all edges with glasspaper. Fig. 39 shows the sizes and modification of design necessary in making a single or a pair of twin bedsteads.

Bedside Cupboard.—A half-tone reproduction of this is shown by Fig. 40. The construction of this piece so closely resembles that of the washstand as to need little comment. A front elevation and section are shown by Figs. 41 and 42. Well-figured stuff should be chosen for

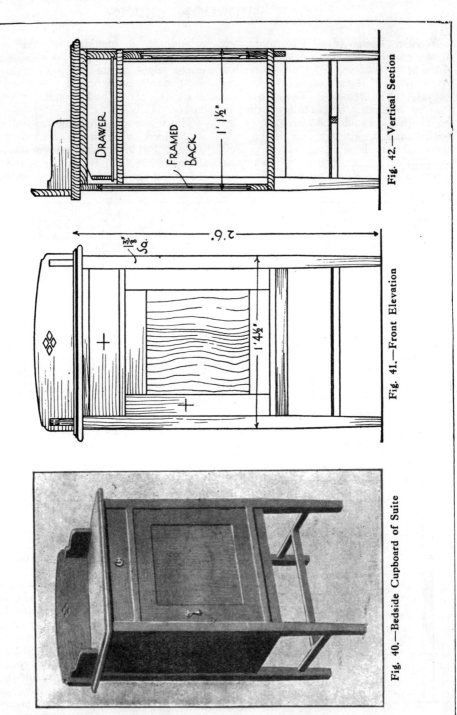

DRAWER

FRAMED BACK

1' 1½"

Fig. 42.—Vertical Section

2' 6"

1⅜" sq.

1' 4½"

Fig. 41.—Front Elevation

Fig. 40.—Bedside Cupboard of Suite

the door panel, and the back need not be framed, although, of course, it would be preferable. The upper drawer is 3 in. deep.

Chair.—The chair is shown in halftone by Fig. 43, and front and side

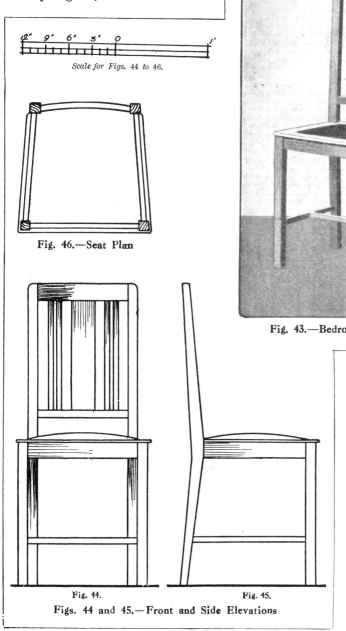

Scale for Figs. 44 to 46.

Fig. 46.—Seat Plan

Fig. 43.—Bedroom Chair of Suite

Fig. 44.

Fig. 45.

Figs. 44 and 45.—Front and Side Elevations

elevations and a plan of the seat are shown by Figs. 44, 45 and 46 respectively. It is quite straightforward in construction; the back, containing an arrangement of vertical slats similar to those of the bedstead, should be jointed and fitted together first. In cutting the back legs a template of $\frac{1}{2}$-in. stuff should first be cut to the shape shown and the legs marked out from this. A thin $\frac{3}{8}$-in. seat is screwed to the seat framing, and a plain upholstered pad tacked to this.

Wardrobes

SMALL WARDROBE WITH LEADED LIGHT

THE small hanging wardrobe shown in three elevations by Figs. 1, 2 and 3, and simple as possible. Figs. 1 and 2 give the principal dimensions.

The construction may be divided into three parts, the main carcase, the framed-up base or stand, and the cornice. In

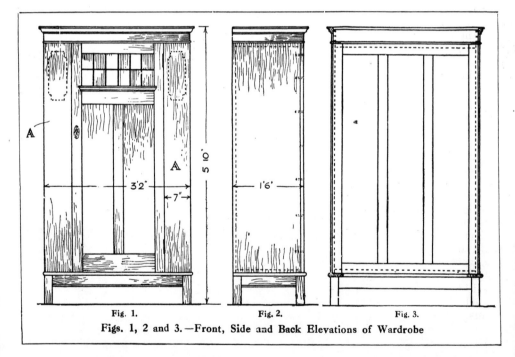

Fig. 1.   Fig. 2.   Fig. 3.

Figs. 1, 2 and 3.—Front, Side and Back Elevations of Wardrobe

of which a photographic reproduction is given by Fig. 4, would be most suitable for construction in oak. An attempt has been made to keep the construction as the main carcase, the ends, top and bottom are of $\frac{7}{8}$-in. material lap-dovetailed together in the usual way. The back should, if possible, be framed up, as in

Fig. 3, and screwed into rebates in the ends. Coming to the carcase front, the two pilasters A (Fig. 1) are dowelled to the ends and at the top and bottom, and are decorated by the inlaying of a suitable mosaic banding (a banding of ebony and boxwood looks well in oak).

The base is 8 in. high, the 2½-in. by 1-in. bearers being tenoned into the legs, which are 2 in. square. These legs are shown plain, but they could have a slight chamfer taken off the edges, or could be turned.

The cornice is a dovetailed frame, faced up and fitted with a cornice moulding, dustboard and frieze moulding, as shown in the section (Fig. 5).

Details of the door are shown in Fig. 6. A leaded light is introduced into the upper part, but to simplify construction, both this and the strip of moulding planted beneath it could be dispensed with, a plain wooden panel being used instead.

The interior fitting can be treated in a variety of ways. In the first place, coat hooks could be screwed to battens about 4 in. wide secured to the carcase back and ends, while triple hooks could also be screwed into the carcase top. As an alternative, lengths of brass tubing could be supported on ledges near the top, from which coat hangers are suspended. A similar arrangement lower down could be used for trousers. The most suitable method of finishing would be to fume the oak (or, as this is likely to be inconvenient, to achieve a similar result by means of a spirit stain), and polish with wax.

4-FT. 6-IN. WARDROBE

The wardrobe to be described is, according to the usual practice and for the sake of portability, designed to be made in three sections, namely, surbase, carcase and cornice. Figs. 7 and 8 show the

assembled wardrobe and give the main dimensions, which, of course, may be varied to some extent to meet individual requirements.

To describe the job in the order in which the work should be undertaken, the surbase (Figs. 9, 10 and 11) claims first attention. This is built up on four 1½-in.

Fig. 4.—Small Wardrobe with Leaded Light

by 1½-in. angle-posts, the lower portions of which are packed out to a size suitable for turning to form the feet, the maximum diameter of which is 3 in. The top rail is dovetailed to the posts as shown in the plan, and the bottom rail and the back board are tenoned into these, the sides being tongued and glued in place. The bottom board has its ends housed to

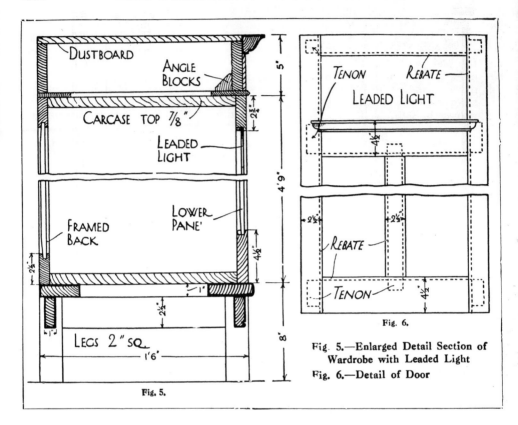

Fig. 5.—Enlarged Detail Section of Wardrobe with Leaded Light

Fig. 6.—Detail of Door

the sides, and, together with the rest of the structure, is stiffened where indicated by a liberal number of angle-blocks. Four fillets and two stops must be fixed where shown in preparation for the drawer, and the two ⅜-in. mouldings planted on the front and both sides. These mouldings are of similar section to that shown on the top frame, and in fixing, it should be borne in mind that the upper member is placed ⅛ in. below the top surface of the bottom rail, to avoid its being damaged and possibly wrenched off with the working of the drawer.

The top frame is mortised and tenoned together, moulded on its three exposed edges, and is held in its place on the surbase with dowels and angle-blocks.

Figs. 12, 13 and 14 deal with the construction of the drawer, the front, back and sides of which are dovetailed together.

The bottom rests in a groove in the drawer front (Fig. 13) and in grooved fillets glued to the sides (Fig. 14), and it is further supported in the middle by the grooved rail which is housed to the drawer front and screwed to the bottom edge of the drawer back. The bottom should be bradded at its back edge only, so as to ensure freedom for possible shrinkage. A suggestion for veneering the drawer front is given in Fig. 7, and the fixing of lock and drawer pulls completes the surbase.

For the next section—the carcase—reference must be made to Figs. 15 to 25, from which it will be seen that the top board is dovetailed to the sides, the bottom board being similarly assembled. The partition is dovetail-housed to the top and bottom boards, and the panelled back (Figs 16 and 17) is screwed to all back edges of the carcase, and keeps this square and rigid. Four locating blocks

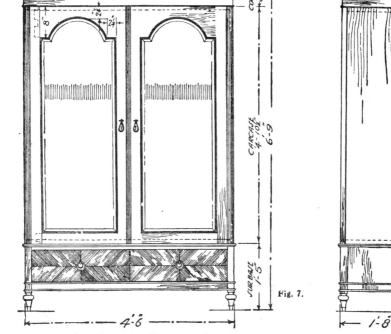

Fig. 7.

Fig. 8.

Figs. 7 and 8.—Front and Side Elevations of 4-ft. 6-in. Wardrobe

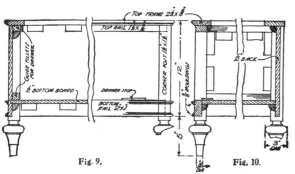

Fig. 9.

Fig. 10.

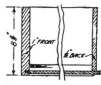

Fig. 13.—Part Cross Section of Drawer

Figs. 9 and 10.—Enlarged Longitudinal and Cross
Sections of Surbase

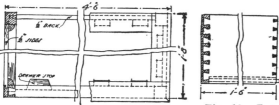

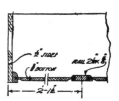

Fig. 11.—Enlarged Plan of Surbase

Fig. 12.—End
Elevation of
Drawer

Fig. 14.—Part Longi-
tudinal Section of
Drawer

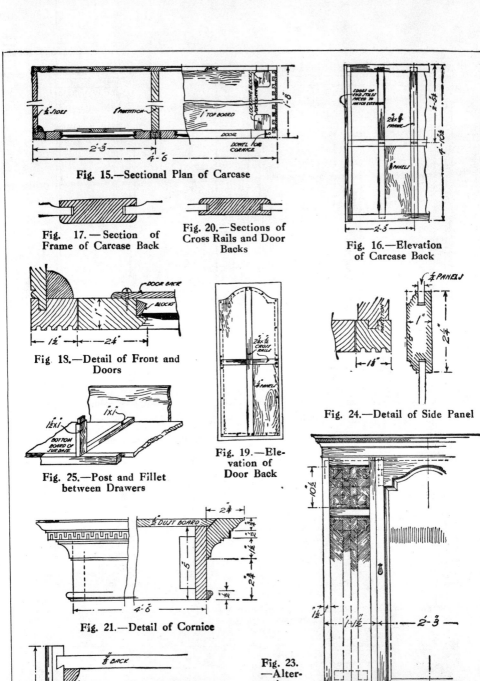

Fig. 15.—Sectional Plan of Carcase

Fig. 17.—Section of Frame of Carcase Back

Fig. 20.—Sections of Cross Rails and Door Backs

Fig. 16.—Elevation of Carcase Back

Fig. 18.—Detail of Front and Doors

Fig. 19.—Elevation of Door Back

Fig. 24.—Detail of Side Panel

Fig. 25.—Post and Fillet between Drawers

Fig. 21.—Detail of Cornice

Fig. 22.—Part Plan of Cornice Frame

Fig. 23.—Alternative Design of Wardrobe

are glued and bradded to the underside of the bottom, and so placed as to fit in the angles of the top frame of the surbase, thereby locating the carcase in correct position on that section. Four similar blocks are placed in suitable positions on the carcase top, for the purpose of fitting on the cornice section. These latter blocks are shown in Fig. 15, as are also the two dowels which further secure the cornice in place.

Details of the front and doors are given in Fig. 18, and it will be seen that the partition is faced with a fluted member to match the end pilasters.

The doors are framed together with haunched tenons—two at the top rails—the moulding being mitred at the angles, and each door is hung on three 2-in. brass butt hinges and fitted with a wardrobe latch. Wedge-shape blocks are pinned at intervals in the rebate to hold the bevelled plate-glass mirror, and here it should be noted that it is advisable to blacken the rebate with stain, to avoid a conspicuous reflection of the rebate surfaces when the glass is in position.

Backs for the doors are constructed as shown in Figs. 19 and 20. A vertical bar runs through with two cross-rails tenoned into it, and the panels fit into grooves in these. The bar and rails must, of course, be halved over the door frame to allow the panels to be screwed down, this being effected with four round-head brass screws placed where indicated. Figs. 21 and 22 give details of the cornice section. This is built up on a frame which may have its front angles mitred and blocked, or, if made of pine, dovetailed and the frame afterwards faced with hardwood. The back rail is dovetail-housed to the sides. The enrichment on the cornice may be fretted out of $\frac{1}{16}$-in. fret-wood, and applied to the moulding by gluing.

Fig. 23 shows an alternative design, being an arrangement for one central door and two drawers, and Figs. 24 and 25 are details relating to this alternative scheme, which may be further varied by moulding the stiles of the side framing as well as the rails, and substituting plain raised panels with chamfered margins about $\frac{3}{4}$ in. wide in place of the veneered work, in which case the veneering should be omitted from the drawer fronts also. These side frames are fixed with dowels and glue, the wardrobe sides being beaded where they abut.

As regards material, the job would look well in walnut, oak, or mahogany. If, however, the choice of timber is quite open, and a suggestion on the matter would be helpful, walnut, finished with a wax-polish, is recommended. In practice it is customary to use oak and occasionally pine or American whitewood for the interior or unexposed work such as the carcase back, partition, top and bottom boards, door backs, and all parts of the drawer excepting the front, and there is, of course, no need for this to be of the superior hardwood, if the suggestion for veneering is adopted. Well-seasoned deal will serve for the dust-board to the cornice, the bottom board of the surbase and the top frame to same, this latter having the hardwood moulding planted on its edges.

WARDROBE WITH DRAWERS AND TRAYS

The wardrobe shown in Fig. 26 is known as a bachelor's wardrobe, and differs from the usual kind inasmuch that there is no hanging space, the whole being utilised by drawers and trays for holding folded clothing. Fig. 27 is a front elevation, and Fig. 28 shows the interior fittings. Suitable woods are mahogany, oak, ash, etc., if it is to be french-polished ; pine or American whitewood if for painting, etc.

The principal measurements are : Extreme height, 6 ft. 10 in. ; width across the front of the carcases, 3 ft. 6 in. ; width of the ends, including the thickness of the doors, 1 ft. 8 in. to 1 ft. 10 in., according to requirements. If hardwood is used, a saving in cost can be made if all the out-of-sight parts are constructed of pine or American whitewood. It is usual, however, no matter what kind of hardwood is selected, to make the inside parts of baywood or Honduras mahogany. In getting out the wood the portions made of 1-in. stuff are : Carcase ends, tops, and bottoms, drawer fronts, tray fronts (*see* Fig. 29), bearers D (Fig. 27), frieze E (Fig. 27), moulding F (Fig. 27), separating the top and bottom carcases and the grooved muntins for the carcase back G (Fig. 30). The parts constructed of $\frac{1}{2}$-in. stuff are : Door panels H (Fig. 31),

(Fig. 28), and then veneer the outer faces. Another method of avoiding veneering is to secret-dovetail the corners. The top and bottom of the upper carcase are dovetailed into the ends, the latter being 3 in. less in width than the lower carcase.

In making the lower carcase containing the drawers, wood can be saved by using

Fig. 26.—Wardrobe with
Drawers and Trays

drawer and tray sides, backs, and bottoms, and grooved slips K (Figs. 32 and 33), frieze moulding L (Fig. 34), carcase backs M (Fig. 30), and the dustboards or divisions N (Fig. 35). The doors are of $1\frac{1}{4}$-in. stuff, finishing about $1\frac{1}{8}$ in. thick.

First make the frieze E (Fig. 27). It is usual to dovetail the front and end pieces together the same as shown in the tray

bearers (Fig. 30), and jointing angular pieces P to them. The arrangement and method of fitting together of bearers, drawer runners, and dustboards between each drawer will be seen clearly in Fig. 35. The division between the two short drawers is tenoned into bearers above and below. The plinth moulding C (Fig. 27) is mitred at the corners as shown

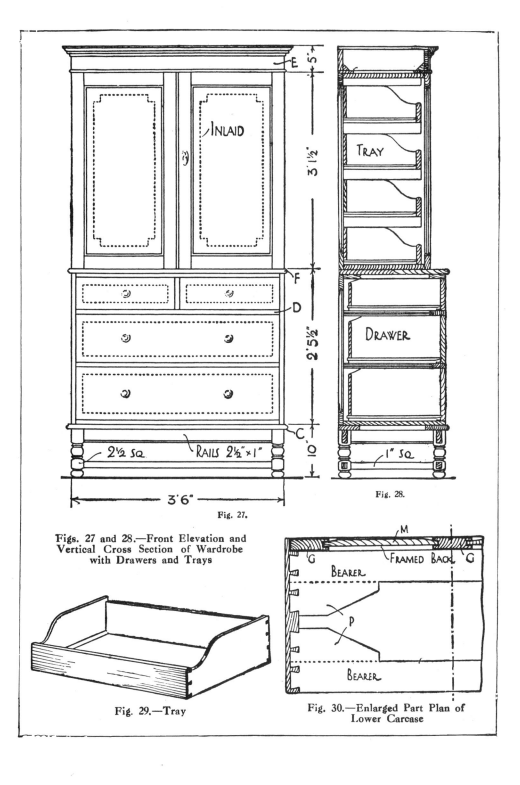

E — 5″

INLAID

3′ 1½″

F

D

2′ 5½″

C

2½ SQ.   RAILS 2½″ × 1″

10″

3′ 6″

Fig. 27.

TRAY

DRAWER

1″ SQ.

Fig. 28.

Figs. 27 and 28.—Front Elevation and
Vertical Cross Section of Wardrobe
with Drawers and Trays

Fig. 29.—Tray

M

G   FRAMED BACK   G

BEARER

P

BEARER

Fig. 30.—Enlarged Part Plan of
Lower Carcase

(*see also* enlarged section, Fig. 36). The mouldings F (Fig. 27) and L (Fig. 34) are treated in the same way ; Fig. 37 is an enlarged section of F (Fig. 27). The cornice moulding can be faced with hardwood and backed with pine (*see* section in Fig. 34), and then mitred at the corners. To prevent dust lodging on the top of the cornice, a ½-in. board (Fig. 34) can be

in position, allowing them to be drawn out the same as drawers.

The doors are mortised and tenoned together, and an ovolo moulding is worked on the inner edges, as shown in Fig. 34 ; or a rebated moulding could be fixed along the edges of the stiles and the rails, and mitred at the corners. The bead which divides the centre stiles of the

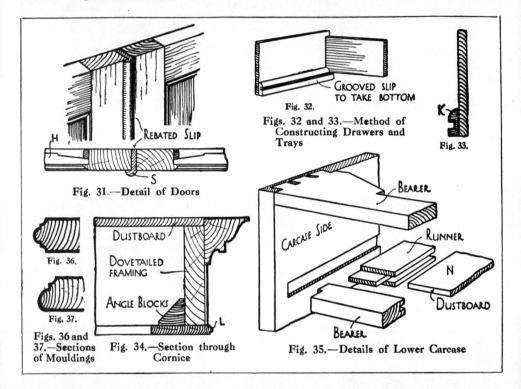

REBATED SLIP

H

S

Fig. 31.—Detail of Doors

GROOVED SLIP
TO TAKE BOTTOM

Fig. 32.

Figs. 32 and 33.—Method of
Constructing Drawers and
Trays

K

Fig. 33.

Fig. 36.

DUSTBOARD

DOVETAILED
FRAMING

ANGLE BLOCKS

L

Fig. 37.

Figs. 36 and
37.—Sections
of Mouldings

Fig. 34.—Section through
Cornice

BEARER

CARCASE SIDE

RUNNER

N

DUSTBOARD

BEARER

Fig. 35.—Details of Lower Carcase

fixed ; it also serves to place any suitable ornaments.

The fronts of the trays for the upper carcase are about 3½ in. wide, and the sides are about 9 in. wide (*see* Fig. 28), the latter being shaped down to the front. This figure also shows the method of dovetailing the trays together. Figs. 32 and 33 illustrate the grooved strips K in which the bottoms of the trays slide. The drawers in the lower carcase are constructed in the same way as the trays. Between the lowest tray and those above, strips of ½-in. stuff are screwed to the carcase ends, and serve to keep the trays

doors is shown at s (Fig. 31). The full thickness of the bead is first glued to the stile, and then it is rebated to receive the other stile. The door panels are decorated by inlaying a mosaic banding as indicated in the elevation (Fig. 27). The drawer fronts are treated in a similar manner. The left-hand door will require flush bolts top and bottom, and the right-hand door a spring lock, with a handle to work the latter.

The stand upon which the wardrobe rests is tenoned together in the usual way, the legs are turned from stuff 2½ in. square, the upper rails being 2½ in. by 1 in., and the lower 1 in. square. The lower carcase is secured to this by pocket screwing from the inside of the rails.

4-FT. WARDROBE WITH MIRROR PANELS

Fig. 38 is a conventional view of a wardrobe which has mirror panels, and which,

A front elevation, a vertical section, and two half-plans are shown by Figs. 39, 40 and 41 respectively, Fig. 40 being on the lines B B and Fig. 41 on the lines A A of the front elevation. Another vertical section, this time of the hanging portion, on the lines C C of Fig. 39 is shown by Fig. 42. The arrangement of the shelves, etc., is clearly indicated in Fig. 43. The

Fig. 38.—4-ft. Wardrobe with Mirror Panels

except for this detail, embodies practically the same constructional work as the three-piece wardrobes described in the preceding pages. It may be mentioned that this wardrobe agrees in design fairly well with a dressing-table and washstand described in a later section.

back of the wardrobe is as shown in the back elevation (Fig. 44). A detail of the top of the door is given by Fig. 45. A detail section of the front on the line L L (Fig. 39) is given by Fig. 46. The construction of the three sections of which the wardrobe is built is made

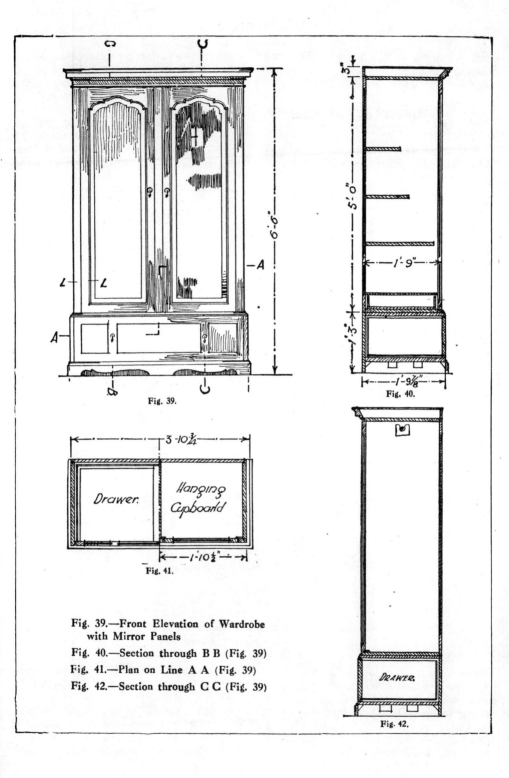

Fig. 39.

Fig. 40.

Drawer.

Hanging Cupboard

Fig. 41.

Fig. 39.—Front Elevation of Wardrobe with Mirror Panels

Fig. 40.—Section through B B (Fig. 39)

Fig. 41.—Plan on Line A A (Fig. 39)

Fig. 42.—Section through C C (Fig. 39)

DRAWER.

Fig. 42.

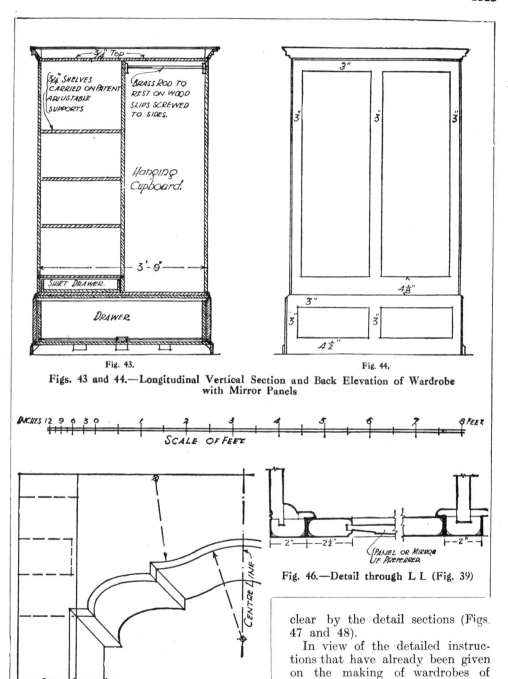

Fig. 43.

Fig. 44.

Figs. 43 and 44.—Longitudinal Vertical Section and Back Elevation of Wardrobe with Mirror Panels

Fig. 46.—Detail through L L (Fig. 39)

Fig. 45 —Detail of Upper Part of Door

clear by the detail sections (Figs. 47 and 48).

In view of the detailed instructions that have already been given on the making of wardrobes of similar construction, a repetition for this would be superfluous, as the drawings will provide sufficient information if studied in conjunction with examples already given.

HANGING WARDROBE

As a substitute, at a comparatively moderate cost, for the ordinary form of whitewood, or deal, the panels being flush on the top side so as to leave no traps for dust.

The construction of the top is shown in Figs. 50, 51 and 52. The two upper members of the cornice are glued and pinned in place, and the 2½-in. by ⅝-in.

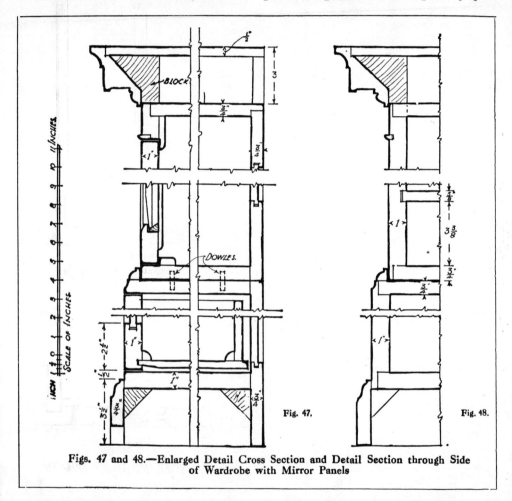

Figs. 47 and 48.—Enlarged Detail Cross Section and Detail Section through Side of Wardrobe with Mirror Panels

wardrobe, the arrangement shown by Fig. 49 may be of interest to many who experience the need for additional hanging accommodation, particularly for items of ladies' attire.

The pillar, feet, and cornice members of the top are intended to be of hardwood, but the top may be framed up in pine, moulded fillet is secured by screwing through the top, the mitred angles being strengthened by glue-blocks as shown in Fig. 51. A 9-in. by 9-in. by ⅞-in. chamfered block is screwed diagonally to the underside of the top to add strength in the fixing of this to the pillar, and four brass brackets of the strong cast type

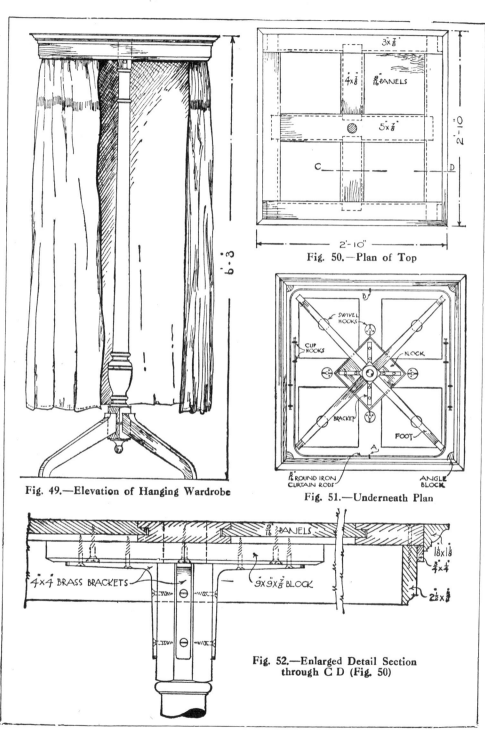

Fig. 49.—Elevation of Hanging Wardrobe

$3 \times \frac{7}{8}$

$4 \times \frac{7}{8}$ $\frac{9}{16}$ PANELS

$5 \times \frac{7}{8}$

C   D

2'-10"

2'-10

Fig. 50.—Plan of Top

SWIVEL HOOKS

CUP HOOKS

BLOCK

BRACKET

FOOT

$\frac{3}{4}$ ROUND IRON CURTAIN RODS

ANGLE BLOCK

B

A

Fig. 51.—Underneath Plan

$\frac{9}{16}$ PANELS

4×4 BRASS BRACKETS

$9 \times 9 \times \frac{7}{8}$ BLOCK

$1\frac{1}{8} \times 1\frac{1}{8}$

$\frac{3}{4} \times \frac{1}{4}$

$2\frac{1}{2} \times \frac{1}{2}$

Fig. 52.—Enlarged Detail Section
through C D (Fig. 50)

are added to afford further support for the top, which, as will be seen from the illustrations, carries the hooks on which the clothes are hung. The angles of the upper squared part of the pillar are planed away to form a face, just wide enough for the fixing of the brackets.

Fig. 53 shows the pillar and feet in detail, the latter being tenoned and pinned to the lower squared part of the pillar which is turned from some 2¾-in. by 2¾-in. stuff. The dotted lines indicate where the stuff must be packed out for turning

Fig. 54.—Recess Wardrobe Fitment

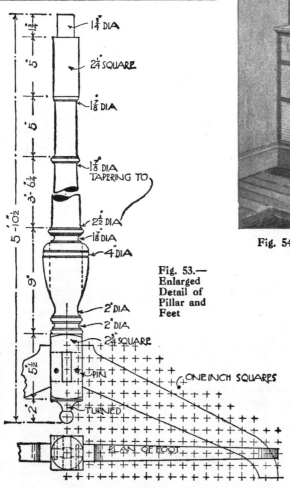

Fig. 53.—Enlarged Detail of Pillar and Feet

to 4 in. in diameter. This method saves material.

As an alternative to the turned pillar, a square pillar tapering from 2¾ in. at the bottom to 2 in. at the top may be used, the angles being chamfered and stopped, say, within 2 in. of the top of the feet, and the same distance from the bottom of the brass brackets.

The curtain rods are of $\frac{5}{16}$-in. round iron, and supported on brass cup-hooks of suitable size, these hooks being closed with pliers when the rods are in position, so as to prevent their being dislodged. It will be seen by reference to Fig. 51 that the rods run by each other at their ends, so as to allow

the curtains to lap at their edges, and sufficient clearance must be allowed between the two sets of hooks for the rings of both curtains to pass.

For access to the wardrobe, the cur-

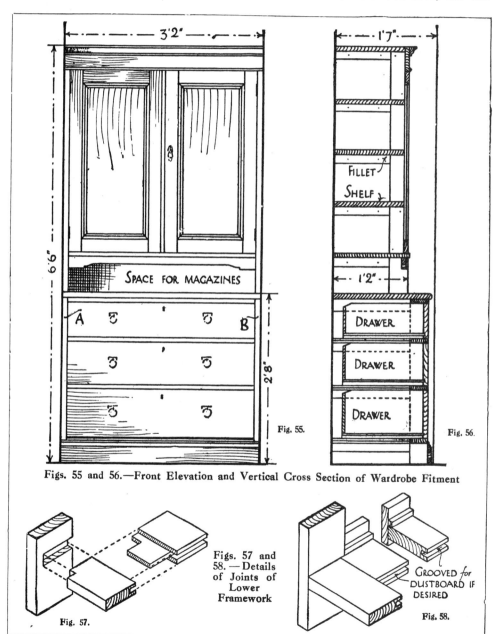

Figs. 55 and 56.—Front Elevation and Vertical Cross Section of Wardrobe Fitment

Figs. 57 and 58. — Details of Joints of Lower Framework

tains are drawn back to the central cup-hooks at A and B. Eight double brass wardrobe-hooks with back plates are

fillets nailed to them, which are in turn nailed to the side walls. The whole of this lower framework should be fitted

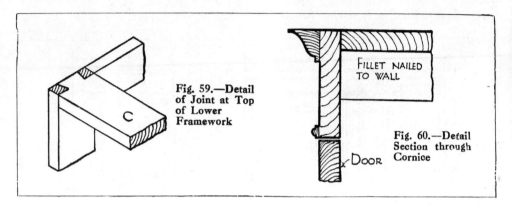

Fig. 59.—Detail of Joint at Top of Lower Framework

FILLET NAILED TO WALL

Fig. 60.—Detail Section through Cornice

DOOR

fixed where shown in Fig. 51, four being on the panels and four on the frame.

RECESS WARDROBE FITMENT

The half-tone reproduction (**Fig. 54**) shows a fitment designed to fill one of the recesses found in most bedrooms. The dimensions given on Figs. 55 and 56 are for a recess 3 ft. 2 in. wide and 1 ft. 7 in. deep ; but the worker will, of course, modify the dimensions to suit his own particular case. The majority of the work is from 1-in. material.

There will in most cases be an existing skirting-board, to which the lower frame-work will need careful adjustment. In this framework the two stiles A and B (Fig. 55) have the drawer rails and run-ners tenoned into them (see details, Figs. 57 and 58), and are connected at the top by the rail C dovetailed into them (see Fig. 59). The runners have 3-in. by $\frac{5}{8}$-in.

together temporarily before being in-serted into the recess and nailed, during which process the runners should be care-fully adjusted to a horizontal position. The top of the drawers, which has a moulded or rounded front edge, can now be prepared and fitted into position. The plinth should be so fitted that it continues the lines of the existing skirting board (see general view, Fig. 54). The drawers are constructed in the usual manner, and guide strips for them should be fitted in the angles formed by the fillets and runners (Fig. 58).

The upper framework for the cupboard should present no difficulties. Fig. 60 shows the arrangement of the cornice. Between the lowest shelf of the cupboard and the top of the drawers a clear space is left. The cupboard doors are framed up with mortise-and-tenon joints, and a moulding is mitred round and pinned on.

Dressing-tables, Chests of Drawers, etc.

DRESSING-TABLE AND WASHSTAND

Dressing - table. — The dressing-table shown in Fig. 1 is designed on the usual lines, the jewel drawers being underneath in order to leave the top as clear as possible for toilet requisites. Two elevations and a part sectional plan are shown by Figs. 2, 3 and 4, whilst a vertical section is given by Fig. 5.

The table is constructed with four $1\frac{5}{8}$-in. square legs tapering to $1\frac{1}{4}$ in., with front and side rails out of 9-in. by $\frac{3}{4}$-in. material, the back rail being $6\frac{1}{2}$ in. by $\frac{3}{4}$ in. The front and side rails are cut to the shapes as shown in Figs. 2, 3 and 6, and are tenoned to the legs as shown in

Figs. 7 and 8. In order to make the table perfectly rigid, it is advisable to frame to the feet of the legs the $1\frac{1}{4}$-in. by $1\frac{1}{2}$-in. rails shown in Figs. 2 and 5.

The construction of the drawers and bearers is detailed in Figs. 6 and 9, Fig. 9 being a detail plan of the drawer, etc., and Fig. 6 being a section through same viewed from the front. The drawer runners ($\frac{3}{4}$ in. by $1\frac{1}{2}$ in.) are stub-tenoned to the front and back rails, and have small guide fillets planted on the top, the two members above the drawers (Fig. 6) being necessary to prevent the drawer tilting when withdrawn. The table-top is 1 in. thick, and is fixed with buttons screwed to same from the underside and tongued to the rails (*see* Fig. 6).

Fig. 1.– Dressing-table

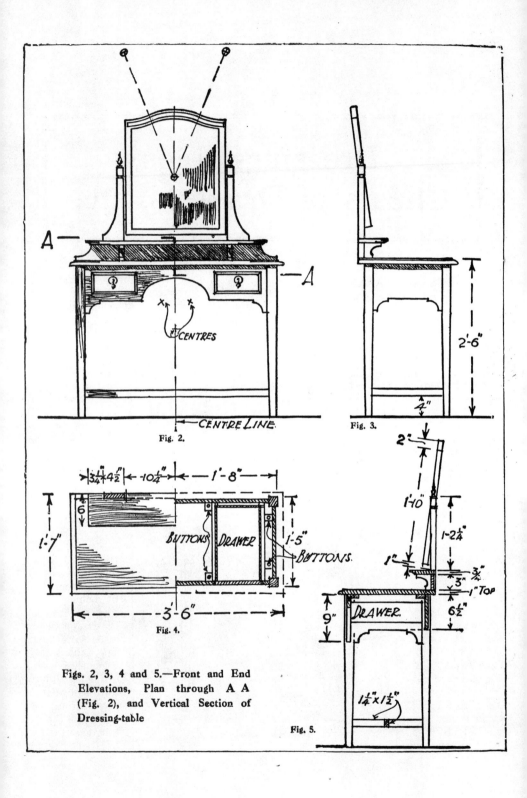

A — | — A

↑ CENTRES

← CENTRE LINE

Fig. 2.

2'-6"

4"

Fig. 3.

|3¼"|4½"|← 10¼" →|← 1'-8" →|

6"

1'-7"

BUTTONS DRAWER

BUTTONS.

1'-5"

← 3'-6" →

Fig. 4.

2"

1'-10"

1'-2¼"

1"

¾"

3"

1" TOP

DRAWER.

6½"

9"

1¼" X 1½"

Figs. 2, 3, 4 and 5.—Front and End
Elevations, Plan through A A
(Fig. 2), and Vertical Section of
Dressing-table

Fig. 5.

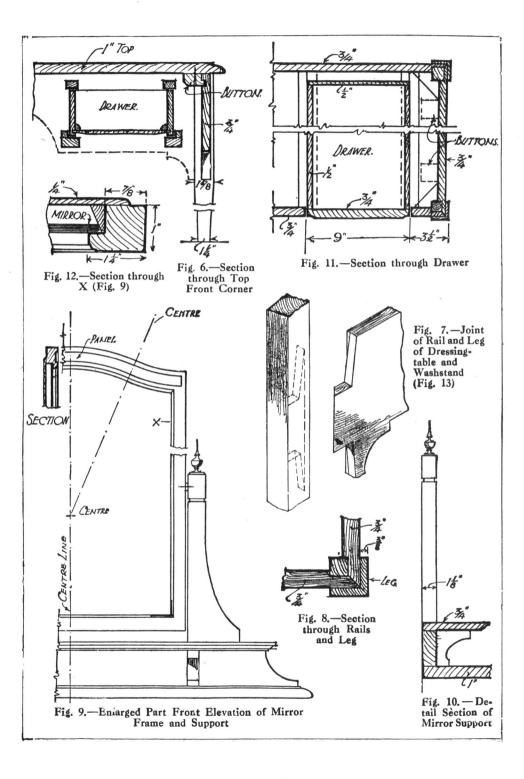

Fig. 12.—Section through X (Fig. 9)

Fig. 6.—Section through Top Front Corner

Fig. 11.—Section through Drawer

Fig. 7.—Joint of Rail and Leg of Dressing-table and Washstand (Fig. 13)

Fig. 8.—Section through Rails and Leg

Fig. 9.—Enlarged Part Front Elevation of Mirror Frame and Support

Fig. 10.—Detail Section of Mirror Support

A detail of the upper portion is shown in Figs. 9, 10 and 11, and is constructed separately from the table and screwed to the top of same from the underside. The mirror frame is formed of 1¼-in. by 1-in. stuff with ovolo moulded and rebated sides (*see* Fig. 12), and bottom members and 2-in. by 1-in. curved top member to match, with small sunk panel in same, as shown in Fig. 9; the frame is mitred and glued at the corners. The mirror is fixed with wedge-shaped blocks, which should be painted black, as should also the inside edges of the frame. The mirror frame should be fixed at a point 1 in. above the centre of

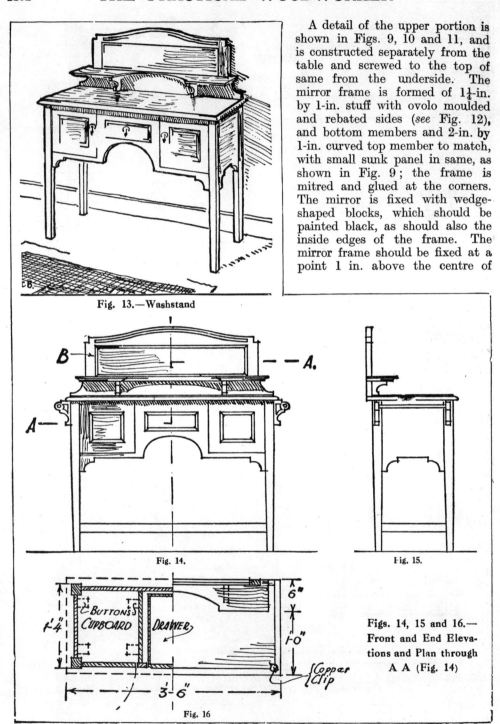

Fig. 13.—Washstand

Fig. 14.

Fig. 15.

Figs. 14, 15 and 16.—Front and End Elevations and Plan through A A (Fig. 14)

Fig. 16.

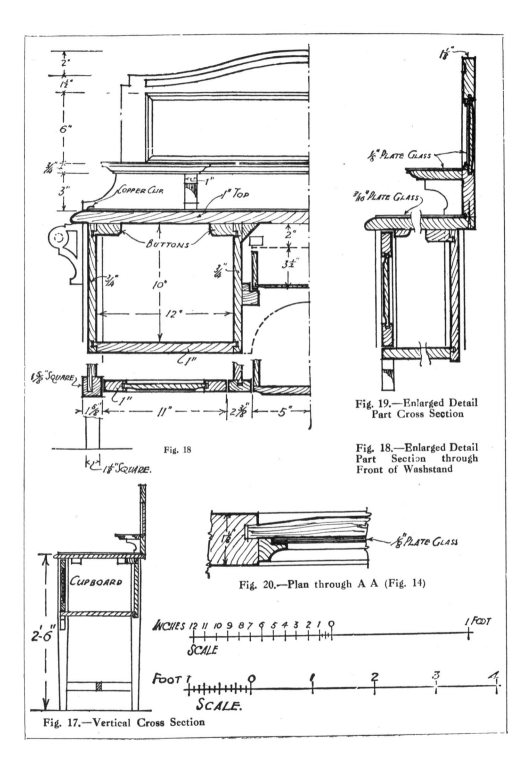

2"
1½"
6"
¾"
3"

COPPER CLIP.

1"
1" TOP

BUTTONS

¾"
10"
¾"

12"

2"
3½"

1"

1⅝" SQUARE

1"
1⅝"
11"
2⅜"
5"

Fig. 18

1⅝" SQUARE.

Fig. 18.—Enlarged Detail Part Section through Front of Washstand

1⅛"

⅛" PLATE GLASS

3/16" PLATE GLASS

Fig. 19.—Enlarged Detail Part Cross Section

CUPBOARD

2'-6"

Fig. 17.—Vertical Cross Section

1⅛"

⅛" PLATE GLASS

Fig. 20.—Plan through A A (Fig. 14)

INCHES 12 11 10 9 8 7 6 5 4 3 2 1 0   1 FOOT
SCALE

FOOT 1   0   1   2   3   4
SCALE.

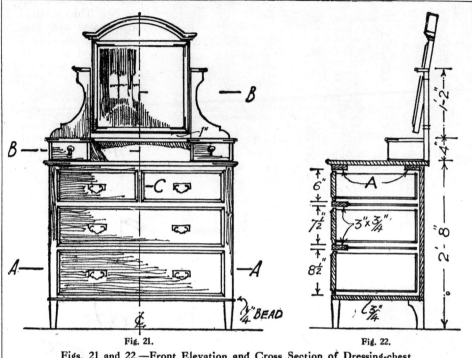

Fig. 21.   Fig. 22.

Figs. 21 and 22.—Front Elevation and Cross Section of Dressing-chest

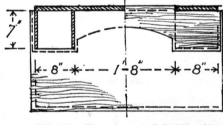

Fig. 23.—Plan through B B (Fig. 21)

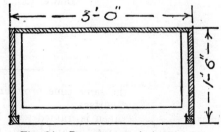

Fig. 24.—Plan through A A (Fig. 21)

the same with pivots in the usual manner.

Washstand.—The washstand is shown by Fig. 13. It is designed *en suite* with the dressing-table already described, being of similar construction in many respects. The principal members are of the same dimensions, and therefore need not be mentioned again. Two elevations and a sectional plan are shown by Figs. 14, 15 and 16, and a vertical section by Fig. 17.

The legs, side, back, bottom rails and table-top should be loosely framed together first and the side toilet cupboards, etc., framed to them as shown in Figs. 18 and 19. The centre of front with perforation for drawer is tongued and grooved to the cupboards and fixed to the table-top. The small curved end pieces which are required in order to match the outline of the dressing-table front are planted on to the bottom of the cupboards and housed to the legs.

The table-top and shelf is covered with clear plate-glass with ground edges, and fitted into the panel of the back screen, as shown in Fig. 20. This method of covering the exposed parts with glass is very effective in practice, allowing as it does the grain of the wood to be clearly

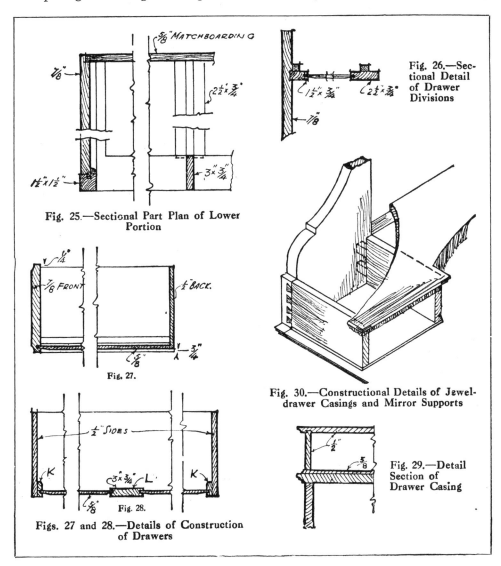

Fig. 25.—Sectional Part Plan of Lower Portion

Fig. 26.—Sectional Detail of Drawer Divisions

Fig. 27.

Figs. 27 and 28.—Details of Construction of Drawers

Fig. 28.

Fig. 30.—Constructional Details of Jewel-drawer Casings and Mirror Supports

Fig. 29.—Detail Section of Drawer Casing

is secured at the back by a small rebate in the bottom of the vertical screen (Fig. 19), and at the front corners with small ornamental copper clips screwed to the table-top. A sheet of similar glass is also seen, and at the same time providing an easily cleansed surface.

The back screen is framed with $1\frac{1}{8}$-in. material with mortise-and-tenon joints at the corners, and a $\frac{1}{4}$-in. panel in the centre with a small moulding planted round (Fig. 20). The shelf is screwed to the screen from the back, and also to the small brackets which rest on the top of the glass. These latter are not fixed to the table-top, so that it is unnecessary to cut the glass round the feet of same.

DRESSING-CHEST

The dressing-chest shown by Figs. 21

treated. The back is of ⅝-in. match-boarding let into the sides, as shown in Fig. 25, and screwed to them.

The drawer divisions are framed together with ¾-in.-thick material grooved for the ⅜-in. panels, the whole being housed, glued and blocked to the sides and back, as shown in Figs. 25 and 26. The drawers are constructed as shown in Figs. 27 and 28, the fronts, sides and backs being dovetailed together, and the

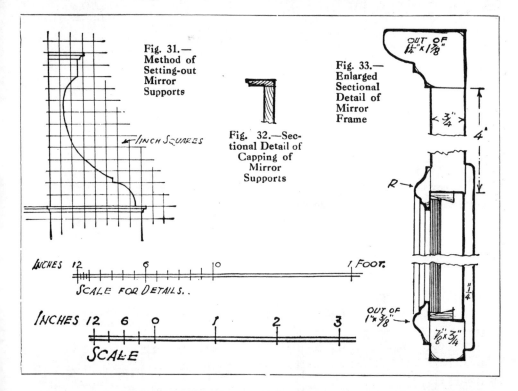

Fig. 31.—Method of Setting-out Mirror Supports

1 INCH SQUARES

Fig. 32.—Sectional Detail of Capping of Mirror Supports

Fig. 33.—Enlarged Sectional Detail of Mirror Frame

OUT OF 1¼"×1⅞"

¾"

4"

R

1"×3/8

OUT OF 1"×3/8"

⅞"×3"/4

INCHES 12   6   0   1 FOOT.
SCALE FOR DETAILS..

INCHES 12   6   0   1   2   3
SCALE

to 24 is a very useful piece of bedroom furniture where space is valuable, combining as it does the purposes of a chest of drawers and washstand.

The lower portion is composed of ⅞-in. sides tongued into the 1½-in. square front legs, with a small fillet glued to the inside-front corner, shown in Fig. 25. The back legs are in one piece with the sides. The ¾-in. bottom is dovetailed at the ends to the sides, the two 3-in. by ¾-in. top members (marked A on Fig. 22) being similarly

bottom panels being housed into fillets (K in Fig. 28), which are screwed to the sides; the long drawers have an additional support in the centre, as shown at L in Fig. 28.

The top is ⅞ in. thick with moulded front and side edges, as shown in Fig. 29, and is fixed by being screwed from the underside through the members A (Fig. 22).

The jewel drawers at the sides and the mirror supports are constructed separately and screwed to the top from the

Fig. 34.—Easily-constructed Chest of Drawers

underside, the drawer casings being constructed as shown in Figs. 29 and 30, and the drawers in the usual manner with $\frac{1}{2}$-in. fronts, sides and backs.

The mirror bearers can be set out as shown in Fig. 31, there being a small capping at the top as shown in Fig. 32. The detail of the mirror frame is given in Fig. 33, and is $\frac{3}{4}$ in. thick with mitred and glued angles, the moulding R being planted on. The mirror is fixed with wedge-shaped blocks, which should be painted black, as should the inside edges of the frame. Various types of fittings are obtainable for fixing the mirror frame to the supports.

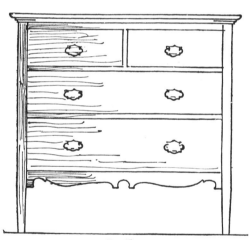

Fig. 35.

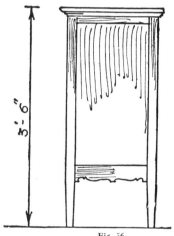

Fig. 36.

Figs. 35, 36 and 37.— Front and End Elevations and Sectional Plan of Chest of Drawers

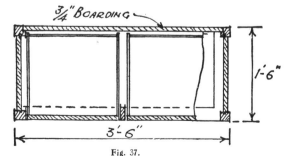

Fig. 37.

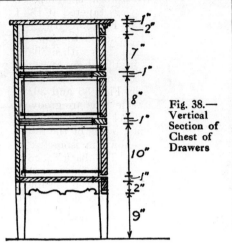

Fig. 38.—Vertical Section of Chest of Drawers

EASILY CONSTRUCTED CHEST OF DRAWERS

With the chest of drawers shown in perspective by Fig 34 an endeavour has been made to obtain a simple but well-proportioned effect, and at the same time to keep the construction as straightforward as this will allow. The drawers are kept well clear of the floor in order to facilitate cleaning, a point which most housewives will appreciate.

Figs 35 and 36 show the front and side elevations respectively, and Fig. 37 shows a plan through the top drawers. Fig. 38 is a vertical section. Details of construction are given in Figs. 39, 40 and 41.

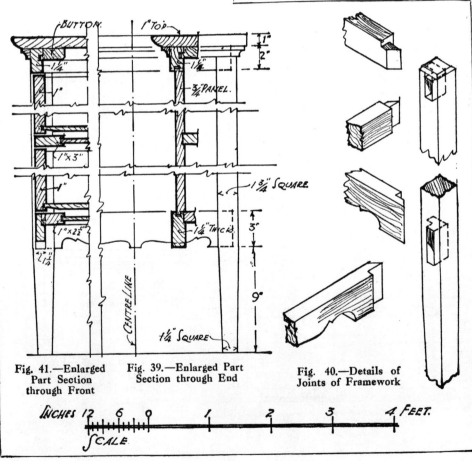

Fig. 41.—Enlarged Part Section through Front

Fig. 39.—Enlarged Part Section through End

Fig. 40.—Details of Joints of Framework

INCHES 12 6 0 1 2 3 4 FEET.

SCALE

Fig. 42.—Queen Anne Chest of Drawers

The framework is composed of four 1¾-in. legs tapered at the feet, as shown in Fig. 39, with 2-in. by 1¼-in. rails tenoned to same at top of front, and sides with similar rails out of 3 in. by 1¼ in. at the bottom, these being cut to the curves as shown on Figs. 35 and 36. The posts and side rails are grooved for the ¾-in. panel as shown in Fig. 39. The tenoned joints of the rails and posts are shown in isometric view in Fig. 40. The back is covered with boarding let into rebates in the posts and screwed to same.

The drawer divisions are constructed of 3-in. by 1-in. framing with ⅜ in. panels, the whole being housed, glued and blocked to the sides. The 1-in. top has a rounded front and side edges, with a small cavetto moulding planted under it,

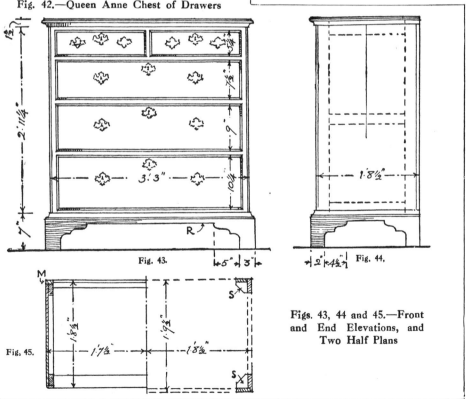

Figs. 43, 44 and 45.—Front and End Elevations, and Two Half Plans

and it is fixed with small buttons screwed to the top from the underside and tongued to the top rails, as shown in Figs. 39 and 41. The drawers are constructed in the usual manner with 1-in.

QUEEN ANNE CHEST OF DRAWERS

The chest of drawers shown by the half-tone (Fig. 42) is a reproduction of a

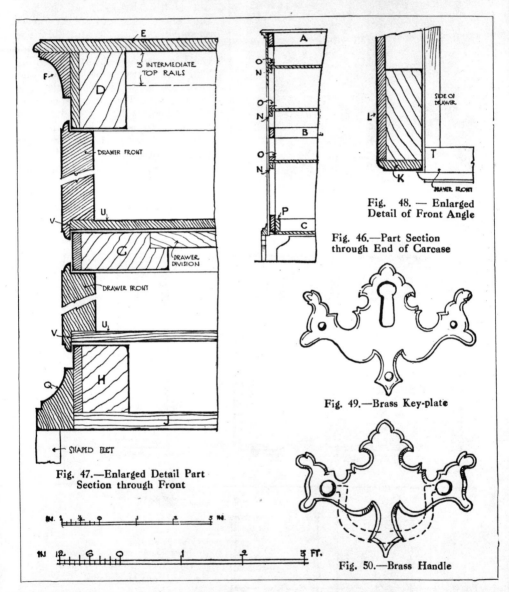

Fig. 47.—Enlarged Detail Part Section through Front

Fig. 48. — Enlarged Detail of Front Angle

Fig. 46.—Part Section through End of Carcase

Fig. 49.—Brass Key-plate

Fig. 50.—Brass Handle

fronts, and $\frac{1}{2}$-in. sides and backs, dovetailed at the corners with $\frac{3}{8}$-in. bottoms tongued to the sides.

similar piece of furniture of over two hundred years of age. The worker will note the liberal and convenient depth from front to back, the projecting fronts of the drawers, and the general simple lines of the whole structure.

Two elevations are given by Figs. 43 and 44, and two half plans by Fig. 45.

The ends are framed up with uprights front and back and three rails, all as dotted in Fig. 44 and in approximately 2½-in. by 1-in. pine. At the back they are connected by similar rails A, B and C (Fig. 46), the spaces between which are afterwards filled in rather roughly with thin boarding. Along the top front edge is a pine rail 1¼ in. by 2 in., faced with oak D (Fig. 47), and supporting three intermediate rails introduced to stiffen the oak top E, which is just over ¼ in. thick, moulded on the projecting edges and finished with a cavetto moulding as at F. Three 2½-in. by 1-in. drawer rails faced with oak and rebated for the divisions G (Fig. 47) are framed between the ends, and also a 1¾-in. by 1¼-in. bottom rail H, beneath which is fixed a rough bottom J.

The front faces of the ends are finished with moulded strips as at K (Fig. 48), covering the ¼-in. oak sides L, which are in two widths with a central butt-joint. The back angles are similarly finished with 1¼-in. by ½-in. oak strips, as at M in Fig. 45. The three drawer divisions are stiffened next the ends by fillets under-neath as at N (Fig. 46), and larger ones above as at O, the latter serving as guides for the drawers. At the bottom is a piece as at P, its upper surface coinciding with that of the rail H in Fig. 47.

The plinth is surmounted by an oak moulding Q (Fig. 47) mitred round and extending to the line R in Fig. 43. Below this are triangular blocks as at S (Fig. 45), dowelled in position and faced with ¾-in.-shaped oak feet as in Figs. 43 and 44. The faces of the latter being in the same plane as the lowest face of the moulding Q, there is a butt-joint where they meet at R.

The fronts of the drawers are 1 in. thick and are rebated and moulded all round on the solid, as in Fig. 47. The sides and back are a trifle less than ½ in. thick, and are dovetailed together and to the fronts at T (Fig. 48). Their lower edges all finish level with the lines marked U in Fig. 47, and 5/16-in. bottoms are bradded on from below without grooves or rebates. It will be noticed from Fig. 47 that the drawer bottoms extend right out to the carcase face at V, thus presenting one smooth wearing-surface.

The key and handle plates should be cut out of thick brass and have bevelled edges. Suitable designs for these are shown by Figs. 49 and 50.

Miscellaneous Bedroom Furniture

SHAVING CABINET

THE shaving cabinet shown by Fig. 1 is 1 ft. 2 in. by 1 ft. by 3 ft. 3 in. high, and, as will be seen, the top consists of two flaps, which open and rest on brackets forming t h e pediment when closed, as shown in Fig. 2. Oak is a most suitable material to use in constructing the cabinet.

In Fig. 3 it will be seen that the top shelf comes below the door stile. This is done partly for appearance, and room must be given for working the holding screw placed above the shelf. If the shaving-glass action has a rim with screw-eyes fixed at the bottom end, it will be necessary to split the shelves in the centre and fix it round the action (see Fig. 4).

SHERATON TOILET GLASS

The design (Fig. 5) for a toilet glass is taken from an antique example of the well-known Sheraton style. The wood is

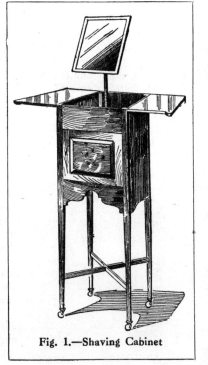

Fig. 1.—Shaving Cabinet

a matter of taste or individual requirements, though probably mahogany would be the most suitable.

The standards are made slightly tapered from 1 in. by $\frac{3}{4}$ in. at the bottom to $\frac{3}{4}$ in. by $\frac{1}{2}$ in. at the top. A small bead is stuck on the front edges, and a small flute runs down the centre of each standard, as shown in Fig. 6. The flute stops 2 in. short of the bottom, and is tapered towards the top as required by the taper of the standards. These standards are tenoned into the feet, and it should be noticed that they drop back from the bottom to the top, 2 in. from the perpendicular in each case. Fig. 7 shows a side elevation, and it will be seen that a small piece, 2 in. high by $\frac{3}{4}$ in. deep, and the width of the standard, is planted on the lower end of each standard, each piece having a shaped top as shown. Fig. 8 shows the setting-out of the feet and lower part of the standards, each square of the diagram representing a square inch. The feet should be made 1 in. thick.

The mirror frame, as in much antique work, is made of deal, 1 in. thick, the front

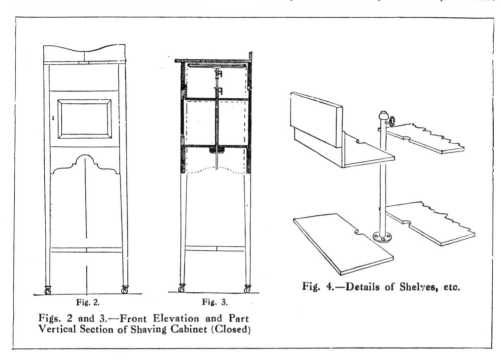

Fig. 2.   Fig. 3.

Figs. 2 and 3.—Front Elevation and Part Vertical Section of Shaving Cabinet (Closed)

Fig. 4.—Details of Shelves, etc.

A spreading piece, $\frac{7}{8}$ in. by $\frac{3}{4}$ in., runs between the standards. This also has a bead worked along both front edges and

being veneered with cross-banding (mahogany) 1 in. wide, and with a capping piece of mahogany veneer along the top edge. The deal is stained where visible, but, of course, the whole frame could be of solid mahogany if desired. Even then it would be better to veneer the front with cross-banding, the shortness of the grain giving a much nicer appearance. If the veneer be at all stout it will form a quite sufficient rebate for the glass, which is kept in position by four angle-blocks about $\frac{1}{2}$ in. thick, glued in the corners. These blocks keep the backing away from the mirror and allow space for the nuts on the pivots.

For these pivots two small brass cabinet handles or cupboard turns, preferably with drops, should be procured, each having a screw about 2 in. long. This screw passes through the standard and mirror frame, with a small wood or leather washer $\frac{1}{8}$ in. thick separating them as at A (Fig. 10), and with a small nut on the

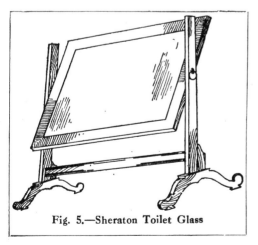

Fig. 5.—Sheraton Toilet Glass

a flute down the centre, as shown in section by Fig. 9.

inside. The nut on the right-hand side should be sunk in the mirror frame, so as to enable the glass to be pivoted to any position desired by tightening the screw on that side.

The mirror used, to be in keeping with the period of the work, should not be bevelled glass, and the work should not be finished off with too high a polish. A small brass or bone finial or knob is

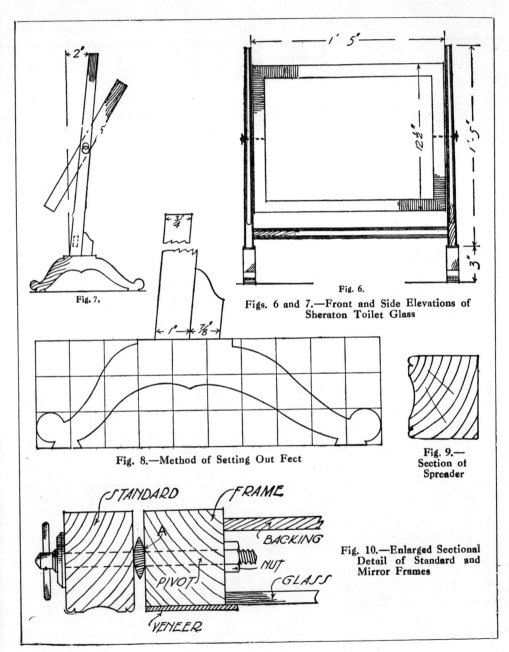

Fig. 7.

Fig. 6.

Figs. 6 and 7.—Front and Side Elevations of Sheraton Toilet Glass

Fig. 8.—Method of Setting Out Feet

Fig. 9.—Section of Spreader

Fig. 10.—Enlarged Sectional Detail of Standard and Mirror Frames

often fixed on the standards in antique examples.

but these may be altered as required. The wood used should be prime-quality

Fig. 11.

Fig. 12.

Figs. 11 and 12.—Front and Rear Views of Bed-rest

SIMPLE BED-REST

The bed-rest shown by Figs. 11 and 12

whitewood. The joints may be mortise and tenon, or dowels may be used, as may be convenient. Three common iron

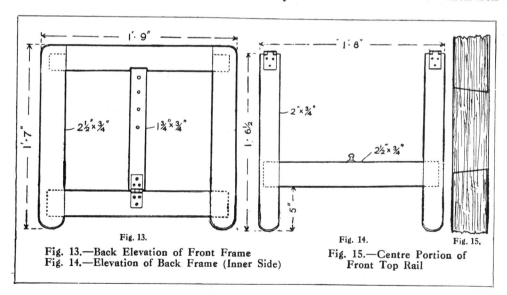

Fig. 13.—Back Elevation of Front Frame
Fig. 14.—Elevation of Back Frame (Inner Side)

Fig. 15.—Centre Portion of Front Top Rail

is simple, convenient, and inexpensive to make. Full particulars as to measurements, etc., are given in Figs. 13 and 14;

flap hinges are required, and a brass stud (as used on baby carriages), which can be obtained at almost any ironmonger's.

As seen in Fig. 13, the unhinged end of the stretcher piece on the front frame fits into a shallow slot cut on the inside edge of the top rail. This slot is slightly dovetail (*see* Fig. 15), and the end made to fit it in such a manner that it will stick in when closed up ; but it is easily pushed out from the front. All corners

(venetian-blind sling tape) fixed with oxidised brass-headed nails, the ends being afterwards turned in.

ANOTHER ADJUSTABLE BED-REST

An alternative type of bed-rest **is**

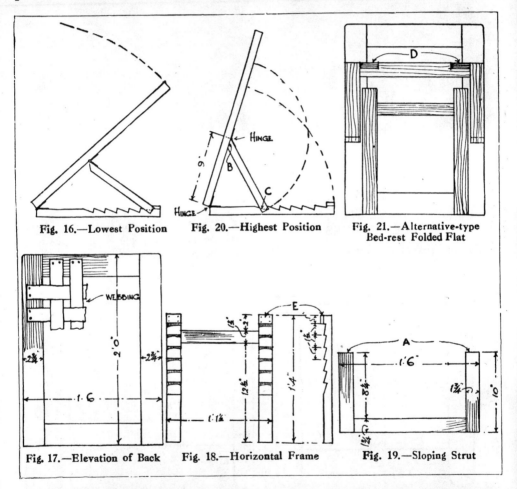

Fig. 16.—Lowest Position   Fig. 20.—Highest Position   Fig. 21.—Alternative-type Bed-rest Folded Flat

Fig. 17.—Elevation of Back   Fig. 18.—Horizontal Frame   Fig. 19.—Sloping Strut

on the ends and edges should be rounded off, and the whitewood will have a nice appearance if finished in its natural colour. To do this the wood is given a coat of clear size and left to get thoroughly dry. Then it is smoothed with fine glasspaper and polished with white polish. The front frame is webbed with strong tape

shown in side elevation by Fig. 16. For this three component parts are required, namely, (1) the back (Fig. 17), a rectangular frame with its top corners rounded, ultimately to be covered with webbing as indicated ; (2) the horizontal frame (Fig. 18) having a series of six notches, and (3) the strut (Fig. 19). These should each be strongly framed and kept perfectly rectangular. Fig. 20 explains how the three are hinged together, and incidentally shows the steepest angle to which the bed-rest can be adjusted, the lowest one being seen in Fig. 16. Back-flap hinges and ¾-in. screws should be used for both connections, that between back and horizontal frame being perfectly simple, while the one at the top of the strut can only be made when the ends of the latter, A (Fig. 19), have been splayed to suit, as at B in Fig. 20. In order properly to engage the notches in the horizontal frame, the strut must be double notched as dotted at c in Fig. 20, where it actually comes over the other notches ; that is to say, where denoted by shading at D in Fig. 21.

The last-mentioned figure shows how the whole can be compactly folded flat when out of use, the strut swinging up against the back frame, and the horizontal frame going just inside it as shown, and as indicated by the curves in Fig. 20. Small pieces of wood about ⅜ in. thick should be fixed to the ends of the horizontal frame, as at E in Fig. 18, in order to hold the strut quite secure when in the rather flat position shown in Fig. 16.

The front should last of all be covered with webbing, about ¾ in. of each end being turned under and fastened with two ¾-in. clout nails. The spaces between should be small, as shown in Fig. 17, where it will be noticed that the webbing is interlaced. Slightly round off all angles, and finish with a light stain and a coat of varnish.

TOWEL HORSE OF SIMPLE CONSTRUCTION

For constructing the towel horse shown by Figs. 22 and 23 almost any hardwood, mahogany for preference, is suitable. The principal parts are two standards, tenoned into shaped feet, and three rails, one fixed to the top of the standards and two to the cross-rails.

The two standards are stop-chamfered to the sizes given in Fig. 24, the length being 2 ft. 10 in., not including the tenon at the foot. The cross-rails are to the same pattern as the top of the standards and half checked to the latter, as shown in Fig. 25. The ⅝-in.-square towel rails are stop-tenoned into cross-rails. A mould of thin wood should be made for the feet to the shape and sizes shown in Fig. 26, which gives a half-shape of the foot. Line out on 1½-in. wood. Mortise the feet to receive the tenons on the standards, as shown in Fig. 27. When these are glued together the small brackets (Fig. 28), which are 1¼ in. thick and 4½ in. high, should be glued in position, thus binding the joint and adding to the appearance. The stretcher is 1½ in. by ½ in., the top edge being slightly rounded, and is tenoned into the standards (see Fig. 29).

ANOTHER TOWEL HORSE

The towel horse shown by Fig. 30 is intended to be 2 ft. 9¾ in. high and 2 ft. 2¼ in. long over the feet, the material required being as follows : Four pieces 2 ft. 7½ in. by 2⅜ in. by 1 in. thick for the standards, two pieces 5¼ in. by 3½ in. by ¾ in. thick for bottom distance pieces, two pieces 4⅜ in. by 3½ in. by ¾ in. thick for the top distance pieces, four pieces 3½ in. by 1¼ in. by 1 in. thick for standard supports A (Fig. 32), two pieces 2 ft. 1¼ in. by 1⅝ in. by 1 in. for towel rails, one 2 ft. 0½ in. by 5¼ in. by 1 in. thick for shelf, two pieces 1 ft. 3½ in. by 3 in. by 1¼ in. thick for feet, one piece 2 ft. 0¾ in. by 1¼ in. by 1 in. thick for bottom rail, and two pieces 8⅝ in. by 1½ in. by ¾ in. thick for capping. Figs. 31 and 32 are front and end elevations.

First of all plane up the four standards, taking care to taper them from top to bottom, the bottom being 2⅜ in. wide and the top 1⅞ in. wide, as shown in Figs. 33 and 34 ; then mark and cut out the tenons top and bottom, the bottom one being 1 in. long ; also mortise all four rails at the top on the inside face to receive the stamp-tenon on the towel rails.

A mould of thin wood should be made for the feet to the shape and sizes shown in Fig. 35 ; line out on 1¼-in.-thick stuff, mortise to take the tenon on bottom of standards, and cut out 1¼-in. groove B

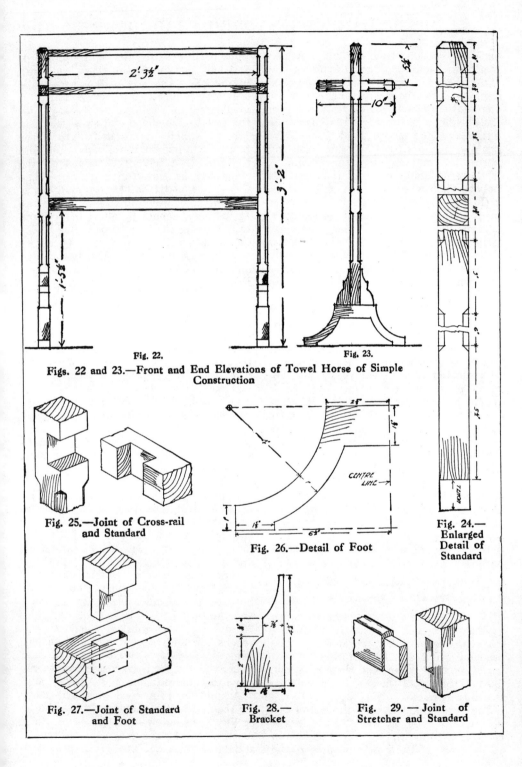

Fig. 22.

Fig. 23.

Figs. 22 and 23.—Front and End Elevations of Towel Horse of Simple Construction

Fig. 25.—Joint of Cross-rail and Standard

Fig. 26.—Detail of Foot

Fig. 24.— Enlarged Detail of Standard

Fig. 27.—Joint of Standard and Foot

Fig. 28.— Bracket

Fig. 29. — Joint of Stretcher and Standard

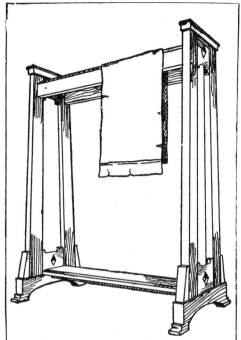

Fig. 30.—Another Design for Towel Horse

on the inside to take bottom rail. Next prepare the four distance pieces to dimensions given in Figs. 36 and 37, give them a slight taper (about $\frac{1}{16}$ in.) to take the slope of the standards; the diamond holes in each can be cut out with a keyhole or fret saw. The wedge-shaped pieces (Fig. 38) are cut out of 1-in. stuff; shoot the bottom edge to take slope of standard. Four of these are required, which can be glued and bradded to the feet and standards. Mortise the capping on the underside to take the top tenon of the standard and finish with moulding, as shown in Fig. 39. Fig. 40 shows a section of the towel rails; these are to have a stump tenon on both ends. The tenons need only be $\frac{5}{8}$ in. long by $\frac{3}{4}$ in. wide; chamfer the two top edges. Mould the edges of the shelf as shown in Fig. 41; the two ends will rest on the feet. The whole can now be framed and glued together, taking care the distance pieces are kept quite flush with the side faces of the standards, to ensure which the bench-cramp may be used with soft-wood blocks between the jaws.

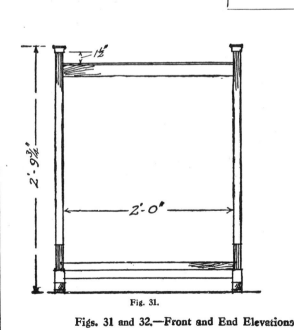

Fig. 31.

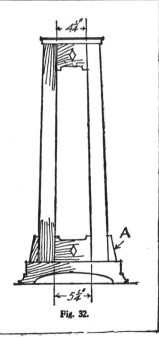

Fig. 32.

Figs. 31 and 32.—Front and End Elevations

TOWEL RAIL FOR WALL

Where space has to be economised, the towel rail shown by Fig. 42 will be found very suitable. It comprises two rails arranged beneath a couple of drawers, a scale of 1 in. to the foot, but this could be departed from in either direction to meet requirements. The end cheeks (Fig. 43) can be readily cut out with the bow saw, and the whole completed without the aid of a lathe, since the pateras

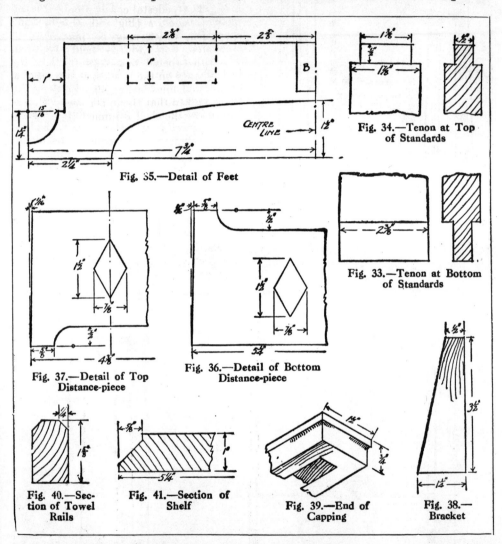

Fig. 35.—Detail of Feet

Fig. 34.—Tenon at Top of Standards

Fig. 33.—Tenon at Bottom of Standards

Fig. 37.—Detail of Top Distance-piece

Fig. 36.—Detail of Bottom Distance-piece

Fig. 40.—Section of Towel Rails

Fig. 41.—Section of Shelf

Fig. 39.—End of Capping

Fig. 38.—Bracket

which in turn are surmounted by a marble shelf (*see* Fig. 42). It is of very simple construction, and being intended to be enamelled to present a cleanly appearance, may be made of inexpensive wood. The details (Figs. 43 to 46) are reproduced to affording a finish to the rail ends and the drop finials depending from the corner pillars can be purchased cheaply and secured by gluing. The other parts and the method of putting together will be understood from the illustrations.

PEDESTAL FITTING WITH DRAWERS

The completed appearance of this useful article is shown in the perspective over-all dimensions suggested will be found marked on the figures.

Figs. 48 to 52 show two elevations, a plan and two sections respectively, one section being on line x (Fig. 48) and the other a vertical section.

The pedestal consists primarily of two sides, A (Fig. 48), about ¾ in. thick, which may be made up of three 6-in. widths held together with tapered oak keys forced into grooves on the insides, shown by the dotted lines in Fig. 49. Care should be taken that the upper key is placed below the shelf E immediately above

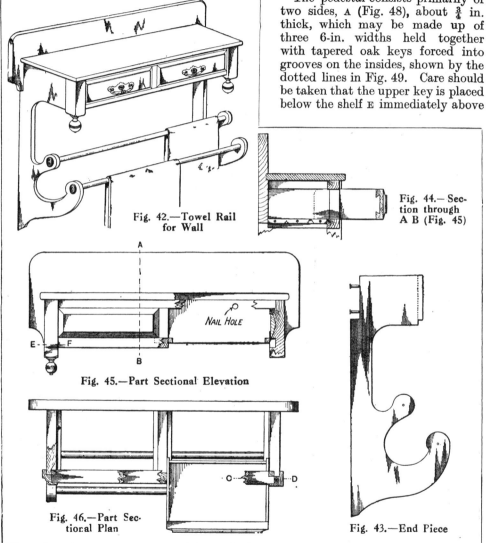

Fig. 42.—Towel Rail for Wall

Fig. 44.—Section through A B (Fig. 45)

Fig. 45.—Part Sectional Elevation

Fig. 46.—Part Sectional Plan

Fig. 43.—End Piece

sketch (Fig. 47), and its construction is explained by the working drawings (Figs. 48 to 59). The height of each drawer may be varied as required; but the general the drawers. The sides are 3 ft. 2 in. high, and cut away on the front edges to the outline shown. A setting out for the bracket part will be found in

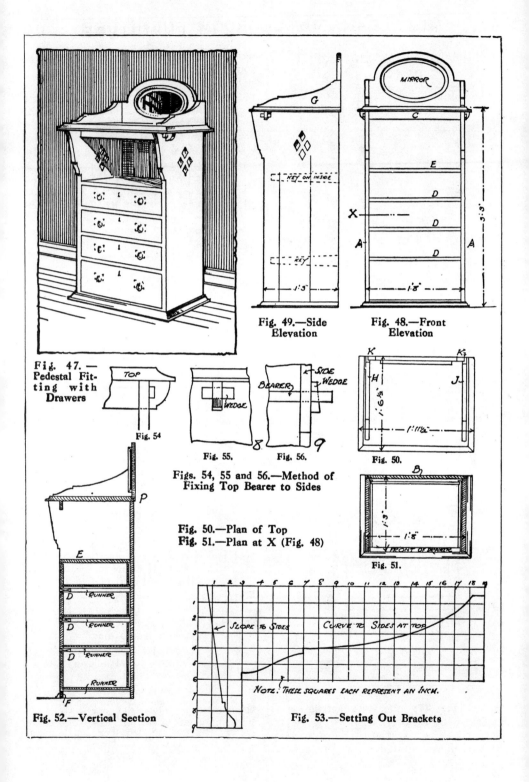

Fig. 47.—Pedestal Fitting with Drawers

Fig. 49.—Side Elevation

Fig. 48.—Front Elevation

Fig. 54

Figs. 54, 55 and 56.—Method of Fixing Top Bearer to Sides

Fig. 55.

Fig. 56.

Fig. 50.

Fig. 50.—Plan of Top
Fig. 51.—Plan at X (Fig. 48)

Fig. 51.

Fig. 52.—Vertical Section

Fig. 53.—Setting Out Brackets

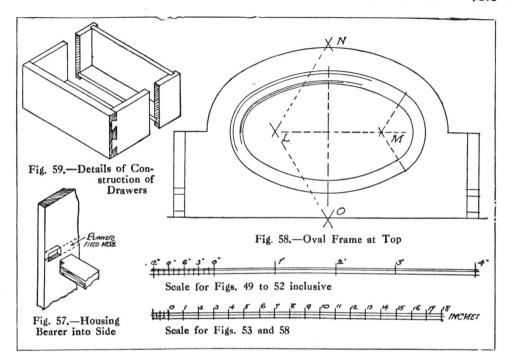

Fig. 59.—Details of Construction of Drawers

Fig. 57.—Housing Bearer into Side

Fig. 58.—Oval Frame at Top

Scale for Figs. 49 to 52 inclusive

Scale for Figs. 53 and 58

Fig. 53, where each square represents an inch on the full-size work, which should be divided into a similar number.

A ⅜-in. rebate is worked along the back inside edge of each side, to take a back (as at B in Fig. 51), which may be of matchboarding, and should be of such a width as will make the outside measurement 1 ft. 8 in. Next a horizontal bearer, C (Fig. 48), 2 in. deep is prepared with shaped ends fitted through slots cut in the sides, and secured with wedges, as shown more clearly in Figs. 54, 55 and 56, which also show the top.

Flat bearers about 2 in. by ⅝ in., D (Figs. 48 and 52), may then be housed into the sides as shown in Fig. 57, and a shelf E similarly fitted with grooves stopped ⅜ in. short of the front edges of the side pieces. A small skirting, F (Fig. 52), is also fitted in front next the floor, and a plinth moulding mitred round the base. Runners, as shown in Fig. 52, preferably of hardwood, should be fixed for the drawers to slide on, in exact lines with the tops of the bearers D.

The top should next be taken in hand,

and consists of a wide shelf 1 ft. 11½ in. by 1 ft. 6½ in. (see Fig. 50), round three edges of which a simple hollow moulding is worked. It is grooved as necessary to take two curved pieces shaped as at G on the side elevation, and shown on the plan at H and J. A setting-out of these pieces is given in Fig. 53, and they should be of the same thickness as the main sides below, and placed immediately over them. They are intended to be rebated along their inner back edges, K (Fig. 50), to take a curved back, shaped to be parallel to an oval picture frame of small section and projection enclosing a picture or mirror. This frame is planted on the surface, and can be obtained through a picture-frame maker or turner. It should be of a shape similar to Fig. 58, which shows it struck from four centres. The centres L and M are 7 in. apart, while N and O have a distance of 11½ in. between them. The sight opening of frame is 11¼ in. A rebate is worked along the edge of the top to suit the back, as at P (Fig. 52). The drawers (Fig. 59) are made in the usual manner.

Bedsteads

INLAID BEDSTEAD

WOODEN bedsteads are now much in favour, and have almost entirely superseded the brass and metal ones so much in vogue during the Victorian period. There was at one time a decided prejudice against wooden bedsteads, due chiefly to the idea that wooden bedsteads could not be kept properly clean ; but the better arrangement of the modern wooden bedstead, whereby wooden laths are superseded by iron fittings, and the old-fashioned box-spring mattress has given way to simple metal fittings, has dispelled this idea, hence their popularity and their undoubted advantage over metal or brass erections for any decorative scheme.

Fig. 1 shows the general design and proportion of the head and foot parts, which differ slightly in construction and a matter of 9 in. or so in height. The construction of the foot part is not dealt with separately, as the features described in connection with the construction of the head part are almost exactly similar.

To construct the head part, all the material should first of all be planed to width and thickness, then the tenons marked on the narrow and the centre splat with corresponding mortises on the top and bottom rails (see Figs. 2 and 3). All of these should then be cut, after which the top and bottom rails should be tenoned into the legs. Next inlaying is proceeded with, each splat having grooves

worked for the stringings, a scratch stock being utilised for this purpose. The top and bottom rails are proceeded with in like manner, and then the stringings are glued down into the grooves and allowed thoroughly to dry. It will perhaps be hardly necessary to note that both the head and the foot parts should be mortised together before proceeding with any of the inlaying.

The next step is to work the mouldings on the rails of each end. Fig. 4 illustrates graphically how this should be effected. Rebates are first worked on the top edges as indicated, and then a cutter is made from $\frac{1}{16}$-in. steel plate, filed to fit the moulding ; this is fixed in the scratch stock as shown by Fig. 5. The cutter just mentioned, and, indeed, all cutters of this type, must be filed in a certain way to obtain the best results. The edge, corresponding to the reverse of the moulding required, should be made perfectly square with the face of the cutter, and a burr is automatically produced on the edge by the action of filing, which really effects the cut. If the edge is not made perfectly flat and square, a part will, of course, bear on the material, and prevent the burr from cutting the material. The bottom edges of all the rails and also the upright splats should be slightly rounded off.

The posts at the top are decorated as shown by Fig. 6. The posts are grooved round about $\frac{1}{16}$ in. deep in order to receive

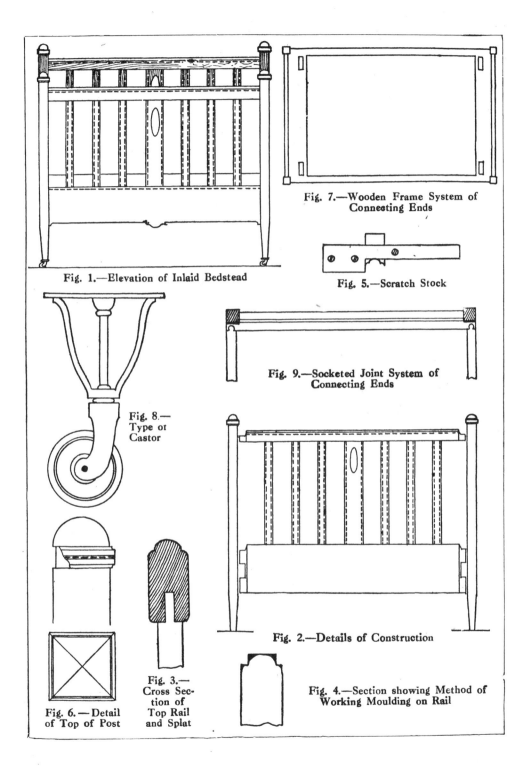

Fig. 1.—Elevation of Inlaid Bedstead

Fig. 7.—Wooden Frame System of Connecting Ends

Fig. 5.—Scratch Stock

Fig. 8.—Type of Castor

Fig. 9.—Socketed Joint System of Connecting Ends

Fig. 6.—Detail of Top of Post

Fig. 3.—Cross Section of Top Rail and Splat

Fig. 2.—Details of Construction

Fig. 4.—Section showing Method of Working Moulding on Rail

a moulding inlaid in the face side. This is prepared in lengths, rectangular in section and gauged to width and thickness. Inlaying should be proceeded with prior to moulding the edges, and both processes may be facilitated by improvising a piece of simple apparatus as follows: After the slips have been planed to size, cut a length of mahogany or other hard wood about 3 ft. long, and shoot one edge perfectly straight and true. Then drive in 1-in. stiff brads at distances of about 6 in. apart, allow the heads to project about $\frac{1}{4}$ in. from the edge, and then file the heads off and joint up the projecting ends with a file. Fix the board in the bench stop, and the slips of wood can then be temporarily secured by pressing the slip down into the points. The pressure exerted during the processes of inlaying and moulding is largely downwards but chiefly forwards ; but it will be found that the slips can be held quite firmly enough by this means. An alternative method of securing the wood is to put $\frac{3}{4}$-in. screws through each end of the slips into the edge of the board, when the inlaying and moulding can be proceeded with without fear of the pieces buckling or breaking. A wooden mitre-cut is, of course, necessary when fixing the mouldings, and a mitre shoot or block should be employed when planing the mouldings to correct lengths.

The question of framing between the ends is the next important item. The French system is a good one for the support of box-spring mattresses, and consists of two wide wooden rails fixed to the posts. The latter is effected by sinking French bolts into the wide rails, the ends projecting through small stub or key tenons worked at each end. Nuts are sunk in the posts. and the whole affair is tightened up and made rigid by the aid of a "tommy" operated from the inside. This system, excellent as it is, is costly, and involves a deal of work and fitting which is obviated by the adoption of methods outlined later. Fittings are obtainable which are economical to purchase and easy to adjust. They also have the advantage of keeping the bedstead thoroughly firm and rigid when the whole is fixed in position. Their action is very simple. Two angle-iron end pieces are screwed inside the head and foot frames, these being notched in order to receive the two side rails. The latter are secured to the end pieces by means of bolts and a key.

Other systems are illustrated. Fig. 7 snows a wooden frame system, this also being used to a large extent in connection with French bedsteads, which run on wheels or rubber-tyred castors such as shown by Fig. 8. It is almost impossible to fix this particular type when iron rails are employed, it, of course, being necessary to set them well back, so as not to show when the bed is erected. They are made of various sizes in order to meet various conditions of height caused by the adoption of certain arrangements of bedding. Generally, it may be said that a chain-spring mattress is placed on the iron or side rails, with a hair mattress above this, and then a feather bed. The arrangement suggested occupies approximately some 12 in. above the side rails, this height being reduced if the feather bed is dispensed with, as some people prefer. When a box-spring mattress is used with a feather bed or loose hair mattress above, the height of the combined pieces is about 14 in., so that before one can determine the best height for fixing the side rails, the type of bedding to be employed must be considered.

To fix the wheeled castors, a large frame is made from 2$\frac{1}{2}$-in. beech, as is illustrated in Fig. 7. This part should be mortised and tenoned together. and when it has been squared up to size it should be dry dowelled into the ends and secured by screwing. The castors are fixed by screwing the plates on to the underside of the frame as indicated in the plan.

A third system of railing the ends together is that shown in part plan in Fig. 9. A socketed rail is firmly screwed to each end of the bedstead which receives the dovetailed side rails. Laths are sometimes introduced, as were generally used on metal bedsteads ; but these are not necessary when chain-spring mattresses are adopted.

With reference to the length and width

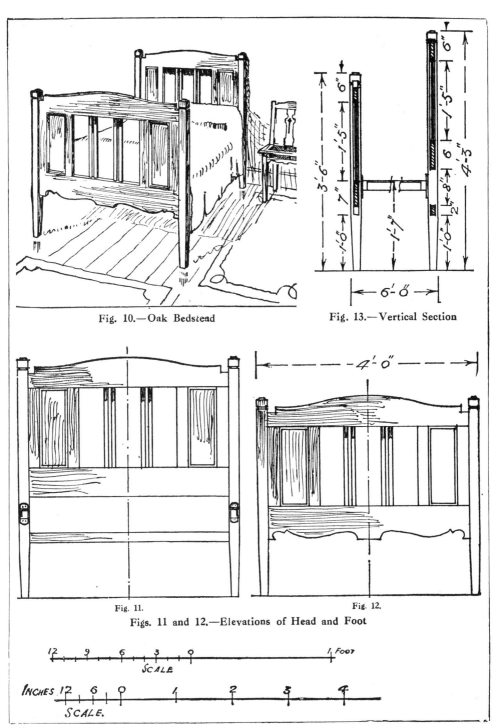

Fig. 10.—Oak Bedstead

Fig. 13.—Vertical Section

Fig. 11.

Fig. 12.

Figs. 11 and 12.—Elevations of Head and Foot

of the bedstead, these sizes can be varied to meet requirements; but it should be noted that after the sizes are settled, the necessary fittings should be obtained previously to making the bedstead so that one will not be faced with any difficulty in obtaining special sizes of fittings. Whether made wider or narrower than the example illustrated (4 ft. wide), no alteration need be made in the design within the limits of 6 in. each way; all that need be considered is the re-spacing of the narrow splats in each end.

CUTTING LIST FOR 4-FT. WIDE BEDSTEAD

No.	For	Lgth.	Wh.	Th.	Wood	Des.	Remarks
1	HEAD PART:	ft. in.	in.	in.			
2	Legs ..	3 8½	2½	2½	mahog.	2	
3	Bottom Rail	3 11	10½	1⅜	,,	1	
4	Top Rail ..	3 11	3	1⅜	,,	1	
5	Centre Splat	2 0	4½	⅞	,,	1	
6	Small Splats	2 0	1½	⅞	,,	6	
7	FOOT PART:						
8	Legs ..	3 3	2½	2½	,,	2	
9	Bottom Rail	3 11	8½	1⅜	,,	1	
10	Top Rail ..	3 11	3¼	1⅜	,,	1	
11	Centre Splat	1 8½	4	⅞	,,	1	
12	Small Splats	1 8½	1½	⅞	,,	6	

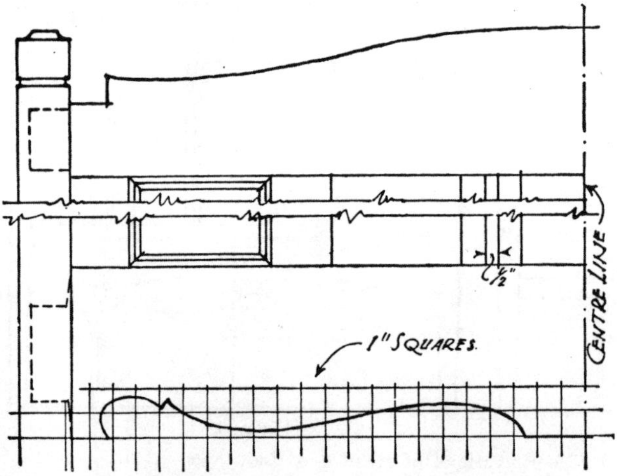

Fig. 14.—Enlarged Part Elevation of Oak Bedstead

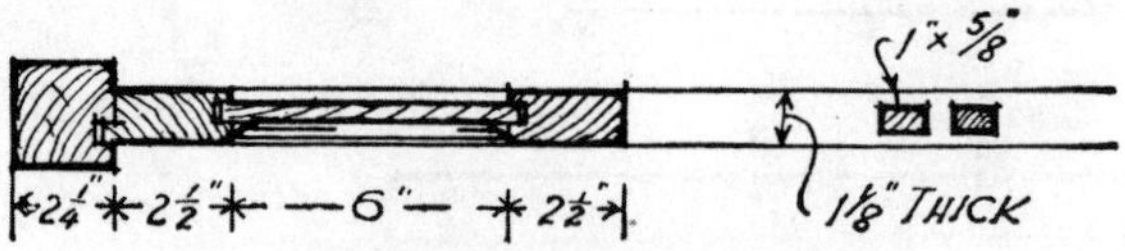

Fig. 15.—Enlarged Part Plan

OAK BEDSTEAD

Fig. 10 is a conventional view of a bedstead that presents a very good appearance if made of oak. Two elevations are given by Figs. 11 and 12, and a section by Fig. 13, and on this last figure the necessary dimensions are given.

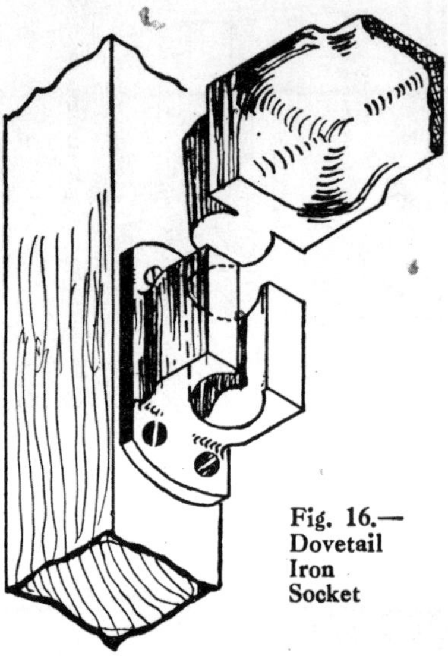

Fig. 16.—Dovetail Iron Socket

The pieces of timber having been cut to their several sizes, each should be planed to the finished dimensions. Then the posts and rails should be set out, and the mortising and tenoning done. The forms of joints for connecting the stiles and rails of the head and foot are clearly shown in the enlarged part elevation and plan (Figs. 14 and 15). On the former figure the method of marking out the curved rails is shown. The joints of the

Fig. 17.—Mahogany Bedstead

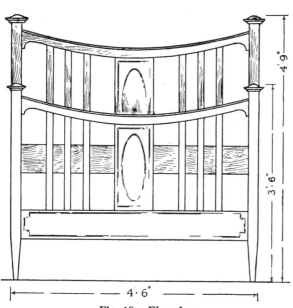

4' 9"

3' 6"

4' 6"

Fig. 18.—Elevation

3½"

Fig. 19.—Detail
Section through
Head or Foot

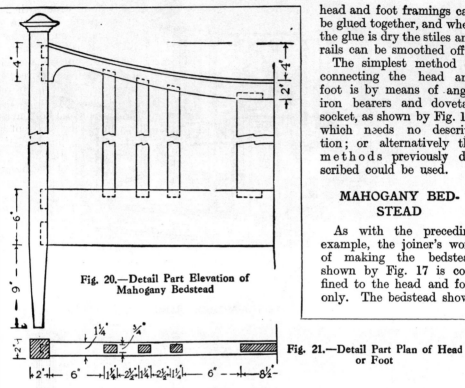

Fig. 20.—Detail Part Elevation of Mahogany Bedstead

Fig. 21.—Detail Part Plan of Head or Foot

head and foot framings can be glued together, and when the glue is dry the stiles and rails can be smoothed off.

The simplest method of connecting the head and foot is by means of angle iron bearers and dovetail socket, as shown by Fig. 16, which needs no description; or alternatively the methods previously described could be used.

MAHOGANY BED-STEAD

As with the preceding example, the joiner's work of making the bedstead shown by Fig. 17 is confined to the head and foot only. The bedstead shown

Fig. 22.—Alternative Design of Mahogany Bedstead

is 4 ft. 6 in. wide with 2-in. square posts, and the dimensions given are for a good, substantial piece of furniture, but if a saving of material is desired, the thickness of the posts may be reduced to $1\frac{1}{2}$ in. by 2 in., and the top and bottom rails to 1 in. thick. A front elevation of the head and foot is shown by Fig. 18.

The whole of the framing is mortised and tenoned together as indicated (see Fig. 19). The dimensions of the various members may be gathered from the enlarged details given by Figs. 18 to 21. A bedstead of this design should preferably

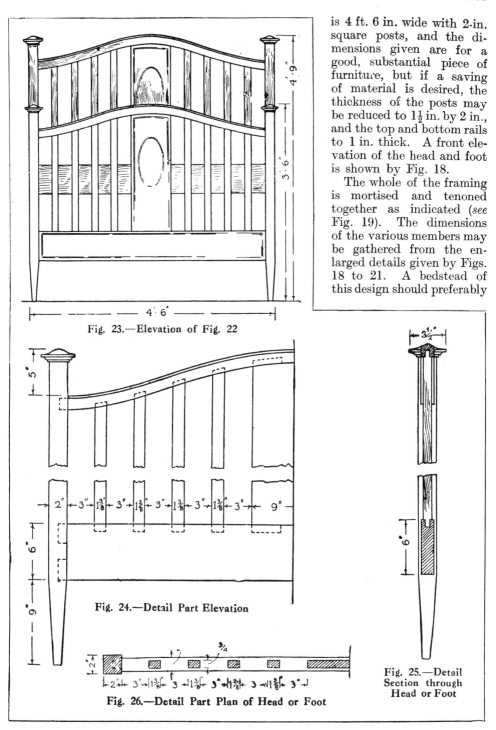

Fig. 23.—Elevation of Fig. 22

Fig. 24.—Detail Part Elevation

Fig. 26.—Detail Part Plan of Head or Foot

Fig. 25.—Detail Section through Head or Foot

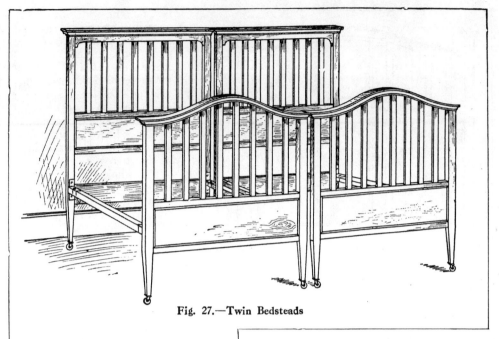

Fig. 27.—Twin Bedsteads

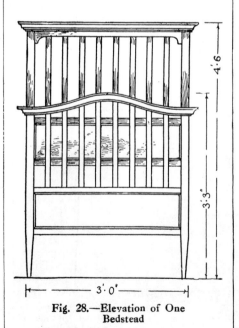

Fig. 28.—Elevation of One
Bedstead

be executed in mahogany, and its appearance would be greatly enhanced if inlay stringings of satinwood were introduced in the posts, and bottom and centre panels.

ANOTHER MAHOGANY BEDSTEAD

An alternative design is shown by Fig. 22, and a front elevation of head and foot by Fig. 23. The constructional details are identical with the preceding one. Figs. 24, 25 and 26 show the necessary dimensions, which, as with the other example, may be reduced slightly if rather lighter construction is desired.

TWIN BEDSTEADS

The twin bedsteads shown in perspective and elevation by Figs. 27 and 28 are based upon the same constructional methods as the examples just described, and the jointing is exactly the same, with the exception of the panels, which in this case are let into ploughed grooves worked in the posts and rails as shown in the details (Figs. 29 and 30).   It

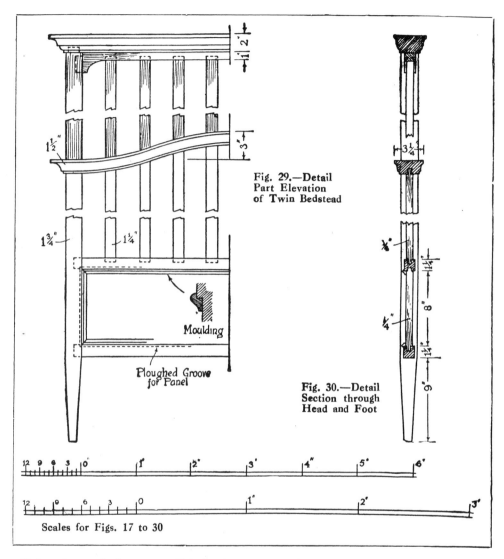

Fig. 29.—Detail
Part Elevation
of Twin Bedstead

Moulding

Ploughed Groove
for Panel

Fig. 30.—Detail
Section through
Head and Foot

Scales for Figs. 17 to 30

will be observed that a small bolection-mitred moulding is planted round the panels. The dimensions are indicated in Figs. 28 to 30.

TEMPORARY BEDSTEAD

The bedstead shown by Fig. 31 is of rough construction intended for temporary use only. As will be seen, the bedstead consists of legs of about 3-in. by 2-in. material 1 ft. $4\frac{1}{2}$ in. long, on which, and secured to them by screwing, is a frame of. say. 3-in. by $1\frac{1}{2}$-in. wood measuring 3 ft. 3 in. by 6 ft. 6 in. over all. It will be noticed that the frame is placed flat, thus allowing ample strength to withstand the inward pull resulting from the weight of the occupant. Struts. $1\frac{1}{2}$ in. by 1 in. and sloping as indicated. can be arranged from the legs to the underside of the frame on the long sides. These are intended to prevent it from bending downwards, and are supported on cleats or brackets on the legs. A "straining piece" is introduced between them at the top as shown, nailed to the underside of the frame and giving still further strength. A piece measuring $1\frac{1}{2}$ in. by 1 in. is next nailed to the legs across the short way of the bedstead, this being to keep the

closely tacked to the underside, preferably with the edge turned in about $\frac{3}{4}$ in., in order to make a neat finish and to obtain extra strength for the nailing. In Fig. 32 is indicated the suggested fitting of a corner without, however, showing the parts turned in along the edges. The

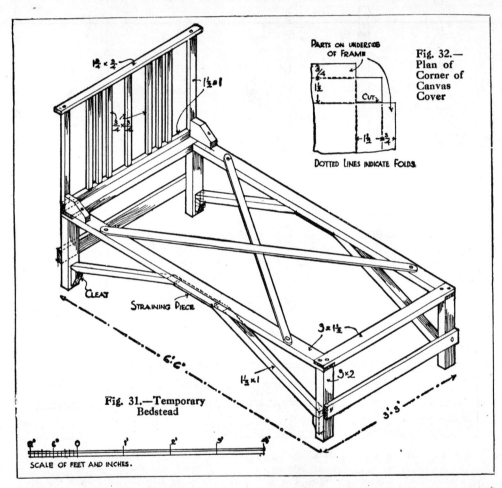

Fig. 32.—Plan of Corner of Canvas Cover

Fig. 31.—Temporary Bedstead

SCALE OF FEET AND INCHES.

legs the correct distance apart and so stiffen the whole.

In order to afford extra support to the surface of the stout canvas cover with which it is intended to cover the frame, two old bed laths are cut to shape, drilled, and screwed to the woodwork crossing diagonally as shown. The canvas is tightly stretched over the frame and

$\frac{3}{4}$-in. margins shown are tacked on the underside of the frame, and the small square piece above the cut is folded round the angle of the frame under the $1\frac{1}{2}$-in. margin shown below it. If iron laths are adopted they might well be covered in, thin strips of material being wound diagonally round them.

A back or head is quite necessary ; but

a foot piece is not essential. The back shown is 2 ft. 1 in. high above the frame, composed of 1½-in. by 1-in. bottom and side rails, with 1¾-in. by ¾-in. top rail and ¾-in. by ¾-in. laths arranged in groups as shown, or at equal intervals. The top rail is placed flat, and rides over the side rails 1¼ in. each side as a simple finish to the work. All these parts are merely strongly screwed together, with the exception of the bottom and side rails; these should be halved and screwed in addition. All

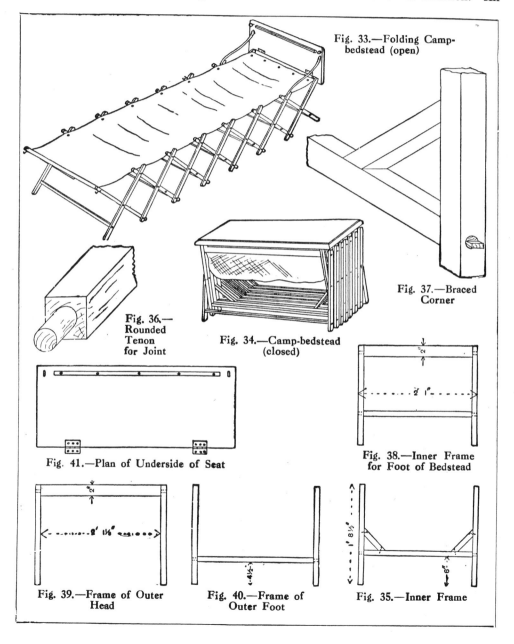

Fig. 33.—Folding Camp-bedstead (open)

Fig. 37.—Braced Corner

Fig. 36.—Rounded Tenon for Joint

Fig. 34.—Camp-bedstead (closed)

Fig. 41.—Plan of Underside of Seat

Fig. 38.—Inner Frame for Foot of Bedstead

Fig. 39.—Frame of Outer Head

Fig. 40.—Frame of Outer Foot

Fig. 35.—Inner Frame

should be of good planed wood, with the exposed angles rounded off, and if finish is desired, should be knotted, stopped, primed, and given three coats of glossy white enamel.

FOLDING CAMP-BEDSTEAD

When not in use, the bedstead illustrated by Fig. 33 can be easily closed up, and fastened by means of hooks and eyes, to the shape of a seat or stool 2 ft. $4\frac{1}{2}$ in. long, $10\frac{3}{4}$ in. wide, and 21 in. high. When extended to a bedstead it is 6 ft. 6 in. long, the seat forming a head board as shown. The pieces for the folding frames are of $\frac{7}{8}$-in. square stuff, and should be of beech wood. All the working joints have $\frac{1}{4}$-in. rivets, washered between the pieces of wood and on each side for the clinching of the rivet.

The bedstead, closed for use as a seat, is shown by Fig. 34. The legs are $20\frac{1}{2}$ in. long, rounded at the top and the bottom ends. The three $\frac{1}{4}$-in. holes for the rivets are bored with a spoon bit $1\frac{1}{2}$ in. from the top end and $6\frac{1}{2}$ in. apart. Fig. 35 shows the construction of the inner frames. The horizontal bar has at each end a $\frac{1}{2}$-in. round tenon as in Fig. 36, which only needs a bored hole for mortising to the leg. The mortise-and-tenon joints should be glued and wedged as shown in Fig. 37, and a brace or strut glued and screwed in the corners to prevent distortion.

The end inner frame for the foot of the

bedstead has an additional piece for a rail, to which the canvas is fixed. This frame is shown by Fig. 38. It will be seen that the outside measurement of the inner frames is 2 ft. 1 in., allowing $\frac{1}{16}$ in. at each side for washers between the pieces. The inside of the outer frames should be 2ft. $1\frac{1}{8}$ in. ; this is required only for making the head and foot frames.

The head frame has the rail for the canvas (see Fig. 39), and the outer frame at the foot has a lower bar for strengthening the projecting legs (see Fig. 40). These rails can be fixed with round mortise-and-tenon joints, as before explained.

The seat has a moulding round the four edges, and a fillet $\frac{1}{2}$ in. square is screwed on the underside $\frac{3}{4}$ in. from the edge for the purpose of clasping the rail of the foot frame when closed, as shown in Fig. 41. The seat is then fixed to the rail of the head frame with brass butt-hinges. Hooks are fixed into the legs of the foot frame, and the eyes for same beneath the seat board, to clasp when folded up. The webbing is fixed as shown in Fig. 33 to keep the board in position.

The canvas for the bed should be strong and of good quality. The edges should be strengthened with a 2-in. hem all round. It is then screwed on the inside of the inner legs near the top, and also to the head and foot rails. The best fixing is made by using an iron and leather washer with each screw, the leather, of course, being next to the canvas.

Cots

FOLDING COT OF SIMPLE CONSTRUCTION

THE child's cot illustrated in Fig. 1 is very simple in construction, and merely requires the ability to plane wood to width and thickness, and to mortise the legs and form tenons on the ends of the side rails. Two elevations are given by Figs. 2 and 3. When not in use the cot can be folded up and placed against a wall. The bottom of the cot A (Fig. 4) serves to keep the cot open as in Fig. 1. When the bottom is lifted out the hinged ends B (Fig. 1) are folded inwards, as shown in the plan (Fig. 4).

As the cot has to carry very little weight, any straight-grained wood free

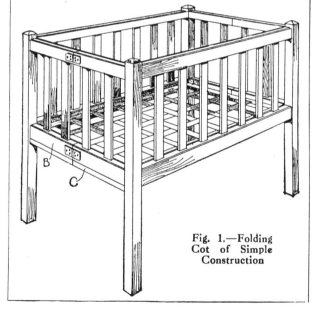

Fig. 1.—Folding Cot of Simple Construction

from knots may be used, such as pine or deal, varnished or french-polished. But for good appearance, mahogany finished with french-polish is recommended. To save expense, iron flap hinges $1\frac{1}{4}$ in. wide may be used; but brass hinges will look better and will not rust. To ensure accuracy of working, it is advisable to make full-size drawings of the plan (Fig. 4), also of half the side elevation (Fig. 2), and half the end elevation (Fig. 3). The dimensions of the cot are: Length, 3 ft. 6 in.; width, 2 ft. 3 in.; height to top rails, 2 ft. 6 in.; height to top edges of rails B (Fig. 1), 1 ft. 4 in.; legs, $1\frac{5}{8}$ in. square; top rail, $1\frac{1}{2}$ in. wide and $1\frac{7}{8}$ in. thick; lower rails B, 2 in. wide by $1\frac{1}{8}$ in. thick; balusters, $1\frac{1}{2}$ in. wide and $\frac{3}{8}$ in. thick.

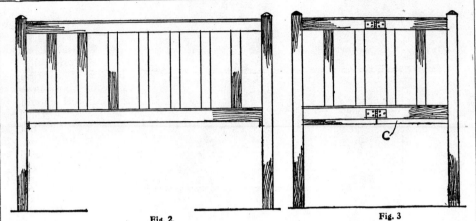

Fig. 2.

Fig. 3

Figs. 2 and 3.—Front and End Elevations of Folding Cot

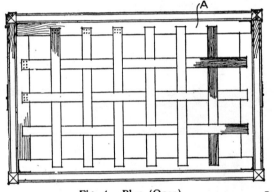

Fig. 4.—Plan (Open)

Fig. 5.—Top of Post
showing Mortise

HINGES

Fig. 7.—Plan (Closed)

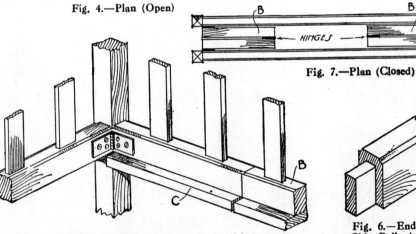

Fig. 8.—Details of Construction showing Method of
Supporting Bottom

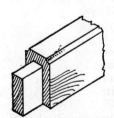

Fig. 6.—End of
Side Rail show-
ing Tenon

Fig. 9.—Another Design of Folding Cot (Open)

sides of the end rails. In folding the ends, as in Fig. 7, the strips c (Figs. 1 and 8) slide under the side rails. To allow for the free working of the strips, the bottom edges of the end rail should be about $\frac{1}{16}$ in. below the level of the side rails. The bottom framing A (Fig. 4) may now be mortised and tenoned together, and then fitted into position, so that it can easily be dropped in or lifted out. When the framing is polished the webbing may be tacked on as in Fig. 4. A suitable webbing is that used by upholsterers for chairs.

ANOTHER FOLDING COT

In the framing of the bottom of the cot, the side rails and the end rails are 2 in. by 1¼ in.

In making, first plane up all the wood to width and thickness, and shape the upper ends of the legs as in Fig. 5. The upper edges of the top and the lower rail are chamfered as in Fig. 6. In marking the legs for the mortises, place all the legs side by side, and draw the lines across with the aid of a square. The same method should be used in marking the tenons on the side rails. It will be seen that the end rails have no tenons, and to facilitate working, the end rails may be kept in one length, while the balusters are fitted and glued together. Then they may be cut in two parts, and the hinges fixed, as shown in Fig. 1. The various positions of the hinges are shown in Figs. 1, 4, and 7.

Support for the bottom framing of the cot can be provided by means of strips of wood c (Fig. 8), 2 in. wide and ¾ in. thick, fixed with screws to the under-

A collapsible cot fixed ready for use is shown by Fig. 9, and partly folded by Fig. 10. Fig. 11 is a side elevation, Fig. 12 an end elevation, and Fig. 13 a plan of the cot. It will be seen that the ends consist of two small gates, each of

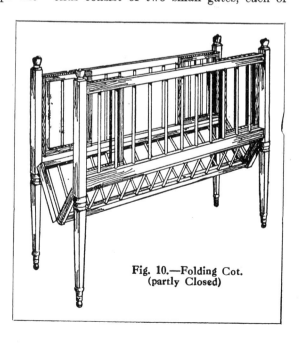

Fig. 10.—Folding Cot. (partly Closed)

which is hinged to a post with a couple of 2-in. brass butts, and folds inwards flat against the sides of the cot. The bottom of the cot also consists of two parts hinged on the upper side along the centre, with three 2-in. brass butts, the manner of fixing these being shown at Fig. 14. The outer edges of the bottom of the cot are hinged with similar-size butts (three on

Having obtained the material the posts and rails should be sawn out, care being taken to cut the former very straight, and ⅛ in. thicker and wider than the finished size. Before planing the posts they should be turned, after which they may be planed to suit the turning. The rails should now be planed to the required sizes and moulded, when the tenons on the rails

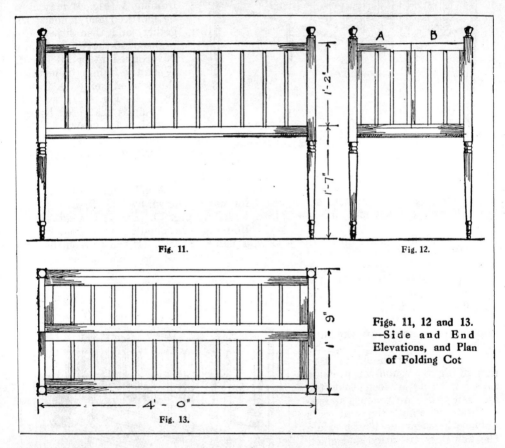

Fig. 11.

Fig. 12.

Figs. 11, 12 and 13.
—Side and End
Elevations, and Plan
of Folding Cot

Fig. 13.

each edge) to fillets fixed to the bottom rails of the cot sides; this is shown in Fig. 15. When the cot is not in use the two sections can be folded flat against each other. As the cot is of a portable character the wood should be light and strong, the most suitable being birch. The illustrations are fully dimensioned, but the sizes may be varied to meet requirements.

and the mortises in the posts may be set out and made. This form of joint is shown in Fig. 16, where it will be seen that the method of fixing is by means of a long-range screw, the head of which is sunk in a hole bored in the face of the post, and fits over a washer which prevents the head sinking into the wood, and also gives it a larger bearing surface. To hide the screw-heads turned wooden buttons are provided. The nut for the screw is inserted in a mortise made in the inner side of the rail. The stiles and rails of the gates are jointed together by means of stub-tenons on the former, glued into mortises made in the latter. A similar method of connecting the rails and stiles is used in the construction of the bottom of the cot.

bored in the framing as indicated in Figs. 15, 17, and 18, getting the upper holes vertically over the lower ones, so that the bars are at right angles to the framing.

When all the various parts are made they should be smoothed off, fitted together, and firmly glued. Then the gates and bottom should be fitted in and hinged.

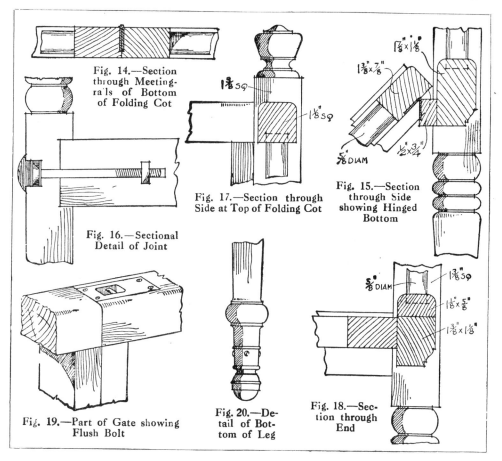

Fig. 14.—Section through Meeting-rails of Bottom of Folding Cot

Fig. 17.—Section through Side at Top of Folding Cot

Fig. 15.—Section through Side showing Hinged Bottom

Fig. 16.—Sectional Detail of Joint

Fig. 19.—Part of Gate showing Flush Bolt

Fig. 20.—Detail of Bottom of Leg

Fig. 18.—Section through End

When the posts, rails, and stiles have all been made the bars should be prepared. In the illustrations they are shown round in section, but those for the bottom may be rectangular, the connection with the sides being by means of a barefaced tenon which causes the upper surface of the bar to be level with the framing. The round bars fit into holes

To keep the gates together when the cot is in use a flush bolt is inserted in the top of one of each pair (see Fig. 19), and a couple of the same type of bolts are used to keep the bottom of the cot horizontal; these are inserted in the underside.

Ball casters will be found very useful for the cot, and should be fitted on the bottom of the legs, as shown in Fig. 20.

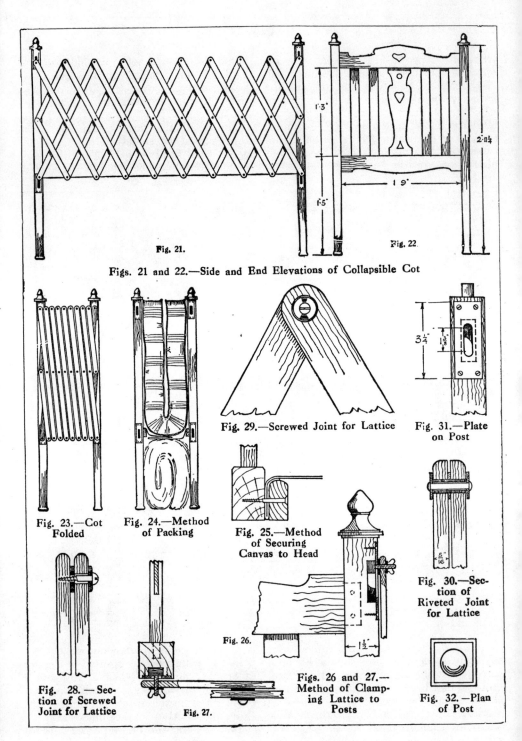

Fig. 21.

Fig. 22.

Figs. 21 and 22.—Side and End Elevations of Collapsible Cot

Fig. 29.—Screwed Joint for Lattice

Fig. 31.—Plate on Post

Fig. 23.—Cot Folded

Fig. 24.—Method of Packing

Fig. 25.—Method of Securing Canvas to Head

Fig. 30.—Section of Riveted Joint for Lattice

Fig. 26.

Figs. 26 and 27.—Method of Clamping Lattice to Posts

Fig. 27.

Fig. 28.—Section of Screwed Joint for Lattice

Fig. 32.—Plan of Post

COLLAPSIBLE COT

The collapsible cot shown by Fig. 21 is 4 ft. long by 2 ft. wide, and has fixed ends (Fig. 22). The sides are formed of thin laths, 1 in. by $\frac{5}{16}$ in., made in lattice work. In Fig. 23 the cot is shown closed, while Fig. 24 illustrates the bedding packed for transit, the lattice being omitted. The mattress is supported by canvas, as shown in Fig. 25. When the cot is fully open and the wing nuts are tightened, the cot is secure in its extended position.

Birch, ash or oak will be a suitable material.

Prepare the four posts from stuff that will clean up to $1\frac{1}{4}$ in. square by 3 ft. long, place them close together on the bench, and square off the dimensions for the mortises of the top and bottom end rails, and set the marking gauge for the width of the mortises. Prepare the rails from stuff 6 in. wide by $\frac{7}{8}$ in. thick, and cut the tenons, which are shown one-fourth full size in Figs. 26 and 27. The balusters are $\frac{7}{16}$ in. thick by $1\frac{1}{2}$ in. wide when finished, and are housed to the rails about $\frac{1}{2}$ in. deep. Clamp the four rails evenly together with their inside edges upwards, square off the lengths of the mortises for balusters, and scribe their width with the marking gauge, fit the balusters to the rails, and see that the distance between the tenons is the same as is marked on the posts; then fit the lot together temporarily.

Now proceed with the laths for the sides, their finished sizes being 1 ft. 10 in. by 1 in. by $\frac{5}{16}$ in.; they should be about $1\frac{1}{2}$ in. longer in the rough to lessen the danger of splitting the ends when boring the holes or riveting up the joints. To ensure uniformity it is advisable to make a template of hardwood or metal, in which holes have been bored of the correct size and distance apart. If of wood the template should be about $\frac{1}{2}$ in. to $\frac{3}{4}$ in. thick; it is clamped to the laths, and the holes are bored in the latter, the template being used as a guide and $\frac{1}{16}$ in. clearance being allowed for the working holes.

A simple joint for the laths is shown in Figs. 28 and 29, where an ordinary round-headed screw and two washers are used. In Fig. 30 the joint is riveted; a thin washer is inserted between the laths, and a brass bush slightly longer than the width of the two laths and centre washer is also used, so that when the rivet is finished the outer washers bear tight on the bush, leaving the laths free to move. This method makes an excellent joint for many purposes, but, of course, it involves a greater amount of labour. Put the lattice sides in their closed position, place them on the posts, and fix the centre screw in each post. Now mark off the position for the slots in the four remaining holes. Next extend the posts until they are 4 ft. apart, and mark through as before; this will give the length of the slot for plates and the groove in the post (*see* Figs. 26, 27, and 31). By a simple method the lattice may be secured with ordinary screws and washers, which must be withdrawn when the cot is closed, and inserted again in the new position caused by closing.

The finials (*see* Figs. 26 and 32) are glued and dowelled on, the rails are glued and pinned to the posts, and the work should be well glasspapered to remove all sharp edges.

Linen Chests

AN OLD-STYLE CHEST

THE chest or " rug-box " shown in the half-tone (Fig. 1) is proposed to be made in oak, quite roughly finished externally, with pegs driven through the various tenoned joints, and the whole stained to a dark dull colour in order to simulate the effect of similar work dating from Tudor times, but without the incised surface

The chest consists of four pieces of framing with rails, etc., finished about ⅞ in. thick, and with panels as shown in Figs. 2 and 3, the usual tenoned joints being secured with two oak pegs each. Fig. 4 shows two half plans and Fig. 5 a cross section. A small ovolo moulding is worked along the edges of each panel, stopped where shown at the top, and dying out on a splay

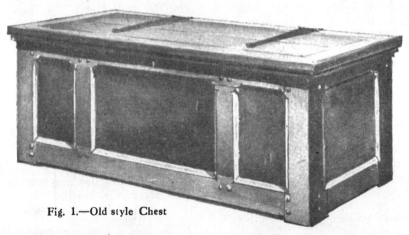

Fig. 1.—Old style Chest

ornament often employed, the presence of which is a matter of taste. The mediæval character will be further enhanced by the treatment of the edges of the framing next the panels, these being worked with mouldings and splays on the solid in the manner adopted by the mason for stonework, rather than that associated with the later developments of joinery.

worked on the top edge of the bottom rail, as at A (Fig. 2). The horizontal joint runs through the small moulding as at B, this being the traditional method. A slightly different finish for the edges of the panels, and one like the first founded on old work, is shown in Figs. 6 and 7, where the ovolo runs right out against the edge of the top rail, while the latter has simply a stopped chamfer. At the back the three panels intended to be formed can suitably have square edges, and at each corner the upright " stiles " project downwards about $\frac{5}{8}$ in. to form feet, which might either serve to conceal small casters or other similar devices for silence if desired. The bottom edge all round c (Fig. 7) might well be chamfered off a little, and the various panels required

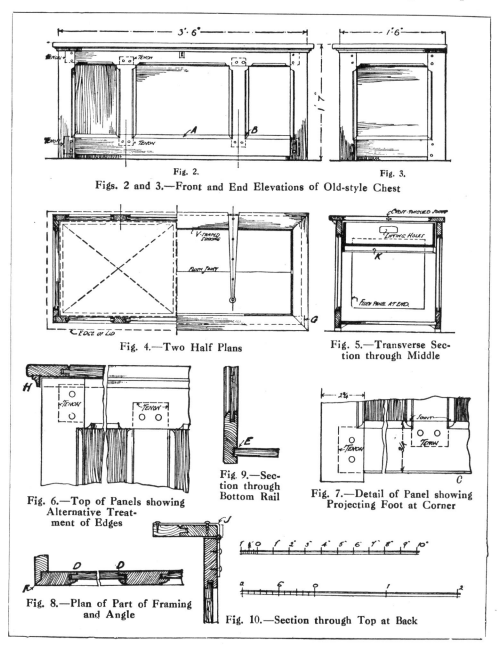

Fig. 2.

Fig. 3.

Figs. 2 and 3.—Front and End Elevations of Old-style Chest

Fig. 4.—Two Half Plans

Fig. 5.—Transverse Section through Middle

Fig. 6.—Top of Panels showing Alternative Treatment of Edges

Fig. 9.—Section through Bottom Rail

Fig. 7.—Detail of Panel showing Projecting Foot at Corner

Fig. 8.—Plan of Part of Framing and Angle

Fig. 10.—Section through Top at Back

can either be quite thin, or rebated as at D in Fig. 8 in order to present a flush internal face, together with greatly increased strength.

When the four pieces of framing have been prepared to the sizes, etc., shown on the illustrations, they should be rebated just above the floor, as at E in Fig. 9, in order to take a wood bottom arranged with its grain running the short way of the box. When this has been made ready, the sides should be mitred together as at F (Fig. 8), this joint being far more practicable for the average craftsman than a lot of concealed dovetailing.

For the lid or top, a piece of framing about $\frac{3}{4}$ in. thick and large enough to overhang the box 1 in. on three sides will be necessary. It might be mitred and have a tenon as G (Fig. 4) at the angles, and is intended to have rounded angles and a small moulding under to fit round the box as at H (Fig. 6). It is suggested that the top be filled in with a panel flush on both top and bottom faces, having a small V-shaped sinking all round, as in Fig. 6, and could be in two widths with a joint longitudinally down the centre as in Fig. 4, this joint being cross-tongued if possible.

Hinges of a fairly rough quality and similar to what are termed "cross-garnets" may be employed, and if, as is proposed, they are required to show on the top of the box, they must be very carefully heated and bent to a right angle as at J (Fig. 10), and small pieces cut out of the lid to suit, the whole being screwed down as indicated. A small chain or strap will probably be of service, if arranged so as to prevent the lid falling back too far, and a small unobtrusive lock and key should be fitted.

It is suggested that instead of carrying the old-style appearance to extremes, the interior should be finished with a natural surface and slightly waxed, this being cleaner than if stained dark; while at a distance down from the top edge of about $4\frac{1}{4}$ in., a small fillet, as at K (Fig. 5), is intended to be fixed all round the box, in order to support two light wooden trays constructed of the very lightest thickness practicable, and are intended to contain small articles. They are each of the square shape indicated by the diagonal lines in Fig. 4. They might have holes cut in their sides as noted in Fig. 5 for easy lifting. In fitting them, the pieces could suitably be mitred together, and secured with a row of fine wire brads.

CARVED LINEN CHEST

Another linen chest, of better finish than the preceding one and with carved panels, is shown by the reproduced photograph (Fig. 11). Figs. 12 to 17 give details of the construction. The accompanying table gives the sizes of the stuff required without any allowance for waste or trimming up. The whole of the work may be carried out in oak; but there is no objection to the use of a softer wood for the back and bottom, and there is an advantage in the reduced weight.

TABLE OF STUFF REQUIRED:

OAK.

	No. of Pieces.	*Thickness*	*Length.*	*Width*
Posts	4	2 in.	1 ft. $4\frac{1}{2}$ in.	$2\frac{1}{2}$ in.
Top	1	$\frac{3}{4}$ in.	5 ft. 3 in.	1 ft. $3\frac{1}{2}$ in.
	2	$\frac{3}{4}$ in.	10 in.	4 in.
Ends	4	1 in.	1 ft. 2 in.	$5\frac{1}{2}$ in.
	2	$\frac{3}{8}$ in.	11 in.	5 in
Front	2	1 in.	5 ft	3 in.
	2	1 in.	1 ft.	$3\frac{1}{2}$ in.
	4	1 in.	1 ft.	3 in.
	2	1 in.	1 ft. $1\frac{1}{2}$ in.	3 in.
	4	$\frac{3}{8}$ in.	$11\frac{1}{2}$ in.	$4\frac{1}{4}$ in.
	2	$\frac{3}{8}$ in.	$10\frac{1}{2}$ in.	$7\frac{3}{4}$ in.
	1	$\frac{3}{8}$ in.	$10\frac{1}{2}$ in.	$8\frac{1}{4}$ in.
PINE.				
Back	2	1 in.	5 ft.	3 in.
	3	1 in.	1 ft.	$3\frac{1}{2}$ in.
	2	$\frac{3}{8}$ in.	2 ft. 1 in.	$9\frac{1}{2}$ in.
Bottom	9	$\frac{3}{4}$ in.	1 ft. 1 in.	7 in.

The front should be finished off first. The carved panels are ploughed into the framing, which has also a $\frac{3}{8}$-in. bead run on at the top and bottom, and on the inside a $\frac{3}{4}$-in. groove must be ploughed to take the bottom. The end pieces are also similarly beaded and grooved. The ends may be put together, draw-bored and plugged to the posts, and when the back is ready the carcase is put together and the bottom fitted. Make the mortises in the posts as convenient, but do not cut too deep so as to damage the faces. The joints of the bottom should be tongued and grooved.

The top is got out in one piece, and the

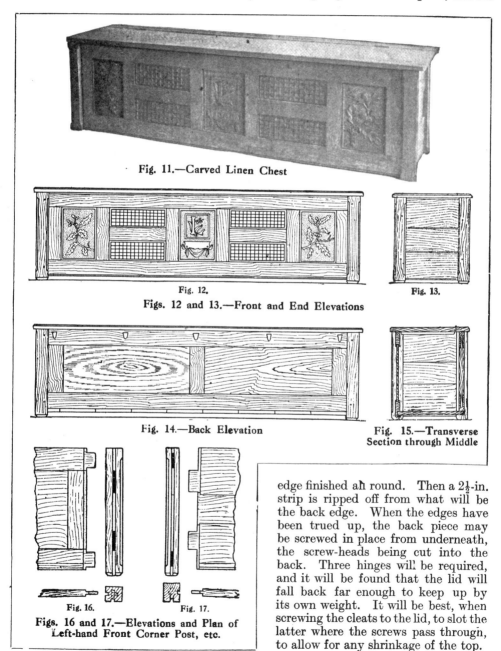

Fig. 11.—Carved Linen Chest

Fig. 12.

Figs. 12 and 13.—Front and End Elevations

Fig. 13.

Fig. 14.—Back Elevation

Fig. 15.—Transverse Section through Middle

Fig. 16.

Fig. 17.

Figs. 16 and 17.—Elevations and Plan of Left-hand Front Corner Post, etc.

edge finished all round. Then a 2½-in. strip is ripped off from what will be the back edge. When the edges have been trued up, the back piece may be screwed in place from underneath, the screw-heads being cut into the back. Three hinges will be required, and it will be found that the lid will fall back far enough to keep up by its own weight. It will be best, when screwing the cleats to the lid, to slot the latter where the screws pass through, to allow for any shrinkage of the top.

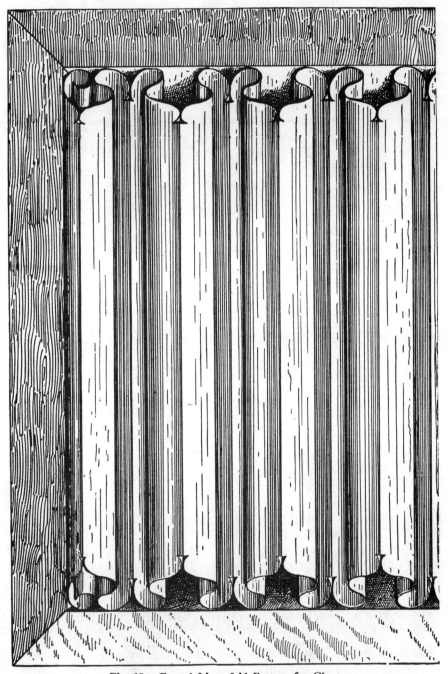

Fig. 18.—Carved Linen-fold Pattern for Chest

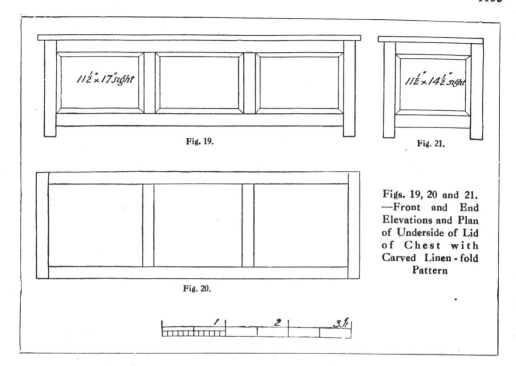

Fig. 19.

Fig. 21.

Fig. 20.

Figs. 19, 20 and 21.
—Front and End
Elevations and Plan
of Underside of Lid
of Chest with
Carved Linen-fold
Pattern

The finishing of the chest is, of course, a matter of taste. A good effect may be obtained by giving the oak a coat of turpentine slightly stained with black japan (just enough to take off the newness of the wood), and then occasionally rubbing over with raw linseed oil. After a time a pleasing dull polish will be the result, and then the ordinary furniture polish will keep it in good trim.

CHEST WITH CARVED LINEN-FOLD PATTERN

The chest shown by Figs. 19, 20 and 21 is given as being one in which the carved linen-fold pattern can be introduced. This pattern (Fig. 18) is at once the most appropriate and traditional of ornaments for this class of article. It was introduced from Flanders and first carved in England in the fifteenth century. The linen pattern is cut with moulding planes, the top and bottom only being worked with carving tools. The actual construction of the chest follows upon similar lines to those already described, and therefore need not be repeated. The finish, similarly, is a matter for the worker's choice, but it will be found that a fumed-wax finish will be in consonance with the design.

Stretchers and Presses

SIMPLE TROUSERS STRETCHERS

THE trousers stretcher shown by the drawings Figs. 1 and 2 consists simply of a pair of clamps, which in operation are clamped on the trousers, and the stretching tension regulated by straining with a piece of strong cord. The clamps are instantly released by giving a quarter-turn to the buttons, and they can be packed up into a space of 3 in. by 3 in. by 1 ft. 6 in., that is, the length of the longest clamp. The clamps are of original form, both being made alike, with the difference that one is made 1 ft. 6 in. and the other 1 ft. 3 in., and with similar buttons on both ends, although only one button end is described. As shown in Fig. 3, each clamp has a bottom bar A, which is planed up $1\frac{1}{2}$ in. wide by 1 in. thick, and is hollowed out on the middle of the upper side about $\frac{1}{4}$ in. deep, as at B, to allow for the extra thickness of trousers seams. Holes $\frac{3}{16}$ in. in diameter are bored through, as shown at C, for the straining cords.

The top strap of the clamp H (Fig. 3) is planed up $1\frac{1}{2}$ in. wide by $\frac{1}{2}$ in. thick, the ends being cut, as shown at A (Fig. 4), to form short tenons about $\frac{1}{4}$ in. long and $\frac{7}{16}$ in. wide, which fit loosely into the counterpart recesses in the end pieces of the clamps, as indicated at A (Fig. 6), to prevent lateral slipping of the top straps when in use. Fig. 5 shows how the tenons are rounded on the top ends, as at A, to prevent the buttons jamming on the corners. The end piece D (Fig. 3) is shown in plan and elevation by Figs. 7 and 8. It is simply a $1\frac{1}{2}$-in. length cut off the top strap. The rounding on the ends can be done when the bottom bars, end pieces, and buttons are bolted together, all being done at one operation. However, the end piece is glued and sprigged on the bottom bar; then the hole for the bolt head ($2\frac{1}{2}$-in. by $\frac{1}{4}$-in. snap-head bolts) being countersunk from the underside with a $\frac{5}{8}$-in. centre-bit, the $\frac{1}{4}$-in. hole is bored through for the bolt, as shown in Fig. 9. This illustration also shows how a washer E is slipped on the bolt between the end piece and the button F (Fig. 3) to make up for the thickness of the clamped trousers, the bolt nut and top washer G completing the fixing arrangement of the clamps.

Figs. 10 and 11 show how the button is cut away at A to permit of the removal of the clamp-top strap when the button gets a quarter-turn backwards, as indicated by the dotted line B (Fig. 6), which shows the button turned at right angles for the removal of the strap. The button is chamfered at the front, as shown in Fig. 11, to permit free entrance over the end of the strap, which then yields to the tightening grip of the flat part of the button. A looped cord (see Fig. 6) is knotted through the centre hole of the short clamps for hanging up when in use. The other clamp has a yard or so of strong cord knotted through it instead of the loop.

To use the stretcher, the clamps are

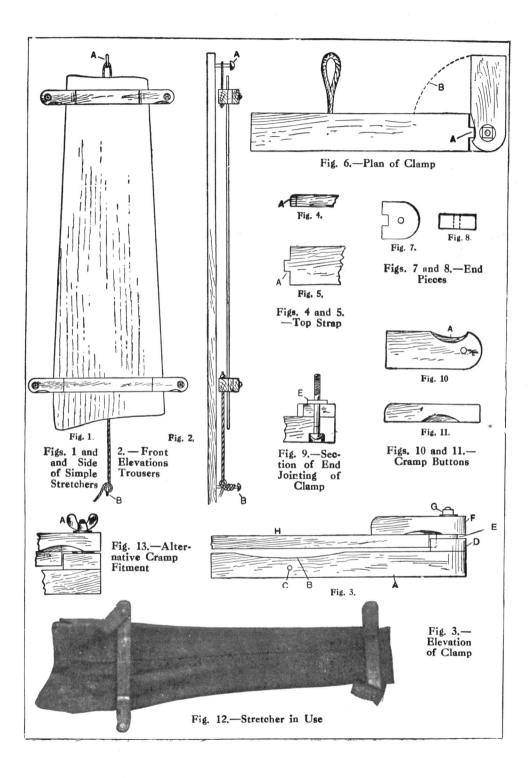

Fig. 6.—Plan of Clamp

Fig. 4.

Fig. 5.

Figs. 4 and 5.
—Top Strap

Fig. 7.

Fig. 8.

Figs. 7 and 8.—End
Pieces

Fig. 10

Fig. 11.

Figs. 10 and 11.—
Cramp Buttons

Fig. 9.—Sec-
tion of End
Jointing of
Clamp

Fig. 1.

Fig. 2.

Figs. 1 and
and Side
of Simple
Stretchers

2. — Front
Elevations
Trousers

Fig. 13.—Alter-
native Cramp
Fitment

Fig. 3.

Fig. 3.—
Elevation
of Clamp

Fig. 12.—Stretcher in Use

placed in any level position, and the trousers, being properly folded, are fixed by slipping on the top straps and giving the buttons a quarter-turn on the straps, which completes the fixing. Then the looped clamp is hung on a hook or nail fixed at a convenient height on a door or wall, and the trousers stretched by strain-

" setting," the top straps having sufficient spring to accommodate trousers of various thickness within reasonable limits.

The butterfly or wing nuts, for tightening the clamps, shown at A (Fig. 13), may be adopted instead of the square nuts. An alternative and more elaborate trousers stretcher is shown by Figs. 14, 15

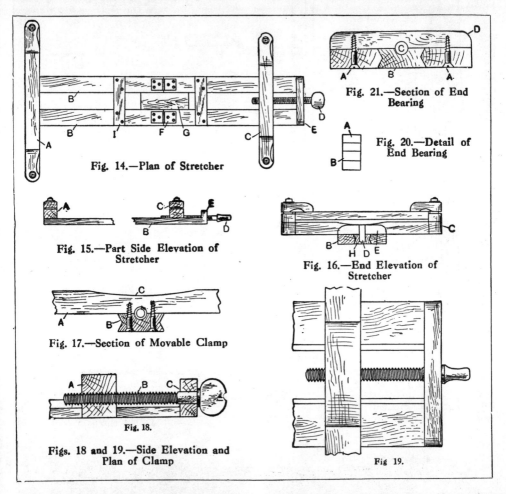

Fig. 14.—Plan of Stretcher

Fig. 21.—Section of End Bearing

Fig. 20.—Detail of End Bearing

Fig. 15.—Part Side Elevation of Stretcher

Fig. 16.—End Elevation of Stretcher

Fig. 17.—Section of Movable Clamp

Fig. 18.

Figs. 18 and 19.—Side Elevation and Plan of Clamp

Fig 19.

ing the lower clamp cord round a similar hook or nail underneath, as indicated at A and B (Figs. 1 and 2). The photograph (Fig. 12) shows the method. The top straps have $\frac{1}{16}$-in. end play between the end pieces, with easy-fitting tenons ; but the buttons need no further adjustment with the bolt and nut after the first

and 16. The clamps, minus the string holes, are made similarly to those just described, but the long clamp A (Fig. 14) is fixed with screw-nails from the underside to the bars B, which form the base of the stretcher. The stretcher is operated by the wooden screw D, which operates through its counterpart—threaded hole, and in this case takes the place of the stretching cord in the short clamp C, a collar piece E being also fixed on the end of the base bars to form a bearing for the screw. The same lettering refers to similar parts in Figs. 14, 15 and 16.

So that the stretcher may fold up handily when out of use, the base is hinged together at F, and the position of the hinges should be so adapted that the clamps clear each other when it is folded. The centre piece G is made V-shaped, and is free to slide stiffly between the bars from end to end between the clamps, working in counterpart with V-edges on the bottom bars. The movable short clamp is also fitted with V-edged centre piece, as shown at H (Fig. 16), so that it works smoothly and parallel to the screws. The centre sliding piece G stiffens the base by sliding it up to the position shown between the hinges, and thus holds the base rigid when the stretcher is in use. The metal strips I (Fig. 14) are fixed across the bars to tie them together, as a precaution against springing apart. To clearly explain the matter, enlarged details of the parts are shown in Figs. 17 to 21. The bottom bars are 2 in. by $\frac{3}{4}$ in. thick, and about 2 ft. 8 in. or so long, with the inner edges planed to an angle of 60°. The centre sliding piece is about 5 in. long, with both edges grooved to similar angle (60°), to suit the bottom bars. In preparing the centre piece it should be made sufficiently long for cutting off the necessary lengths for fixing underneath the movable clamp and the end bearing for the screw ; also, it is advisable to fix a centre piece at the long clamp end to facilitate the width adjustment of the bottom bars.

Fig. 17 gives a sectional view of the short clamp A, with the V-groove piece B fixed on underneath to form the slide ; the central hole is bored on the junction line of the clamp and V-piece, as at C, and tapping size for $\frac{5}{8}$-in. woodscrewing tap. Figs. 18 and 19 show the adjustment of the movable clamp A by means of the screw B working through the end bearing C. The end bearing, as shown in Figs. 20 and 21, is $\frac{3}{4}$ in., and of

a length equal to the overall width of the bottom bars, on which it is glued and fixed with screws from the underside, as at A (Fig. 21). The centre piece B is glued between the bars and also to the end bearing, of which it forms the lower half. The hole C is bored centrally, in alignment to the clamp-screw hole, and the upper ends of the bearing are finished by rounding off as at D.

Six inches or so is ample for the screw, which is best made of birch or beech, and the neck end of it is left uncut with the screw for working in the end bearing. The screw may be prepared from $1\frac{1}{2}$-in. square stuff, in which case the head will be turned ball-shape, and afterwards dressed to shape something similar to an enlarged violin peg. Or it can be turned from a piece of $\frac{3}{4}$-in. thick stuff, leaving the head end with enough for turning to shape and finishing as detailed. The two plates may be prepared from sheet brass about $\frac{1}{16}$ in. thick, with holes drilled and countersunk, for fixing with $\frac{5}{8}$-in. brass screw-nails. For appearance, the stretcher can be twice varnished.

TROUSERS STRETCHER WITH SCREW

The trousers stretcher shown by Fig. 22 consists chiefly of two pairs of clamps which are forced apart by a long screw worked by a loose handle. Fig. 23 is a plan of the top pair of clamps, and Fig. 24 shows in detail the rods and brackets. The clamps are prepared from either ash or beech, the top pair being 1 ft. 5 in. long by $1\frac{3}{4}$ in. wide by 1 in. thick at the centre and $\frac{5}{8}$ in. thick at the ends. A recess about $\frac{3}{32}$ in. deep by $2\frac{1}{4}$ in. long is made on the inside at the centre in both pairs of clamps (see Fig. 25), to allow for the extra thickness of the seams in the trousers, and also to obtain a uniform grip across the leg ; plush may be glued on the inside of the clamps, to prevent injury to the cloth. Patterns should be made for the wing-nuts and bracket (Fig. 26), which should be cast in brass ; the bolts are 3 in. long by $\frac{3}{8}$ in. in diameter (Whitworth thread), with snap heads, and

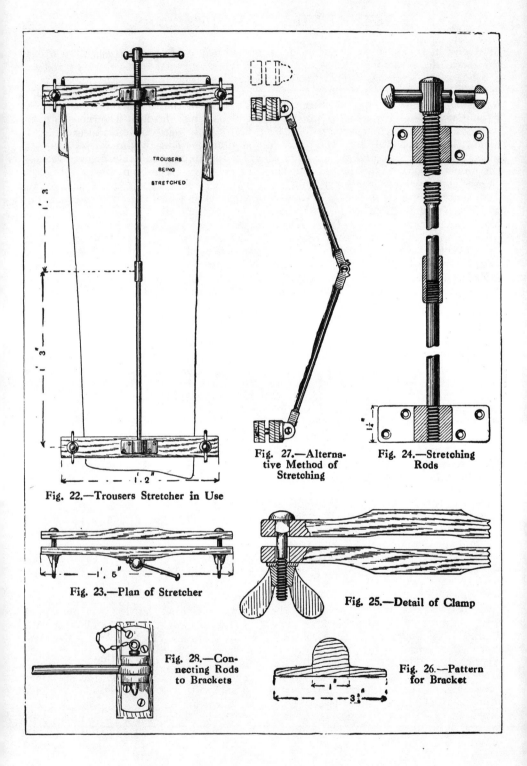

TROUSERS
BEING
STRETCHED

Fig. 22.—Trousers Stretcher in Use

Fig. 23.—Plan of Stretcher

Fig. 27.—Alternative Method of Stretching

Fig. 24.—Stretching Rods

Fig. 25.—Detail of Clamp

Fig. 28.—Connecting Rods to Brackets

Fig. 26.—Pattern for Bracket

square on the shank to prevent them turning.

The lower bracket is drilled for ⅜-in. tapping, the rod screwing tightly into it. On the upper end of the rod is screwed a piece of ¼-in. gas tube 1¼ in. long, which forms a guide socket for the forcing screw. The latter is made by welding a piece of ½-in. round iron or mild steel rod to a ⅜-in. length ; the thread when finished

with removable pins attached, as shown in Fig. 28.

TROUSERS PRESS

A plan of the top of the trousers press is shown by Fig. 29. The woodwork of the press consists of two mahogany boards 1 ft. 9 in. by 6 in. by ⅝ in. for the top, and two boards of the same dimensions for the bottom. The iron straps are 1 ft.

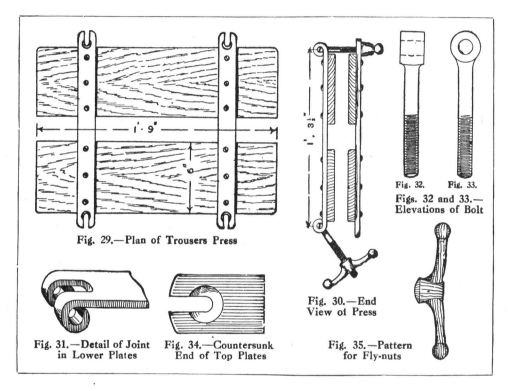

Fig. 29.—Plan of Trousers Press

Figs. 32 and 33.—Elevations of Bolt

Fig. 32.   Fig. 33.

Fig. 30.—End View of Press

Fig. 31.—Detail of Joint in Lower Plates

Fig. 34.—Countersunk End of Top Plates

Fig. 35.—Pattern for Fly-nuts

is 6 in. long, and works in the top bracket, which forms its nut. A loose vice-handle 5 in. long, made from ¼-in. steel rod, is fitted as shown, the ends being shouldered down for riveting on the semi-spherical ends.

An alternative method of expanding the clamps is shown by Fig. 27, the action being much quicker than the screw described above. The dotted outline on the left shows the position of the clamps when the knuckle-joint is straightened. To facilitate packing, the rods may be fitted

5½ in. by 1¾ in. by ¾ in. Fig. 30 is an end view. The clamping bolts being pivoted, the wing-nuts need only be slacked back sufficiently to clear the countersunk part, when they will swing clear through the slot. Fig. 31 shows the shape of the lower bars that receive the pins, which should fit tight in the bars, while the holes in the bolts (*see* Figs. 32 and 33) should be slightly larger. Fig. 34 shows the end of one of the top plates ; the $\frac{7}{16}$-in. clearing hole is drilled first, then countersunk, and finally the slot is cut.

Fig. 35 is a pattern in wood for the fly-nuts; the distance across the wings is 4½ in.

The metal-work of the press should be filed and polished with emery-cloth, and then nickel-plated. The woodwork should be finished by french-polishing or varnishing.

LINEN PRESS

A perspective drawing of a linen press operated by two ⅞-in.-diameter square-thread joiner's bench screws is given by Fig. 36. In the carcase are fitted two drawers of equal size, and at each end drop leaves are attached, which are supported with hinged brackets. If desired, the press could be made in a dwarf or table form, that is, the drawers and drop leaves being dispensed with; the posts need only be 4 in. to 6 in. below the top of the carcase, which would simplify the construction considerably.

The most suitable wood is one of the hardwoods, such as oak, teak, or ash, and next in favour comes pitchpine. Fig. 37 is a front elevation of the cabinet with the leading dimensions. The following are some of the principal sizes of material. The posts are 3 ft. 7 in. long by 1¾ in. by 2 in. in section, and tapered at their lower extremities, as shown in Figs. 36 to 38. All the sizes given are to be taken as the finished sizes of material, therefore allowance must be added for cutting and planing. The front and back rails are 1 ft. 6 in. long between the shoulders, and 1½ in. by 1¾ in. in section; the bottom rails are 1¼ in. thick by 1¾ in. wide. Fig. 38 is a vertical cross section of the press near the centre, but showing the carcase with the drawers removed. Fig. 39 is a part sectional plan.

The side rails are 1 ft. 2 in. between the shoulders and of the same section as the front rails. Prepare the cross pieces A (Figs. 37 and 38), which are 1 ft. 2 in.

long from the faces of the shoulders, 3 in. deep by 2¾ in. thick at the centre, and diminishing to 2¼ in. thick at each end. Lay the posts on the bench, and mark the positions for the mortises which are to receive the tenons of the various rails. Commence with the lower mortise at 1 ft. 6 in. from the floor end of the posts. Next measure up a distance of 1 ft. 4½ in. for the top face of the top rail; then midway between these mor-

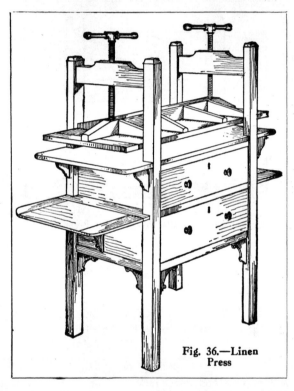

Fig. 36.—Linen Press

tises set out a mortise (on the front posts only) for the reception of the parting rail between the drawers. This rail is ⅞ in. thick by 1¾ in. wide. The measurement having been marked off on one post first, the remaining posts can be brought close together, and the lines produced across their faces with a try square. The rails can then be turned over, and the mortises for the end rails set out in the same way. This will economise time and give true results, providing the posts are planed up true and square. Then cut the mortises, shape the tenons as shown at Figs. 40, 41 and 42, and fix them all together temporarily.

Next prepare the top of the carcase from boards 6½ in. wide by 1¼ in. thick, or 1 in. if hardwood is used. The boards can be grooved and tongued, jointed, or dowelled as preferred, the ends being clamped in the usual way. At the centre

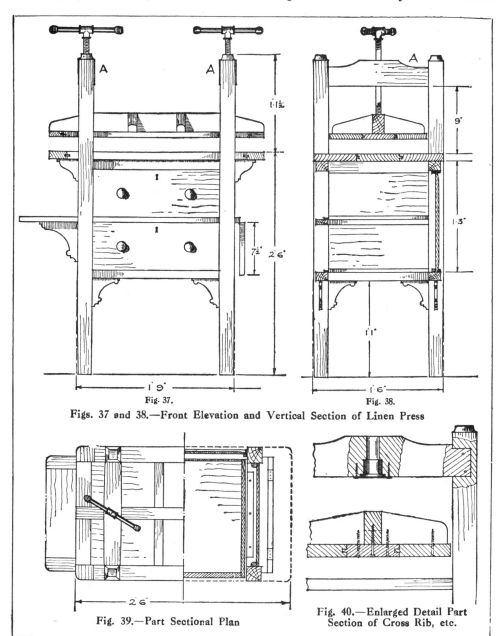

Fig. 37.

Fig. 38.

Figs. 37 and 38.—Front Elevation and Vertical Section of Linen Press

Fig. 39.—Part Sectional Plan

Fig. 40.—Enlarged Detail Part Section of Cross Rib, etc.

underside of the carcase top a batten, 2 in. wide by 1¼ in. thick, is screwed to the boards and also notched to the front and back top rails as shown at Fig. 43. Next bore the holes in the top cross pieces A for the reception of the nut and screw; a 1-in. hole should be bored for a ⅞-in. diameter

faces of the posts. The brackets which support the leaves are cut with the grain running vertically, and short dowels formed on each end nearest to the carcase, fit into holes bored in the top projecting fillet and to the top edge of the lower rail respectively. Next fit and brad

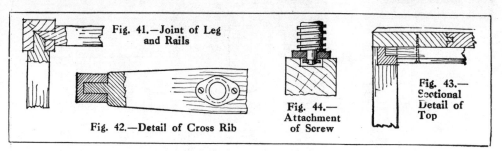

Fig. 41.—Joint of Leg and Rails

Fig. 42.—Detail of Cross Rib

Fig. 44.—Attachment of Screw

Fig. 43.—Sectional Detail of Top

screw, while the hole for the nut should be of such diameter that it will stand driving in. If the nut is provided with ribs as shown in Fig. 39, corresponding grooves must be cut in the cross pieces to receive them. The nut is kept in position and prevented from dropping out (in the event of the wood shrinking) by a light metal plate fixed with two screws. The square thread screws are 10 in. long, the lower end being shouldered down, as indicated in Fig. 44, to receive a metal plate ⅛ in. thick and of similar shape to that shown in the plan at Fig. 42. The part projecting through this plate is also shouldered down to receive a suitable washer, and finally this end is riveted over. The reduced part on which the metal plate fits should be about $\frac{1}{32}$ in. longer than the thickness of the plate.

To ensure the screw working freely after the washer has been riveted over, the screws with the plates attached and drilled for the wood screws must be in the cross pieces before they are finally framed to the posts. Then the drawer runners and guide fillets and stops can be fixed. Also, the carcase ends and backing, cut from stuff ⅜ in. thick, can be fitted and blocked in, as shown in Fig. 39.

The drop leaves are 7½ in. by 1 ft. 3 in. by ¾ in. thick, and are hinged to the fillet which supports the top drawer. These fillets project slightly beyond the outer

the small shaped angle brackets under the lower rails and projecting ends of the top. For the drawers, the fronts are cut from stuff ¾ in. thick, and the sides and back are of ½-in. stuff, while the bottoms are ⅜ in. thick. Wood or earthenware knobs or drop handles and locks can be fitted as desired.

The rise-and-fall top of the press is made up similar to the top of the carcase. Three boards are planed up true both on the faces and the edges, and are either grooved and tongued or secured with dowels. The two ends are clamped and wedged, then the ribs are secured to the rising top to stiffen it when in use, and also to distribute the pressure of the screws more uniformly over the top of the press. The central rib is 2 ft. 6 in. long by 3 in. deep and 1¼ in. thick, and is notched to fit tightly over the four cross ribs. All the ribs are secured with countersunk screws driven from the under face of the press (see Fig. 39). The screws are attached to the rising top by the oval plates referred to in Fig. 42. By this means the top is raised and lowered with the screws, the pressure being taken first on the oval plates, which should be preferably of sheet brass. A little french chalk can be used on the screws, and will be cleaner than oil or any other kind of lubricant. The woodwork can be stained and sized and varnished, or filled up and polished.

Aquaria

SIMPLE AQUARIUM WITH FOUNTAIN

THE wood-framed aquarium shown in front and end elevations and plan by Figs. 1, 2, and 3 can easily be made by anyone who has mastered the making of mortise-and-tenon joints. It must, of course, be perfectly watertight, and sufficiently strong to resist the pressure against the sides from the weight of water. The size of the aquarium is 2 ft. 6 in. long by 1 ft. 6 in. wide by 1 ft. 3 in. high. The bottom is ¾ in. thick, moulded on the edge, and grooved on the upper face to receive the tongue or the bottom rail as shown. The framing forming the sides is composed of bars grooved and tongued together, as shown in Fig. 4, each separate piece being grooved to receive the plate glass. Each piece of the top and bottom rails is tongued on the edge (Fig. 5) and tenoned into the stiles. The glass is cut to the exact size and fitted and fixed in position previous to the framing being glued up. After being glued together they are allowed to stand for two days until the glue has set hard. The glass is then stopped in with a composition of white-lead, red-lead, and gold-size.

The sides and ends are then fitted together, the tongue and groove being painted with a thin coat of the composition made more liquid by the addition of linseed oil. The whole of the framework is put together, and the joints tightened by means of brass screws. The face is then cleaned off level, and the tongue fitted into the grooves in the bottom. When this has been done, the bottom is covered with No. 14 gauge zinc, and a hole cut through the centre to allow the tube which supplies the fountain to pass through. A hole in the angle, through which the tube for the waste passes, is also formed.

The sides of the aquarium may now be secured to the bottom. Well cover the zinc, groove and tongue with the composition, and draw up the joint tight with screws from the underside. The top rim is moulded on the outer edge, rounded on the inner edge, mitred at the angles, and secured with round-headed screws to the top rail. The outer faces are blacked with stain and polished, the inside faces being painted with bath enamel. If desired, the teak framework may be left in its natural colour and french-polished. The tubes for the fountain and waste pipe are secured to the bottom with back nuts (Fig. 6), the tubes being threaded for the purpose. The fountain may be supplied from an overhead cistern kept filled with river water. A plumber would supply the necessary parts, which, after being fitted and fixed, should be enamelled, and the zinc bottom similarly treated. The enamel must, of course, be allowed to stand until quite hard before the aquarium is used.

If preferred, several coats of good copal varnish could be applied in place of the white enamel. In this case a brass pipe and fittings would be used.

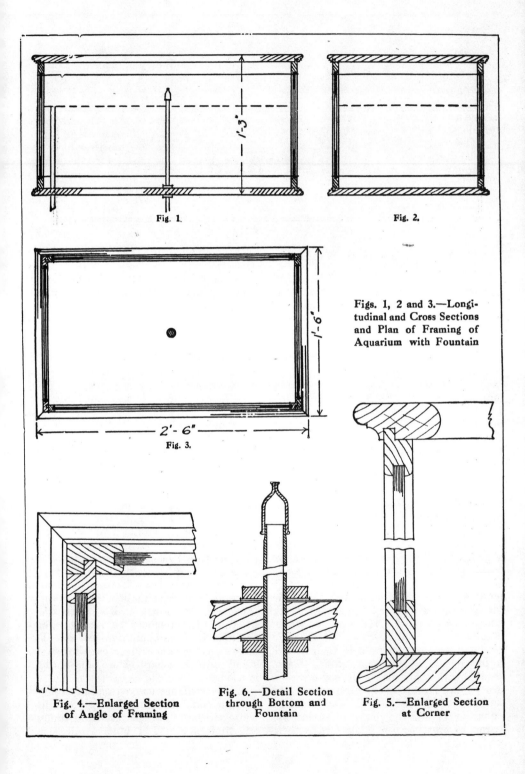

Fig. 1.

Fig. 2.

1'-3"

1'-6"

2'-6"

Fig. 3.

Figs. 1, 2 and 3.—Longitudinal and Cross Sections and Plan of Framing of Aquarium with Fountain

Fig. 4.—Enlarged Section of Angle of Framing

Fig. 6.—Detail Section through Bottom and Fountain

Fig. 5.—Enlarged Section at Corner

COMBINED JARDINIERE AND AQUARIUM

An aquarium of more elaborate construction, and combining in the one article a jardiniere and aquarium, is shown in side and end elevations by Figs. 7 and 8. The construction of the aquarium will first be dealt with. A convenient size for the aquarium is 2 ft. 6 in. long by $10\frac{1}{2}$ in. wide by $11\frac{3}{4}$ in. deep (outside square

connecting rails. The mortises for the top rails should be $\frac{5}{8}$ in. long by $\frac{3}{8}$ in. wide by $1\frac{3}{16}$ in. deep, and $\frac{7}{8}$ in. from the end; and for the bottom rails $\frac{7}{8}$ in. long by $\frac{3}{8}$ in. wide by $1\frac{3}{16}$ in. deep, and 2 in. from the end. An isometric view of the top and bottom of the post showing these mortises is given in Fig. 9. When the mortises have been made, gauge the posts for the rebates, which should be $\frac{7}{8}$ in. from the inside edge and $\frac{3}{8}$ in. deep, and stopped $1\frac{3}{4}$ in. from the

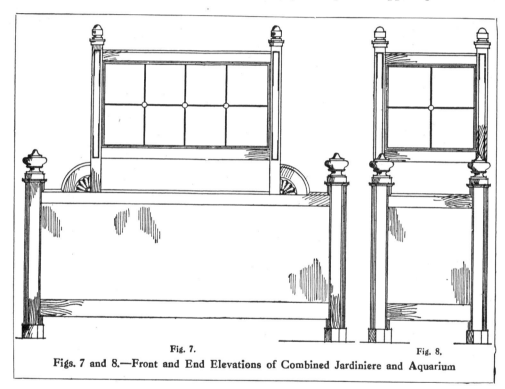

Fig. 7.   Fig. 8.

Figs. 7 and 8.—Front and End Elevations of Combined Jardiniere and Aquarium

corner posts and without feet), and the jardiniere above 1 ft. 6 in. long. $10\frac{1}{4}$ in. wide, and 10 in. deep, the two together standing 2 ft. $2\frac{1}{4}$ in. high without the terminal at the top.

In choosing the wood, great care must be taken to select only those pieces that are perfectly sound and free from knots, and for preference it should be teak, oak, or mahogany. For the corner parts, prepare four pieces 1 ft. $2\frac{1}{2}$ in. by $1\frac{1}{4}$ in. square and set them out for the mortises for the

top and $3\frac{1}{4}$ in. from the bottom (*see* Fig. 9). As the length of the post is not sufficient to enable the rebating to be done with a plane, a good method is to cut the gauge lines down with a cutting gauge, and then chisel out the wood to the required depth. The top rails should be each $1\frac{1}{4}$ in. by 1 in., with a moulding worked on the top face, as shown in section in Fig. 10; the front and back rails measure 2 ft. $3\frac{1}{2}$ in., and the side rails 8 in. The bottom rails should be $1\frac{1}{2}$ in. by 1 in. As these lengths are

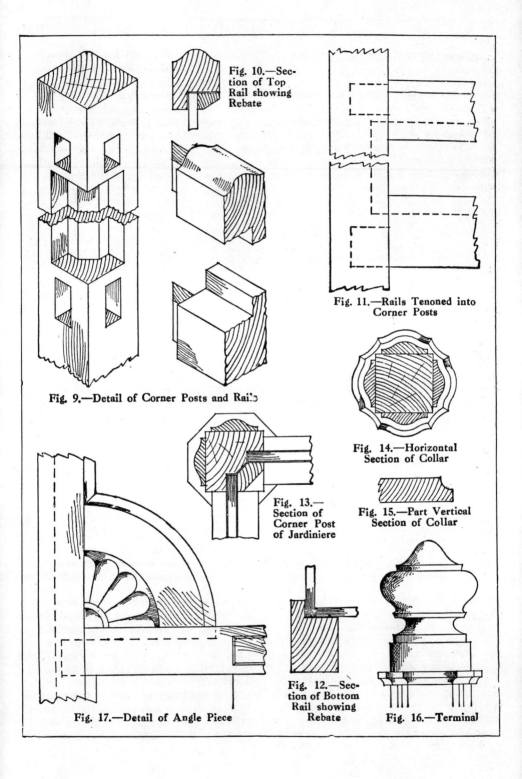

Fig. 10.—Section of Top Rail showing Rebate

Fig. 9.—Detail of Corner Posts and Rails

Fig. 11.—Rails Tenoned into Corner Posts

Fig. 14.—Horizontal Section of Collar

Fig. 13.—Section of Corner Post of Jardiniere

Fig. 15.—Part Vertical Section of Collar

Fig. 17.—Detail of Angle Piece

Fig. 12.—Section of Bottom Rail showing Rebate

Fig. 16.—Terminal

taken between the corner posts, sufficient allowance must be made at each end of the rails for the tenons ; and, roughly, 2 in. added to the length of each piece will suffice. When these rails are planed up square to their respective sizes, the tenons should be set out, the sizes being taken from the mortises. An elevation showing the positions of the tenons in dotted lines is given in Fig. 11. The tenons meet in the corner post, and are mitred together. The rebates on the rails should be $\frac{11}{16}$ in. long by $\frac{3}{8}$ in. deep, as shown in Figs. 10 and 12. In the centre of the bottom rails a bearer $1\frac{1}{4}$ in. by $\frac{7}{8}$ in. should be tenoned from the front to the back.

The various pieces of the framework should now be smoothed up, glasspapered, fitted together with glue and cramped, and when dry, the joints should be further strengthened by driving in a $2\frac{1}{4}$-in. brass screw from each side, the head of the screw being slightly sunk below the surface. As the corner posts are necessarily somewhat heavy, to detract from this appearance they should be ornamented, as shown in Fig. 7. Run off a length of moulding 1 in. by $\frac{1}{4}$ in. and to the section shown at Fig. 13, and cut off strips 1 ft. $1\frac{1}{4}$ in. long. These should be planted on the two outside faces of each corner post (leaving a space of $1\frac{1}{4}$ in. at the bottom for the feet) and fixed with glue and tacks, the heads of the tacks being punched in and the holes filled with stopping. Small pieces of moulding should also be fixed on the inside faces of the corner posts, above the top rail and below the bottom rail. The feet are formed of rectangular pieces planted on and mitred at the corners as in Fig. 13. The collar (Fig. 8) is $\frac{1}{4}$ in thick and $2\frac{1}{4}$ in. across each way, and should be shaped and moulded as shown in Figs. 14 and 15. The former is a section through the corner post looking up at the collar (see Fig. 8), and the latter is a section of the collar. The terminal, of which Fig. 16 is an enlarged view, is $2\frac{3}{4}$ in. high and $2\frac{1}{4}$ in. at its widest part, and is fixed with a dowel through the collar into the corner post.

Polished plate glass $\frac{3}{16}$ in. or $\frac{1}{4}$ in. thick

will be most suitable for the sides and bottom. It will be seen, on reference to Fig. 12, that the side glasses butt against the bottom of the rebate, and the bottom glass butts against the side glasses. Bed the glass in the rebates with a cement composed of one part of red-lead and two parts of white-lead, mixed together with sufficient gold-size to make the whole workable. The edges of the glass should be first coated with gold-size so as to make the cement adhere better ; only sufficient cement should be used to make the joint firm. After the glass is inserted in the rebates, it should be pulled up tight to the corner posts and top rails by means of an angle fillet as shown in Figs. 10 and 13. These fillets should previously be given a thin coat of cement. When the whole has thoroughly dried, give the angles two coats of enamel, and then over this two coats of shellac varnish ; let the varnish extend $\frac{1}{8}$ in. beyond the enamel.

The jardiniere, which should be made separately so as to be taken off when the aquarium is required to be cleaned out, is fitted to the top rails of the latter by four tenons, one in each leg. The four corner posts should each be 1 ft. $3\frac{3}{8}$ in. long by 1 in. square, and the connecting rails 1 in. by $\frac{7}{8}$ in., the front and back rails being 1 ft. 4 in. long and the side rails $8\frac{1}{4}$ in. long. Sufficient allowance should be added to the length of the above pieces for the tenons. The rails are tenoned into the corner posts $2\frac{3}{8}$ in. from the top and 3 in. from the bottom. The tenons on the bottoms of the corner posts should be each $\frac{1}{2}$ in. long, and the mortises for these on the top rails of the aquarium should be made $4\frac{3}{4}$ in. from the corner posts. To make the jardiniere perfectly rigid, dovetail-house an ornamental angle piece into the side of each corner post, and in a line with the bottom, as shown in Figs. 17 and 18. This piece has a radius of $2\frac{7}{8}$ in., and should have a moulding worked on the outside circular edge, of the same section as that on the top rail of the aquarium with which it mitres. The front and back top rails of the aquarium are notched to receive the feet of the corner posts and the angle pieces as shown. The carving is cut to the depth of $\frac{1}{8}$ in., and within a radius of $1\frac{5}{8}$ in.

Before finally fixing together the frame-work of the jardiniere, the corner posts should be ornamented on the two outside faces with a sunk moulding as shown in Fig. 19, this being stopped $2\frac{5}{8}$ in. from the top and 3 in. from the bottom. The remaining portion at the top should be square cut and shaped to form a terminal with a neck mould planted on and mitred. The bottom is of $\frac{3}{8}$-in. or $\frac{1}{2}$-in. material and as it is not seen, it could be of American whitewood or pine. To form rebates for the reception of the bottom, screw fillets on the sides of the rails as shown in Fig. 20, which is a section through the bottom corner of the jardiniere. To fix in the tiles, screw fillets all round the inside of the four frames as shown in Fig. 20, and also vertically at the three inter-sections to which the brass studs are secured, and fix them in the front with a $\frac{1}{4}$-in. moulding. To ensure against any liquid drainage from the flower pots find-ing its way into the aquarium, a zinc tray should be provided to fit inside the jardiniere. This should be fitted with

two folding handles on the inside for lifting purposes, and given two coats of paint or japan to prevent it rusting.

The best finish for the woodwork is perhaps french-polish. If the wood used is oak or teak, it should be left in its natural colour and " egg-shell " finished, using green tiles for the jardiniere. But if any other hardwood is used, it should be coloured in the usual way to get the desired tone.

Before using the aquarium for fish, it should be allowed to remain for some days alternately full and empty, so as to take off the taint from the paint, cement, etc. Cover the bottom to a thickness of $\frac{1}{2}$ in with river sand or fine gravel, that has been thoroughly cleansed till the water runs from it quite clear, and over this lay small pebbles. As well as the fish, two or three aquatic plants, such as the *Vallisneria spiralis*, spiked water milfoil, or common hornwort, and a few water snails are essential to the welfare of the aquarium ; the snails act as scavengers, and eat away the surplus plant growth. The plants are anchored by tying them to pebbles which are pushed into the gravel. For emptying the water. use a syphon made from a piece of composition tubing.

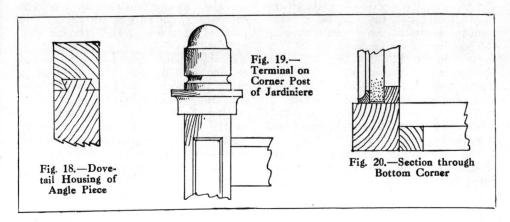

Fig. 18.—Dovetail Housing of Angle Piece

Fig. 19.—Terminal on Corner Post of Jardiniere

Fig. 20.—Section through Bottom Corner

Bagatelle and Billiard Tables

BAGATELLE TABLE

BAGATELLE tables are made in sizes varying from 6 ft. to 10 ft. in length by from 1 ft. 6 in. to 3 ft. in width. The bed of the table, which is ordinarily of slate or mahogany, should be covered with fine green West of England cloth. At the upper end, which is rounded, there are nine holes or cups, numbered from 1 to 9. The sides and circular end have elastic cushions, and nine balls are required, eight white and one red.

The construction of the table about to be described is wholly of wood, but if a slate bed is desired reference should be made to the instructions on making a billiard table given in later pages of this chapter. Fig. 1 shows a table on an ordinary wooden frame, Fig. 2 being the plan.

To construct the table, first, on rods, set out the longitudinal section and cross section (Figs. 3 and 4), and draw two parallel lines, 1 in. apart, to represent the thickness of the bed. At one end set out a rail 3⅜ in. wide with a tongue ⅜ in. long, and on the inner edge fill in the groove for the tongue on the panel ⅜ in. wide by ½ in. deep. Then, from the shoulder line at A

(Fig. 3), measure off 8 ft. 10 in. to the opposite shoulder ; form the tongue beyond this length as before, and fill in the grooves. From the remaining 8 ft. 4 in. deduct the width of the three cross-rails, which will be 9 in., leaving 7 ft. 7 in. This divided again by 4 leaves the space for the four panels 1 ft. 10¾ in. each between the shoulders. Divide the spaces as shown, and fill in the rails with grooves. Then draw two parallel lines as before for the

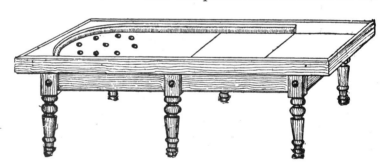

Fig. 1.—Bagatelle Table

cross section, fill in one end, and measure off 2 ft. 7 in. The intervening space will measure 2 ft. 1 in. ; from this deduct 5 in. for the width of two muntins, leaving 1 ft. 8 in. Divide this by 3, which leaves 6$\frac{11}{16}$ in. " bare " between the shoulders of the panels ; fill these in, and the rods are complete.

The mahogany required is as follows : Two stiles, 9 ft. by 3½ in. by 1⅛ in. ; three rails, 2 ft. 8 in. by 3⅜ in. by 1⅛ in. ; two

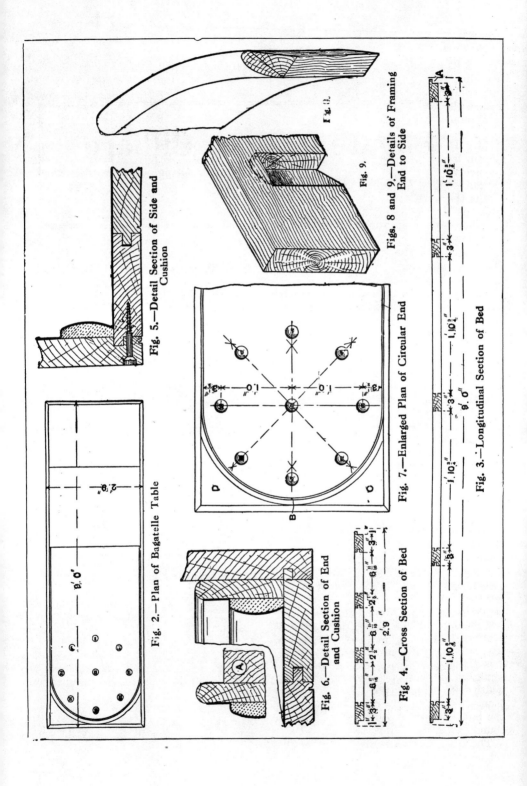

Fig. 8. — Detail Section of Side and Cushion

Figs. 8 and 9. — Details of Framing End to Side

Fig. 9.

Fig. 2. — Plan of Bagatelle Table

2' 0"

9' 0"

Fig. 7. — Enlarged Plan of Circular End

1' 0"   1' 0"

B

D   C

Fig. 6. — Detail Section of End and Cushion

A

Fig. 4. — Cross Section of Bed

3" 6¹⁄₁₆" 2¹⁄₂" 6¹⁄₁₆" 2¹⁄₂" 6¹⁄₁₆" 3¹⁄₁₆"

2' 9"

Fig. 3. — Longitudinal Section of Bed

A

3" 1' 10¾" 3" 1' 10¾" 3" 1' 10¾" 3" 1' 10¾" 3"

9' 0"

rails, 2 ft. 8 in. by $3\frac{1}{2}$ in. by $1\frac{1}{8}$ in. ; eight muntins, 2 ft. 2 in. by $2\frac{5}{8}$ in. by $1\frac{1}{8}$ in. ; and twelve panels, 2 ft. by $7\frac{3}{4}$ in. by $1\frac{1}{8}$ in. Frame these together as in Figs. 5 and 6, the tenons fitting very tightly in the mortises, as it is essential that all joints be rigid. The framework is ploughed with a $\frac{3}{8}$-in. iron $\frac{1}{2}$ in. deep on all inner edges to receive the tongue on the panel ; be careful to allow for the depth of this groove, minus the width of the muntin or rail in each case. The frame, when knocked together dry, should be allowed to stand for a few days in a drying-room, where a current of air can pass through it. The

plan of the circular end. For the latter, 1 ft. $3\frac{7}{8}$ in. from the outer edge of the tongue on the bed, make a mark on the face, this being the centre of the board. From the top end at B (Fig. 7) measure 1 ft. $4\frac{1}{2}$ in., cutting the centre line at the 9 hole ; from this centre mark a square line across the bed. The cups are arranged and numbered in the following order :—

<pre>
            5
        3   2
    8   9   7
        4   6
            1
</pre>

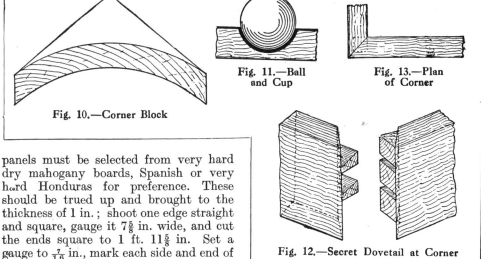

Fig. 10.—Corner Block

Fig. 11.—Ball and Cup

Fig. 13.—Plan of Corner

Fig. 12.—Secret Dovetail at Corner

panels must be selected from very hard dry mahogany boards, Spanish or very hard Honduras for preference. These should be trued up and brought to the thickness of 1 in. ; shoot one edge straight and square, gauge it $7\frac{5}{8}$ in. wide, and cut the ends square to 1 ft. $11\frac{5}{8}$ in. Set a gauge to $\frac{7}{16}$ in., mark each side and end of the panel, and work the tongue to the gauge line. Then place the panels in position to ascertain whether they fit properly. When they have stood for a few days in the frame the whole may be thoroughly well glued together, and, when dry, cleaned off flush at both sides. After this the outer edges may be shot quite straight and parallel to the required width (2 ft. $7\frac{3}{4}$ in.) and length (8 ft. $10\frac{3}{4}$ in.). Run a gauge set to $\frac{3}{8}$ in. along the edges on the bottom face, and work the tongue all round to it.

Then place the bed on the bench and set out the sinkings for the cups and the

With 9 as centre and a radius of 12 in. describe a circle, marking the positions 1, 5, 7 and 8 ; bisect the arc 1 to 8 in 4, 5 to 8 in 3, 5 to 7 in 2, and 1 to 7 in 6, and from each of these points as centres describe circles 2 in. in diameter. Then with 9 as centre and radii of 1 ft. $3\frac{1}{2}$ in. and 1 ft. $4\frac{1}{8}$ in. describe semicircles to get the shape of the mahogany for the circular end (see Fig. 8). The depth of the rim being 4 in., the circular end must be $2\frac{1}{2}$ in. wide ; therefore prepare a thin mould and cut the rim in two pieces, making a butt joint in the centre at B (Fig. 7), and framing it to the rim as shown in Figs. 8 and 9. Good fixing may be obtained for this end by inserting screws from the front side, which will be covered by the cushion. The corners C and D (Fig. 7) are filled with

bed, and similarly for the short pieces for the ends. Secret dovetail these together, as shown, and plough the groove on the inner lower edge to receive the tongue on the bed, and when

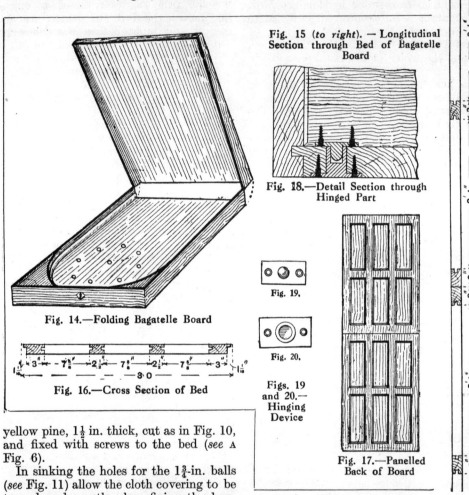

Fig. 15 (*to right*). — Longitudinal Section through Bed of Bagatelle Board

Fig. 18.—Detail Section through Hinged Part

Fig. 14.—Folding Bagatelle Board

Fig. 16.—Cross Section of Bed

Fig. 19.

Fig. 20.

Figs. 19 and 20.— Hinging Device

Fig. 17.—Panelled Back of Board

yellow pine, 1½ in. thick, cut as in Fig. 10, and fixed with screws to the bed (*see* A Fig. 6).

In sinking the holes for the 1¾-in. balls (*see* Fig. 11) allow the cloth covering to be turned underneath when fixing the boxwood cups, so that no raw edges are left; and when setting out the holes always consider the thickness of the cushion. Next the rim will require two pieces of dry, straight-grained mahogany 9 ft. long, 4⅛ in. wide, and 1⅛ in. thick, and two pieces 2 ft. 9 in. long, 4⅛ in. wide, and 1⅛ in. thick; face these true and straight, and set out the longer pieces from the shoulder on the

the corners (Fig. 12) are mitred, etc., fit each piece in place as in Fig. 13.

The cloth is fixed securely behind a loose mahogany bead on the upper inner edge, the bead being secured with very fine pins. The rim is glued and fixed permanently to the bed with screws, the bead being covered with pellets. The cloth round the circular end is fixed along the top edge in a sinking in the mahogany just sufficiently deep for the cloth when fixed to be flush. The bed is first covered with the cloth, the cushions of any section being covered and fixed afterwards, and the exposed parts of the mahogany are french-polished.

FOLDING BAGATELLE BOARD

A folding bagatelle board is shown partly open in Fig. 14. Figs. 15 and 16 illustrate the setting out of the rails for a folding board 10 ft. long by 3 ft. wide ; the previous instructions on setting out may be followed, but the double rail framed in the centre must be noted. The panels will be bead and flush on the outer side (see Fig. 17), and the whole of the outer part french-polished. When closed the board is 5 ft. long and 6 in. deep, and it is necessary to fill the open space with a movable end, which is prepared to fit tightly ; it is fixed by means of brass studs and plates, as in Fig. 18. The studs are fixed to the movable end, one at each corner, and the plates are let in from the outside of the board and screwed, the inner edge being flush with the bed. Without these plates constant use wears away the wood, making a large hole and tearing away the cloth covering. Fig. 19 shows an underneath plan of the top plate, and Fig. 20 a top plan of the bottom plate. The hinge is let in flush with the edge.

FULL-SIZED BILLIARD TABLE

The standard billiard table of this country is 12 ft. long and 6 ft. wide, and encloses a space between its cushions made up of two squares, each 5 ft. 10¼ in. across. The table is supported on eight legs, and is 3 ft. high from the floor level to the top of the cushion rail. The finest Welsh slate is used for the bed, which is planed to a regular thickness in order that it may have a perfectly true surface. The slate is afterwards covered with green cloth. Six pockets are provided, one at each corner and one half-way along each of the long sides. At a distance of 2 ft. 4 in. from the lower or bottom cushion a line, called the baulk line, is drawn across the table, and from the centre of this line a semicircle, having a radius of 1 ft. 9 in. to 1 ft. 11 in., is described between it and the lower end of the table, the space so enclosed being called the baulk. In the middle of the baulk line is marked the baulk spot, in the middle of the table the centre spot, and in line with these and 1 ft. 1 in. from the upper end of the table the red ball spot. The cushions are made of indiarubber, and are of different shapes. On the old style of table the cushions were made much higher than they are at present ; that in general use is called the low cushion, and enables the player to strike the ball much nearer the centre.

One of the chief matters to consider in connection with the erection of a billiard table is whether the floor on which the table is to stand is perfectly level. This is an absolute necessity. Fig. 21 is a side elevation, and Fig. 22 an end elevation of the table about to be described. If the floor is framed together in the usual way with fir joists and batten flooring, it is possible that there will be vibration, which must be prevented, as the table needs to stand quite rigid and firm. If the room is on the ground floor, it will be wise to put in a bed of concrete below the joists, finishing it off with neat cement, in order that it may be level. On the top of this are placed, in position for the legs, blocks of well-seasoned hardwood, each 7 in. or 8 in. square, and as long as required. The blocks should be placed with the end grain up, and the floor should be cut round them, but must not be fixed to them in any way, as they have to stand quite independently of it. The blocks must be levelled with a straightedge and spirit level. If the floor is to be made of concrete, stone blocks with a concrete bed can be used, the blocks being placed in position before the concrete floor is laid. The following are the smallest dimensions for rooms to suit tables of various sizes, exclusive of all projections : A 12-ft. by 6-ft. table requires a room 15 ft. by 21 ft. ; a 10-ft. by 5-ft. table, a 14-ft. by 19-ft.

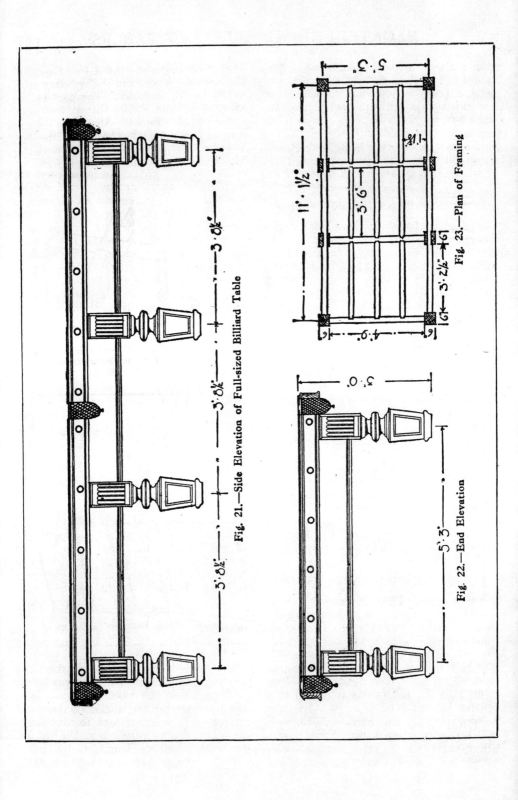

Fig. 21.—Side Elevation of Full-sized Billiard Table

Fig. 22.—End Elevation

Fig. 23.—Plan of Framing

room ; a 9-ft. by 4-ft. 6-in. table, a 13-ft. 6-in. by 18-ft. room ; an 8-ft. by 4-ft. table, a 13-ft. by 17-ft. room ; a 7-ft. by 3-ft. 6-in. table, a 12-ft. by 16-ft. room ; and a 6-ft. by 3-ft. table, an 11-ft. by 14-ft. room.

The rramework of the table is composed of the following stuff : Legs, 8 in. square ;

the intermediate legs occur (*see* Fig. 25). The ends are tenoned in the ordinary way with a double shoulder. The part below is intended to be square turned, but may be altered as desired. Allow 2 in. from the face of the rails to the face of the leg, and set out a mortise for a $1\frac{1}{4}$-in. tenon in the centre of the rail. A large tenon is

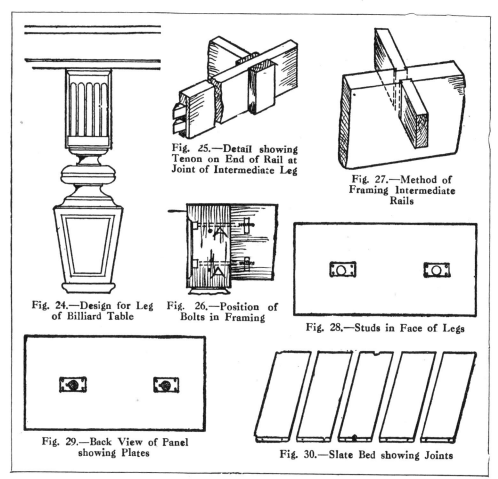

Fig. 24.—Design for Leg of Billiard Table

Fig. 25.—Detail showing Tenon on End of Rail at Joint of Intermediate Leg

Fig. 26.—Position of Bolts in Framing

Fig. 27.—Method of Framing Intermediate Rails

Fig. 28.—Studs in Face of Legs

Fig. 29.—Back View of Panel showing Plates

Fig. 30.—Slate Bed showing Joints

rails, 11 in. by $2\frac{1}{2}$ in. ; and intermediate rails, $4\frac{1}{2}$ in. by $2\frac{1}{2}$ in. On the plan of the framework (Fig. 23) the legs are shown 6 in. square, which is correct, as the extra 2 in. is taken up by the projecting turned portion below the rails, as shown in Fig. 24. The side rails are continuous, and are shouldered on the front side only wher?

necessary for the purpose of strength, especially as part of it is cut away when boring holes for the bolts.

Fig. 26 shows the position of the bolts in framing the outer legs to the rails. When the leg is panelled in the square part, as shown, the length of the panel must be determined by the positions of the bolts. Assuming that Fig. 26 represents the bolts fixing the end rail, those which are to fix the side rails must also pass through the same leg but at a different level, as shown by the black dots A. The panel is made longer than is actually needed in order that it may cover the heads of the bolts. The intermediate cross-rails, which are framed into the legs, are fixed in the same manner.

When making a table, first frame the outer rails and legs, as this enables the length of the longitudinal minor rails to be easily obtained. The latter are dove-tailed into the transverse rails as shown in Fig. 27. No glue is used in putting the table together, the work being left dry, so that they may be readily taken apart when required. If preferred, the panel hiding the heads of the bolts in the legs may be fixed on the face by means of brass studs and plates (see Figs. 28 and 29), allowing the panels to be easily removed.

The slate bed shown in Fig. 30 is placed on the frame in the manner illustrated, the joints being brought together carefully so that the dowels, which are of copper, enter the holes easily. The bed is composed of five specially selected slate slabs, and can be purchased fitted, etc., ready for use. When placing the bed in position, be careful to see that it overhangs an equal distance on all four sides; also that the surface is perfectly level. If the bed is unequal, the inequalities can be remedied by driving in wooden wedges between the slate and the table framework. When quite accurate and level, the bed is ready to be covered with cloth, which is stretched over it and tacked to a deal fillet fixed on the underside of the bed close to the edge by means of screws. The slate is drilled and countersunk to allow the screws to pass through from the top side, the heads of the screws being covered by the cushion. If the cloth is tacked on the edge of the fillet the work must be done neatly, so that the heads are quite level and the cushion rail is allowed to fit tight to the bed. This makes a much simpler job than when the cloth is tacked underneath, although the result is the same.

The rails may now be prepared; there is no hard and fast rule laid down as to their size. Figs. 31 to 34 are sections of different varieties of rails and cushions, and details of fixings. Figs. 31 and 32 show fast cushions for a full-size table. The cushion shown by Fig. 31 is built up of eight layers of vulcanised sheet rubber of different widths; this gives the elasticity required for a quick cushion. The other illustrations show solid rubber cushions of various shapes.

The rails are either prepared in the solid or are built up in sections, the joints being made where the square in the moulding occurs; they are then cut to the lengths required, according to the size of the pockets. Fig. 35 gives dimensions for a very useful size pocket, and shows the pocket plates and the canted corner of the cushion. The plate is let into the top edge of the rail, and fixed by means of a screw from the underside of the rail. Pockets vary in size, those on a match table being always smaller than those on a public table. The cushion is built in the manner shown, its deal foundation being determined by the section of the rubber, and being screwed to the rail; the rubber is cemented to it. A groove is made along the back side of the top edge of the deal, in which a slip of wood A (Figs. 32 and 33) is fitted just loose enough to allow a thickness of cloth to be inserted.

When the rubber has been fixed, the whole cushion is covered with two thicknesses of flannel, glued on the top and bottom edges. The cloth covering for the cushion is fixed in the groove along the edge of the rail at B, and the slip A hammered tightly home. The cloth is then stretched over the rubber, being carefully drawn over the cant without any puckers, and is fixed underneath with glue. The rail is now ready to be fixed to the table with screws, as shown in Fig. 31. It is bored for the screws, including the heads, the slate bed is drilled, and a nut is inserted from the underside and held in place by running some lead into the hole. The screw is turned into the nut, and the whole thus securely fixed. A turned patera is fitted in the hole made for the head of the screw in order to cover up the latter.

The pocket plates and pockets may now be fixed. The plate is lined with leather in order to prevent the ball being chipped when it strikes the plate. The cord pocket is suspended from the plate.

SMALL BILLIARD TABLE FOR DINING-ROOM

A small billiard table suitable for placing on a dining-room table is shown by Fig. 37.

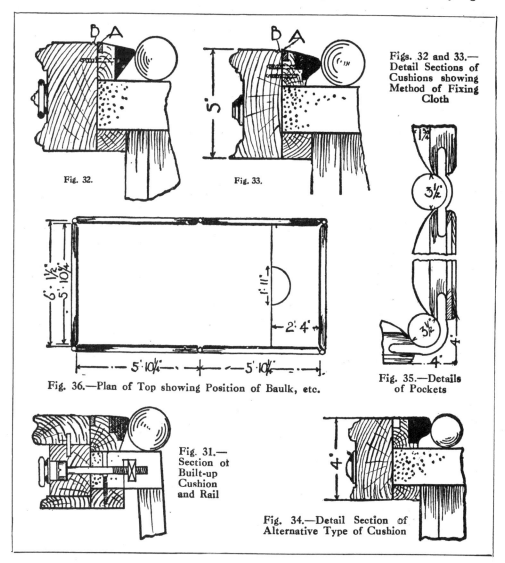

Figs. 32 and 33.—Detail Sections of Cushions showing Method of Fixing Cloth

Fig. 32.

Fig. 33.

Fig. 36.—Plan of Top showing Position of Baulk, etc.

Fig. 35.—Details of Pockets

Fig. 31.—Section of Built-up Cushion and Rail

Fig. 34.—Detail Section of Alternative Type of Cushion

The positions of the spot and the baulk are marked as shown by Fig. 36. After this has been done the cloth bed should be ironed, beginning from the baulk end of the table.

The size is 6 ft. by 4 ft. 6 in. between the rails, the slate bed and under-framing (Fig. 38) being of the same dimensions. The rails are 4 in. wide by $1\frac{1}{2}$ in. thick, sunk and moulded as in Fig. 39, which shows a corner cut for the pocket. The cushion is low, as used on modern tables.

The under-framing is made of deal, 1¼ in.

slate bed, to which the cloth is secured. The fillet is screwed to the slate, suitable holes being drilled for this purpose. The

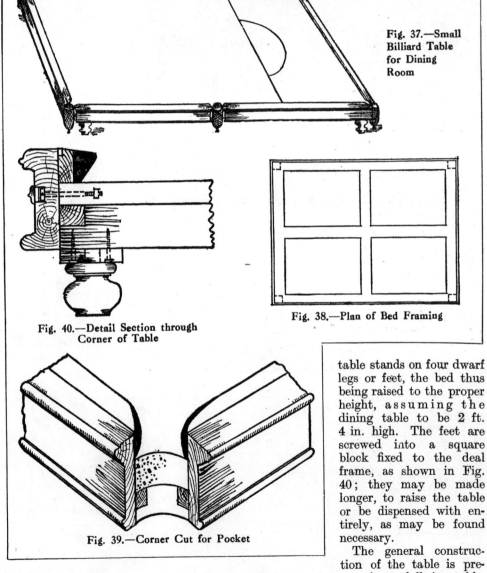

Fig. 37.—Small Billiard Table for Dining Room

Fig. 40.—Detail Section through Corner of Table

Fig. 38.—Plan of Bed Framing

Fig. 39.—Corner Cut for Pocket

table stands on four dwarf legs or feet, the bed thus being raised to the proper height, assuming the dining table to be 2 ft. 4 in. high. The feet are screwed into a square block fixed to the deal frame, as shown in Fig. 40; they may be made longer, to raise the table or be dispensed with entirely, as may be found necessary.

The general construction of the table is precisely the same as for a full-size table, instructions on making which are given on page 1219.

thick, skeleton framed. Each edge is rebated ¾ in. deep by 1 in. wide to receive the fillet fixed to the underside of the

Made and Printed by The Greycaine Book Manufacturing Company Limited
Watford.